Reading Ladders
for Human Relations

NCTE Committee on Reading Ladders for Human Relations

Eileen Tway, Miami University, Ohio, *Chair*
James Duggins, San Francisco State University
Ruth Gallant, The University of North Dakota
Nancy Gropler, Lloyd Mann Elementary School, Loveland, Ohio
Lucille Michael Hart, Georgetown High School, Georgetown, Ohio
Janet Hickman, Ohio State University
Darlene Hughes, Bristow High School, Bristow, Oklahoma
Maia Pank Mertz, Ohio State University
Edith H. Newhart, Oakland Unified School District, Oakland, California
Marilyn Little Tall, Dayton Public Schools, Dayton, Ohio
Roy R. Wilson, University of Oklahoma
Sr. Rosemary Winkeljohann, St. Ursula Villa School, Cincinnati, Ohio
Charlotte S. Huck, Ohio State University, *Consultant*
Virginia M. Reid, University of California Extension, Berkeley, *Consultant*

Contributors

Joan Atterbury, Norman, Oklahoma
Jeanette Barnum, Purcell, Oklahoma
Kim Burns, University of Oklahoma
Susan Ercanbrack, Oklahoma City, Oklahoma
Elaine Fulton Hale, Norman, Oklahoma
Susan Hepler, Ohio State University
Janet Lanier, University of Oklahoma
Kathy Latrobe, Moore, Oklahoma
Linda Levstik, Ohio State University
Madalyn Shannon Long, Bethany, Oklahoma
Mary Ann McConnell, Ohio State University
Robert Mertz, Ohio Department of Education
Martha Graham, Noble, Oklahoma
Sara Pfaff, Bexley High School, Columbus, Ohio
Donna Skvarla, Norman Public Library, Oklahoma
Stacey Smith, Norman, Oklahoma
Gertrude Wessman, Sun City, Arizona
Mary Louise Wilson, Southwest Indian School, Peoria, Arizona
Jane Zaharias, Ohio State University
Students of Children's and Adolescent Literature at the University of North Dakota

Reading Ladders
for Human Relations

6th Edition

Eileen Tway, Editor

American Council on Education
Washington, D.C.

National Council of Teachers of English
1111 Kenyon Road, Urbana, Illinois 61801

NCTE Editorial Board: Paul T. Bryant, Marilyn Hanf Buckley, Thomas J. Creswell, C. Kermeen Fristrom, Jane M. Hornburger, Robert F. Hogan, *ex officio,* Paul O'Dea, *ex officio*

Book Design: Tom Kovacs

NCTE Stock Number 38942

© 1981 by American Council on Education
One Dupont Circle, Washington, D.C. 20036

Library of Congress Cataloging in Publication Data

Main entry under title:
Reading ladders for human relations.

   Includes indexes.
   1. Intercultural education—Bibliography.
2. Children's literature—Bibliography. I. Tway, Eileen.
II. National Council of Teachers of English. Committee on Reading Ladders for Human Relations.

Z5579.R4 1981 [LC1099] 016.302 81-1828
ISBN 0-8268-1414-X   AACR2

9 8 7 6 5 4 3 2 1

PRINTED IN THE UNITED STATES OF AMERICA

Contents

Preface	vii
Statement of Purpose	3
Ladder I: Growing into Self	15
Developing a Positive Self-Image	18
Growing into Maturity	33
Identifying with One's Heritage	51
Developing Personal Values	59
Ladder II: Relating to Wide Individual Differences	79
Understanding the Aging	82
Understanding the Handicapped	92
Understanding the Gifted	112
Understanding Male and Female	117
Understanding Economic Differences	134
Ladder III: Interacting in Groups	147
Family Relationships	149
Friendships	184
Peer Relationships	203
Other Social Groups	214

Ladder IV: Appreciating Different Cultures — 223

Ethnic Cultures — 227
Religious Cultures — 255
Regional Cultures — 265
World Cultures — 278

Ladder V: Coping in a Changing World — 317

Understanding Life Cycles — 319
Learning from the Past — 329
Meeting Personal and Political Crises — 338
Interacting in a Technological World — 351
Facing the Future — 358

Directory of Publishers — 367
Author Index — 373
Title Index — 383

Preface

The purpose of the sixth edition of *Reading Ladders for Human Relations* is essentially the same as stated for all the previous editions: to advance the cause of better human relations. Appropriately enough, this new edition, like the one before it, was prepared by a team approach; it was an endeavor in human relations. Each Ladder had a team of two specialists in working with children and young adults. These teams represented different geographic areas and diverse interests in literature. The task of putting together such a unique booklist is enormous, and team members and the people who assisted them in reading the hundreds of books required for wise selection deserve more credit than I can possibly give them here. They believe in the purpose of *Reading Ladders* and believe enough to give unselfishly of their time for the months and years it takes to do a revision.

Other dedicated people who have supported the work and who deserve special mention are Virginia Reid, Oakland, California, editor of the fifth edition, whose advice was invaluable; and Charlotte Huck, Columbus, Ohio, who helped immeasurably in getting the new edition started. Both served throughout our work as consultants to the *Reading Ladders* committee.

Still others who gave of their time and expertise include Charlotte Leonard, Head Children's Librarian of the Dayton and Montgomery County Public Library, and E. Jane Porter, Ohio State Department of Education, who served as liaison between our committee and the Children's Book Council. Two advisers, Ruth Kearney Carlson and Elizabeth Guilfoile, who cared deeply about the work of *Reading Ladders* and who helped with the sixth edition, must be remembered posthumously. Their advice is treasured and their contributions are now a part of all that *Reading Ladders* stands for. Students of children's and adolescent literature classes assisted committee members, and those at the University of North Dakota, in particular, contributed many reviews. My thanks go to all of them and to my own students at Miami University who so generously shared their instructor's time with *Reading Ladders*.

I am personally indebted to Nancy Gropler, Lloyd Mann Elementary School, Loveland, Ohio, and Cara Park, Miami University, who assisted in the organizational aspects of the project; to the librarians of the Lane

Public Library, Oxford, Ohio; and to Ruth Miller of the Heckert Media Center, McGuffey Laboratory School, who helped in procuring and checking the books. The committee and I are also grateful to Patricia Cianciolo, Michigan State University; Marilou Sorensen, University of Utah; and John Stewig, University of Wisconsin at Milwaukee, who gave support and encouragement throughout.

Book publishers are central to the compiling of a booklist and our thanks go also to all the publishers who sent books for review and who took time to make suggestions about Ladder placement of the books.

Certainly, the Editorial and Production Services Department of the National Council of Teachers of English receives our praise for their thoroughness and patience in the project. Special recognition must go to Miami University, the Department of Teacher Education, and my colleagues there for aid and encouragement, both tangible and intangible, that enabled me to complete the work.

Many people have made this book possible, and it is the hope of our committee that many more will continue the work by building on the suggestions here for promoting better human relations.

Eileen Tway, *Chair*
Miami University, Ohio

Reading Ladders
for Human Relations

Statement of Purpose

Reading Ladders for Human Relations is a specialized booklist and teaching aid for parents, librarians, and teachers who want to promote better human relations. Notwithstanding a long tradition, *Reading Ladders* is revitalized with each new edition. The current, sixth edition consists mainly of books printed since the last edition, with the exception of outstanding books that are pertinent, in spite of copyright date, for each new group of children.

The first *Reading Ladders* was a pamphlet that grew out of a project to find materials and techniques for improving human relations. The project, sponsored by the American Council on Education and called "Intergroup Education in Cooperating Schools," no longer exists, but *Reading Ladders* is continuing evidence of its work. A pamphlet with that title still in use today appeared as the project's first publication in 1947. Its reception by schools and libraries prompted a revision and enlargement in 1949. In both pamphlets, books were annotated or listed according to themes in human relations. The compilers chose to call these themes "Ladders," perhaps because they saw them as necessary steps to take along a continuum of ever-increasing contacts with others.

Hilda Taba wrote in the preface to the 1949 edition that one important purpose of education is to increase sensitivity toward people, their values, and their ways of living. She stressed that books, especially fiction and drama, can deepen understanding. She wrote again in the preface to the third edition in 1954 that "none of the people involved in producing the first published *Ladders* in 1947 knew exactly what role this tool was to play in creating a new vision in education, or the response that it would produce among teachers across the country. Both the idea of using literature to extend sensitivity and the method of organizing books around themes important in human relations proved quite popular." Thus, a tradition was born. *Reading Ladders* appeared in a fourth edition in 1963 and a fifth in 1972.[1]

---

[1] Editors for the earlier editions included Margaret Heaton who prepared the first pamphlets for publication; Margaret M. Heaton and Helen B. Lewis, 1954; Muriel Crosby, 1963; and Virginia M. Reid, 1972.

The 1981 edition has five Ladders, or themes, beginning with understanding the self and radiating outward from immediate associations to ever-widening circles of others. The Ladder, "Growing into Self," is included in this book about understanding others because it is believed that only as one understands the self can one truly understand others. The second Ladder, "Relating to Wide Individual Differences," is new in this revision, although some of the categories have appeared in earlier editions. With the current emphasis on topics such as understanding aging, helping the handicapped, and removing stereotypes of sex roles, a reading list of the eighties must include the increasing number of good books that bring special insight into wide individual differences. The third Ladder, "Interacting with Others," lists books that bring the reader outside the unique one-to-one contacts and into close associations with family and others. The fourth Ladder, "Appreciating Different Cultures," encourages readers to go beyond provincialism and to appreciate cultures quite different from their own, whether nearby geographically or faraway. Finally, books listed in the fifth Ladder, "Coping in a Changing World," have to do with how human beings cope in historically changing times, in the technological world of today, and in facing the unknown and only partially predictable future.

Design of the Ladders

In this edition, *Reading Ladders* has extended its scope to include books for pre-school youngsters, wherever possible, so that the range is now from pre-school years through high school. However, the separate mature designation which appeared in the previous edition has been omitted. Since literature for young people has become increasingly frank and problem-oriented in the last few years, the distinction between adult and children's literature has become blurred. A book for middle graders may contain so-called mature language, and certainly, books for advanced high school students will be mature in theme and content. John Rowe Townsend wrote as early as 1971 that "books are, in fact, continually finding their way on to the children's lists which, in another age, would have been regarded as general fiction."[2] A separate category labeled "mature" seems redundant for contemporary children's and adolescent literature.

Each Ladder has sub-categories and in each sub-category books are grouped in the age-range steps along the continuum from pre-school through high school years. In each of the steps, books are arranged alphabetically by author. Books are sometimes cross-referenced across Ladders and categories with the full annotation appearing under the most pertinent category. If only the author's name and title of the book are given, the main entry can be found by checking the title index. The page containing the full annotation will appear in italic type. The books, however, are never cross-referenced across age levels, so that the teacher or other adult using the book as a reference must use personal judgment as to the suitability of a book for a particular age level. This is always the case, in any event, for the users of a booklist know best the children with whom they work. Moreover, some books can be appreciated across many age levels at different levels of understanding. For this reason, the age designations are not meant to be limiting; they are intended to be a guide. To further emphasize the precariousness of assigning age designations to books, the age levels are listed in overlapping stages. *Reading Ladders* provides a framework, or scope of reference, and it is left to the readers of this reference to decide how and when to use a book that is listed.

Criteria Used in Selecting Materials

The reviewers who helped to put this booklist together kept in mind the fact that while good literature often teaches, it goes beyond the functions of informing, entertaining, and providing emotional release; it exists in its own right as art. Their aim in selecting books was a dual one, to choose books that would promote sensitivity in human relations and to choose books that would exemplify good literary quality. In some areas of concern, scarcity of titles forced reviewers to list available books, not necessarily those of highest literary merit. Within these limitations, reviewers followed as best they could the following selection criteria:[3]

1. Books that contain the essentials of all good literature; for fiction: well-developed plot, characterization, setting, theme, and style; for nonfiction: clear, logical writing and accurate information; for poetry: lyrical beauty of language or poetic statement of truth.
2. Books that are positive and fair in their presentation of all people, both in text and illustration, and that belittle no people either through condescension, deprecatory statements, or ridicule.
3. Books that are natural and convincing instead of contrived and suggest superficial treatment in solving difficult problems human beings face.

---

[2] From Introduction to *A Sense of Story* (1971), reprinted in *A Sounding of Storytellers,* New York, J.B. Lippincott, 1979, p. 10.

[3] These are largely the same as followed in earlier editions. See especially pages 8-10 in the 1972 edition.

4. Books in which the illustrations supplement the text in adding content or contributing to the mood.
5. Books that help prevent the carrying forward of old prejudices and stereotypes into the new generation.
6. Books that recognize minority groups' participation in and contribution to history and culture of our country.
7. Books that can help each reader to a realization of identity, an appreciation of individuality, and a respect for heritage.
8. Books that contain subject matter appropriate to the age levels given.
9. Books that show women in active, interesting roles rather than stereotypic ones; books that avoid sex role stereotyping, in general.
10. Books that contain an honest and authentic portrayal of the human condition, including different stages in the life cycle, different lifestyles, and life in different cultures.

In spite of the use of these criteria, the selections for *Reading Ladders* may not appeal to all or be useful in all cases. Certainly, they are not meant to be all-inclusive. Some excellent books are sure to be omitted, even with the best of intentions, and old favorites may be left out, inadvertently or due to space consideratons. In addition, good books are being published and will be published beyond this copyright date. For these reasons, all parents, teachers, and librarians who refer to this book are urged to use it as a springboard to further looking for books appropriate to their needs.

No matter how carefully books are selected, no matter how enlightened the era, there are certain to be choices offensive to some, since tastes and mores vary so widely from community to community and from individual to individual.

The reviewers of *Reading Ladders* believe in students' right to read and express, and that the first amendment brooks no age limits. They urge users who anticipate questions or who are faced with criticism or censorship of their use of books to read NCTE's *The Students' Right to Read* for help and support in their efforts to encourage students to know more about themselves, others, and their world. It is only in knowing that people are free to improve their own lives. Real life is not without problems, and since literature both reflects and illumines life, it explores the problems of human experience. Young people can be better helped in their own problem-solving by reading about how others have coped, by looking at varying points of view, and by gaining hope and perspective for improving life than by being unrealistically protected by an attempt to hide the problems of living.

Statement of Purpose 7

The reviewers met the challenge of what is sometimes called the new realism in literature for children with careful deliberation. There are few, if any, taboos in literature for young people today. The problems that young people face in present-day existence—including drug abuse, sexual concerns, value conflicts, and physical and social malignancies—are realistically treated in their literature. At the same time, censorship appears to be on the increase, and parents, teachers, and librarians are faced, perhaps as never before, with the dilemma of honoring youth's right to know versus the responsibility of determining appropriate reading matter. Book selection can be seen as a form of censorship in itself when some books are chosen and some are not. We all walk a fine line between censorship and guidance.

Each person using *Reading Ladders* must make the final selections. Some books have descriptive sexual scenes, language that is not generally socially acceptable, explicitly tragic events, or other passages that are potentially offensive to many people. There are also the beautiful passages, examples of unquenchable human spirit, and solutions to problems that offer our young people hope. The beautiful and the ugly are all part of life, and the reviewers have included the literature if it seemed to promote the cause of better human relations.

Using This Book

Reading Ladders is about books and human relations, and it follows that those who use it will do so because they are concerned about all kinds of human relationships. A relationship of first consideration must be the one between the adult who uses this book and the young person or persons with whom the adult is working. Much as they believe in the value of literature, parents, teachers, and librarians cannot impose books on young people any more than they can impose other values. How then *can* they work with young people and books?

Example, of course, is the best precept. The adult who reads in front of and to children will show that reading is a valued experience. Children are never too young or too old to enjoy and benefit from reading as a shared experience. Parents begin, and teachers and librarians continue to build awareness of the kinds of experiences literature affords the reader. Sometimes it will be as easy as responding to a child's question or concern, such as, "Where can I find a book about what it feels like to be blind?" or "Do you know a good book about being friends?" At other times the child or young adult does not or cannot voice the questions. A caring parent, teacher, or librarian, sensitive to the concerns of young people, will try to select books for the personal, school, or public library that deal honestly and sympathetically with human behavior. Books will then be available to offer assurance to readers that they are not alone in their problems and to offer perspective for a broader view, possible solutions, hope, and sometimes humor about the human condition. At still other times, an adult will want to read a book to a group because of a particular concern, either explicit or implicit in the group's interaction. *Reading Ladders* is designed to help in the selection of books to meet these needs, whether for a particular child, for family sharing, for classroom reading, or for the library.

As trust and mutual respect grow, young people will rely on the suggestions of others for good reading. Book talks—short, provocative introductions to satisfying books—are helpful, and they are not only the prerogative of the librarian. Teachers and students can give book talks to good advantage. It can be an important use of class time to let students give recommendations to their peers. Hughes Mearns expressed just how important this time could be many years ago when he said, "Youth calls to youth with an inspiring influence we elders can never hope to match."[4]

Several annotations in *Reading Ladders* give suggestions for other ways to extend experience. Literature that inspires drama or acting out can promote understanding and insight. As children put themselves in Annabel Andrews' place, for example, they can imagine what it would be like to turn into their mothers for a day, as it happened to Annabel in *Freaky Friday*. Puppets can also help youngsters work their way into understandings and satisfying interaction with others. Feelings can be projected and worked through with the puppet or book character in the spotlight until maturity and new understandings are ready for real relationships.

Literature can help people write their way out of problems. There are those who find that they are able to work out solutions to problems through writing down their feelings and concerns. Many teachers effectively promote the idea of journals. Books, such as *Nabby Adams' Diary,* can give young people ideas for recording their own experiences and thoughts. Other stories or poems may stimulate the creation of further stories. Young people may create vicarious experiences through their writing that aid in their understanding of themselves or others.

All these and many other literature-related experiences can grow out of the suggestions in *Reading Ladders,* but mostly it will be the province of the user to see the possibilities according to the particular human relations involved.

To sum up, several important human relations occur in the sharing of books, and cannot be ignored in any discussion of using this booklist. First, parents can exert a positive influence on a child's future experiences

---

[4]Hughes Mearns. *The Education of Youth in the Creative Arts.* New York: Dover, 1929, p. 253.

with reading by introducing books at an early age. Studies show that children who are read to are the better readers later on, especially children who are encouraged to respond to and talk about the experience.[5] As the parent reads and the child responds with comments and questions, important learnings are taking place. Along with whatever content is being discussed, the child is learning what reading is all about and learning to value reading.

Another important relationship is that between the listener and the teacher or librarian who reads aloud or tells stories. Experienced bibliophiles know that nothing sparks reading interest like a good story. In addition, the dialogue or discussion about the story becomes a vital means of clarifying feelings and values.

Still another relationship that must not be overlooked is that between and among readers. Libraries and classrooms are no longer places of silence; they are places where people talk about books and what books mean to them. When there is truly shared communication about books, students will recommend books to adults, as well as to each other. Adults will not be the only ones recommending books; it will be a two-way communication.

And, of course, some of the finest of all relationships can exist between an author and a reader via the shared ideas of a book. The possibilities are almost limitless. Only through books can one enter the thoughts of another and live there for awhile. Quietly, fearfully, angrily, sadly, playfully, joyfully, or thoughtfully, a reader lives for awhile in the life or lives of others. Books provide access to human relations and understandings that would otherwise be impossible.

Reading Ladders for Human Relations contains all kinds of suggested books about a variety of human relations. Some of the books will have satisfying conclusions; others will provoke thought about possible solutions to problem relationships. Above all, *Reading Ladders* is meant to be a catalyst to help parents, teachers, and librarians bring books and young readers together in the quest for better human relations.

Additional General References

Bechtel, Louise S. *Books in Search of Children: Essays and Speeches* (edited by Virginia Haviland). New York: Macmillan, 1969.

Carlsen, G. Robert. *Books and the Teenage Reader: A Guide for Teachers, Librarians, and Parents.* 2nd rev.ed. New York: Harper and Row, 1980.

---

[5]See Cohen, Dorothy. "The Effect of Literature on Vocabulary and Reading Achievement." *Elementary English*, 45 (February, 1968): 209-213, 217, and Cullinan, Bernice E., Angela Jaggar, and Dorothy Strickland. "Language Expansion for Black Children in the Primary Grades: A Research Report." *Young Children,* 29 (January, 1974): 98-112.

Carlson, Ruth Kearney. *Literature for Children: Enrichment Ideas.* Dubuque, Iowa: William C. Brown, 1970; 2nd ed., paper, 1976.

Chan, Julia M. T. *Why Read Aloud to Children?* International Reading Association Monograph Series. Newark, Delaware: International Reading Association, 1974.

Cianciolo, Patricia, ed. *Adventuring with Books: A Booklist for Pre-K-Grade 8.* Urbana, Illinois: National Council of Teachers of English, 1977.

Coody, Betty F. *Using Literature with Young Children.* Dubuque, Iowa: William C. Brown, 1973; 2nd ed., paper, 1979.

Cullinan, Bernice E. and Carolyn W. Carmichael, eds. *Literature and Young Children.* Urbana, Illinois: National Council of Teachers of English, 1977.

Davis, James E., ed. *Dealing with Censorship.* Urbana, Illinois: National Council of Teachers of English, 1979.

Donelson, Kenneth, ed. *Books for You: A Booklist for Senior High School.* Urbana, Illinois: National Council of Teachers of English, 1976.

Donelson, Kenneth, ed. *The Students' Right to Read.* Urbana, Illinois: National Council of Teachers of English, 1972.

Dreyer, Sharon S., ed. *The Bookfinder.* Circle Pines, Minnesota: American Guidance, 1977.

Fader, Daniel N. and Elton B. McNeil. *Hooked on Books: Program and Proof.* New ed. New York: Berkley Publishing Corporation, 1977.

Greene, Ellin and Madalynne Schoenfeld, eds. *A Multimedia Approach to Children's Literature. A Selective List of Films, Filmstrips, and Recordings Based on Children's Books.* Chicago: American Library Association, 1972; 2nd ed., paper, 1977.

Hopkins, Lee Bennett. *The Best of Book Bonanza.* New York: Holt, Rinehart, and Winston, 1979.

Huck, Charlotte S. *Children's Literature in the Elementary School.* 3rd rev. ed. New York: Holt, Rinehart, and Winston, 1979.

Landau, Elliott D., Sherrie Landau Epstein, and Ann Ploat Stone, eds. *Child Development Through Literature.* Englewood Cliffs, New Jersey: Prentice-Hall, 1972.

Larrick, Nancy. *A Parent's Guide to Children's Reading.* 4th rev. ed. New York: Doubleday, 1975.

Leonard, Charlotte. *Tied Together: Topics and Thoughts for Introducing Children's Books.* Metuchen, New Jersey: Scarecrow, 1980.

Purves, Alan C. and Richard Beach. *Literature and the Reader: Research in Response to Literature, Reading Interests, and the Teaching of Literature.* Urbana, Illinois: National Council of Teachers of English, 1972.

Reid, Virginia M., ed. *Reading Ladders for Human Relations.* 5th ed. Urbana, Illinois: National Council of Teachers of English, 1972.

Rosenblatt, Louise M. *Literature as Exploration.* 3rd ed. New York: Modern Language Association, 1976.

Sebesta, Samuel Leaton and William J. Iverson. *Literature for Thursday's Child.* Chicago: Science Research Associates, 1975.

Shapiro, Jon E. *Using Literature and Poetry Effectively.* Newark, Delaware: International Reading Association, 1979.

Stewig, John. *Children and Literature.* Chicago: Rand McNally, 1980.
Stewig, John. *Read to Write.* New York: Hawthorn, 1975.
Stewig, John and Sam L. Sebesta, eds. *Using Literature in the Elementary Classroom.* Urbana, Illinois: National Council of Teachers of English, 1978.
Sutherland, Zena, ed. *The Best in Children's Books.* Chicago: University of Chicago Press, 1973. *University of Chicago Guide 1973*-1978, Supplement, 1980.
Sutherland, Zena and May H. Arbuthnot. *Children and Books.* 5th ed. Glenview, Illinois: Scott, Foresman, and Co., 1977.
Tiedt, Iris M., ed. *Drama In Your Classroom.* Annotated bibliography. Urbana, Illinois: National Council of Teachers of English, 1974.
Townsend, John Rowe. *A Sounding of Storytellers.* New York: J.B. Lippincott, 1979.
Walker, Jerry L., ed. *Your Reading: A Booklist for Junior High Students.* Urbana, Illinois: National Council of Teachers of English, 1975.
White, Mary Lou. *Children's Literature: Criticism and Response.* Columbus, Ohio: Charles E. Merrill, 1976.

Book Review Sources

The Booklist and Subscription Books Bulletin. American Library Association.
Bulletin of the Center for Children's Books. University of Chicago.
English Journal. National Council of Teachers of English. (secondary focus)
The Horn Book Magazine. The Horn Book, Inc.
Interracial Books for Children. Council on Interracial Books for Children.
Language Arts. National Council of Teachers of English. (elementary focus)
New York Times Book Review. New York Times Co.
Publishers' Weekly. "Children's Book Number." R. R. Bowker and Company.
Saturday Review. Marco Communications Corporation.
School Library Journal. R. R. Bowker and Company.
School Media Quarterly. American Association of School Librarians, American Library Association.
Top of the News. Association for Library Service to Children and the Young Adult Services Division of the American Library Association.
The WEB: Wonderfully Exciting Books. The Reading Center, The Ohio State University.
Wilson Library Bulletin. The H. W. Wilson Company.

Ladder I

Growing into Self

To witness young people's frustrating encounters in the reality of life is a never ending shock to those adults whose role it is to guide the growing-up experiences. Today, concerns with the ecological environment, air, water, chemical wastes, land use, and the general aesthetics of life in terms of goods and services loom before our young people as never before. The young are meeting with the confusions and contradictions of values between countries, within our country, and even within the family. Many of the scientific achievements and technological innovations of the past are, in part, becoming the destructive forces of the future. We are asking the young to rethink values and reorder priorities within this context of far-reaching global concerns. This section of *Reading Ladders for Human Relations* is an attempt to give teachers, parents, librarians, and other concerned adults a guide to books that give readers a better understanding of their world and the potential for individual growth in the face of enormous challenges.

The first category in Ladder I, "Developing a Positive Self-Image," focuses on books in which characters provide a model in the developing of self concept. As these characters learn to recognize their strengths and weaknesses and to build on their strengths, readers may identify and accept their own abilities and limitations. Acceptance of one's strengths and weaknesses is the beginning of a positive self image—and the path to maturity.

The second category in Ladder I, "Growing into Maturity," is intended to show how people can grow through their own failures and accomplishments. Acceptance of these actions and learning from such actions is a maturing process. In Louise Fitzhugh's *I Am Five,* a little girl describes her activities and feelings on the day after her fifth birthday. She shares a great deal of herself with the reader or listener: her feelings of being sad, things that make her laugh, and the things that she dislikes most. Young people will recognize their own likes and dislikes, and realize that others have had the same feelings and that these feelings are acceptable. They are growing into maturity as they learn more about themselves and the universality of experience.

Mari Evans' *Jim Flying High* tells the experience of a flying fish who is caught in a tree and too proud to admit that he needs help. Children who read this story will be reassured that it is all right to need help, that there are times when we all need help, and that it is no reflection on self integrity.

The older child can identify with Marcy in Paula Danziger's *The Cat Ate My Gymsuit,* as she works through her problems with her parents, her social life, and her weight. Life for Marcy gains purpose and meaning as Ms. Finney, a remarkable English teacher, comes into her life and helps her appreciate her uniqueness. Books such as this one mirror for the reader the positive growth of persons much like themselves.

The third category in this Ladder, "Identifying with One's Heritage," covers an issue of great concern in the United States. At one point in our history, even twenty or thirty years ago, families and ideas could age like wine. The family settled in one part of the country and contributed to the growth of community and nation, secure in an established identity. As our country has grown and mobility has increased, the family is scattered. Children do not always know their relatives, even close relatives such as grandparents. Books can contribute to a sense of roots, of family, and of history.

Peter Spier, in *The Legend of New Amsterdam,* has given the child living in New York City a portrait of that city's life over three hundred years ago. *Corn Is Maize: The Gift of the Indians* by Aliki reveals to the elementary school reader in a picturesque way one contribution of the Indians. Laurence Yep and Virginia Hamilton, along with others, have given us books through which children can identify with the heritage and contribution of their ethnic and racial cultures.

The cliché that "attitudes are caught, not taught" fits our fourth category, "Developing Personal Values." Values cannot be didactically presented to children. But the ideals and values presented in fiction challenge the young reader to a recognition of the personal values that they can choose to nourish within themselves. For example, the many fine books of Byrd Baylor, such as *The Way to Start A Day* and *Guess Who My Favorite Person Is,* present values that are secure, refreshing, and wholesome.

Many of the books that we read contribute to the development of a positive self image and help with the process of growing into self. The books chosen for this Ladder have a special contribution to make in this area, while in several cases they can be cross-referenced with other Ladders and categories. Literature which fosters respect for individuality helps young people explore human potential to the fullest.

Well chosen books provide a rich reservoir for the growing person to dip into; a reservoir where one encounters all of life, its problems and its promise. In reading, one is challenged to try on new roles, choose new models, and visualize oneself as full of untapped potential and unlimited possibilities. We need, now as never before, individuals who are confident in themselves if they are to confront world issues with any hope for the future.

Sister Rosemary Winkeljohann
and Ruth Gallant

Developing a Positive Self-Image

Ages 1 to 5

Ets, Marie Hall. **Just Me.** Illus. by author. Puffin 1978.

> A little boy finds it satisfying to imitate the various animals on the farm, but when he sees his dad, and runs to him, it is as himself, "just me." He knows, and is glad, that he is like nobody else at all. This is an excellent book for young children to act out, culminating in the special role of being themselves.

Hallinan, P. K. **I'm Glad to Be Me.** Illus. by author. Childrens 1977.

> This book shows young children many of the reasons why they should be glad to be themselves. Full page illustrations and large print make this an especially good book for sharing with the very young.

McNaughton, Colin. **The Rat Race: The Amazing Adventures of Anton B. Stanton.** Illus. by author. Doubleday 1978.

> Anton B. Stanton is a Tom Thumb-sized boy who follows a rat down a rat hole and enjoys adventures in which his size is not a drawback but an asset. The detailed, imaginative drawings will fascinate very young readers, while suggesting a better self image to children of small stature.

Moncure, Jane Belk. **All by Myself.** Illus. Frances Hook. Childrens 1976.

> The children featured here are proud of accomplishing things by themselves. Their efforts demonstrate the pride and challenge in managing to dress and play games without help.

Schwartz, Delmore. **"I Am Cherry Alive," the Little Girl Sang.** Illus. Barbara Cooney. Har-Row 1979.

> "Each morning I am something new." Poet and child continue an exploration of being "cherry alive" to the world about them. Barbara Cooney's illustrations complement the song of the child, the celebration of life set forth in the poem.

Developing a Positive Self-Image

Simon, Norma. **Why Am I Different?** Illus. Dora Leder. A Whitman 1976.

"I'm different! I'm getting a big front tooth. What's different about you?" Various children offer answers to the question, and explain why they are different in school, home, or other everyday situations. Each one examines personal preferences, family life, or physical attributes, and shows acceptance of these differences.

Skorpen, Liesel Moak. **Michael.** Illus. Joan Sandin. Har-Row 1975.

Michael has two problems: he is afraid of storms, and he can't seem to do anything right in his father's eyes. When he finds a baby rabbit, his father seems uncaring, and will not allow it in the house. Michael takes care of the small animal and becomes concerned about its safety during a storm. He overcomes his fears in order to help the bunny, and at the same time finds a new side to his father.

Stanton, Elizabeth, and Henry Stanton. **Sometimes I Like to Cry.** Illus. Richard Leyden. A Whitman 1978.

A child tells of the many occasions when he has cried. The story leaves the reader or listener with the impression that in growing up there are appropriate times for tears.

Stren, Patti. **Hug Me.**

Wulf, Kathleen. **I'm Glad I'm Little.**

Ages 5 to 8

Adoff, Arnold. **Big Sister Tells Me That I'm Black.** Illus. Lorenzo Lynch. HR&W 1976.

A boy and his sister discuss what they must be when they grow to adulthood. They want to be proud of being black, brave, strong, and smart; they want to be proud of themselves.

Ambrus, Victor. **Mishka.** Illus. by author. Warne 1978.

Mishka, an eight-year-old fiddle player, sets out to show his talents to the world by joining a circus. No one believes in his talent as a musician, so he becomes an odd jobs boy. One day he seizes the chance to show an audience his talents and is an overwhelming success.

Armstrong, William. **The Tale of Tawny and Dingo.**

Bach, Alice. **Grouchy Uncle Otto.** Illus. Steven Kellogg. Har-Row 1977.

>Oliver Bear is chosen to take care of Uncle Otto, who is sick. In spite of Oliver's memory of how Uncle Otto hates him, he goes—because he's an A-1 bear, so they say. Ronald, Oliver's brother, likes to think that he is the smartest one. When Ronald and Oliver switch places at Uncle Otto's house, Ronald does his best to make everything go wrong so that Oliver looks bad. Primary children find out who the smart bear is and how Uncle Otto's feelings change because of this little venture.

Bach, Alice. **Millicent the Magnificent.** Illus. Steven Kellogg. Har-Row 1978.

>Millicent, Girl Wonder, is a circus acrobat. She can hurtle through the air faster than any bear. When she offers to let Oliver be her assistant at the Bear Festival, he is delighted to become her pupil. But Oliver's twin brother, Ronald, wants no part of Millicent's training program. He decides to teach himself to be the best acrobat in the forest. This is the success story of a boy who doesn't always shine just like his twin brother.

Bach, Alice. **The Smartest Bear and His Brother Oliver.** Illus. Steven Kellogg. Har-Row 1975.

>In this story of two young brother bears, Ronald is the intellectual. By reading through a set of encyclopedias he hopes to become the smartest bear in the world. Oliver, on the other hand, simply rejoices in eating. The contrasting situations make for a humorous story about individuality.

Baylor, Byrd. **Hawk, I'm Your Brother.**

Bond, Gladys Baker. **Boy in the Middle.** Illus. Trina Hyman. Ginn 1972.

>Mick is unhappy because he thinks he has no identity. In appearance, he is exactly like his two brothers and nobody, not even his family at times, can tell them apart. The book deals with Mick's need to develop a concept of himself as separate and unique. At the end of the story he realizes that he is not merely a copy of his brothers, but an individual personality.

Bottner, Barbara. **Dumb Old Casey Is a Fat Tree.** Illus. by author. Har-Row 1979.

>In time, says seven-year-old Casey, she will be a "skinny as a song" ballet dancer. However, there is a more immediate problem: who

Developing a Positive Self-Image

wants to be a plump tree when one could be a princess, a queen, or an evil prince in the dance recital? Written and illustrated with humor and empathy.

Bulla, Clyde Robert. **Daniel's Duck.**

Bulla, Clyde Robert. **Keep Running, Allen!** Illus. Satomi Ichikawa. T Y Crowell 1978.

Youngest and smallest, Allen has difficulty keeping pace with his brothers and sister. Chasing after them, he trips. The grass feels good so he lies there, contentedly examining worm, bluejay, and cloudy sky, to the consternation of older, and presumably wiser siblings. The reversal of roles in "follow the leader" is eminently satisfying.

Bunting, Eve. **St. Patrick's Day in the Morning.**

Delton, Judy. **Two Good Friends.** Illus. Giulio Maestro. Crown 1974.

Bear loves to bake, and his friend Duck is an immaculate housekeeper. Each has a quality that the other needs and wants. In this simple story, Bear and Duck compensate for each other's shortcomings by sharing their talents and friendship.

Dumas, Philippe. **The Story of Edward.** Illus. by author. Parents 1977.

Edward is a dancing donkey who puts on quite a show, along with his musician master, Angelo Dupas. Just before Angelo dies he tells Edward to make it on his own but to never let anyone see his long ears. After entering the real world, Edward gets a job and falls in love with a human being. Then his secret is discovered. He flees the policemen, resumes his life as a donkey, and lives happily as himself.

Fassler, Joan. **Howie Helps Himself.** Illus. Joe Lasker. A Whitman 1975.

Howie is a physically handicapped child who wants more than anything to operate his own wheelchair and move about as other children do. Although he still can't walk, after a great deal of practice he tries with all his strength and is finally able to move the wheelchair with his hands.

Freschet, Berniece. **The Happy Dromedary.** Illus. Glen Rounds. Scribner 1977.

At first, the dromedary's body is not suited for life in the desert. He asks the King of the Animals to adjust his feet so he can walk easily on the sand, and to give him a hump on his back to store food and water. When the other animals see the results, they laugh. He again asks for help. The King gives it to him by proportioning his neck and nose to the rest of his body. From then on, the dromedary holds his head high and walks proudly. Discussion of this myth may prompt the writing of other "why and how" stories.

Hallinan, P. K. **Just Being Alone.** Illus. by author. Childrens 1976.

A little boy enjoys being alone. He can do anything he wants to do—think, daydream, or maybe just sleep the day away. He can run through a meadow at top speed, or follow a bee while it is gathering honey. The story illustrates that being alone is a good way to find out special things about oneself and the world.

Hallinan, P. K. **Where's Michael?** Illus. by author. Childrens 1978.

Michael wears his pig suit one day and everyone laughs. He thinks it's great that everyone notices him, so he wears another costume the next day, but people don't laugh as much. Each day he wears a different costume and people laugh less and less. At last he puts them all together to make one great costume, only to find himself trapped inside. Nobody notices him. When Michael admits to everyone that he wants to be himself again he is set free.

Hoff, Syd. **The Littlest Leaguer.**

Holding, James, Jr. **The Ugliest Dog in the World.** Illus. Marilyn Miller. Xerox Ed Pubns 1979.

Eight-year-old Caroline loves her dog Algernon very much. But "Algy" feels that he is ugly and doesn't amount to anything. He sets out to find the "secret to success." He asks many friends for their advice and each one gives a different answer. He is sad because he doesn't possess any of the qualities his friends do. It is not until Caroline is in danger and Algy shows his bravery that he discovers his own worth.

Hopkins, Lee Bennett, editor. **Girls Can Too! A Book of Poems.** Illus. Emily McCully. Watts 1972.

These poems celebrate active, curious, noisy, and not-so-noisy girls (and boys). The title poem and two others are by Hopkins. Also included are poems by David McCord, Myra Cohn Livingston, Aileen Fisher, and other favorite authors. Verses and illustrations both explode the stereotypical images of sex-typed behavior for children.

Kent, Jack. **The Wizard of Wallaby Wallow.** Parents 1971.

A mouse, dissatisfied with his lot in life, decides to buy a magic spell from the Wizard of Wallaby Wallow. He dreams of becoming something other than a mouse. However, the Wizard has only an unlabelled potion for him, and as the mouse speculates about the possible creatures he may become, he decides that the life of a mouse is not so bad.

Krasilovsky, Phyllis. **The Shy Little Girl.** Illus. Trina Schart Hyman. HM 1970.

Anne, shy and unhappy, doesn't like herself. She feels awkward and plain, and lacks self-confidence. Then one day she makes friends with a new girl at school and her life changes. By sharing herself with her friend, she develops confidence in herself and her abilities and begins to fit in with the other children at school. Most of all, she comes to like herself.

Kraus, Robert. **Leo the Late Bloomer.**

Kuskin, Karla. **Any Me I Want to Be.** Illus. by author. Har-Row 1972.

In the words of the author, these poems were written to encourage children to try on different lives—those of a whale, a bicycle, a broom, a parrot, the night, the moon, or a tree rooted in one spot "come rain, wind, snow, sleet, thaw, spring, summer, winter, fall, blight, bug, day, dark." They motivate children to express their own imaginings.

Molarsky, Osmond. **Song of the Empty Bottles.** Illus. Tom Feelings. Walck 1968.

Thaddeus, a young black boy, spends his Thursday afternoons at the Neighborhood House where children gather to sing. He does not sing, but listens to the director playing a guitar. After a talk with the director, he learns that if he can save $15, he can have a guitar of his own. Determined to own the instrument, he collects empty bottles and newspapers to save money. Later he grows discouraged and is ready to give up, until he composes a song for which he is paid. This is wonderful for a boy who loves music: his talent enables him to become the proud owner of a guitar.

Moncure, Jane Belk. **About Me.** Illus. Linda Somers. Childs World 1976.

Through rhyme and the use of first person narrative, a child relates what she is capable of enjoying with each of her senses. She takes delight in the many things she can do with her feet, hands, ears, and eyes. Through her senses, she identifies with the world around her and perceives beauty in her environment. With this awareness she is able to draw conclusions about her own feelings.

Peter, Diana. **Claire and Emma.**

Robinet, Harriette. **Jay and the Marigold.** Illus. Trudy Scott. Childrens 1976.

> Jay is eight years old and has cerebral palsy. He watches the other children play and feels sorry for himself because he is unable to talk or play with them. Then a marigold that manages to grow out of the corner of the concrete steps gives him something to care for all summer. It helps him see that there are ways of blooming in spite of handicaps.

Ross, Geraldine. **The Elf Who Didn't Believe in Himself.** Illus. Kurt Werth. Steck 1966.

> A small elf believes in everyone and everything, except himself. When he encounters two young boys who do believe in him, his whole self-concept changes.

Steinmetz, Leon. **Clocks in the Woods.** Illus. by author. Har-Row 1979.

> A greedy porcupine wants to get rich and decides to sell every animal in the woods a watch. He says, "with a watch you will always know when to get up and when to go to sleep. And you will never miss your dinner." The gullible animals buy watches, only to discover that they have bought trouble. When they discard them, they find that their natural gifts are all they need.

Waber, Bernard. **You Look Ridiculous Said the Rhinoceros to the Hippopotamus.** HM 1966.

> When she compares herself to the other jungle animals, a hippopotamus decides that she must look ridiculous. She lacks the handsome qualities of the other creatures and this makes her sad. She wishes she could look like them. When her wish comes true in a dream, she realizes that she doesn't look ridiculous at all, and accepts her identity.

Williams, Margery. **The Velveteen Rabbit: Or How Toys Become Real.** Illus. William Nicholson. Avon 1975.

> A splendid velveteen rabbit arrives in a little boy's Christmas stocking and is at first a favorite gift. Being naturally shy and made only of velveteen, he is soon snubbed for more expensive toys. Old, wise, and experienced Skin Horse tells the little rabbit how to become real. He finds that to be real he must be loved. This is nursery magic with a message on how to become real and loved in our world.

Developing a Positive Self-Image

Wise, William. **The Cowboy Surprise.** Illus. Paul Galdone. Putnam 1961.

> Mike and Sally are unhappy because they have to wear glasses. Sometimes the other children make fun of them. Everything changes, however, when Wild Bill, a famous cowboy, and his horse come to town to perform. The other children become envious because Mike and Sally wear glasses just like Wild Bill's.

Ages 8 to 11

Allen, Alex B. **Basketball Toss-Up.** Illus. Kevin Royt. A Whitman 1974.

> Jamie is faced with a personal struggle when his twin brother, Jack, begs him to join his boys' club basketball team. The big game of the year is at stake and two key players are out with the flu. Jamie has the talent to fill the spot, but must overcome the haunting fears that resulted from a mistake that cost last year's team the championship.

Blume, Judy. **Otherwise Known as Sheila the Great.** YB. Dell 1978.

> Sheila is a young girl who thinks she is great at everything. Yet she is afraid of dogs, the dark, swimming, and noises. She learns to overcome these fears and admit that she isn't so great. The result is a more accepting, realistic view of herself.

Blume, Judy. **Tales of a Fourth Grade Nothing.** Illus. Roy Doty. YB. Dell 1978.

> Peter Hatcher has quite a large problem—namely, his two-year-old brother, whom everyone calls Fudge. Peter thinks that the adults in his life do not realize how difficult it is living with someone that age. When Fudge swallows Peter's pet turtle and has to go to the hospital, Peter learns that his parents understand more than he suspected.

Bradbury, Bianca. **The Young Loner.** Illus. John Gretzer. Schol Bk Serv 1971.

> A young boy finds it difficult to get along with his older brother, who excels in all sports. He finds himself a summer job and is able to buy his own boat. He discovers that there are some things his brother can help him with and there are other things that he can do better himself. Realizing this, he is able to develop a friendship with his brother.

Byars, Betsy. **After the Goat Man.** Illus. Ronald Himler. Avon 1976.

> Harold Coleman is fat and miserable. Meeting Figgy and his eccentric grandfather, the goat man, helps Harold see problems that are

bigger than his own. The displacement of Figgy and his grandfather for the sake of an interstate highway provides the plot for a story about friends, their feelings, and their adventures.

Byars, Betsy. **The Cartoonist**

Christopher, Matt. **Glue Fingers.** Illus. Jim Venable. Little 1975.

Billy Joe loves to play football, but he won't play on a regular team because he is ashamed of his stuttering. After much support from his family, he successfully tries out for the team. When the first game is over, Billy has not only helped his team, but he realizes that he doesn't have to be afraid of stuttering anymore.

Cleary, Beverly. **Ramona the Brave.** Illus. Alan Tiegreen. Morrow 1975.

Ramona Quimby, who is in first grade, thinks she has many problems. Her sister Beezus, a fifth grader, seems to be favored by her teachers, parents, and neighbors. Ramona wants to be liked too, and tries hard to be brave and spunky, but most of her efforts are in vain. Then one day she takes a new route to school, has an encounter with a German shepherd, and discovers new strength in herself.

Conaway, Judith. **Will I Ever Be Good Enough?** Illus. Bruce Witty. Raintree Pubs Ltd 1977.

A young girl wonders if she'll have what it takes to be a scientist, an explorer, a model, a photographer, or an Olympic athlete. She doubts that she will ever be good enough to be anything at all. The girl her friend Meg then do several things together. The result is that she overcomes her envy of Meg, and develops enough self-confidence to say "You know, if I really wanted to, I think I could."

Cretan, Gladys Yessayan. **All Except Sammy.** Illus. Symeon Shimin. Little 1966.

Coming from a very musical family is great—if you are also musical. This is Sammy's problem: he can't seem to play an instrument of any kind. A solution begins to evolve while Sammy is touring an art gallery on a homework assignment. Intrigued with the skill of painters, he decides he wants to learn the art himself. The next family picture shows Sammy in the center of his family, displaying the poster he made for the family concerts. At last a part of the artistic family, Sammy realizes that playing an instrument isn't the only thing a boy can do.

de Paola, Tomie. **The Clown of God.** Illus. by author. HarBraceJ 1978.

> Little Giovanni is a poor, homeless child who discovers that he can please people by juggling. He joins a troupe of traveling players as a clown. He becomes famous, and entertains people until he is an old man. One day his talents fail him and he drops his yellow Sun-in-Heaven ball. He is rejected, and becomes a beggar once more. When he takes refuge in a church one Christmas Eve, a miracle occurs and he offers his talents as a gift to the Christ child.

Dionetti, Michelle. **Thalia Brown and the Blue Bug.**

Fogel, Julianna A. **Wesley Paul, Marathon Runner.** Illus. Mary S. Watkins. Lippincott 1979.

> Wesley Paul broke the record for nine-year-olds in the New York City Marathon. He describes the training, the race, and his dream of being an Olympic runner. An atmosphere of sportsmanship and encouragement of others permeates the text.

Friis-Baastad, Babbis. **Kristy's Courage.**

Girion, Barbara. **Joshua, the Czar, and the Chicken Bone Wish.**

Green, Phyllis. **The Fastest Quitter in Town.** Illus. Lorenzo Lynch. Young Scott 1972.

> Johnny Colmer quits playing baseball every time he starts. As soon as things do not go his way, he quits. Yet when his great-grandfather loses a diamond ring, and a search begins, this is one time Johnny does not quit. He knows how much the ring means to his great-grandfather and keeps looking long after the others have given up, discovering that he is not a quitter, after all.

Hicks, Clifford B. **Alvin's Swap Shop.** Illus. Lisl Weil. Schol Bk Serv 1977.

> Alvin Fernald is a twelve-year-old boy known as Magnificent Brain because he can think of fantastic ideas. With his sister and another friend, he opens a swap shop for the summer and they get involved in trying to solve a murder. Alvin catches the murderer in his swap shop and solves the mystery. Readers can compare Alvin's experiences with other stories of youthful competence.

Hunt, Irene. **The Lottery Rose.**

King, Cynthia. **The Year of Mr. Nobody.** Illus. Malcolm Carrick. Har-Row, 1978.

> Everyone in the family gets used to Mr. Nobody except Mother, who says, "Frankly, I don't like Mr. Nobody. He's a troublemaker." Abbot knows that Mr. Nobody doesn't start trouble; he just comes when trouble comes. For example, when other people think you're too little to go out after dark on Halloween, or too little to know when you aren't sick any more, it's nice to have a friend like Mr. Nobody to back you up. However, on the night when a young bull comes into the yard, Abbot finds that only a real person can take action: he must begin to depend on himself.

Levitin, Sonia. **A Sound to Remember.**

Levy, Elizabeth. **Lizzie Lies a Lot.** Illus. John Wallner. YB. Dell 1977.

> Lizzie is a compulsive liar who doesn't realize that her lies keep growing. Her best friend Sara begins to suspect her, and their friendship is hurt. Lizzie's grandmother knows what the problem is and tries to do something, but her actions are resented. The problem is brought out in the open when Lizzie's parents help her see why she is lying and understand herself better.

Little, Jean. **From Anna.**

Mark, Jan. **Under the Autumn Garden.**

Petersen, Palle. **Sally Can't See.** Illus. Jeremy Finlay. John Day 1977.

> Born blind, twelve-year-old Sally goes to school for the blind where she learns by using her other senses. For example, her fingertips help her read Braille letters and numbers. The picture book format, visually descriptive, can prompt a discussion of the many things that Sally is able to do for herself.

Rosen, Winifred. **Henrietta, the Wild Woman of Borneo.** Illus. Kay Chorao. Four Winds. Schol Bk Serv 1975.

> Henrietta is having a very difficult time pleasing members of her family, especially her older sister Evelyn, who has beautiful silky reddish hair and is "pretty enough to be on television." Henrietta, on the other hand, has braces on her teeth and her hair is brown and bushy. Whenever she comes in from the park, her mother says, "Henrietta, you look like the Wild Woman of Borneo!" She decides to fix up a crate and ship herself off to Borneo, for surely no one

Developing a Positive Self-Image

would criticize her there. Her "journey to Borneo," and what she discovers about Evelyn and their parents makes a funny, heartwarming story.

Sachs, Marilyn. **Marv.** Illus. Louis Glanzman. YB. Dell 1973.

Marv is always dreaming about building new inventions. Meanwhile, his teacher considers him stupid and his sister, whom he adores, constantly criticizes his behavior. He fails to please her time after time because she, like others, doesn't see his genius. Due to their low expectations, he considers himself a failure. Actually he has great potential which needs fostering. This book gives insight into the problems of being different in this special way.

Smith, Doris Buchanan. **Kelly's Creek.**

Smith, Robert Kimmel. **Chocolate Fever.** Illus. Gioia Fiammenghi. YB. Dell 1978.

Henry Green has no ordinary love of chocolate; he practically lives on it. He loves chocolate so much that he even puts it on his mashed potatoes and noodles. Poor Henry's love of chocolate results in a "rare disease" and he runs away from home. This is a humorous and tender story about the many misunderstandings that we all face at some time in our life.

Sperry, Armstrong. **Call It Courage.** Macmillan 1971.

Mafatu, son of a South Seas island chief, grows up with a fear of the sea, the result of his near-drowning in a storm which took his mother's life. Mafatu's fear is especially disastrous since the islanders must make their living from the sea. When he can no longer face the derision at home, he sets out across the sea in spite of his fear, finds a lonely island where he proves his courage in the face of many dangers, and eventually returns to his father's island.

Yolen, Jane. **The Boy Who Had Wings.** Illus. Helga Aichinger. T Y Crowell 1974.

In a story that combines the power of Greek myth and psychological insights, Jane Yolen taps the deep and universal roots of every child's dreams. When Aetos is born with wings, his parents and older brothers are amazed and they reject him. A black cloak is made to conceal the wings, and he is advised to keep the secret. He is glad to hide his "differentness." But when his herdsman father is trapped in the snows of the high mountains only Aetos is able to help, and the boy suddenly realizes his unusual gift. As he lifts his father to safety in one great thrilling flight, he lifts himself, too, out of his loneliness and feelings of insignificance.

Ages 11 to 14

Branscum, Robbie. **The Ugliest Boy.**

Cunningham, Julia. **Come to the Edge.** Avon 1978.

>Gravel Winter was ten when his father left him at the foster farm. Until then, he had lived with his drunken father and never had a good friend because they moved around all the time. At the farm he and a boy called Skin become close friends. After four years Skin leaves without telling him and without saying good-bye. Gravel is devastated and runs away from the home. He knows that his father doesn't want him, and now that his best friend is gone he is struck by fear, a feeling of grayness, and a feeling of worthlessness. He goes on to befriend four people and conflict develops when he's afraid to get too close for fear of losing them. He has to learn to accept loving people again.

Distad, Audree. **The Dream Runner.** Har-Row 1978.

>An old man's recollection of the "vision quests" of Indian youth seeking inner power spurs Sam into the mountains on a similar search. Awed by the freedom and strength of the wild horses and befriended by the maverick Mrs. Em, he survives storm and injury on his lonely climb and finds hidden reservoirs of strength within himself.

Donovan, John. **I'll Get There: It Better Be Worth the Trip.**

Gessner, Lynne. **To See a Witch.**

Haynes, Betsy. **Slave Girl.**

Hentoff, Nat. **This School Is Driving Me Crazy.** LFL. Dell 1978.

>Sam Davidson is a student at the private Bronson Allcott School in New York City, and he is very unhappy there partly because the headmaster is his father. He gets into trouble when one of the younger students tells him about three school bullies who are trying to get money from the little kids. Because he has promised not to tell, and because his father is the headmaster, it develops into a big episode for Sam—a time of personal decision making.

Joseph, Stephen M., editor. **The Me Nobody Knows: Children's Voices from the Ghetto.** World Pub. Avon 1972.

Sensitive teachers with a positive attitude toward learning and children inspired these perceptive writings. The ghetto children tell it like it is—about themselves, their neighborhood, their world.

Van Leeuwen, Jean. **I Was a 98-Pound Duckling.** YB. Dell 1974.

Kathy McGruder, her family, and friend Beth Hardy spend a few weeks at their lake cabin every summer. Thirteen-year-old Kathy weighs ninety-eight pounds and feels she is an ugly duckling compared to Beth. With all her beauty problems, she believes that no boy will want to date her. However, she does meet a boy who asks her out, and he wants to write to her when summer is over. Kathy develops a more positive self-image and realizes that although her beauty problems still exist, she can deal with them.

Lipsyte, Robert. **One Fat Summer.** Bantam 1978.

An overweight boy builds confidence in himself by getting a summer job. He doesn't tell his father at first in case he fails at it. In spite of the hard work, a difficult employer, and a bully, he is able to do the job. By working so hard at his job, he is able to lose some weight. His success at work also gives him the strength to watch his diet. He realizes he will have weak moments but he has learned how to say "no" to food. He begins to feel better about himself and his future.

Steele, Mary Q., and William O. Steele. **The Eye in the Forest.**

Thiele, Colin. **Blue Fin.** Illus. Roger Haldane. Har-Row 1974.

This story deals with the relationship between an awkward, fourteen-year-old boy named Snook and his hard-nosed, sea-going father, whom he greatly admires. Ridiculed at school and dismissed by his father as "good for nothing," Snook has grave doubts about his own abilities. But he discards his negative self-image and his clumsiness forever, and wins the respect of his father in an exciting rescue at sea.

Ages 14 and Up

Green, Hannah. **I Never Promised You a Rose Garden.**

Madison, Winifred. **A Portrait of Myself.**

O'Dell, Scott. **Carlota.** HM 1977.

A fearless and competent horsewoman, Carlota is the pride of her father, Don Saturnino, and a scandal to her proud, domineering grandmother. She joins her father and the other rancheros in the war for possession of California, but her valor is touched with pity for the one gringo soldier she lances. At this point, she assumes control of her heritage—of land and power and herself.

Terris, Susan. **The Drowning Boy.** Doubleday 1972.

Reacting to the passivity of his mother and the competitiveness of his father and sister, Jason refuses to excel in any way. Apprenticed to a teacher-carpenter, Sam Slavin, he shares in the care of Slavin's autistic nephew, Buddy. He attempts to shock Buddy into recovery by introducing him to Gammer who, in her senility, is beyond all caring and knowing. The attempt ends in disaster and Jason retreats into total despair. But his summer of caring has made a difference. He begins to manage his own life, including the relationships within his family.

Growing into Maturity

Ages 1 to 5

Arnstein, Helene S. **Billy and Our New Baby.** Illus. M. Jane Smyth. Human Sci Pr 1973.

When Billy's mother and father bring home the new baby, he becomes very jealous. To receive the attention he wants from his mother, Billy starts to act like a baby himself. But after his mother explains how much better off he is being a big boy rather than a baby, he realizes his new status, begins to love the new baby, and welcomes him to the family.

Barrett, Judi. **I Hate to Go to Bed.** Illus. Ray Cruz. Four Winds. Schol Bk Serv 1977.

Children's feelings about going to bed, both pleasant and unpleasant, are captured in the text and the colorful, realistic illustrations. The text lends itself to young readers sharing their own similar experiences and feelings.

Carrick, Carol. **The Accident.** Illus. Donald Carrick. Seabury 1976.

Christopher is disconsolate when his dog, Bodger, is hit by a truck. He accuses his father of not caring for either Bodger or him. It is a gentle story in which an understanding father lets anger give way to tears, and tears to the comfort of shared memories and love.

Clifton, Lucille. **Some of the Days of Everett Anderson.** Illus. Evaline Ness. HR&W 1970.

"Daddy's back is broad and black and Everett Anderson loves to ride it." Who is Everett Anderson? He is any child who has ever missed his daddy, played in the rain, been afraid of the dark, or wondered about the stars.

Corey, Dorothy. **You Go Away.**

Dauer, Rosamond. **Bullfrog Grows Up.** Illus. Byron Barton. Greenwillow 1976.

> A family of mice raises a tadpole, but when he turns into a bullfrog, he begins to eat enormous amounts of food. The mice come to terms with their foster child and ask Bullfrog to move out and make a life of his own.

Delton, Judy, and Elaine Knox-Wagner. **The Best Mom in the World.** Illus. John Falkner. A Whitman 1979.

> Lee Henry thinks he has the best mom in the world—until today, when she is working late. He must now learn to do everything she usually does for him. As he is learning to help himself, he realizes why he does have the best mom in the world.

Fitzhugh, Louise. **I Am Five.** Illus. by author. Delacorte 1978.

> The day after her fifth birthday, a little girl delightfully describes her likes, dislikes, and activities. She shares a great deal with the reader: her swimming suit, her feelings of being sad, her knowledge of how to laugh, and the three things she dislikes most.

Hazen, Barbara Shook. **The Gorilla Did It.** Illus. Ray Cruz. Schol Bk Serv 1974.

> A gorilla in the bedroom? Mommy doesn't understand that he just comes to play at night, and he doesn't mean to make a big mess. This book deals with a young boy's imaginary playmate, who is "responsible" for whatever goes wrong in the boy's life.

Iverson, Genie. **I Want to Be Big.** Illus. David McPhail. Unicorn. Dutton 1979.

> This story presents a little girl who wants to be big enough to dress herself, catch the school bus, be in the first grade, reach the right elevator button, watch monster movies, and eat supper at a friend's house. But she does not want to be big enough to stay overnight at her friend's house, or sleep without a night light, and not too big for her mother's lap or fuzzy bathrobe.

Little, Lessie Jones, and Eloise Greenfield. **I Can Do It by Myself.** Illus. Carole Byard. T Y Crowell 1978.

> Donny's birthday gift for his mother is a plant which he intends to buy and carry home on his own. A rough looking, loudly barking bulldog stands between him and the realization of his plans. Even Wade, his big brother, takes pride in Donny's determined independence.

Growing into Maturity

MacLachlan, Patricia. **Through Grandpa's Eyes.**

Ages 5 to 8

Allard, Harry. **It's So Nice to Have a Wolf Around the House.** Illus. James Marshall. Doubleday 1977.

> An old man living with a cat, a dog, and a tropical fish, advertises for a housekeeper to take care of them and be a companion in their last years. Cuthbert Q. Devine, looking very much like a wolf, answers the ad, is hired, and brings cheer to the household. When it is discovered that he is wanted for bank robbery, he explains that everyone expected him to be bad because he was a wolf; then he has an attack of nerves, and faints dead away. This leads to an interesting examination of good and bad behavior, and the chance to be forgiven.

Blegvad, Lenore. **Moon-Watch Summer.**

Carlson, Natalie Savage. **Runaway Marie Louise.** Illus. Jose Aruego and Ariane Dewey. Scribner 1977.

> A little brown mongoose named Marie Louise runs away from home after her mother spanks her for being naughty. She feels that she is no longer loved. In the course of her search for a new mother, she visits the homes of many of her friends, but fails to find a mother who wants another child. Eventually she talks to the witch toad who leads her back to her real mother.

Delton, Judy. **It Happened on Thursday.**

Evans, Mari. **Jim Flying High.** Illus. Ashley Bryan. Doubleday 1979.

> Jim, the flying fish, is caught in a tree and too proud to admit his need for help. "Everyone knows he in trouble," says the storyteller. Family and friends don't wait to be asked for help, so the tale ends on a strong note of community support and interdependence. The use of black idiom increases the effect of oral narration.

Hoban, Lillian. **Arthur's Honey Bear.** Illus. by author. Har-Row 1974.

> Arthur is a small monkey who decides to clean out his old toys and have a tag sale. He is willing to part with the hula hoop, yo-yo, marbles, and even Baby King Kong. But when it comes to his Honey Bear, which he received from his father when he had chicken pox, Arthur has second thoughts. After an afternoon of no sales, his sister

Violet buys Honey Bear for 31¢! His misery is compounded when she dresses Honey Bear in girls' clothes. After much consideration, he discovers a solution—since he is Violet's brother, he is Honey Bear's uncle, so they can spend a lot of time together.

Holmes, Efner Tudor. **Amy's Goose.** Illus. Tasha Tudor. T Y Crowell 1977.

Amy is a lonely child who waits every spring and fall for the geese to stop at her farm. One fall, a fox attacks the flock and injures a goose. She grows attached to it as she and her father nurse it back to health. When the flock prepares to leave, one gander remains behind, calling to it. Amy wishes she could keep the goose but realizes that it must join its mate. Tearfully, she sets it free.

Hopkins, Lee Bennett. **By Myself.** Illus. Glo Coalson. T Y Crowell 1980.

A collection of appealing poems that deal with concerns of growing up: relationships with parents, explorations with nature, and discoveries of self. The ending of Myra Cohn Livingston's poem, "Tomorrow," sums up the essence of all: "It is the growing up, The tomorrow, Of me."

Horvath, Betty. **Will the Real Tommy Wilson Please Stand Up.** Illus. Charles Robinson. Watts 1969.

Brian Hopper does everything well and Tommy Wilson wants to be just like him. So, he dresses like him, talks like him, acts like him, and even begins to look like him. However, one day at school his mother mistakes Brian for her son, and Tommy unhappily discovers that the real Tommy Wilson no longer exists. When his mother finally recognizes him, he sees that it is best to just be himself.

Hutchins, Pat. **Don't Forget the Bacon!** Illus. by author. Puffin 1978.

A seven-year-old boy goes grocery shopping for his mother. As he is walking to the store he tries to remember the grocery list, but he is distracted by all the things on the way. The list grows as he walks along, and it's surprising what he takes home.

Kay, Helen. **An Egg Is for Wishing.** Illus. Yaroslava. Abelard 1966.

Nikolas' mother would like to paint a Ukranian Easter egg for him, but because he is so afraid of the rooster, he is unable to bring her a hen's egg. He collects eggs from many types of birds and finally manages to throw corn to the rooster and get a hen's egg. To his surprise it hatches. His mother explains that the chick needs the hen for warmth and protection, and in his concern for it he walks past the rooster, unafraid, to return the chick to its mother.

Keeping, Charles. **The Nanny Goat and the Fierce Dog.** Illus. by author. S G Phillips 1973.

A little nanny goat is left to fend for herself after her mother is killed by a fierce dog. She is frightened, and conscious of the danger that lies outside the protection of the fence. When spring arrives and she comes face to face with the dog, she proves what a brave and independent little goat she has become.

Kellogg, Steven. **Much Bigger Than Martin.** Illus. by author. Dial 1976.

Being a little brother has its problems, and Henry wishes he were bigger. He tries various means, including watering himself and eating apples, but he doesn't seem to grow. His parents and big brother Martin help him realize that Martin was once his size, and could not hit the basketball hoop, either. Henry accepts himself more as he realizes that he, too, will grow with time.

Krahn, Fernando. **April Fools.** Illus. by author. Dutton 1974.

Two eight-year-old boys build a monster to scare the townspeople on April Fools' Day, and it appears mysteriously all over town. When they get themselves into trouble, they have to use their monster to get out.

Kroll, Steven. **That Makes Me Mad!** Illus. Hilary Knight. Pantheon 1976.

Humor is used to illustrate situations which make young children angry with their parents. Nina's anger comes out as: "I need to stay up late and it's always my bedtime," or "I try very hard and it doesn't come out right." She also expresses the fact that it makes her happy when her parents let her tell them how angry she gets sometimes.

Kuskin, Karla. **The Bear Who Saw the Spring.** Illus. by author. Har-Row 1961.

This book deals with the change of the seasons, running parallel with the changes living things go through as they grow to maturity. The child learns that it is natural for animals to be born, to live, and then to die.

Moskin, Marietta. **Lysbet and the Fire Kittens.** Illus. Margot Tomes. Schol Bk Serv 1973.

Home from school on a holiday, Lysbet is supposed to take care of the house until her father returns, but she leaves to go skating. When she returns to take care of her kitten, she discovers a fire in her home, and realizes how important it is to carry out one's responsibilities.

Power, Barbara. **I Wish Laura's Mommy Was My Mommy.** Illus. Marylin Hafner. Lippincott 1979.

Laura's mother gives cookies and candy for after school snacks; Jennifer's mom gives fruit. Laura's family eats in the dining room with flowers and candles; Jennifer's eats in the kitchen because her little brothers are messy. When Jennifer sleeps over at Laura's, they stay up very late and have pillow fights. At Jennifer's house they must go to bed and be quiet so they won't wake up the babies. Jennifer wishes she lived with Laura, until Laura's mother comes to babysit, and the restrictions placed on her by her own mother are now enforced by Laura's mom.

Prager, Annabelle. **The Surprise Party.** Illus. Tomie de Paola. Pantheon 1977.

Nicky arranges his own surprise birthday party, only to find that his friends have made other plans for him.

Reinach, Jacquelyn. **Who Stole Alligator's Shoe?**

Riley, Susan. **Afraid: What Does It Mean?** Childs World 1978.

In this series book, a boy hides behind the door because he's afraid to come out. He tells what he's afraid of—the dark, heights, shots, storms, thunder, lightning, and doing things for the first time, like going to school or being in a parade. After talking about these things he's not afraid anymore, so he comes out from behind the door. He conveys the idea that if you talk about your fears, you'll feel much better about them.

Sharmat, Marjorie Weinman. **I Don't Care.** Illus. Lillian Hoban. Macmillan 1977.

Jonathan's smiling blue balloon is fun to play with, until one day it slips through his fingers and disappears. He repeatedly assures his family and friends that it doesn't matter, but in the evening, he can't eat supper, some tears appear, and he begins crying. His pent-up feelings about the loss of his balloon are released.

Sharmat, Marjorie Weinman. **I'm Not Oscar's Friend Anymore.** Illus. Tony Deluna. Dutton 1975.

This is a humorous, yet sad, account of how it feels to lose a best friend after a fight. The little boy feels that it will take forever to make up. "Forever, like never. Because I will never make up with Oscar." He misses their friendship so much, however, that he finally swallows his pride and makes a phone call. Learning that his friend has already forgotten the fight, he thinks, "Oscar can't remember anything unless I remind him. Yes sir, without me Oscar is a sinking ship."

Skorpen, Liesel Moak. **His Mother's Dog.** Illus. M. E. Mullin. Har-Row 1978.

A boy gets a long-awaited dog only to have it give its loyalty and love to his mother instead of to him. He continues to take care of the dog and be responsible, as he promised he would, but it remains his mother's dog—until his baby sister arrives. In adjusting to this new development, the boy and his mother's dog become companions.

Skorpen, Liesel Moak. **Kisses and Fishes.** Illus. Steven Kellogg. Har-Row 1974.

Erwina's mother was swallowed by a fish and her father, trying to save his wife, was swallowed by the sea. She lives alone in her house and with no one to boss her about, does whatever she likes. After all the good food in the house is gone, she eats seaweed. She spends the holidays and her birthday by herself. Finally she dreams that the sea feels sorry for her and gives her back her parents. Erwina wakes up, and her parents are there. This is a good story about both independence and interdependence.

Thomas, Ianthe. **Hi, Mrs. Mallory!**

Thompson, Jean. **I'm Going to Run Away.**

Viorst, Judith. **Try It Again, Sam.** Illus. Paul Galdone. Lothrop 1970.

A mother has faith in her son's ability to walk to David's house safely. Sam promises to turn right around and come home if he gets into any trouble on the way. He does get into trouble by disobeying the rules for safe-walking and, consequently, returns home many times. But his mother is very understanding, tells him to "try it again," and finally he succeeds.

Waber, Bernard. **Ira Sleeps Over.** HM 1972.

Ira is invited to sleep overnight at Reggie's but there is one problem:

he can't sleep without his teddy bear. He goes through great deliberations about whether or not to take the bear. After a scary story session, both boys make a decision that helps them sleep through the night.

Williams, Barbara. **If He's My Brother.**

Ages 8 to 11

Asch, Frank. **Gia and the One Hundred Dollars Worth of Bubblegum.** Illus. Russell Alan Busah, Linda Galle, and Pat Galle. McGraw 1974.

Gia is a young girl who likes to help others. When she and her friends go to the circus one day, they help a dog in need of medical attention. The dog rewards Gia's helpfulness by giving her one hundred dollars, with which she buys bubblegum. She and her friends chew and blow bubbles until they blow away with the sticky gum. A bird pops their bubble and helps them get back to the safety of the circus. This story contrasts maturity and immaturity in a humorous way.

Buchan, Stuart. **When We Lived with Pete.** Scribner 1978.

This well-written narrative helps the reader understand Tommy's innermost feelings about his mother's breakup with Pete, his need for a father, and his gradual realization that other people have needs, too, although they may take different forms. Elements such as a deserted Hollywood estate, a horrendous fire, a daring rescue, and a reunion with Pete carry the story to a satisfactory climax.

Bulla, Clyde Robert. **Shoeshine Girl.** Illus. Leigh Grant. Schol Bk Serv 1975.

Sarah Ida, troublesome at home, arrives in Palmville to stay with her Aunt Claudia for the summer. Wanting her independence, she gets a shoeshine job with a man named Al. Through her job, she begins to learn the value of money and of friendship. When Al has to spend a long time in the hospital, Sarah keeps the business open for him. At the end of the summer, she goes home, a more mature and wiser person.

Byars, Betsy. **Good-Bye, Chicken Little.** Har-Row 1979.

First the death of his father, and then the drowning of his Uncle Pete leave Jimmie fearful and anxious, a self-dubbed Chicken Little.

His family, celebrating the Uncle Pete of their memories, provides the antidote for his fears.

Calhoun, Mary. **Ownself.** Har-Row 1975.

Laurabelle Morgan feels unappreciated and forgotten by her large family. There is no place for her between four brothers and two sisters. Even her father, with whom she once felt a closeness, has turned against her. When she summons up a fairy, she is laughed at, scolded, and scorned. But through it all, she learns the meaning of "ownself" and resolves the conflict with her father. There are some good references to what life may have been like at the turn of the century in a small Missouri town.

Clymer, Eleanor. **Me and the Eggman.** Illus. David K. Stone. Dutton 1972.

Ten-year-old Donald decides to run away from home. His home is crowded and he is tired of Aunt Lizzie continually bossing him around. He runs away to Mike the Eggman's farm, where he finds out that farm life is hard work. However, helping the elderly farmer proves to be a growing experience with much self-satisfaction involved.

Colman, Hila. **The Secret Life of Harold the Bird Watcher.** Illus. Charles Robinson. T Y Crowell 1978.

Harold is a nine-year-old boy who has a secret world. He spends most of his time alone in a small cove at the lake watching the wildlife and letting the imagination run wild. He is very anxious to make his parents proud of him, so he dreams of situations in which he is the hero. In an unexpected turn of events he does become a hero in real life and learns an important lesson.

Grisé, Jeannette. **Robert Benjamin and the Great Blue Dog Joke.** Illus. Alex Stein. Westminster 1978.

Robert is continually playing practical jokes on his classmates, school principal, and family. There is one joke that gets him into deep trouble with the biggest, strongest boy in the fifth grade: he paints Lester's art project, a leather dog, blue. Through this experience he matures, and comes to realize that a good joke shouldn't ruin anything and shouldn't make people mad—it should help make them happy.

Hays, Wilma Pitchford. **Trouble at Otter Creek.** Illus. Marilyn Miller. Xerox Ed Pubns 1978.

Ten-year-old Sam Story, his mother Ann, and his four brothers and sisters leave their home in New Hampshire to live in the cabin their father built near Otter Creek. Sam's father was killed by a falling tree that he was cutting down while building the cabin. From the time the family leaves New Hampshire, many exciting and dreadful things happen. The family shows great courage and love as they survive in their new home.

Irwin, Hadley. **The Lilith Summer.**

Jones, Adrienne. **Sail, Calypso.** Illus. Adolph Le Moult. Little 1968.

A lonely summer, an abandoned boat, and two boys make a wonderful story of friendship. Clay, a black boy whose family are migrant workers, is the first to find the boat and makes plans to return and spend his time fixing it up. The white boy, Paul, finds the boat a day later, but also claims his right to fix it up. Refusing to work at the same time, they agree upon the plan of taking turns alone with the boat on an every other day basis. After considerable antagonism they realize that the boat can be fixed much faster if they work together. As the boys become united in their efforts, they find that friendship is even more valuable than the boat they worked all summer to restore.

Konigsburg, E. L. **From the Mixed-Up Files of Mrs. Basil E. Frankweiler.** Atheneum 1968.

A delightful account of two runaways, Claudia and Jamie Kincaid. Claudia masterminds the trip which takes them to the Metropolitan Museum of Art. A new statue called "Angel" mesmerizes Claudia with its beauty and she becomes engrossed in discovering the maker. This leads them to Mrs. Frankweiler's house and files. The grand old dame gives her the key to unlock the secret, thus making it possible for Claudia to return home.

Kurelek, William. **A Prairie Boy's Summer.**

Langton, Jane. **The Fledgling.**

Le Guin, Ursula K. **Wizard of Earthsea.** Illus. Ruth Robbins. Bantam 1975.

The boy, Sparrowhawk, later to become Ged, learns the rules and the means of wizardry, and his own heart, as he faces his destiny in this powerful fantasy-allegory. Though set as prose, the rhythms of the language are truly and consistently poetical.

Lexau, Joan M. **Me Day.** Illus. Robert Weaver. Dial 1971.

It is Rafer's birthday and he is very excited about getting out of chores, choosing the TV shows he'll watch, and having cake for supper. But even with all these good things he has a growing feeling of disappointment. His parents are divorced and he misses his dad. He waits for the mailman, but there is no letter. After his mother gets a phone call, she sends him on a mysterious errand to pick up a package at the fruit stand. His Dad is waiting there to see him! He reassures Rafer that despite the divorce, he and Rafer are tight as glue and will be spending the day together.

Rawls, Wilson. **Summer of the Monkeys.**

Silman, Roberta. **Somebody Else's Child.** Illus. Chris Conover. Warne 1976.

Ten-year-old Peter had been adopted as a baby by loving and understanding parents. However, he begins to question his own sense of belonging, when a special friend, his bus driver, makes an innocent remark about bringing up "somebody else's child." As the story develops, these two people—one young, one old—gain insight into the love and warmth between parents and adopted children.

Simon, Norma. **We Remember Philip.** Illus. Ruth Sanderson. A Whitman 1979.

When their teacher's son Philip dies in a mountain-climbing accident, Sam and his classmates are bewildered—about death, about coping with death, and about showing their concern to the family of the dead person. They send letters to Mr. Hall, but when he returns to school they don't feel he is the same man; he is sad and quiet—not "his old, cheerful, friendly self." The children work with their parents and principal to give Mr. Hall and his family a lasting memorial to Philip.

Stolz, Mary. **Ferris Wheel.** Har-Row 1977.

Nine-year-old Polly is desolate when her best friend moves to California. Quarreling with her seven-year-old brother adds to her summer moodiness. But when she sees that Rusty needs help, and her new neighbor lacks friends, she comes to the rescue of both.

Terris, Susan. **No Boys Allowed.** Illus. Richard Cuffari. Doubleday 1976.

Being the youngest child and the only boy in a family with four older sisters can be frustrating. Thinking about "boys' lib," Tad decides to set out on his own to buy his mother a birthday present. This leads to a terrifying, but nevertheless educational experience for Tad.

Tobias, Tobi. **The Quitting Deal.** Illus. Trina Schart Hyman. Viking Pr 1975.

Mother and daughter vow to help each other give up their respective bad habits of smoking and thumb-sucking. After many attempts and strategies, they both realize they must "kind of sneak up on quitting, a little bit at a time."

Tolles, Martha. **Katie and Those Boys.** Illus. Lisl Weil. Schol Bk Serv 1974.

Katie, a ten-year-old girl, is tired of having only boys to play with; she is the only girl on Apple Street. She invites girls to play with her but her brothers and their friends are always picking on them. Even when they play in the vacant summerhouse, a ghost scares them away. When the house next door comes up for sale, Katie sees an opportunity to find someone with a daughter to buy the house. The story points up the importance of relating to both sexes in growing up.

Wolkstein, Diane. **The Red Lion: A Tale of Ancient Persia.**

Yolen, Jane. **The Transfigured Hart.** Illus. Donna Diamond. T Y Crowell 1975.

The three characters in this work are Richard Plante, a loner who has trouble with his heart; Heather Fielding, an enjoyer, and the only girl in a family of boys; and the hart, an albino deer who is weak and frightened. Different as they are, Richard and Heather become friends as the opening day of deer-hunting season approaches. They find themselves with an urgent common cause—saving the white deer from the hunters. Together, they learn about themselves, and the strange secret of the mysterious hart.

Ages 11 to 14

Blume, Judy. **Deenie.**

Clifton, Lucille. **The Times They Used to Be.** Illus. Susan Jeschke. YB. Dell 1976.

A black woman is recounting the summer of her twelfth year to her children. Adventures with her best friend in the summer of 1948 involve fun, ghosts, love, and the thoughts of a girl blossoming into womanhood.

Colman, Hila. **Tell Me No Lies.** Crown 1978.

When Angela's mother marries Larry and he offers to adopt Angela, she discovers that there was no previous marriage, no divorce, and no father in Saudi Arabia. Instead, her father is a bus ride away, and he has never known of her. In seeking him out, she decides that growing up is both more painful and more rewarding than she had expected.

Cooper, Gordon. **A Second Springtime.**

Danziger, Paula. **The Cat Ate My Gymsuit.** LFL. Dell 1976.

Marcy, a junior high student, has problems with her parents, her social life, and her weight. Her life gains purpose and meaning through contact with a remarkable English teacher. When Ms. Finney is not rehired for the next school year, the students protest. She and Marcy help the students understand issues of teacher independence and student protest. Under Ms. Finney's influence, they all grow.

Fitzhugh, Louise. **Nobody's Family Is Going to Change.** Illus. by author. YB. Dell 1975.

Their father's chauvinistic resistance to Willie's dream of becoming a dancer and Emma's plan to become a lawyer finally indicates to Emma where the roots of her problems lie: unless she herself does the changing, and makes the most of her life, she will always be the loser.

Frank, Anne (translator B. M. Mooyart). **Anne Frank: The Diary of a Young Girl.** Doubleday 1967.

Few are unfamiliar with Anne Frank, thirteen years of age, documentor of a secret life and Nazi terror. Forced into hiding by the Nazi occupation of Amsterdam, eight Jews lived in fear of discovery and death for two years. They faced almost unbearable conditions of material and spiritual deprivation, yet their lives, and especially Anne's, are an everlasting monument to human courage, faith, and hope.

Hinton, S. E. **Rumble Fish.**

Hopkins, Lee Bennett. **Wonder Wheels.** Knopf 1979.

> Mick Thompson, personable and open, is the star of the roller rink. His friend, Kitty Rhodes, is quiet and preoccupied. His family life is secure; hers is in turmoil. The two share many interests and problems, but she has one secret. In the days before a skating competition, however, Katie's secret is uncovered by a sudden tragedy. A teenager coping with a problem is portrayed realistically as Mick struggles with his feelings.

Hunter, Mollie. **The Third Eye.**

Keith, Harold. **The Obstinate Land.**

Kirkpatrick, Doris. **Honey in the Rock.**

Kjelgaard, Jim. **Big Red.**

Lee, H. Alton. **Seven Feet Four and Growing.** Westminster 1978.

> Bill is fifteen, is over seven feet tall, and is still growing. His father was a star basketball player, and Bill is expected to follow in his footsteps. However, he is more interested in animals and caring for them. He has trouble accepting his size, and runs into a conflict when it comes to girls. Then he meets a woman who is a veterinarian. She helps Bill to see that the most important thing is for him to be himself and set goals for things he wants to do.

LeShan, Eda. **What's Going to Happen to Me? When Parents Separate or Divorce.** Illus. Richard Cuffari. Four Winds. Schol Bk Serv 1978.

> Children of divorced or separated parents will find their concerns clearly expressed. Understanding and accepting emotions, communicating honestly, and genuine caring are offered as general guidelines for adult/child relationships. The advice given is very open and candid, realistic, and easy to read.

Mazer, Harry. **Snow Bound.** Delacorte 1978.

> A young boy and girl survive being lost in a snowstorm in Upstate New York, and in the process do some growing up. In the end, the girl says that they are now bound together as brother and sister, that they have given birth to themselves in the ordeal.

Peck, Robert Newton. **A Day No Pigs Would Die.**

Pevsner, Stella. **A Smart Kid like You.**

Reiss, Johanna. **The Upstairs Room.**

Rodgers, Mary. **Freaky Friday.**

Say, Allen. **The Ink-Keeper's Apprentice.** Har-Row 1979.

>A young Japanese teenager who lives alone in Tokyo is accepted by Tokida, a famous comic-strip artist, as an apprentice. Kiyoi attends class and becomes involved in political street demonstrations. Suddenly he receives a letter from his father, a successful merchant who has emigrated to America, and the boy must decide whether to go to him. Western influences on modern Japan are shown along with significant events in the maturation of a self-reliant adolescent.

Shyer, Marlene Fanta. **Welcome Home, Jellybean.**

Smith, Doris Buchanan. **Kick a Stone Home.**

Stewart, A. C. **Dark Dove.**

Stolz, Mary. **Lands End.** Illus. Dennis Hermanson. Trophy. Har-Row 1973.

>Twelve-year-old Joshua Redmond likes to talk and read encyclopedias. His family and friends think he talks too much, so he keeps to himself. A new family moves into town and accepts him as he is. His relationship with his own father is bad, but this changes when his parents help the new family survive in a hurricane.

Stoutenburg, Adrien. **Where to Now, Blue?** Four Winds. Schol Bk Serv 1978.

>Blueberry's attempt to run away from her poor home in Minnesota —with a six-year-old orphan tagging along—ends in frustration, but also in more realistic plans for the future. She learns that dashing off without thinking where you are going is foolish.

Taylor, Theodore. **Teetoncey.** Illus. Richard Cuffari. Camelot. Avon 1975.

>Despite his mother's opposition, Ben longs to be a surfman, responding to ships in distress off the Carolina coast, as his heroic father had done. Mother and son acknowledge each other's strong compassionate qualities in the process of rescuing and caring for a young, shipwrecked girl. Regional character and setting are vividly established.

Uchida, Yoshiko. **Journey Home.** Illus. Charles Robinson. Atheneum 1978.

Yuki longs for the day when she can return to her old home in Berkeley—the home from which she and her family were uprooted when the United States declared war on Japan. But when her brother, Ken, comes home wounded and bitter after serving as a soldier in the U.S. Army, she senses that there is more to coming home than being together in a particular place. The indignities suffered in World War II by Japanese citizens, despite their loyalty to the United States, is sensitively portrayed.

Wersba, Barbara. **Tunes for a Small Harmonica.**

Wilkinson, Brenda. **Ludell.**

Ages 14 and Up

Arrick, Fran. **Steffie Can't Come Out to Play.**

Cameron, Eleanor. **To the Green Mountains.** Dutton 1975.

"You don't love my father. And he has never loved me." Face the truth, Cath urges Mama, and set us free. Mama has always acted with courage—managing the small town hotel, encouraging the head waiter in his dreams of a career as a lawyer, pitting her dignity and personal convictions against criticism, gossip, and advice from chauvinistic men. Yet Cath wants to cut through to the truth. Her friend Herb has shown her that doing so is a source of strength. It could also help her dreams come true.

Donovan, John. **Remove Protective Coating a Little at a Time.** Har-Row 1973.

Harry finds himself growing up alone. His parents treat him more like a friend. Furthermore, his father is rarely home, and his mother suffers a nervous breakdown. He befriends Amelia, an old lady who lives in condemned buildings before they are torn down, cons people for food money, and generally scrounges to stay alive. Through this relationship, Harry begins to sort out his feelings and courageously face what lies ahead after his first fourteen years.

Greene, Bette. **Morning Is a Long Time Coming.**

Hurwood, Bernhardt. **Born Innocent.** Ace Bks 1975.

Chris, a fourteen-year-old runaway, finds herself faced with the fact that her family has rejected her and she is being sent to a girls'

Growing into Maturity 49

>state school for juveniles. Neglect, brutality, lesbianism, and rape change Chris from a sensitive, naive child to a tough, hard-shelled teenager fighting for survival and leadership.

Jenkins, Peter. **A Walk Across America.**

Joffo, Joseph. **A Bag of Marbles.**

LeRoy, Gen. **Cold Feet.** Har-Row 1979.

>After her father's death, Geneva Michillini poses as a boy so she can take a job in an arcade. Her boss is involved with big time gamblers. He likes her work, and offers her more money to work for the gambling ring. She doesn't always like what she sees, and life becomes dangerous. Her mother worries because she's not like other girls. Nor does she have any girlfriends at school. She finally reaches a point where she feels she must break away, and it is a move toward increased independence.

Madison, Arnold. **Runaway Teens.**

Neigoff, Mike. **It Will Never Be the Same Again.**

Potok, Chaim. **My Name Is Asher Lev.**

Samuels, Gertrude. **Run, Shelley, Run!**

Skármeta, Antonio. **Chileno!**

Steinbeck, John. **The Red Pony.** Viking Pr 1959.

>Though Jody is the dominant character in this book, it is not just about him. It is the story of the pain of becoming an adult; it is the story of a child's wisdom and a man's foolishness; it is the age-old story of birth and death, love and hate, pleasure and pain. The boy encounters all these things in the painful process of becoming a man.

Sutcliff, Rosemary. **Sun Horse, Moon Horse.** Illus. Shirley Felts. Dutton 1978.

>The famous White Horse of Uffington in England was the stimulus for this tale of a heroic tribal artist. Lubrin, the only remaining son of the Chief, has the right to bargain with Cadroc the Conqueror for the freedom of what remains of his tribe. In exchange for their freedom, he makes the Sun Horse—a horse cut out of the downsland turf, white against the green, half a hillside high—and gives his life.

Windsor, Patricia. **Diving for Roses.** Har-Row 1976.

Jean tells of a relationship with her mother that keeps them both isolated, dependent on each other, and hostile, and of the stranger in the forest who puts her in touch with the truth. Her mother is not a mad woman; she is an alcoholic. When the mother conquers her particular demon, Jean must accept being set free and stop holding it against her mother for making it possible.

Young, Alida E. **Land of the Iron Dragon.**

Identifying with One's Heritage

Ages 5 to 8

Aliki. **Corn Is Maize: The Gift of the Indians.** Illus. by author. T Y Crowell 1976.

>The history of corn is revealed to elementary readers in a picturesque way. It starts with the seed being planted by the Indians and goes through the history of when it was discovered by the Indians and how it was used. Each illustration shows the stages of growth starting beneath the soil, to how the Indians harvest, store, and grind the corn to survive. Readers are also told of the importance of corn in the world today.

Bollinger, Max (translator Rosenna Hoover). **The Fireflies.** Illus. Jiri Trnka. Atheneum 1970.

>For Prosper, the young firefly, growing up does not come all at once. He must learn to fly in a wind, to find his way when he is lost, to know what to fear and what not to fear. Finally he must learn to answer for his own children the questions he asked when he was young.

Brenner, Barbara. **Wagon Wheels.** Illus. Don Bolognese. Har-Row 1978.

>In this true story, a family of black pioneers leaves the South after the Civil War to take advantage of the Homestead Act. Arriving at free land in Kansas, they face starvation the first winter but are saved by Osage Indians. The father moves farther west, then sends for his boys, and they must brave traveling one hundred and fifty miles alone.

Brodsky, Beverly. **Secret Places.**

Eisenberg, Phyllis Rose. **A Mitzvah Is Something Special.** Illus. Susan Jeschke. Har-Row 1978.

>One grandmother excels at strudel, quilts, and weddings; the other wears tinted contacts, has two wigs, and plays the flute. This in itself

Fleischman, Paul. **The Birthday Tree.** Illus. Marcia Sewall. Har-Row 1979.

> is a mitzvah, a very big blessing. Lisa enjoys the specialness of both worlds.

Fleischman, Paul. **The Birthday Tree.** Illus. Marcia Sewall. Har-Row 1979.

> Grieving for their three sons lost at sea, a sailor and his wife move inland. They have another son, Jack, and celebrate his birth by planting an apple seedling. As both Jack and the apple tree grow, there seems to be a strange connection between them. When he goes to sea, the tree reflects his fortunes and misfortunes.

Greene, Laura. **I Am an Orthodox Jew.**

Greenfield, Eloise. **Africa Dream.**

Hopkins, Lee Bennett, editor. **Merrily Comes Our Harvest In.** Illus. Ben Shecter. HarBraceJ 1978.

> This collection of poems with Thanksgiving themes evokes images of the colonists and Indians of the first Thanksgiving, an abundance of delicious things to eat, what life was like for a settler's child, and thankfulness itself.

Jackson, Louise A. **Grandpa Had a Windmill, Grandma Had a Churn.** Illus. George Ancona. Parents 1977.

> A girl remembers following her grandparents around their farm as they do the daily chores. They use tools and equipment from another era—and many illustrations show the uses of these "antiques." The relationship between the granddaughter and her grandparents is one of love and mutual respect.

Newman, Shirlee P. **Tell Me, Grandma Tell Me, Grandpa.** Illus. Joan Drescher. HM 1979.

> A very young girl asks her grandmother what her mother was like when she was young. She asks her grandfather what her father was like. Then she visualizes her parents acting like babies at their present age—throwing cereal, crying all night, and having tantrums at the grocery store.

Raynor, Dorka. **This Is My Father and Me.** Illus. by author. A Whitman 1973.

> Photographs from many different countries are presented with brief captions. Scenery and clothing are international, while the relationships between fathers and their children are universal.

Roy, Ronald. **A Thousand Pails of Water.** Illus. Vo-Dinh Mai. Knopf 1978.

> A young Japanese boy struggles to save a stranded whale, the very animal his father must hunt and kill for a living. Yukio finds he cannot save the whale by himself, but his promise to bring it a thousand pails of water is fulfilled by his father and the rest of the village.

Showers, Paul. **Me and My Family Tree.** Illus. Don Madden. T Y Crowell 1978.

> The process of heredity is introduced, with a child's family tree used as an illustration. The author discusses the famous pea-plant experiment conducted by George Mendel, and how his discoveries contributed to our understanding of the genetic traits we pass down.

Spier, Peter. **The Legend of New Amsterdam.** Illus. by author. Doubleday 1979.

> Life on Manhattan Island over three hundred years ago is the subject of this detailed portrait. The story takes the reader on a tour of the city—its buildings, businesses, and legends.

Waber, Bernard. **But Names Will Never Hurt Me.** Illus. by author. HM 1976.

> Alison Wonderland resents her name when classmates tease her about it. Her parents explain how the surname was derived from "Voonterlant," her immigrant grandparents' name, and how her first name was given to her with love and after much deliberation. She learns to accept her name as part of her heritage and as part of the person she is.

Yolen, Jane. **The Seeing Stick.**

Ages 8 to 11

Clifton, Lucille. **The Lucky Stone.**

Glubok, Shirley, and Alfred Tamarin. **Olympic Games in Ancient Greece.** Har-Row 1976.

> In an outstanding introduction to world cultures, the authors invite the reader to join the excited crowds at the Olympia for a celebration of the Games. The Olympic Games—in ancient Greece just as in the

modern world—are supreme tests of skill for young athletes. The history of the Olympic Games is inseparable from the history of ancient Greece, and using the Games as a vantage point, the reader finds the history of a disciplined civilization enhanced by beautiful vase painting, statues, and magnificent architecture. The Olympic Games are surrounded by the rich panorama of Greek life, literature, and culture.

Goble, Paul. **The Girl Who Loved Wild Horses.**

Griffin, Judith Berry. **Phoebe the Spy.** Illus. Margot Tomes. Schol Bk Serv 1977.

In 1776, most black people in New York were slaves, but not Phoebe and her father. He was a trusted man and the owner of a tavern that was the popular meeting place of the patriots. This is an historically accurate account of a young, free, black girl's experiences in helping save General Washington's life, and of her silent dream of freedom for the slaves.

Hamilton, Virginia. **Zeely.** Illus. by Symeon Shemin. Macmillan 1971.

Imaginative eleven-year-old Geeder is stirred when she sees Zeely Tayber, who is dignified, stately, and six and one-half feet tall. Geeder thinks Zeely looks like the magazine picture of the Watusi queen. Through meeting Zeely personally and getting to know her, Geeder finally returns to reality.

Johnston, Johanna. **Harriet and the Runaway Book.** Illus. Ronald Himler. Har-Row 1977.

This biography tells the story of how Harriet Beecher Stowe grew up to write the famous anti-slavery novel, *Uncle Tom's Cabin*. Motivated by experiences with slavery and beliefs about freedom, she created the book which President Lincoln said helped start the Civil War.

Jordan, June. **Fannie Lou Hamer.**

Larrick, Nancy. **On City Streets.** Illus. David Sagarin. M Evans 1968.

Children from rural and suburban areas can catch a vivid glimpse of life in the city from the clear photographs and the well-written poems. Children from the big city can see themselves in the poetry and photographs.

Lewiton, Mina. **Candita's Choice.** Illus. Howard Simon. Har-Row 1959.

Identifying with One's Heritage 55

An eleven-year-old girl leaves her Puerto Rican home to start a new life in New York City. There she must learn a new language and new customs, as well as overcome her shyness. With help from a teacher, a neighbor boy, and a nurse's aid, Candita develops her self-image and finds happiness and security in her decision to remain in the United States.

Sorensen, Virginia. **Plain Girl.** Illus. Charles Geer. Schol Bk Serv 1972.

A young Amish girl is forced by law to go to school against her family's beliefs. As she is exposed to other people she develops many questions about her own customs. Her self-doubts grow and she fears that she may take the first steps toward breaking away as her brother did. Eventually she understands many of the customs and decides that it is best for her to live as her family does.

Yarbrough, Camille. **Cornrows.**

Ages 11 to 14

Adoff, Arnold. **Black Out Loud: An Anthology of Modern Poems by Black Americans.**

Bunting, Eve. **The Wild One.**

Clark, Ann Nolan. **To Stand Against the Wind.**

Clifton, Lucille. **The Times They Used to Be.**

Fisher, Leonard Everett. **Across the Sea from Galway.**

George, Jean Craighead. **Julie of the Wolves.** Illus. John Schoenherr. Trophy. Har-Row 1973.

Miyax/Julie, a thirteen-year-old Eskimo bride, runs away from her retarded husband's home to join her pen pal, Amy, in California. When she realizes that she is lost on the tundra, she courageously makes friends with a wolf pack who gradually accept, feed, and protect her. Her resourcefulness in the Arctic wilderness teaches readers much about the region, and Eskimo life and customs. In the course of her experiences, Julie learns to appreciate her heritage.

Hamilton, Virginia. **Arilla Sun Down.** Greenwillow 1976.

Arilla, twelve years old and interracial, tells her own story partially in half-remembered, almost dreamlike snatches in the voice of a seventh-grader living in a small midwestern town. Arilla is typical: she fights with her brother, Jack Sun Run Adams; complains about homework; and sometimes disobeys her mother (most flagrantly with the off-limits indulgence of her secret passion for roller-rink figure skating). This is the story of her awakening to who she is and where she fits within her interracial family.

Hamilton, Virginia. **M. C. Higgins, the Great.**

Hickman, Janet. **Zoar Blue.**

Hilton, Suzanne. **Who Do You Think You Are? Digging for Your Family Roots.** Sig. NAL 1978.

With this step-by-step guide, readers can trace their origins far into the past. It tells how to find and use all the resources available, whether human memories or official records; how to spot vital clues that can lead to startling discoveries; how to dig for people whose origins are difficult to uncover: adopted and divorced people, American Indians, Puerto Ricans, and blacks; and how to organize all these findings into a coherent pattern.

Kaplan, Bess. **The Empty Chair.**

Lehmann, Linda. **Better Than a Princess.** Nelson 1978.

Tilli, traveling from Germany to America to be reunited with her parents, believes her mother must be a rich princess. The journey is filled with bewilderment and excitement. Her enthusiasm and dreams are shattered momentarily when she sees that her mother is neither rich nor a princess. But after a few minutes, motherly love and understanding prove to be "better than a princess."

Monjo, F. N. **A Namesake for Nathan.** Illus. Eros Keith. Coward 1977.

Joanna reads the fiery words of Thomas Paine as she spins flax for the shirts of Captain Nathan Hale, her older brother. A thread of sorrow runs through this warm family tale, set in Revolutionary days, foreshadowing the hanging of Nathan Hale as a spy. His heroic death is seen in the sharp perspective of its meaning for the cause and for the family.

Taylor, Mildred. **Roll of Thunder, Hear My Cry.**

van Iterson, S. R. **The Spirits of Chocamata.**

Yep, Laurence. **Child of the Owl.**

Identifying with One's Heritage

Yep, Laurence. **Dragonwings.** Trophy. Har-Row 1977.
> Moon Shadow leaves China to join his father, Wind Rider, in San Francisco. Survival in the land of demons is difficult, but in time, he masters his fears. The descriptions of the immigrant Chinese of the early 1900s dispel many stereotypical images.

Ages 14 and Up

Astrov, Margot. **American Indian Prose and Poetry.** Putnam 1962.
> The contents of this volume are selected from ten areas of Indian culture in North and South America. Those represented are the northern woodlands, the basin area, the great plains, the deserts of the Southeast, California, the Northeast, the Far North, Mexico, Central America, and Peru. The poetry is selected from the ritualistic observances of Indian life. The prose represents speeches, childhood recollections, and similar narratives.

Bond, Nancy. **Country of Broken Stone.**

Ellis, Mel. **Sidewalk Indian.**

Goldston, Robert. **Next Year in Jerusalem: A Short History of Zionism.**

Haley, Alex. **Roots.**

Harris, Janet. **Thursday's Daughters: The Story of Women Working in America.** Har-Row 1977.
> Starting with the women who pioneered in the settlement of the thirteen colonies, and ending with the women's liberation movement of the 1960s and '70s, the author traces the role of women in the social, political, and economic history of our country. The writing is anecdotal; the details fascinating. A final chapter summarizes broad social changes in America and their effects on women's lives.

Levin, Meyer. **The Harvest.**

Means, Florence C. **Our Cup Is Broken.** HM 1969.
> Sara, a Hopi Indian, goes to live with a white family for nine years after the death of her parents. After an unhappy love affair with a white boy, she returns to the reservation in the hope that she can leave behind the white man's ways and adopt the life of her ancestors. However, she is unable to accept the Indians' ancient religion and way of life, and the Hopi cannot accept what in her seem to be

eccentricities. A Hopi boy rapes her and she bears a daughter who is blind. Ultimately she marries, but her life, while not without hope, is fraught with the tragedy of being caught between two cultures.

Momaday, N. Scott. **House Made of Dawn.** Har-Row 1977.

The Pulitzer award winner in 1969, this novel is a post-World War II account of a Kiowa Indian who cannot come to grips with reservation life following his service as a G.I. He commits a senseless murder and is given a light sentence on the condition that he resettle in Los Angeles under an Indian rehabilitation service. He continues to drink heavily to cover up for a life that has no meaning. He returns to the reservation with hopes of finding himself.

Silko, Leslie Marmon. **Ceremony.**

Wangerin, Walter, Jr. **The Book of the Dun Cow.** Har-Row 1978.

The story is centered around a chicken coop animal kingdom and set in an ancient time when evil, in the form of a giant Wyrm, lay trapped in the center of the earth. It can be described as an allegorical fantasy rich in Christian meaning and tradition—a powerful story of love, friendship, courage, and of the strength of these qualities in meeting and overcoming adverse conditions.

Developing Personal Values

Ages 1 to 5

Asch, Frank. **Monkey Face.** Illus. by author. Parents 1977.

> Monkey draws a picture of his mother in school. On the way home he shows it to several of his friends. They are critical and each suggests an improvement. Arriving home, he timidly shows it to his mother. She loves it! She values it for what it means to her.

Hazen, Barbara Shook. **The Gorilla Did It.**

Odor, Ruth. **Sarah Lou's Untied Shoe.** Illus. Helen Endres. Childs World 1976.

> Sarah Lou has a broken arm and finds out that she is incapable of performing even simple tasks. When two people walk right past her and don't offer to tie her shoe, she learns that life can be very unkind. She feels bad until one little girl comes and offers her assistance. Then she learns that there are also people who care.

Scott, Ann Herbert. **On Mother's Lap.** Illus. Glo Coalson. McGraw 1972.

> Michael shares his mother's lap with a doll, a boat, and a puppy, all snugly wrapped in his reindeer blanket. There is no room for his baby sister, he says. But mother's love—and lap—accommodates Michael and his sister and toys. Full page illustrations of Eskimo homelife add to the value of this picture book.

Wulf, Kathleen. **I'm Glad I'm Little.** Illus. John Nelson. Childs World 1976.

> Tommy is always too little for the things he wants to do, like playing ball with his older brother Kevin. A talk with his father helps him realize that being little has advantages too. The text and illustrations depict many activities available to little people.

Ages 5 to 8

Allard, Harry. **It's So Nice to Have a Wolf Around the House.**

Anno, Mitsumasa. **The King's Flower.** Illus. by author. Collins Pubs 1979.

> An enormously wealthy king wants everything that is the biggest and the best—until a seed planted in the largest flower pot ever made produces a tiny but beautiful flower. He sees that biggest is not always best.

Bach, Alice. **The Day After Christmas.** Illus. Mary Chalmers. Har-Row 1975.

> Children will identify with Emily's feeling of dejection and disappointment on the day after Christmas. All the surprise and suspense is over. The colorful decorations and special dishes are being put away. She dwells on the fact that Christmas is now a whole year away, until her best friend visits and helps her discover how to enjoy herself.

Bartoli, Jennifer. **The Story of the Grateful Crane.** Illus. Kozo Shimizu. A Whitman 1977.

> In this Japanese folktale, an old man helps a crane escape from a trap. The next day it comes to live with the old man and his wife, disguised as a strange and beautiful girl. She spins, and works for hours on a loom making beautiful and valuable silk. They have promised not to watch her while she works, but when they break that promise she turns back into a crane.

Baylor, Byrd. **The Way to Start a Day.**

Blegvad, Lenore. **Moon-Watch Summer.** Illus. Erik Blegvad. HarBraceJ 1972.

> A family changes with the day by day, chapter by chapter development of Jenny and Adam. Their personal growth includes the growth of values.

Bonsall, Crosby. **Mine's the Best.** Illus. by author. Har-Row 1973.

> Two five-year-old boys argue over who has the best water toy. As they argue, their toys are destroyed. Each concludes that his own was the best.

Byars, Betsy. **The Lace Snail.** Illus. by author. Viking Pr 1975.

> The Lace Snail makes lace and gives it to her friends on the way to

Developing Personal Values

the pond. She feels that everyone deserves lace. In this way, she makes the most of her special abilities.

Charlip, Remy, and Lilian Moore. **Hooray for Me!** Illus. Vera B. Williams. Parents 1975.

This colorful book deals with a child being "me." It develops the relationship of the child to family, friends, and pets, and shows that who you are depends partly on your life with others.

Conaway, Judith. **I'll Get Even.** Illus. Mark Gubin. Childrens 1977.

A young boy wants the acceptance of his older brother. He wants to help his brother and friends build a kite, but is told to go away. The story shows how he copes with his feelings of being left out.

Cosgrove, Stephen. **Hucklebug.** Illus. Robin James. Serendipity Pr 1975.

Barry Hucklebug feels that he is being picked on when the mayor of his village asks him to do his share of the work. He decides to run away from his responsibilities. Warned not to go near the village of the giants, he goes anyway. When he finds out that he is in danger, he barely escapes. Back in the village, he decides that work isn't so bad.

de Paola, Tomie. **Helga's Dowry: A Troll Love Story.** Illus. by author. HarBraceJ 1977.

Lars asks Helga, a troll, to marry him, but she doesn't have a dowry. She fears that he will marry rich Inge, instead, leaving her an unmarried troll maiden who must wander the earth forever. She decides to go out and earn herself a dowry, and in doing so learns a lesson about true love.

Duvoisin, Roger. **Petunia's Treasure.** Illus. by author. Knopf 1975.

Petunia discovers a treasure chest on the river bottom, and believes the unseen contents have made her wealthy. Her barnyard friends share in the excitement and begin begging for gifts from her. The story describes the problems that come with new-found wealth as well as their resolution.

Gackenbach, Dick. **Do You Love Me?** Illus. by author. Seabury 1975.

Walter accidentally kills a hummingbird when he tries to capture it for a pet. His big sister tells him to respect animals and not try to keep them, because some animals are meant to be free. When he receives a puppy, he is terrified that he will hurt her the way he hurt the hummingbird. He is happy to find that the dog responds to his love.

Gray, Nigel. **It'll All Come Out in the Wash.** Illus. Edward Frascino. Har-Row 1979.

> A little girl wants to try a number of grown-up jobs. As she attempts these tasks she grows frustrated. She floods the kitchen floor with soap suds, and spills breakfast all over her father—among other minor disasters. Her mother becomes upset, but her father maintains that it's all right to make mistakes, and that trying is most important.

Isadora, Rachel. **Willaby.** Macmillan 1977.

> Willaby loves to draw more than anything. When her first-grade classmates make cards for their teacher who is ill, Willaby draws a picture instead. Later she is sorry she did not make a card, and remembers that she didn't even sign the picture. She is reassured when her teacher returns and there is a thank you note on her desk for the get-well picture. The mutual concern of teacher and pupil is expressed.

Johnson, D. William. **The Willow Flute: A North Country Tale.** Illus. by author. Little 1975.

> Lost in a snowstorm, Lewis Shrew finds shelter in an abandoned cottage where he spies a willow flute amidst the debris. With its first bird-like trills, winter retreats, and there among the glacier lilies is Lewis' home. This gentle tale evokes the magic of beauty and spring.

Lionni, Leo. **Frederick.** Illus. by author. Pantheon 1973.

> Some field mice are very industrious and put away corn, nuts, wheat, and straw for winter. One mouse doesn't do any work, however; he sits gathering the sun's rays. Frederick says they will need the colors of the rays in the gray winter. That winter, when the food is eaten, he tells them to close their eyes and imagine the colors. He warms them all with his storyteller's magic. Children can discuss how Frederick was different from his friends, but still had an important contribution to make.

Martin, Bill, Jr. **David Was Mad.** Illus. Symeon Shimin. HR&W 1967.

> David is angry, and takes it out on everyone else—which makes his day even more miserable. He admits to Grandma, "This was an awful day. I got mad first and then everybody else got mad." His Grandma explains, "Yes, that's how it goes. Anger is like wet paint. It rubs off on everybody who touches it."

Merriam, Eve. **Unhurry Harry.** Illus. Gail Owens. Four Winds. Schol Bk Serv 1978.

Developing Personal Values

Harry finds that everyone wants him to hurry, but there are other things he'd rather do—daydream, read, watch workmen, and wonder about things. His predicament is one that many youngsters have experienced. When he finally gets some unhurried time, young readers will understand its value.

Miles, Miska. **Hoagie's Rifle-Gun.** Illus. John Schoenherr. Little 1970.

Ira and Hoagie live in Appalachia. Their father is looking for work, and in the meantime the family is living on potatoes. The boys are given permission to go hunting for meat, but they can find nothing. Hoagie decides to shoot Old Bob, a bobcat who is their neighbor. He shoots and misses though he has not missed a shot since he was ten years old. The fact is that he cannot shoot Old Bob—he's too much like a friend. The parents accept this, even as they sit down to another meager meal.

Ness, Evaline. **Marcella's Guardian Angel.** Illus. by author. Holiday 1979.

A guardian angel succeeds in her attempt to change Marcella's inconsiderate, rude behavior. The angel's new game "flip-flop" turns the girl from bad to good, rude to polite, and greedy to generous. Marcella notices other pleasant developments: she has more friends, and receives more hugs from her mother.

Pinkwater, Daniel Manus. **The Big Orange Splot.** Illus. by author. Hastings 1977.

When a seagull drops a can of orange paint on a house in a neat, quiet neighborhood, the owner decides it is time for a change. His decision stirs up more than paint as the change takes effect. Best of all is the change in himself as he asserts his individuality.

Reinach, Jacquelyn. **Who Stole Alligator's Shoe?** Illus. Richard Hefter. HR&W 1977.

Accusing Alligator is one of the twenty-six animal characters who live, work, and play in the town of Sweet Pickles. Alligator blames everybody but herself when she cannot find her left shoe. She learns responsibility for her own belongings.

Riley, Susan. **Angry: What Does It Mean?** Childs World 1978.

A little boy, running away from home, thinks about all the angry remarks that have been directed at him. Then he begins to think about situations that make *him* angry, and he realizes that he can't blame others if they are bothered sometimes by what he does. He accepts the fact that anger is a normal feeling, and finds a positive way to deal with it.

Sarton, May. **A Walk Through the Woods.** Illus. Kazue Mizumura. Har-Row 1976.

A boy walks through the woods with friends in tow, and becomes aware of the sights and sounds.

Sendak, Maurice. **Higglety Pigglety Pop! Or There Must Be More to Life.** Illus. by author. Har-Row 1979.

Jennie is a dog who has everything—her own sweater, two bowls, two windows, and a nice home. Nonetheless, she is unhappy and leaves home in search of something more in life. She meets a pig who promises her the lead in The World of Mother Goose Theater, after she gains some experience. She sets out, and in the course of things she becomes a nurse for baby, sticks her head in a lion's mouth, and eventually ends up out in the cold with nothing. At this point her old friends inform her that she is now the new leading lady in The World of Mother Goose Theater. Early primary children will enjoy the wordplay and the exaggerated circumstances.

Sendak, Maurice. **Where the Wild Things Are.**

Sharmat, Marjorie Weinman. **I'm Terrific.** Illus. Kay Chorao. Schol Bk Serv 1977.

Jason Bear never does anything wrong, and he gives himself gold stars whenever he does something terrific. Unable to impress Henrietta with his perfection, however, he turns himself into mean Jason Bear. This new image fails, too. He finally discovers that all he needs to do in order to make friends is just be himself.

Skorpen, Liesel Moak. **Michael.**

Vigna, Judith. **Anyhow, I'm Glad I Tried.**

Waterton, Betty. **A Salmon for Simon.**

Weil, Lisl. **Gertie & Gus.** Illus. by author. Parents 1977.

Gus the bear loves to fish, and he goes fishing every day. His ambitious wife surprises him with a net to help him catch even more fish. Later she gives him a boat, and still later, a whole fleet of boats. Finally she goes too far. He gives it all up and returns to the simple way of fishing.

Developing Personal Values

Williams, Barbara. **If He's My Brother.** Illus. Tomie de Paola. Harvey 1976.

> A young boy feels that if something belongs to him, he should be able to do as he chooses with it. "If it's my room, why can't I paint it any way I want? If he's my brother, why can't I punch him?" These are good questions for discussion.

Yolen, Jane. **The Simple Prince.** Illus. Jack Kent. Parents 1978.

> The prince is unsatisfied with court life; he wants to live simply. Setting off to do so, he finds it more difficult than he'd expected. He returns to the court eagerly, a wiser and humbler prince.

Ages 8 to 11

Adkins, Jan. **Moving On: Stories of Four Travelers.** Illus. by author. Scribner 1978.

> Four adventures involving fishing, skiing, backpacking, and bicycling make up this book. In each story, the author evokes the joy of being in nature.

Alexander, Lloyd. **The Four Donkeys.** Illus. Lester Abrams. HR&W 1972.

> This uniquely illustrated book brings the Tailor, the Baker, and the Shoemaker together on one road. They are all going to the fair to make themselves rich. On their way, they run into misfortune, and it soon gets worse because of their greed. Finally they begin to understand that they can accomplish more by working together than by acting selfishly.

Babbitt, Natalie. **Tuck Everlasting.**

Baylor, Byrd. **Guess Who My Favorite Person Is.** Illus. Robert Andrew Parker. Scribner 1977.

> Two friends play the game of naming their favorite things. The mood is one of rapport, as they share a lazy afternoon in an alfalfa field, "sort of lying down watching ladybugs climb yellow flowers." It is an afternoon of taking time for things that are important to them.

Bornstein, Ruth. **The Dancing Man.** Illus. by author. Clarion Bk. Seabury 1978.

> In the village of the orphan boy, Joseph, no one laughs and no one

dances. Yet he longs to dance, seeing the movement of sea and trees and clouds. A gift of silver shoes sends him on his nimble way—lightening hearts, easing pain, and returning, years later, to the same seashore where another wistful child awaits the silver shoes.

Bunting, Eve. **Magic and the Night River.** Illus. Allen Say. Har-Row 1978.

Yoshi cherishes the scenes on the night river, the fires blazing in iron cradles off the sailboats, and his grandfather's gentle handling of the captive cormorants. He knows that his grandfather's loss of dexterity may end their fishing trips. Then, a costly tangle of birds and cords reveals the power of the old man's kindly ways.

Chaikin, Miriam. **I Should Worry, I Should Care.**

Christopher, Matt. **Power Play.** Illus. Ray Burns. Little 1976.

A young boy, Rabbit, is only an average basketball player, and snide remarks from a fan bother him. He feels terrible about his playing until he finds a candy bar that promises instant power to the eater. His newfound success creates more problems than he bargains for, and the story tells of how he copes with them.

Cleary, Beverly. **Ramona and Her Father.**

Clymer, Eleanor. **Luke Was There.** Illus. Diane DeGroat. HR&W 1973.

First Julius' dad leaves him, then his uncle, and then his stepfather. When his mother goes to the hospital, he is sent to a children's home. Here he meets Luke, another adult whom he loves and trusts. When Luke leaves, Julius runs away. The tables are turned for Julius when he finds someone whom he must care for.

Fisher, Ronald M. **A Day in the Woods.** Photographs by Gordon W. Gahan. Natl Geog 1975.

Harley and Joan spend a day in the forest learning about the wonders of nature—as shown through the photographs. Carrying boxes for collecting specimens, they stop to look at animals, insects, and plants. They find the forest filled with life.

Godden, Rumer. **The Rocking Horse Secret.** Illus. Juliet Stanwell Smith. Viking Pr 1978.

Tibby and her mother live in Miss Pomeroy's great house, the closest thing to a home they have ever known. Tibby does not mind being forbidden to see Miss Pomeroy, who is old and ill, because she has found an attic full of wonderful toys. Best of all, there are Noble, the rocking horse, and Jed, the handyman, who tells her tales of the great Pomeroy Place stables and hunts. When the old lady dies, there are terrible changes. "If only she had left a will," says Ma. Tibby knows that a secret was left with Noble—something that could make all the difference to them. She wonders whether she should share a secret not her own.

Goodman, Robert B., and Robert A. Spicer. **The Magic Brush.** Illus. Y. T. Mui. Island Her 1974.

In this story Ma Lien, a poor Chinese orphan boy, a woodgatherer clothed in rags, feeds largely on his dream of becoming an artist. He gets no help: the art teacher scorns him, and the village children taunt him. Undaunted, he pursues his dream and receives the gift of a magic paintbrush. Through the powers in the brush, his paintings come to life, and with them, he answers the needs of his poor neighbors. Hearing of his special power, the greedy Emperor summons him to Peking. There, in spite of the Emperor, Ma Lien remains true to his dream of using the magic brush only "for the good of the people."

Greaves, Margaret. **A Net to Catch the Wind.** Illus. Stephen Gammell. Har-Row 1979.

A beautiful white colt is the center of family conflict as the king and his daughter each look upon it in a different manner. The king views the animal as an object to be possessed; the daughter believes that it should be free. As differences in opinions develop, each character is faced with the difficult task of dealing with personal values.

Greene, Bette. **Philip Hall Likes Me. I Reckon Maybe.** Illus. Charles Lilly. Dial 1974.

Would Philip Hall like her if she was first and he was second best? Beth ponders this as she leads—and he follows—in the business of catching turkey thieves and running a roadside stand. Winning is hard work she decides; so is losing, says Philip.

Greene, Constance C. **The Unmaking of Rabbit.**

Hickman, Janet. **The Stones.** Illus. Richard Cuffari. Macmillan 1976.

A boy grows up without a father during World War II, and gets involved in the group persecution of someone who is different. He and his friends, carried away with misplaced patriotism, harass and torment an elderly neighbor of German descent. When the old man saves the boy's sister at great personal cost, the children see themselves, the old man, and what they have done more clearly.

Hopkins, Lee Bennett. **Mama.** Knopf 1977.

Mama doesn't like questions, so her young son doesn't ask about the boxes and bags of goodies that come from her place of work. But he worries. What if she is arrested and sent to prison? If he loves her enough—and he does—will she change? Can love change this wide, and confusing world? A neighbor says he must show his mother that he loves her for herself, not for the things she brings home.

Hopkins, Lee Bennett, editor. **My Mane Catches the Wind.** Illus. Sam Savitt. HarBraceJ 1979.

Twenty-two poems about horses at all stages of life express both their differences and their feelings. The enjoyment of a sense of freedom is stressed.

L'Engle, Madeleine. **A Wrinkle in Time.**

Mayer, Marianna, retold by. **Beauty and the Beast.** Illus. Mercer Mayer. Four Winds. Schol Bk Serv 1978.

All that Beauty asks of her father is a single rose, but that rose, taken from the Beast's garden, is costly: she must choose to live with the Beast in exchange for her father's life. This traditional tale of the power of love is greatly enhanced by vivid word pictures and richly detailed full-page illustrations.

Paterson, Katherine. **Bridge to Terabithia.**

Pfeffer, Susan Beth. **Kid Power.** Illus. Leigh Grant. Schol Bk Serv 1977.

Janie is eleven years old and wants a new bike, but her mother has lost her job. To raise money, she opens a business called Kid Power, and does all kinds of odd jobs for people. The business expands so much that she has to hire her friends to work for her. Her mother then opens an adult version. It is a story of self-sufficiency.

Robinson, Barbara. **The Best Christmas Pageant Ever.** Illus. Judith Gwyn Brown. Har-Row 1972.

This humorous book tells of the misadventures at a simple Christmas pageant. The starring roles are taken over by a family known as the Herdmans, people who are constantly in trouble for everything from beating up fellow students to smoking cigars in the girls' bathroom. The production becomes the talk of the town—even the fire

Developing Personal Values

department appears unexpectedly—yet suddenly, during the commotion, the message of Christmas is revealed to both readers and pageant participants.

Shecter, Ben. **The River Witches.** Har-Row 1979.

This tale of good and bad witches, of good versus evil, is set in New York's Hudson Valley, where superstition is rampant. Unhappy Andrew Van Aken is sent to help his mother's dear friend in her apothecary shop. Auntie Lizard, as he secretly calls her, is a witch. She plans to make him her apprentice by initiating him at the "night of the Crescent Moon" party. Her plan is foiled when Pooter, his dog, and Peter Bronck, the pastor's assistant, deliver Andrew's prayer book to him, thus spoiling the effects of the initiation.

Steig, William. **Abel's Island.** Illus. by author. FS&G 1977.

Torn from his gentle spouse and luxurious home by torrential rains—in a gallant attempt to retrieve his wife's gauzy scarf—a gentleman mouse finds himself the lone castaway on an island. The year-long exile marks his metamorphosis from sybaritic heir to resourceful adventurer and talented sculptor.

Steiner, Jörg. **Rabbit Island.**

Wallace, Barbara Brooks. **Hawkins.**

Wallace, Barbara Brooks. **The Secret Summer of L.E.B.** Illus. Joseph Cellini. YB. Dell 1976.

Lizabeth Elvira Bracken has found social acceptance in her new sixth-grade class at Anderson Bays School. She is not always in agreement with her classmates, but this doesn't really bother her until she finds Creepy Douglas, the class outcast, in an old, deserted house. As they become good friends, she must examine her feelings and values—she must weigh her standing in the social group against her new friendship.

Wilde, Oscar. **The Star Child.** Illus. Fiona French. Four Winds. Schol Bk Serv 1979.

In this medieval fairy tale, a child learns compassion and humility. Beautiful and selfish, the Star Child rejects his mother, an ugly beggar-woman. For this he is transformed into a toad. He realizes that unless he finds his mother he will never be restored. Three years of wandering pass before he finds her, and gains forgiveness.

Williams, Margery. **The Velveteen Rabbit.**

Ages 11 to 14

Arkin, Alan. **The Lemming Condition.** Illus. Joan Sandin. Har-Row 1976.

> Today was the day: lemmings everywhere were heading west, past the cliffs and into the ocean. Why? asks Crow. Taken aback, Bubber is first angry, and then puzzled. Why indeed? Questions of conformity and survival haunt him, and he seeks advice from his elders. But the decision to conform remains his alone.

Beyer, Audrey White. **Dark Venture.** Illus. Leo Dillon and Diane Dillon. Knopf 1968.

> Demba, a twelve-year-old African boy, is captured by an enemy tribe and sold into slavery. Transported to Barbados, he and Adam White, the ship's surgeon, become friends. Although Demba is treated as less than human at times, he remains honest, loyal, and proud, as his father had taught him to be. The story displays the feelings of both whites and blacks who were caught in the web of slavery and shows how its various facets affect their characters.

Blume, Judy. **Then Again, Maybe I Won't.**

Bosse, Malcolm J. **The 79 Squares.** T Y Crowell 1979.

> Eric is strangely fascinated by an old man he meets while on probation. The old man assigns him the task of mapping every inch of his garden. He becomes interested in spite of himself and begins reading books on nature so that he can identify and record everything correctly. When it is learned that the old man is an ex-convict, Eric must defend him against his parents, the town, and even his own friends. Through his experiences Eric gains new understanding of himself and others.

Bridgers, Sue Ellen. **Home Before Dark.**

Brittain, Bill. **All the Money in the World.** Illus. Charles Robinson. Har-Row 1979.

> A farm boy catches a hundred-year-old leprechaun by accident and gets a magic wish. He wishes for all the money in the world, and it is piled high in his backyard. Problems develop that he isn't ready for, including international warfare. The leprechaun grants him another wish, and the money goes back to where it belongs.

Carew, Jan. **The Third Gift.** Illus. Leo Dillon and Diane Dillon. Little 1974.

Developing Personal Values

In "long-time-past days," the black prophet, Amakosa, led his people to the foot of Nameless Mountain. The mountain is climbed by all the young men of the Jubas in search of the gifts of wonder. They obtain the gifts of work and of beauty, and lastly, and most precious, the gift of imagination.

Constant, Alberta Wilson. **Does Anybody Care About Lou Emma Miller?**

Edmonds, Walter D. **Bert Breen's Barn.**

Garrigue, Sheila. **Between Friends.**

Gilbert, Harriett. **Running Away.** Har-Row 1979.

The premature birth of another brother devastates Jane Rockham. "Plain-face" Jane does not like the responsibilities of being the oldest child. Neither does she like being in a boarding school away from her family. After a series of crises, she begins to take charge of her life; she learns the meaning of friendship and responsibility.

Hamley, Dennis. **Pageants of Despair.**

Heide, Florence Parry. **When the Sad One Comes to Stay.**

Hunt, Irene. **Across Five Aprils.** Illus. Albert John Pucci. G&D 1978.

The "five Aprils" of the title are those of the Civil War—1861–1865. A family living in southern Illinois is one of many split by sympathy for either the North or the South. Young Jethro Creighton becomes the man of the family when his brothers enlist in the Union and the Confederate armies and his father falls ill. He learns to understand himself and his role within the family as he accepts the responsibility of the farm work, and copes with the reactions of the neighbors to a family with sons fighting on both sides.

King, Clive. **Me and My Million.** T Y Crowell 1979.

Ringo is a young lad who finds himself holding onto a valuable painting stolen by his older half-brother. While trying to carry it back to his brother, he gets lost in the heart of London. A series of humorous adventures follows, as he keeps just one step ahead of some shady people who want to get their hands on the painting. He is finally helped by a crusty old canal boat skipper, and they become friends while trying to figure out what to do.

Kjelgaard, Jim. **Outlaw Red.**

Kornfield, Anita Clay. **In a Bluebird's Eye.**

Miles, Betty. **The Real Me.** Camelot. Avon 1975.

>Barbara Fisher does not want to be a feminist, stand up before a crowd, or take particularly courageous stands. The pursuit of her own identity does cause her to become involved in women's rights advocacy, however. She wants to keep her brother's paper route and take tennis, rather than Seventh Grade "Slimnastics." Readers will learn what it costs to be "different" as they follow Barbara's struggle to be "the real me."

O'Dell, Scott. **The 290.**

Paterson, Katherine. **The Great Gilly Hopkins.**

Paterson, Katherine. **The Master Puppeteer.** Illus. Haru Wells. T Y Crowell 1975.

>Famine engenders violence in the streets of old Osaka. But Jiro, an apprentice to the master puppeteer, Yoshida, escapes the struggle. In time, his mother's plight jolts him into recognition of the ties between the imaginary world of the stage and the desperation in the streets.

Pevsner, Stella. **Cute Is a Four-Letter Word.**

Sebestyen, Ouida. **Words by Heart.**

Thiele, Colin. **The Shadow on the Hills.** Har-Row 1977.

>While tending his rabbit traps in the hilly rangelands of South Australia, Bodo meets a fellow trapper, Ebenezer Blitz—aged, deranged, and self-exiled. Bodo rescues him after a fall and is entrusted with his plans for revenge on the town swindler. The young boy's decision to reveal all that he knows at the jury trial is weighed against his fears, the cost to his family, and his compassion for Ebenezer.

Ullman, James Ramsey. **Banner in the Sky.** Archway 1967.

>People in the little Swiss village think no one can climb the Citadel. Rudi, whose father had lost his life trying, joins the party of Captain Winter, who believes the mountain can be conquered. The story shows a boy's struggle to develop independence and become a man.

Van Steenwyk, Elizabeth. **Rivals on Ice.** Illus. Rondi Anderson. A Whitman 1979.

Developing Personal Values

>Tucker Cameron practices her ice-skating daily, despite the lack of parental interest and the lack of money for a coach. Her dream is to be "numero uno" in the Novice Competition. It seems possible until Sara Mars, the Midwest champion, moves into town. She has everything—money, a good coach, a mother who is always at practice, and talent. Tucker's jealousy and fear of losing are diminished by Sara's sincere attempts to be her friend. Eventually, though, she must decide whether or not to encourage her friend to compete against her, or to let her default—which would mean a sure win for Tucker.

Walsh, Jill Paton. **Children of the Fox.**

Yolen, Jane. **The Hundredth Dove and Other Tales.** Illus. David Palladini. T Y Crowell 1977.

>Jane Yolen's lyrical stories have the terse wisdom of folktales. A merman tempts Borne into the underwater world; a sorcerer is thwarted by the fidelity of young lovers; and Merdock loses his seven sons to the silchie, one of the seal folk. Fantasy is set against the sharp edge of truth in all seven tales.

Ages 14 and Up

Butterworth, W. E. **LeRoy and the Old Man.**

Cormier, Robert. **I Am the Cheese.** LFL. Dell 1978.

>Adam Farmer is a teenager on an arduous journey. Questions arise: What is he looking for? Why does he have two birth certificates? Why is there a sudden move to a new town? and What about the strange Mr. Gray who keeps reappearing? An innocent young Victim tells a horrifying tale of government corruption, espionage, and counter-espionage. Suspense builds throughout the book.

Craven, Margaret. **I Heard the Owl Call My Name.**

Crawford, Charles P. **Letter Perfect.**

Dickinson, Peter. **Tulku.**

George, Jean Craighead. **Going to the Sun.** Har-Row 1976.

>Marcus' father argues that hunters keep the animal population in balance—but when Marcus spends a summer with Melissa, meticulously observing and recording the behavior of the Rocky Mountain

goats of Montana, he is converted from hunter to protector. A tale of young love amid family feuding is interspersed with details about the majestic goats.

Gordon, Barbara. **I'm Dancing As Fast As I Can.** Har-Row 1979.

Barbara Gordon, successful career woman and award-winning television producer, thought she had everything. What she didn't know was that on the night of the Emmy awards, she would be in a mental institution fighting drug addiction and an intolerant, vengeful lover. But she survives, and tells the story of her struggle. With the aid of a dedicated psychologist, two close friends, and a fellow inmate, she is able to save her mind and her life.

Greene, Bette. **Summer of My German Soldier.**

Guy, Rosa. **The Friends.**

Hesse, Hermann (translator Michael Roloff). **Peter Camenzind.** FS&G 1969.

This book captures the tragic beauty of bitter experiences with friendship, love, and death. Peter, a Swiss poet, develops a deeper appreciation of humanity from his relationship to nature. As he learns to climb the mountains of his country, so he learns to surmount the obstacles of life.

Jones, Adrienne. **The Hawks of Chelney.** Illus. Stephen Gammell. Har-Row 1978.

To the fishermen of Chelney, the return of the osprey is a curse. Their conspiracy to trap fourteen-year-old Siri and his beloved fish-hawk is thwarted by the Old Woman, his mother. He survives alone until he rescues Thea, the hawk. She rekindles the ire of the villagers but brings reconciliation and love to the Old Woman and Siri. This novel is touched with the mystery of man's primordial relationship to nature.

Knowles, John. A Separate Peace. Delta. Dell 1962.

The boys in Devon School view the war as something remote—they have their own battles to fight, their own enemies to conquer. They are engaged in the struggle to find themselves and their place in the world. This is the story of two of these boys. One, the narrator, mistakes his fellow man as the enemy. Too late, he discovers that he is his own worst enemy. He is too late because he destroys his friend.

Developing Personal Values

This is a moving story, deep in understanding of the adolescent boy and his painful search for a sense of values.

Lindbergh, Anne Morrow. **Gift from the Sea.** Vin. Random 1978.

The author has written these lyrical essays as musings while on a walk along the seashore. Using metaphors of the tides, shells, and waves, she ponders the many patterns and relationships of life.

O'Dell, Scott. **The Hawk That Dare Not Hunt by Day.**

Paterson, Katherine. **Of Nightingales That Weep.**

Peyton, K. M. **A Midsummer Night's Death.** Collins Pubs 1978.

Jonathan's teacher and hero, Charles Hugo, proves that he has "clay feet" when he stands by while the English teacher drowns, and then lets the authorities believe the death was a suicide. Jonathan discovers the truth and endures a traumatic and soul-searching time while he decides what to do. At the same time, he is able to help a troubled classmate. He emerges strong and ready to be head prefect of his school.

Stevenson, Robert Louis. **The Touchstone.** Illus. Uri Shulevitz. Greenwillow 1976.

In this fable two brothers compete for a fair maiden. Each searches for the touchstone in whose light "the seeming goes, and the being shows, and all things besides are worthless." Using a mirror, the younger brother wins the maiden. The elder continues his search and finds the stone whose light penetrates worldly facade to inner truth. Both language and concept are mature.

Teague, Bob. **Letters to a Black Boy.** Walker & Co 1968.

A father describes in detail his bitter experiences as a victim of racial prejudice, with the hope of preparing his son for the indignities he may encounter. Written by a news commentator at NBC-TV for his son to read at the age of thirteen, this book affords insight into what it is like to grow up black, and the courage it takes to live in a biased world.

Tolstoy, Leo. **Anna Karenina.** Bantam 1978.

Written between 1873 and 1877, this long novel with a double plot presents upper-class Russian society of the nineteenth century. Anna Karenina becomes involved in a love triangle which ends in her suicide. Konstantine Levin, the hero of the alternate tale, learns to appreciate the values of the peasants who toil on his estate. The contrast in moral values between Anna and Konstantine may be less apparent today than when this novel was written, but the lesson in value appreciation remains poignant.

Wheeler, Shirley P. **Dr. Nina and the Panther.** Dodd 1976.

Nina Case struggles constantly toward one goal: becoming a doctor. As a young girl, she has only her mother to take care of her and give her early schooling. Later she is abandoned, and lives with several different families while getting enough money for school. Forced to marry—not for love, but for money and the chance to finish medical school—Nina finally realizes her childhood dream of being a medical doctor.

Professional References

Axline, Virginia M. *Dibs: In Search of Self.* New York: Ballentine Books, 1976.

Favat, F. Andre. *Child and Tale.* Research Report # 19. Urbana, Illinois: National Council of Teachers of English, 1977.

Johnson, Ferne, ed. *Start Early for an Early Start: You and the Young Child.* Chicago: American Library Association, 1976.

Kircher, Clara J. *Behavior Patterns in Children's Books.* An annotated list of books for children, preschool through grade nine. Westminister, Maryland: Christian Classics, Inc., 1966.

Squire, James R. *The Responses of Adolescents While Reading Four Short Stories.* Research Report #2. Urbana, Illinois: National Council of Teachers of English, 1964.

Terry, Ann. *Children's Poetry Preferences.* Research Report # 16. Urbana, Illinois: National Council of Teachers of English, 1974.

Ladder II

Relating to Wide Individual Differences

> The success of the human species is due notably to its biological diversity. Its potential lies in this diversity .... From it stems the need to respect the other person and the differences in social life ....
>
> Francois Jacob

When one considers the magnificent diversity of human beings, one can see clearly why the category "Relating to Wide Individual Differences" was included in this new edition of *Reading Ladders for Human Relations.* Seemingly the coquettish attention of a society flits from one aspect of itself to another, gazes for awhile, then glances away. The books in this Ladder were chosen to mirror some uniquenesses long ignored by our society and our schools.

Writers and their literature also reflect that careless attention. In recent years, more than ever before, the individuality of each human being has been stressed. This heightened awareness of the uniqueness of each and every one of us has been a facilitating current to bring attitudinal changes to American society as well as to many different parts of the world. It is reflected in legislation and in our changing life styles; it is a truism that demands to be recognized and accepted.

The books in this section were chosen to focus attention upon some differences and to show the similarities of "the different" to us all. In addition to the literary consideration of plot, characterization, setting, and imagery, the reader will be influenced by the underlying central theme of this Ladder that we have called "understandings."

The topics included here are those most currently of interest in America: understanding aging, male and female role changes, the handicapped, the gifted, and the economically different. In many cases the lists included are imperfect—sometimes because the amount of material available is inexhaustible, sometimes because very little has been written.

Because these topics have become prominent in literature only in the last decade, there may be inherent difficulties for the teacher who would develop a full unit around them. Some caution must be advised. For example, while it is enormously important, the subject of aging necessarily also gets into death and dying. In dealing with changing roles of males and females, hardened stereotypes almost certainly will be met. Although we consider the themes presented here as among the most exciting and vital of new literature, each of them presents certain problems in the classroom.

The relationship of young and old, subsumed under the category "Understanding Aging," is of tremendous importance to the development of the young who often notice more difference than similarity between themselves and elders. Books such as Chester Aaron's *Better Than Laughter* and Stephanie Tolan's *Grandpa and Me* provide extraordinary opportunities for the young to gain insights into the human process of aging. Again, certain particulars of this literature are difficult to face. Senility, death, dying, and suicide are not easy to handle in life, or in literature. They are, however, facts of both and appear not infrequently in books portraying the relationships of young and old. Whether it is Little Bits' loss in *Hi, Mrs. Mallory* or Geneva Reade's in *The Eyes of the Amaryllis,* young readers today are presented portraits of persons who die. Nearly every classroom will contain young readers who have experienced the loss of someone dear. Teachers and librarians can and should help with insights about that commonality we all share in love and grief. These books can explicate some of those feelings, but they must be approached with the tenderness and care the subject deserves.

The number of stories about economic differences and stories about the gifted present a peculiar insight into life in the United States. There is an abundance of literature about the problems of poverty and intellectual shortcomings, but relatively little suggests concern for the problems of children who grow up rich or gifted. There is no doubt that such young people do have unique growing pains. It may be symbolic that neither writers nor our society consider those differences problematic. Teachers will want to be watchful for such new titles that will balance human relations units involving economic and intellectual differences.

Our list of books around the central theme of "understanding the handicapped" is only a small sample of what is available. Today, with mandated national mainstreaming legislation, this is not a subject any teacher can ignore. The dilemma of the classroom teacher will be in selectively choosing a reading list devoted to specific disabilities from the vast amount of literature that is available. Beyond this book, further references can be obtained from sources such as publishers, librarians, resource teachers, and officials in organizations for the handicapped.

The topic of "male and female" developed here about literature that portrays young people in roles of non-stereotypic gender also presents some difficulties. Differences in sexual preference, occupational and family roles are not always easily accommodated in local communities. Again, they are matters of the gravest importance, but must be approached sensitively. This Ladder, too, in its imperfections, mirrors our society. There is much, for instance, to provide understanding of the girl who wants to be a doctor, but little for the boy who would be a nurse. We are beginning to see stories of men who care for the children, stories of gay men and lesbian women, stories of females at war and male ballet dancers, but such books are just now appearing in any quantity. Teachers are advised to review these materials carefully for quality as well as content before their presentation.

Finally, the divisions included in this Ladder (aging, handicapped, gifted, male and female, and economic differences) will no doubt frequently overlap with the other four Ladders. Teachers, librarians, and parents using this book should make their recommendations to students based on what seems best for them. We have striven for quality rather than quantity, but in some instances books were chosen for the content. This is especially true for the books for younger children.

> Books *can* play a significant role in the life of the young child, but the extent to which they do depends entirely upon adults . . . . There is a great store of literature to share with the young, but the wealth could go unused if adults disregard their responsibilities. Adults must sing the songs, say the rhymes, tell the tales, and read the stories to children to make literature and all its benefits central to children's lives.[1] (p. 1)

It is with this thought that this portion of *Reading Ladders* has been approached so that adults, teachers, librarians, or parents might have a ready reference to books that will help—to sensitize perceptions of individual difference, enhance language, stimulate imagination, and provide encouragement to dream a little.

James Duggins and Edith Newhart

---

[1] Cullinan, Bernice E. and Carolyn W. Carmichael, eds. *Literature and Young Children.* Urbana: National Council of Teachers of English, 1977.

Understanding the Aging

Ages 1 to 5

Anders, Rebecca. **A Look at Aging.** Photographs by Maria S. Forrai. Lerner Pubns 1977.

> The joys, problems, contributions, and physical changes of the elderly are vividly rendered through photographs, and reinforced by the simple text. The photographs can be used by a creative teacher to develop inference skills, even with pre-school age children.

MacLachlan, Patricia. **Through Grandpa's Eyes.** Illus. Deborah Ray. Har-Row 1980.

> John discovers that he has a different perspective on his every day world if he tries to "see" it as his blind Grandfather does—by hearing, smelling, and feeling. The sensitive drawings will be especially appealing to young listeners.

Seuling, Barbara. **The Teeny Tiny Woman.** Illus. by author. Viking Pr 1976.

> This old English ghost tale is about an aging woman who lives alone. Alliteration is used throughout to develop the story of her way of life.

Skorpen, Liesel Moak. **Mandy's Grandmother.** Illus. Martha Alexander. Dial 1975.

> At their first meeting, Mandy and her grandmother have nothing in common. As time passes, however, they both realize that they can live and learn through each other. Mandy learns to knit, and her grandmother learns to accept a granddaughter who is not always a typical little girl. Outstanding illustrations add to the story.

Ages 5 to 8

Bach, Alice. **Grouchy Uncle Otto.**

Understanding the Aging 83

Berger, Terry. **Special Friends.** Photographs by David Hechtlinger. Messner 1979.

In this account of a young person's rewarding and enjoyable relationship with an elderly neighbor, photographs are used to enhance a crisp text.

Burch, Robert. **Two That Were Tough.** Illus. Richard Cuffari. Viking Pr 1976.

An old man who has been strong and independent all his life faces the inevitable dependence that will come when he moves to the city to live with his daughter. He sees himself in the fierce independence of a wild chicken that lives in the countryside around him. He wants to take the chicken with him when he leaves, but at last decides not to disturb its freedom, not to "take the risk out of living" for the wild one.

Jeschke, Susan. **Mia, Grandma and the Genie.** Illus. by author. HR&W 1978.

This tender folktale will help children understand why grandparents sometimes appear strange. After Grandma goes to the hospital, Mia discovers that she really did have a Genie. The tale lends itself to the discussion of fact and fantasy with young children.

LaFarge, Phyllis. **Granny's Fish Story.** Illus. Gahan Wilson. Parents 1975.

Julie's grandmother is different—she wears blue jeans and sneakers. Sarah and Julie visit her in the country, and she helps them get over their fears about thunderstorms. In the end, Sarah wishes she had a granny like Julie's.

Lasky, Kathryn. **I Have Four Names for My Grandfather.** Illus. Christopher G. Knight. Little 1976.

This story portrays the special love of a grandfather and grandson for each other. Their differences in age, wisdom, and physical size are indicated in words and pictures. Because they openly express their love, the book is well-suited to helping those who are inhibited about communicating such emotion.

Lundgren, Max (translator Ann Pyk). **Matt's Grandfather.** Illus. Fibben Hald. Putnam 1972.

This story of a little boy and his grandfather has an up-beat conclusion that makes it a treat for adults as well as children. The illustrations are part and parcel of the impact.

Matsuno, Masako. **A Pair of Red Clogs.** Illus. Kazue Mizumura. Collins Pubs 1960.

A grandmother reminisces about the time she cracked her new red clogs as she played the weather game, and almost did something dishonest so that her mother would buy her a new pair. This charming family story of Japan is told with warm sympathy and gentle humor.

Miles, Miska. **Annie and the Old One.** Illus. Peter Parnall. Little 1971.

Annie and her grandmother are Navajos. The Old One says she will die when Annie's mother finishes weaving the rug, so Annie tries to prevent her from completing it. Gradually the Old One helps Annie understand that there is a pattern to life which includes dying.

Skorpen, Liesel Moak. **Old Arthur.** Illus. Wallace Tripp. Har-Row 1972.

Old Arthur is too old to be of help on the farm, but he is not too old to be a friend and companion to a little boy named William. This gentle story of an aging dog with endearing ways will help young children appreciate and understand both animals and people as they grow old.

Stevens, Margaret. **When Grandpa Died.** Illus. Kenneth Ualand. Childrens 1979.

This story considers both the closeness possible between young and old, and coping with the separation of death. A little girl who has enjoyed the companionship of her grandfather is angry when he dies. While others are crying, she is angry with Grandpa for leaving her. Finally, she is able to cry and talk about his dying.

Stren, Patti. **There's a Rainbow in My Closet.** Illus. by author. Har-Row 1979.

When Emma's mother leaves for two months in Europe, her grandmother comes from Florida to stay with Emma and her father. Emma is very resentful until she discovers that "gramma" is a person who not only likes her drawings and understands her need to draw, but is also fun to be around. With her grandmother's help, she comes to understand herself and her own talents better.

Thomas, Ianthe. **Hi, Mrs. Mallory!** Illus. Ann Toulmin-Rothe. Har-Row 1979.

This is the story of L'il Bits and her best friend, a very old woman named Mrs. Mallory. All the marvelous things they have in

Understanding the Aging

common—their shared snacks and conversations, and their love for each other—are recounted. L'il Bits visits every day after school until one day, when Mrs. Mallory does not answer her call. This book helps to develop the marvel of relationships between the young and old, and to introduce the difficult subject of death.

Ages 8 to 11

Ancona, George. **Growing Older.** Dutton 1978.

In this long photographic essay, the life cycle of older people is evoked with then-and-now pictures. Thirteen Americans from diverse parts of the country and diverse ethnic backgrounds are shown at work, with their families, and in their daily routines. Teachers will be able to use this book to demonstrate the great variety of American people and the potential vibrancy of old age.

Blue, Rose. **Grandma Didn't Wave Back.** Illus. Ted Lewin. Watts 1972.

A family comes face to face with a grandmother's growing senility. The story shows some of the problems of coping with aging family members. Although the elegant nursing home may be too simplistic a solution, the problems are very real and will provoke discussion.

Buck, Pearl. **The Beech Tree.** John Day 1955.

A whole family is faced with the adjustment of grandfather's coming to live with them. Mother is unhappy about the situation, feeling it would be best for all if he went to a nursing home, but Mary Lou explains how he is like the beech tree, giving life to the little trees around it. She also notes that grandfather is the only one who has time for her. This portrayal of a serious social problem is sensitive and realistic.

Byars, Betsy. **After the Goat Man.**

Byars, Betsy. **The House of Wings.**

Byars, Betsy. **Trouble River.** Illus. Rocco Negri. Avon 1978.

A young boy takes his grandmother forty miles down Trouble River to escape from Indians in the Old West. Aided by the advice of this rather crotchety old woman, Dewey evades the enemy, fights wolves, and travels through rapids. A philosophy of not giving up, and a sense of real love and family solidarity predominate.

Clymer, Eleanor. **Me and the Eggman.**

Girion, Barbara. **Joshua, the Czar, and the Chicken Bone Wish.** Illus. Richard Cuffari. Scribner 1978.

> The kids think Joshua can't do anything well, and he agrees. He's the "klutz" of the fourth grade. But new friends at the nursing home where his mother works find qualities to praise, and his very special friend, The Czar, teaches him a skill—how to win when breaking a wishbone. His self-confidence begins to show, and he takes charge of an emergency situation on the class field trip. The story is both sensitive and upbeat.

Greene, Constance C. **The Unmaking of Rabbit.**

Herman, Charlotte. **Our Snowman Had Olive Eyes.** Dutton 1977.

> When Sheila's grandmother, Bubbie, arrives, the bedroom must be shared. Although she has to give up half her closet, half her dresser, and the bed next to the window, she finds that there are many good things about sharing with the old woman. No one else is so helpful and understanding. As for Bubbie, she finds Sheila the most supportive member of the family; she wants to be self-sufficient, and she also wants to meet secretly with a gentleman friend. Young readers will find out about some of the joys and problems of aging.

Houston, James. **Akavak: An Eskimo Journey.** Illus. by author. HarBraceJ 1968.

> A grandfather and his grandson make a treacherous journey over miles of frozen land to fulfill a promise. The wisdom of the old man and the physical endurance of the boy, coupled with the moral courage of both, enable them to reach their destination.

Irwin, Hadley. **The Lilith Summer.** Feminist Pr 1979.

> Twelve-year-old Ellen wants a ten-speed bike, and in order to earn the money she agrees to spend her summer as a companion to Lilith Adams, a seventy-seven-year-old woman. Ellen gradually discovers that Lilith is very interesting. She is a strong and entertaining person, in spite of being older than anyone Ellen has ever known. The two learn from each other, but Ellen, especially, becomes aware of life from an older person's perspective: coping with loneliness and needing to give and receive love.

Mahy, Margaret. **Ultra-Violet Catastrophe!** Illus. Brian Froud. Parents 1975.

> Sally and Great-Uncle Magnus share an afternoon of freedom and

Understanding the Aging 87

abandon on a walk through the countryside, and give readers a glimpse at the easy companionship of the young and the old.

Mathis, Sharon Bell. **The Hundred Penny Box.**

Wallace, Barbara Brooks. **Hawkins.** Illus. Gloria Kamen. Abingdon 1977.

Harvey is ten, and an avid collector of anything free. He wins the free services—for one month—of Hawkins, a gentleman's gentleman. In that month he learns about devotion to duty, high standards of job performance, and versatility. He also catches a glimpse of the special problems and viewpoints of two elderly people.

Ages 11 to 14

Aaron, Chester. **Better Than Laughter.** HarBraceJ 1972.

Allan and Sam Collins have everything—the best house in town, a pool, summer camp, and all the sports equipment they can use. However, they are not given time, and love, and understanding. The story of their one-day protest about this is set against a narrative of materialism and waste. The boys meet Horace, the eighty-five-year-old keeper of the town dump. The old man is struggling with his own problems of love, age, and consumerism. Young readers will be able to compare different value systems as they clash.

Babbitt, Natalie. **The Eyes of the Amaryllis.** Skylark. Bantam 1979.

Geneva Reade, her grandmother, her father, George, and her deceased grandfather—a seacaptain who died at sea thirty years before—are all involved in an adventure with an underwater treasure and an unpopular old legend. The similarities and differences of the two women, one old and one young, are striking.

Bales, Carol Ann. **Tales of the Elders: A Memory Book of Men and Women Who Came to America As Immigrants, 1900-1930.**

Bosse, Malcolm J. **The 79 Squares.**

Cleaver, Vera, and Bill Cleaver. **Queen of Hearts.** Lippincott 1978.

Granny Lincoln, a cantankerous and spiteful seventy-nine-year-old, cannot live alone without the help of her twelve-year-old granddaughter. The girl is mature enough, and unselfish enough, to seek solutions that will truly help the old woman look forward to more years of life. One by one, housekeepers and attendants leave. Wilma, who comes to understand both the old woman and herself, stays on. Adolescents will see here some of the processes of aging, with some of its problems and some of its joys.

Hall, Lynn. **The Siege of Silent Henry.** Follett 1972.

Robert Short is a young man who wants to be rich. He is clever enough to charm adults into giving him what he wants at school, in town, and at home. Because he is selfish and a loner, he is lonely. An old man, Silent Henry Leffert, owns the secret to fabled and wealth-producing beds of Ginseng roots. Robert sets out to befriend him in order to discover the secret. Each of the men knows that he is playing a game to benefit himself. Ultimately, both of them discover what they have become. Teachers can use this book to project comparisons of either old and young, or different value systems.

Heide, Florence Parry. **When the Sad One Comes to Stay.** Bantam 1976.

In this story of a move to a new town, the only friend the heroine has is an old woman who fantasizes that the girl is her own daughter. Conflict develops because the poor and eccentric old woman cannot gain the approval of the girl's mother, a social-climber. In the end, the girl betrays her one friend as she assumes her mother's values.

Mazer, Norma Fox. **A Figure of Speech.** Delacorte 1979.

When no one else seems to care about Grandpa, Jenny cares. The old man is physically weak, and senile. His son's family—with whom he lives—wants to put him in a home for senior citizens. Neither Jenny nor the old man can accept this; they run away to the farm on which he grew up. But the place is not the same; the farmhouse is decrepit, windowless, and beyond restoration. At this point, the old man gives up and dies. Jenny will inspire compassion in other young people.

Moskin, Marietta D. **A Paper Dragon.** John Day 1968.

When her father's job takes him out of the country, sixteen-year-old Karen Stevens reluctantly moves to New York to live with her grandmother and her older sister, Wendy. Favoritism towards Wendy and restrictions placed on Karen cause her to think of her grandmother as a dragon. Relations with an adopted aunt and the family of a new friend help her understand her grandmother and sister.

Newton, Suzanne. **Reubella and the Old Focus Home.** Westminster 1978.

Reubella is the mainstay of the run-down house/hotel her lazy father owns. She has just decided to run away when she meets three old ladies whose combined ages total two hundred and twenty-eight. They change not only her father, but the entire town of Shad, North Carolina. In this portrayal, they are the youngest folks around. Even Reubella's father learns to give and receive love in a mature way after associating with the young oldsters.

Rogers, Pamela. **The Rare One.** Nelson 1974.

An unhappy adolescent boy secretly befriends an old man who lives in the woods. He writes a prizewinning "scientific" essay, learns about the press and TV, and then discovers that winning at the expense of his friend's privacy is not satisfying. A supportive family helps him grow toward maturity and understanding.

Thiele, Colin. **The Hammerhead Light.**

Thiele, Colin. **The Shadow on the Hills.**

Tolan, Stephanie S. **Grandpa—and Me.** Scribner 1978.

Eleven-year-old Kerry Warren discovers her love for her grandfather when she believes that he is crazy. He has lived with her family since she was three. One day she finds him doing queer things, things that embarrass her in front of her friends. In the process of sorting it all out, Kerry learns a great deal about herself and her relationships. The family must decide what to do about grandpa, but the options—a home or a full-time nurse—seem cruel. In this story, grandpa makes his own decision.

Wersba, Barbara. **The Dream Watcher.**

Wilkinson, Sylvia. **A Killing Frost.** PB 1978.

The late autumn of Miz Liz's life is lovingly and understandingly detailed by her thirteen-year-old granddaughter, Ramie. The strong-willed, single-minded old lady contrasts with the sensitive, artistic Ramie, as revealed through her vivid perceptions and descriptions of the world of rural North Carolina.

Zindel, Paul. **The Pigman.** Har-Row 1968.

Two teenagers take turns chapter by chapter relating the story of their friendship with a lonely old man. Although they are very fond of Mr. Pignati and aware at times of their need for his company, one thoughtless act on their part has a great deal to do with his death. It is only afterwards that John and Lorraine realize the enormity of their irresponsibility, and attempt to explain it by writing the book. The lesson is all the more painful when told from their point of view.

Ages 14 and Up

Bach, Alice. **Mollie Make-Believe.** Dell 1976.

Mollie is perfectly respectful and good until her favorite grandparents meet a crisis. Events take place in the apartment of her dying grandmother. Set against the emotionality of the situation is Mollie's maturity in her views toward herself, her parents and relatives, and a young man she meets in the park. Through her eyes, young readers will see the pain of growing up and becoming independent.

Bryant, Dorothy. **Miss Giardino.** Ata Bks 1978.

Miss Giardino is a retired school teacher living where she always has, near the school where she taught for forty years. Told as a flashback—after she has been mugged on her old school ground—this is the story of a first generation Italian-American, from childhood through teaching career. As she regains her memory readers learn how much she and the world have changed. Young people will perceive that one is never too old to change, or begin again.

Cummings, Betty Sue. **Let a River *Be*.** Atheneum 1978.

An old woman struggles with developers to save the environment on a Florida river. In the process, she saves a retarded man from the backwater townspeople for awhile. The reader gains insight into differences of perception, zeal in the defense of values, human cruelty, and human love.

Denker, Henry. **Horowitz and Mrs. Washington.** Putnam 1979.

Seventy-year-old Samuel Horowitz is a completely independent widower until, in an encounter with muggers, the old man receives a knife wound and a paralyzing stroke that change his life. He has a choice to make: go to a nursing home or employ a nurse and housekeeper. The black woman who fulfills both of these roles is as proud and independent as Horowitz. This lively and humorous story demonstrates the warm affection the two develop as they learn to live with each other.

Sarton, May. **As We Are Now.** Norton 1973.

The terror and despair of an old but healthy mind trapped in a nearly useless body is communicated in this first person account. Miss Spencer, a heart attack victim at the age of seventy-six, is put away to live in a "rest" home. She describes her fight with the managers to keep her own mind intact, and to be allowed to die with dignity. The conclusion is stunning and terrible; Miss Spencer has hidden her journals in the Frigidaire, to be published after her death.

Schulman, L. M., editor. **Autumn Light: Illuminations of Age.** T Y Crowell 1978.

This collection of short stories by well-known twentieth-century writers highlights some of the problems of older people—senility, fear, immobility, and most of all, loneliness. Each of the stories is a lyrical and poignant message—the perception of one who suddenly becomes conscious of aging. It is perhaps one-sided to present only the problems, never the joys, of growing old. However, teachers as well as young readers will grow more sensitive to older people as a consequence of sharing these stories.

Scott, J. M. **In a Beautiful Pea Green Boat.** Chilton 1969.

Vacationing Jonathan Bordas is desperate: plans for his own bookshop have bankrupted him, and his inability to relate to others has left him utterly alone. He swims miles from the Portuguese coast, intending suicide, but instinct forces him to clutch a rubber raft which drifts within his reach. Inside is seven-year-old Bonnie, whose dependence on Bordas requires his own survival, both physical and emotional. Their adventure on the sea has both beauty and violence; its dramatic conclusion is haunting.

Understanding the Handicapped

Ages 1 to 5

Cauley, Lorinda Bryan. **The Ugly Duckling.** Illus. by author. HarBraceJ 1979.

> The author's artistic ability enhances her retelling of the well-known story of an ugly duckling that grew up to be a beautiful swan. Large and colorful illustrations make this an especially good book to read and show to young listeners.

Fanshawe, Elizabeth. **Rachel.** Illus. Michael Charlton. Bradbury Pr 1975.

> Rachel can do many of the things other boys and girls do: she can swim, make birthday cards, go to meetings of the Brownies, and feed the gerbils. But she must do most of them in a wheelchair. Teachers can use this book with young readers and pre-schoolers to explain how disabled people are both different from and similar to others.

Peterson, Jeanne Whitehouse. **I Have a Sister: My Sister Is Deaf.** Illus. Deborah Ray. Har-Row 1977.

> Poetic text and appealing illustrations are used to portray a little sister who is deaf. What she can and cannot do in everyday living is sensitively described. Young children will become aware of her feelings as she copes with a "normal" world.

Ages 5 to 8

Arthur, Catherine. **My Sister's Silent World.** Illus. Nathan Talbot. Childrens 1979.

> Vivid photographs show that deaf children look and act like "normal" children. The easy-to-read text helps young readers to understand why deaf children can't speak fluently and how they use sign language to communicate.

Bouchard, Lois. **The Boy Who Wouldn't Talk.** Illus. Ann Grifalconi. Doubleday 1969.

Understanding the Handicapped

Carlos, who comes from Puerto Rico, is frustrated by the problems of adjusting to a new city and a new language. To the distress of his family, his friends, and his teacher, he decides to stop using words at all until he becomes friends with Ricky, who is blind and cannot read Carlos' signs and gestures. A sensitive "boy's eye" view of the problems of a child facing a new urban environment.

Fassler, Joan. **Howie Helps Himself.**

Hoban, Russell. **Ugly Bird.** Illus. Lillian Hoban. Macmillan 1969.

Ugly Bird is a very ugly bird; he is so ugly in fact that only his mother loves him and all the other birds make fun of him. Looking for an escape from his ugliness, the little bird changes himself into a handsome stone, a shiny fish, a little pebble, and a buzzing bee. In the process, he finds out that it is not so bad to be himself after all.

Keats, Ezra Jack. **Apt. 3.** Illus. by author. Macmillan 1971.

"Someone in the building playing a harmonica" starts Sam and Ben off on a search. Before they find the blind man with the secrets in Apt. 3, they discover some secrets of their own. The apartment interiors depicted are more somber than those in *Hi Cat* and *Goggles* but they convey that special feeling for ghetto life unique to Keats.

Kraus, Robert. **Leo the Late Bloomer.** Illus. Jose Aruego. Windmill. Dutton 1973.

Leo the Tiger cannot do anything right, not even talk. His mother has faith that he will bloom in his own good time, and encourages his father to be patient. Leo's late but triumphant blooming should be reassuring to all, whether they are slow starters or waiting for slow starters to bloom.

Larsen, Hanne. **Don't Forget Tom.** Illus. by author. T Y Crowell 1978.

The author's color photographs supplement this story of a six-year-old boy and his family. Tom is mentally handicapped, and some things are harder for him than for other children his age. The story is told with empathy and understanding. Young readers and listeners will be more sympathetically aware of this common handicap.

Lasker, Joe. **He's My Brother.** Illus. by author. A Whitman 1974.

Peer and family relationships affect the way Jamie copes with his mental handicap; sometimes he has difficulty being accepted. Readers see his experiences and reactions through the eyes of an older brother.

Litchfield, Ada B. **A Cane in Her Hand.** Illus. Eleanor Mill. A Whitman 1977.

> Valerie is a visually-impaired child who tries to cope with her handicap. She receives special help in school and learns to use a cane. She roller skates, swims, takes dancing lessons, and does many of the same things other children do. She discovers that although seeing with your eyes is important, it is not everything.

Mack, Nancy. **Tracy.** Illus. Heinz Kleutmeier. Raintree Pubs Ltd 1976.

> Since birth Tracy has been afflicted with cerebral palsy. She goes to school, but is confined to a wheel chair or crutches most of the time. With the aid of therapy she is learning to function in the "normal" world. Though her movement is limited, she is able to participate in some activities with her peers. Her acceptance is reflected in the manner in which they tease her.

Montgomery, Elizabeth Rider. **The Mystery of the Boy Next Door.** Illus. Ethel Gold. Garrard 1978.

> The neighborhood children think the new boy next door is unfriendly and does not want to play with them. Then they discover that he is deaf and can only communicate through sign language. The simple text and attractive illustrations make this a good introduction for young readers to the problems of being deaf. A chart of the alphabet in sign language is included.

Montgomery, Elizabeth Rider. **"Seeing" in the Dark.** Illus. Troy Howell. Garrard 1979.

> Kay, a blind primary student, must adjust to her new school. In her own language, she describes both her fears and the responses of other children to her. Ultimately she is accepted. Indeed, the prejudices of the others disappear as she heroically leads them from a burning building because she can "see" through the smoke-filled halls. Teachers can use this book to suggest the possibility of strength in disability, as well as the cruelty of some children toward the handicapped.

Peter, Diana. **Claire and Emma.** Illus. Jeremy Finlay. John Day 1977.

> Four-year-old Claire and two-year-old Emma are sisters who were born deaf. They wear hearing aids and take lessons in lipreading and speaking. Many of the difficulties of being deaf are described, yet we see the girls doing a lot of the same things other children do.

Renter, Margaret. **My Mother Is Blind.** Illus. Philip Lanier. Childrens 1979.

A young boy describes the changes in his family life that occur when his mother goes blind. Photographs illustrate how he and his father help her, and how she learns to cope with her handicap.

Robinet, Harriette. **Jay and the Marigold.**

Smith, Lucia B. **A Special Kind of Sister.** Illus. Chuck Hall. HR&W 1979.

At the age of seven, Sarah must cope with school, friends, and family. In addition, her brother Andy is retarded. This story describes the different feelings and problems she must sort out to discover who she is and what her life will be. Young readers can learn about retardation as they learn about Sarah.

White, Paul. **Janet at School.** Illus. Jeremy Finlay. T Y Crowell 1978.

Color photographs lead us through the day with five-year-old Janet, who was born with *spina bifida*. There is a simple explanation of her handicap, and an easy flowing text to accompany the excellent color photos.

Yolen, Jane. **The Seeing Stick.** Illus. Remy Charlip and Demetra Maraslis. T Y Crowell 1977.

The emperor is sad, because his beloved daughter cannot see the beauty surrounding her. In fact, she can see nothing at all, for the princess Hwei Ming is blind. A mysterious old man dressed in tatters claims he can cure her. The magic in the old man's "seeing stick" is not what anyone expects, and the story's ending is a striking surprise. The sorrowful, self-centered princess learns to see, not with her eyes, but with her fingers and, more significantly, with her mind and her heart.

Ages 8 to 11

Armer, Alberta. **Screwball.** Illus. W. T. Mars. G&D 1963.

Intense sibling rivalry keeps twins in a competitive stance, a not uncommon occurrence. In this case, such a relationship doesn't provide much base for supporting one of the twin's development of self-confidence since developing polio at the age of three. A severely weakened right side of the boy's body does not interfere with his flare for things mechanical and building imaginative and inventive toys. The winning of a soap box car race gives the boy insight into his strengths.

Bawden, Nina. **The Witch's Daughter.** Lippincott 1966.

An exciting suspense story involving much more than the capture of jewel thieves. Perdita, a lonely orphan, is rejected by the other children because of her unusual power to see into the future. Through the arrival of a blind girl, Janey, and Janey's brother Tim, Perdita comes to realize that her powers are not a sign of witchcraft, but a special talent.

Byars, Betsy. **Summer of the Swans.** Camelot. Avon 1974.

A beloved mentally retarded younger brother is lost and fourteen-year-old Sara is faced with the longest day in her life. Help comes from an unexpected source as she learns to understand herself and others a little better. This is a realistic, perceptive, nonsentimental story with a touch of romance.

Christopher, Matt. **Long Shot for Paul.** Illus. Foster Caddell. Little 1966.

Glenn Marlett is determined to make Paul, his mentally retarded brother, a good enough basketball player to make the local team. Finally Paul does make the team, but his acceptance by the other boys takes more time. As Paul is given the opportunity to prove himself, he is recognized as a valuable asset to the team. This book could be used to help students learn to view retardation more holistically.

First, Julia. **Flat on My Face.** Camelot. Avon 1975.

This charming story unfolds the trials of a tomboy and her enthusiasm for "boys'" sports. In the care she gives a cerebral palsied child she learns to accept her differences and win the admiration of others. Teachers can use this to teach readers to better understand both those who are different and themselves.

Fleischman, Paul. **The Half-a-Moon Inn.** Illus. Kathy Jacobi. Har-Row 1980.

This is a dramatic tale of a young mute boy, kidnapped by the proprietress of an inn. Surrounded by deception and intrigue, Aaron tries desperately, and finally successfully, to escape this bizarre world and find his mother. The haunting line drawings set a sinister mood.

Friis-Baastad, Babbis. **Kristy's Courage.** Illus. Charles Geer. HarBraceJ 1965.

Understanding the Handicapped

Kristy is a small girl who has been hit by a car and must learn to live with a scar and nearly unintelligible speech. Teased or ignored by the children in her school, Kristy learns to accept herself and deal with her classmates' reactions.

Garfield, James B. **Follow My Leader.** Illus. Robert Greiner. Viking Pr 1957.

This is the story of blindness following an accident with a firecracker. Young readers will empathize with the dramatic changes that must be encompassed by those who lose their sight as well as understand the trauma that comes to one who has caused such an accident. Teachers can use it to help children learn what the experience is like and to help others who live in a world of darkness.

Hermes, Patricia. **What If They Knew?** HarBraceJ 1980.

By describing one girl's way of coping with epilepsy, this book will help children understand how modern medicine can keep the illness under control. Jeremy is finally able to accept herself and to talk openly about epilepsy to her friends.

Hickok, Lorena A. **The Story of Helen Keller.** Illus. Jo Polseno. G&D 1974.

This is the tender, moving story of the life of Helen Keller. A child left deaf, dumb, and blind after an illness at two years of age overcomes her plight and becomes one of the most remarkable women of all time. Miss Keller's acceptance of self and the way she matured despite her handicaps should be an inspiration to anyone reading this book.

Hirsch, Karen. **My Sister.**

Hunt, Irene. **The Lottery Rose.** Scribner 1976.

Georgie is an abused child, disfigured from beatings, emotionally unstable, tagged as retarded on school records, but his love of flowers in a picture-book is the tiny spark that can't be extinguished. Winning a rosebush at the grocery lottery is his first step along the "road back." This story will develop or strengthen the reader's sensitivity to the physically disfigured, the retarded, and those suffering from loss of loved ones, and shed light on the possible causes of anti-social behavior.

Kamien, Janet. **What If You Couldn't . . . ? A Book About Special Needs.** Illus. Signe Hanson. Scribner 1979.

Asking the reader to imagine that he or she has a disability (mental, physical, or emotional), this book then provides experiments that will help one understand how it feels to have that disability. The book is also useful as background information in preparing a classroom for mainstreaming.

Levitin, Sonia. **A Sound to Remember.** Illus. Gabriel Lisowski. HarBraceJ 1979.

Jacov was known throughout his village as a slow, clumsy boy who stuttered and stumbled. Children made fun of him, adults felt sorry for him, and they were all surprised when the Rabbi chose Jacov to sound the ram's horn on Rosh Hashanah. When no sound was produced, the villagers were sure that the Rabbi would choose someone else to sound the Shofar for Yom Kippur. What the Rabbi chose to do is both a surprise and unforgettable. The superb illustrations will inspire much discussion and oral expression.

Little, Jean. **From Anna.** Illus. Joan Sandin. Trophy. Har-Row 1972.

Although well-loved by her capable, efficient family, five-year-old Anna knows that they do not understand her inability to learn to read and that her constant clumsiness is a source of annoyance. However, once Anna starts wearing glasses, she amazes her family and herself with the variety of things she can do. Anna's being part of a German immigrant family gives an added dimension to this touching story of a lonely, misunderstood child.

Little, Jean. **Mine for Keeps.** Illus. Lewis Parker. Little 1962.

Sally Copeland adjusts to living at a special school for children with physical handicaps. When she learns she is going home to live, she is filled with fear and apprehension for she knows being the only cerebral palsied child in a family and a school would cause many difficulties. With the help of an understanding family, she acquires new attitudes about herself, and when she begins to be thoughtful of others her life becomes more satisfying.

McDonnell, Lois Eddy. **Susan Comes Through the Fire.** Illus. Jim Walker. Friend Pr 1969.

Young Susan is on an outing with her parents and a girl friend when she accidentally pours gasoline on their campfire, instead of water. The resulting burns put Susan in the hospital for many months. Resentment builds as Susan is confined to bed. After a few trips to a playroom where other injured children play, Susan realizes that many others have been hurt more than she has. This is the beginning of Susan's road to recovery. She overcomes her grief and begins to help other children at the hospital. After she leaves, Susan returns to help with the other children in the ward.

Petersen, Palle. **Sally Can't See.**

Robinson, Veronica. **David in Silence.** Illus. Victor Ambus. Lippincott 1965.

Deaf and dumb, David suffers fear and the derision of the young people of his new neighborhood. With Michael as a friend, David is finally able to win their respect by proving his worth as a person. Realistically and tenderly written, this book shows true sympathy and understanding for the deaf.

Slote, Alfred. **Hang Tough, Paul Mather.**

Smith, Doris Buchanan. **Kelly's Creek.**

Southall, Ivan. **Let the Balloon Go.** St. Martin 1968.

A spastic child, stifled by his overprotective mother and friends is determined to accomplish a feat which would tax the endurance of any boy. The result is nearly tragic, but John Summer's achievement makes a real difference in the way his parents respond to him.

Ages 11 to 14

Albert, Louise. **But I'm Ready to Go.** Dell 1978.

This is the story of the minimally disabled, the learning handicapped. In this story, Judy *feels* more than *knows* what her learning disability is when she is compared with her more average sister, Emily. Judy's great dream is to be able to compete with her peers in their everyday and school tasks. The diary she keeps of her secret dream to run away and the failures she meets provide an unusual insight into those whose handicaps are not visible.

Baldwin, Anne Norris. **A Little Time.** Viking Pr 1978.

It takes some time for a young adult to learn to know her feelings and those of her family when their home is shared with a brother who has Down's syndrome. As Sarah learns to love and to share love, she also learns the importance of family. Her values mature and become clarified through the relationship with her retarded brother Matt. This book will help young people understand what it is like to grow up in a family with a handicapped sibling.

Beckwith, Lillian. **The Spuddy.** LFL. Dell 1978.

> The Spuddy, nicknamed for his intelligence, is a dog who loves Andy, a mute boy deserted by his mother. This story tells of the hardships and joys of the sea and fishermen as Andy learns love and grief in growing up in that environment. His speech is returned when he faces the trauma of burying his dog at sea. Young people will gain insight into the difficulties of muteness and communication.

Blume, Judy. **Deenie.** Dell 1977.

> Deenie, a beautiful junior high school girl, is being pressured by her mother to become a model when she develops scoliosis, a progressively deteriorating curvature of the spine. In this story, a girl who abhors handicaps must face four years in an ugly, awkward body brace. The way she responds before and after her misfortune will provide insight for discusssion about physical handicaps.

Bridgers, Sue Ellen. **All Together Now.**

Brooks, Jerome. **The Big Dipper Marathon.** Dutton 1979.

> In a freak incidence, Ace gets polio. Because of all the mixed feelings parents experience with handicapped children, Ace is told alternately to overcome and to be careful of his disabilities. A trip to Chicago gives him a week in which he learns to do those things he can and to accept help in those things he cannot. When he returns to California, he must still deal with his parents' feelings. This book can help teachers explain to "normal" children some of the differences handicaps make.

Carpelan, Bo (translator Shela La Farge). **Bow Island: The Story of a Summer That Was Different.** Delacorte 1971.

> Johan has come to the Baltic Sea coast with his family to spend their summer vacation. He soon meets Marvin, a mentally retarded boy, who lives on Bow Island. Through his companionship with Marvin, Johan learns much about nature, people, and how to cope with cruelty and fear. Teachers can use this book to demonstrate the differences handicaps do and do not make.

Cook, Marjorie. **To Walk on Two Feet.** Westminster 1978.

> Carrie Karns has suffered the amputation of both legs. In this story she becomes independent again despite the frustration and despair she feels in trying to face her former friends and her family. Part of

her ultimate survival is wound up in solving a town mystery—a gang of thieves who break into schools and steal equipment. Teachers will find the book valuable in combating negative attitudes toward the handicapped because it is never apologetic.

Corcoran, Barbara. **A Dance to Still Music.** Illus. Charles Robinson. Atheneum 1974.

A fourteen-year-old, suddenly deaf, struggles to stay out of schools for the deaf. After running away from home, she finds her way to an experimental program of education. Readers will understand what it's like to be deaf and the reasons for mainstreaming handicapped children.

Fleischer, Leonore. **Ice Castles.** GM. Fawcett 1978.

Lexie Winston wants to ice-skate more than anything else in the world. Through the efforts of a has-been skater who has become a town eccentric, she achieves her dream. A freak accident that blinds Lexie almost destroys her future. This novel traces the courage and determination of an exceptional young woman who goes on to win regional skating trials without any of the judges knowing that she is blind. Teachers will want to use this movie-based novel as demonstration of personal triumph over what might have been an overwhelming handicap.

Forbes, Esther. **Johnny Tremain.** YB. Dell 1973

This classic story of a talented silversmith apprentice at the time of the American Revolution builds an understanding of the attitudes of people toward the handicapped when Johnny suffers a crippled hand. It takes all the boy's conviction and courage to overcome his despair. Teachers of social studies and English can use the book for values clarification as well as a portrait of the American Revolution.

Friis-Baastad, Babbis (translator Lise S. McKinnon). **Don't Take Teddy.** Scribner 1967.

Mikkel Grasbeth is a sensitive thirteen-year-old with an older brother who is mentally retarded. What the family has always feared happens one day. Teddy throws a rock and knocks out a boy's tooth. With echoes of "lock him up" and "call the police" in his ears, Mikkel decides to run away to protect Teddy. The long hard journey across the Norwegian countryside helps Mikkel to better understand his brother's needs and to do what would be best for him and for the whole family.

Garfield, Leon. **Smith.** Illus. Antony Maitland. Pantheon 1967.

Twelve-year-old Smith is one of the best pickpockets in all of eighteenth-century London. One day he steals a document from an old gentleman minutes before the man is murdered. Determined to discover why the document is valuable, he sets out to learn to read. Befriending a blind judge whose daughter tutors him, Smith finds himself accused of killing the man whose document he stole.

Garrigue, Sheila. **Between Friends.** Bradbury Pr 1978.

After moving to Massachusetts, Jill must make new friends. She chooses to be friends with Dede, a retarded girl, to the disgust of her more "normal" peers. Making some basic decisions about values, loyalties, and human compassion is not easy for this teenager who sacrifices many fleeting pleasures to continue the relationship so important to Dede. Young people can learn, as Jill did, that some retarded persons ". . . may never be a ballerina . . . but know more about being a friend than anyone else. . . ."

Green, Phyllis. **Walkie-Talkie.** A-W 1978.

Richie Fassinger, a highly unstable fourteen-year-old, befriends a cerebral-palsied boy. His tragi-comic antics are simultaneously creative and funny and desperately cruel. After a fearful thunderstorm, Richie commits the ultimate cruelty upon his handicapped "friend." His final realization of the scope of this cruelty does not make it better, but he learns a great deal about himself.

Jones, Ron. **The Acorn People.** Bantam 1977.

Handicapped children experience summer camp with the help of warm and loving young counselors. The children and the counselors learn what handicaps are and are not as they imitate the kind of experiences other children have during a summer in the woods. Special to children without handicaps will be the insight this story provides about adjustments that can be made by those with disabilities.

Lee, Mildred. **The Skating Rink.**

Levoy, Myron. **Alan and Naomi.**

Long, Judy. **Volunteer Spring.** Archway 1977.

At fourteen, Jill is caught up in the concerns normal to young women. She feels that her life has little meaning and that her future is uncertain, but her life takes on new values when she signs on as a volunteer worker in an institution for the retarded. Many young people will see themselves differently when they experience with Jill the needs of her institutionalized patients.

Melton, David. **A Boy Called Hopeless by M.J.** Schol Bk Serv 1977.

Jeremiah, a brain injured child, is termed hopeless by medical authorities and misunderstood by a special education program. He is helped by a rigid professional program, a tenacious family, and many volunteers for several years. His progress is related through the eyes of his sister, M.J., who never gives up on her little brother. Her own and her family's vision, selflessness, love and concern, and hard work help Jeremiah become a "normal" boy.

Neufeld, John. **Lisa, Bright and Dark.**

Platt, Kin. **The Boy Who Could Make Himself Disappear.** LFL. Dell 1971.

Twelve-year-old Roger, unloved, unwanted, and handicapped by a severe speech impediment, withdraws into a world of schizophrenia.

Rivera, Geraldo. **A Special Kind of Courage: Profiles of Young Americans.** Bantam 1977.

In this collection of short stories, all of the main characters, boys and girls, have overcome poverty, prejudice, hardship, and disease. Teachers may use these stories to provide insight into the meaning of difficulty and achievement.

Sachs, Marilyn. **Dorrie's Book.** Illus. Anne Sachs. Doubleday 1975.

Dorrie's beautiful micro-world is replaced by a harsher, larger reality when her mother has triplets, the family moves to a cheaper living area, and two neglected neighbor children move in with them. Now, one of six, after eleven years as the only child, she matures as she makes the adjustment. This is another glimpse of what life is like for abused children.

Sherburne, Zoa. **Why Have the Birds Stopped Singing?** Morrow 1974.

While exploring her great-great-grandmother's house, Katie has an epileptic seizure that sends her back one hundred years. Living as her ancestor, Kathryn, she is held prisoner by her own family who want to hide her epileptic condition. In discussing this book, students will gain insight into the negative attitudes held about certain handicapping conditions, and also into traditional superstitions about illness.

Shyer, Marlene Fanta. **Welcome Home, Jellybean.** Scribner 1978.

How Neil's life is drastically changed when his mentally retarded thirteen-year-old sister comes home to live is sensitively told in this first person narrative. The ambivalent feelings that Neil has, the embarrassment he feels, the resentment that builds up, is realistically expressed. Neil's father leaves home when he can no longer cope with such a stressful situation and Neil almost joins his father. Why he doesn't is a remarkable indication of Neil's growth as a compassionate human being.

Smith, Gene. **The Hayburners.** Illus. Ted Lewin. Delacorte 1974.

Joey, a thirty-year-old man with the mind of a ten-year-old, comes to live with and work for Will's family for the summer as part of a special program involving the mentally retarded. At first, Will looks down on Joey, but his awareness of Joey as a person takes a turn for the better when, in a fit of anger, he calls Joey an idiot and witnesses the man's deep hurt. Will's acceptance increases as he comes to admire Joey's gentleness and determination in caring for a 4-H steer, which Will himself had neglected.

Sutcliff, Rosemary. **Warrior Scarlet.** Walck 1966.

Drem has a crippled arm: how can he ever become a warrior and earn the right to wear the scarlet cloth that is reserved for the men of his tribe? In spite of many setbacks, Drem's courage and grim determination enable him to win the respect of his people and the right to wear the scarlet robe. The book provides an accurate view of life and customs in Bronze Age Britain.

Weik, Mary Hayes. **The Jazz Man.** Illus. Ann Grifalconi. Atheneum 1968.

The music of the jazz man helps a young man escape the loneliness of his world. The boy has a lame leg and must spend many hours alone each day. The music he hears from across the court helps him to create dreams that fill the time and emptiness of his room. Young people will come to a greater appreciation of both the beauty and cruelty sometimes caused by physical handicaps.

Winthrop, Elizabeth. **Marathon Miranda.** Holiday 1979.

Miranda has been a loner all her life. She is poor at group sports in school because she suffers from asthma. In this story she meets a girl who becomes her best friend. But, her new friend, Phoebe, is a jogger preparing for a six mile marathon. With Phoebe's encouragement, Miranda decides to jog to build her lung power and to achieve in a way she never has before. As important as the handicap are the personal relationships developed in this story. Rich and poor, old and young, being loved and wanted, are all treated with humanity and humor.

Yep, Laurence. **Sweetwater.** Illus. Julia Noonan. Camelot. Avon 1975.

This science fiction thriller delineates the struggles of a half-submerged city on another planet attacked by alien hydras. Tyree, a young flautist, encourages friendships with spider beings thus violating the code of his people. Caley, his blind sister, provides a rounded glimpse into what is missing and what remains for the handicapped.

Ages 14 and Up

Baker, Louise M. **Out on a Limb.** McGraw 1946.

Louise Baker finds herself out on a limb, as she humorously puts it, when at the age of eight she loses her leg in an automobile accident. How she skates, skis, rides horseback, and, despite her grandmother's grim prediction that "Louise will never get a man," marries twice, is a tale full of fun and courage, a reproof to those inclined to pity themselves.

Beim, Lorraine. **Triumph Clear.** HarBraceJ 1966.

A seventeen-year-old girl is stricken with polio just as she is ready to enter college. Through the treatment, she comes to grips with the reality of changing her career plans of studying acting. Feelings of rejection, despair, and hopelessness, even anger, are dealt with in a story that sustains interest by focusing on the interpersonal relationships among crippled teenagers and adults. Value clarification is a central point in this story.

Brancato, Robin. **Winning.** Bantam 1978.

A high school football star suffers an accident which leaves him paralyzed from the neck down. The novel revolves around his effort to deal with the many changes the accident brings—with his girlfriend, his parents, and a new relationship with a young high school teacher. Gradually he overcomes the despair and hopelessness of his plight to cope with the new life he must lead.

Brooke, Joshua. **Just a Little Inconvenience.** Dell 1978.

Kenny Briggs and Frank Logan, high school ski champions, were best friends until Kenny returned from Viet Nam missing an arm and a leg. Moreover, Kenny blames Frank's cowardice for the war incident that caused the double amputation. Together the men conquer skiing on one leg and regain their friendship. In addition to the drama between the men, readers will experience the triumph of overcoming a disability.

Buchanan, William. **A Shining Season.** Bantam 1979.

John Baker has it all. Among the top indoor milers of the world, the young athlete puts most of his time and energy into his rewarding sports career, until he finds out that he has cancer. Despite his personal physical and emotional agony, John spends the last eighteen months of his life helping younger athletes, delinquent as well as handicapped. This story will be an inspiration for young people, helping them understand the meaning of perseverance.

Campanella, Roy. **It's Good to Be Alive.** Little 1959.

This is the courageous story of a famous, professional baseball player in his long struggle to conquer paralysis. An equally important aspect of the book is the historic documentation of race relations in professional sports. Carefully introduced, the story could be used to inspire students.

Carson, Mary. **Ginny.** Popular Lib 1971.

Ginny is a popular high school girl struck down by a truck. Her struggle with herself, her relationships with peers and adults as she faces paralysis, is keenly portrayed. Students are led to understand the courage it takes for her to return to school.

Clewes, Dorothy. **Guide Dog.** Illus. Peter Burchard. Coward 1965.

At the age of nineteen, Roley Rolandson has a bomb blow up in his face causing permanent blindness. How can he become a doctor now? Roley would have given up but for his two friends, Susan and Steven, who encourage him to get a guide dog. The adjustment to the loss of sight and to using a guide dog makes this a moving and meaningful story.

Copeland, James. **For the Love of Ann.** Ballantine 1976.

This book traces the determined fight of a family to help their autistic girl's recovery. The feelings of the girl after twenty years of autism and the parent's continuing love and concern is clearly shown. Teachers may examine with their classes the heartbreak and day-to-day struggle such a disease brings to parents and siblings.

Crichton, Michael. **The Terminal Man.** Bantam 1974.

> A psychotic with psychomotor epilepsy has a computer surgically implanted in his brain. A malfunction in the computer causes this "terminal man" to kill three minutes each day. Readers are led, in this fast moving thriller, to consider the dangers of overmedication and surgery.

Cummings, Betty Sue. **Let a River** *Be.*

D'Ambrosio, Richard. **No Language but a Cry.** Dell 1971.

> Thousands of children are victims of desertion and child abuse every year. This is the story of the physical and emotional scars that result from such treatment. Dr. Richard D'Ambrosio tells the story of his attempt to rescue Laura, a patient in an institution as a result of early mistreatment. Senior high school readers will learn many of the causes of emotional and physical handicaps and the compassion necessary to cure these handicaps through this fictionalized case study.

Dooley, Thomas A. **The Night They Burned the Mountain.** FS&G 1960.

> The young American doctor, who after the war returned to the remote villages of Laos, tells of the personal battle he fought against the cancer which ultimately claimed him while he was healing the sick in the jungles of Asia.

Elliott, David. **Listen to the Silence.** Sig. NAL 1969.

> An emotionally disturbed boy tells of the long climb back to reality. Vividly described are the conditions, the sights, and sounds of institutionalized life. Teachers may use this book to share with students the facts of mental illness, and the philosophy which supports mainstream classes.

Greenberg, Joanne. **I Never Promised You a Rose Garden.** Sig. NAL 1977.

> Deborah's everyday surroundings become a gray shadow world as she slips deeper into her secret Kingdom of Yr. Once a pleasant retreat from reality, Yr is now a frightening place which claims increasingly larger segments of her days. Deborah is ill, and treatment in a mental hospital is necessary. With the help of her doctor, Deborah finds strength to fight her way back to health. Told with deep understanding and compassion, Deborah's story provides a rare glimpse into the world of those who suffer from mental illness.

Greenberg, Joanne. **In This Sign.** Avon 1977.

> A girl grows up as the hearing daughter of two deaf parents. The

attitudes and values, the confusion and despair of the hearing impaired, are clearly presented. Readers will learn what it means to be deaf as well as many facts about a world without sound.

Greenberg, Joanne. **The Monday Voices.** Avon 1972.

This book tells the story of a rehabilitation counselor and the variety of mental, social, and physically handicapped clients he works with. Most sensitively described is the progress that is expected and that is sometimes made as the handicapped attempt to use their lives in meaningful ways. The realistic portrait of these handicapped persons who do not always achieve is given.

Hanlon, Emily. **It's Too Late for Sorry.**

Heide, Florence Parry. **Secret Dreamer, Secret Dreams.** Lippincott 1978.

Although Caroline is autistic, she tries desperately but unsuccessfully to communicate. Her life and lack of communication deeply affect her family—a frustrated mother, an alternately loving and hating sister, and a loving, patient father. Caroline can communicate only with her dog, Brumm. Teachers will want to use this first person narrative to explain Caroline's world to those who can communicate.

Hill, Grace L. **A Patch of Blue.** Bantam 1980.

Set in what appears to be the rural South, the story contrasts the life of Selina, a blind teenage white girl living with her prostitute mother and drunken grandfather, with a world of beauty as described by Selina's only friend, Gordon, a kind and gentle young black man.

Hugo, Victor. **The Hunchback of Notre Dame.** Sig. Classics. NAL 1965.

In this classic story of revolutionary France, one sees the cruelty of social class and disabling handicaps as the hunchback of Notre Dame struggles to be accepted. The futility of his position is made clear as he attempts to help a woman who does not know he exists.

Keyes, Daniel. **Flowers for Algernon.** Bantam 1970.

This is the story of a mentally retarded man who is the loved, if foolish, pet of his peers. Through experimental surgery he becomes brilliant, finds real love and self-esteem, but loses the friends of his former life. Finally, he regresses to his retarded self. The book could be helpful in unveiling the perceptions people have of retarded and gifted persons.

Killilea, Marie L. **Karen.** P-H 1962.

A gallant mother and a courageous and devoted family help a little girl, born with cerebral palsy, to conquer her disability.

Krents, Harold. **To Race the Wind: An Autobiography.** Putnam 1972.

Blindness need not be a handicap to achievement. In this story a blind man cheerfully overcomes his disability to become a graduate of Harvard law school. The reader cannot help but admire the achievement of this man surmounting enormous difficulties.

Lawrence, Marjorie. **Interrupted Melody: The Story of My Life.** S Ill U Pr 1949.

Marjorie Lawrence tells her own story as she worked to become a famous opera singer from her beginnings in a less than distinguished Australian family. At the height of her career, she is stricken with polio. She tells of her brave struggle to come back, to sing in public again. Readers gain insight into the faith and persistence required to overcome handicaps.

Mancini, Pat McNees, editor. **Friday's Child.** Sig. NAL 1977.

These short stories all share one central theme: the difficulties and sometimes the joys of the retarded person. Collected from works as diverse as Marjorie Kinnan Rawlings, Eudora Welty, and John Steinbeck, the stories show that major writers of the twentieth century have felt compassion for the less fortunate. Some of the stories deal with institutionalization, so recently understood in this country's efforts toward mainstreaming. It is in this context, bringing understanding to mainstream classrooms, that teachers will find this collection most helpful.

Mathis, Sharon Bell. **Listen for the Fig Tree.** Viking Pr 1974.

Poverty and physical disability are not the end of the world. The death of her father causes this blind black girl to mature quickly to gain the strength to aid her troubled mother. Young readers will be inspired by the courage of this young woman.

Maugham, W. Somerset. **Of Human Bondage.** Penguin 1978.

An ambitious and sensitive young man with a deformed leg attempts to find love despite his handicap. The issue of his deformity is raised primarily as a cause for his becoming sensitive to the actions of others and his isolation from the mainstream of human interaction.

Nason, Michael, and Donna Nason. **Tara.** Hawthorn 1974.

This is the story of a family with a brain-injured child. Through love, extensive therapy, and belief in God, this family saves that child from permanent disability. Of particular value for the reader's consideration is the effect upon the rest of the family when one member is handicapped.

Pepe, Phil. **Winners Never Quit.** P-H 1968.

This is a group of short stories all featuring an athlete who succeeds despite great adversity. The struggles these men make to overcome physical handicaps provide a challenge for all would-be athletes.

Rodowsky, Colby F. **What About Me?** Dell 1978.

Dorrie, a normal young adult, has a handicap. Her handicap is her eleven-year-old mongoloid brother. This story tells of the feelings of deprivation that come to the family who must place major emphasis on the care of the severely handicapped. As Dorrie faces the love and guilt that come from her seeming selfishness in trying to prevent her own life from being ruined, young readers will gain greater insight into the impact of the handicapped upon those about them. Teachers can use this book to help young people examine the values of family love and caring for others.

Spencer, Elizabeth. **The Light in the Piazza.** McGraw 1960.

This is the story of cruelty and greed. A mentally retarded American woman falls in love with a noble, but impoverished, Italian man in Florence. For separate reasons, their families arrange the wedding. Readers will anticipate ironic, subtle results of the marriage.

Steinbeck, John. **Of Mice and Men.**

Sullivan, Tom, and Derek Gill. **If You Could See What I Hear.** Sig. NAL 1975.

Rather than take the easy way out, when Tom Sullivan loses his sight he chooses the sighted world and music as his life. This personal account recreates his growth, school and college, his ultimate happy marriage and career. Young adults will appreciate his tenacity and courage.

Trumbo, Dalton. **Johnny Got His Gun.** Bantam 1970.

In this bitter anti-war novel, a young soldier is the victim of quadruple amputations. In addition, he has lost all senses except feeling. Young readers will relive this man's attempts to communicate with the outside world.

Walton, Todd. **Inside Moves.** Doubleday 1978.

> Returning war veterans with handicaps of all kinds congregate for companionship in a bar in San Francisco. They give to each other what they need most, an ersatz family of real love. Through surgery, one of their member's legs is repaired. He goes on to become a professional basketball player. The relationships among these men and their women provide insight into the "normalcy" of persons with handicapping conditions.

Wharton, Edith. **Ethan Frome.** Scribner 1968.

> Ethan tries to escape the stultifying world of Starkfield, Massachusetts, but he is prevented from doing so by his obligations first to his parents, then to his hypochondriac wife Zeena, and finally by an accident which injures him and a young cousin Mattie to whom he is attracted. In an ironic twist, Mattie becomes the querulous invalid and Zeena cares for both Mattie and Ethan.

Williams, Tennessee. **The Glass Menagerie.** New Directions 1945.

> This lyrical and tenuous play centers on a mother and daughter who live in their illusions. Laura, the daughter, uses her crippled leg as a shield against reality; Amanda, the mother, lives in a world populated by gracious Southern ladies and gentlemen of a bygone era. Tom, the son, is torn between the mundane reality of his job at the shoe factory and the poetic feeling in his soul.

Yates, Elizabeth. **The Lighted Heart.** Dutton 1960.

> This is a story of a middle-aged couple. The man, an international businessman, is going progressively blind. He and his wife begin again, with a new life on a farm in New Hampshire. The newly handicapped will see from their story that it is possible to cope with disability; sighted readers will learn some new things about the world of the blind.

Understanding the Gifted

Ages 5 to 8

Gripe, Maria (translator Paul Britlen Austin). **Hugo and Josephine.** Illus. Harald Gripe. SeyLawr. Delacorte 1969.

Hugo is a bright six-year-old whose independent thinking opens up a whole new world for his friend and classmate, Josephine.

Stren, Patti. **There's a Rainbow in My Closet.**

Ages 8 to 11

Cretan, Gladys Yessayan. **All Except Sammy.**

Duncan, Lois. **A Gift of Magic.** Illus. Arvis Stewart. Little 1971.

Nancy has a special way of knowing, called ESP or extra-sensory perception. She learns to live comfortably with her gift, to accept and appreciate it without undue anxiety.

Fuller, Miriam Morris. **Phyllis Wheatley: America's First Black Poetess.** Illus. Victor Mays. Garrard 1971.

From slave, to being an acknowledged poetess, to dying as a pauper is the story of Phyllis Wheatley who lived during the Revolutionary War. Her eventful but tragic life gives readers a glimpse of the prejudice Phyllis encounters as well as the strength she shows as she attempts to overcome insurmountable odds.

Keller, Beverly. **The Genuine, Ingenious, Thrift Shop Genie, Clarissa Mae Bean & Me.** Illus. Raymond Davidson. Coward 1977.

Marcie becomes best friends with Clarissa, and shares the special life of a "free-spirit" in the world of ballet. Delightful story, compellingly told, that lifts the reader out of ordinary life to soar with someone whose future holds fame, and whose present is already very special.

Konigsburg, E. L. **(George).** Atheneum 1974.

> Ben is a bright, gifted boy with problems—both family and school—compounded by (George). Up to now (George) and Ben had existed compatibly in the same body (Ben's), and in fact (George) probably had a great deal to do with Ben's brilliance. Now Ben feels the need for visible, peer acceptance and (George), in a huff, goes silent. Ben suffers suspicion of theft at school and cruel treatment by his stepmother. He finds a thought-provoking solution to his problems by assuming the blame and punishment for the crime he did not commit to spare an older boy who had been exploiting him. Some incidents and characters are unreal but the author's skill holds it all together.

Krumgold, Joseph. **Henry Three.** Atheneum 1968.

> Henry doesn't want it known that he has an I.Q. of 154. He and his family have just moved into a high-toned suburb and they all want more than anything to make good with the "right" crowd. Henry has discovered that when people know how smart he is, they tend to shy away from him. No one finds out about his brilliance and he is accepted by the "right" crowd until his family has a bomb shelter installed in their backyard. He figures that the only way to solve his problems is to find a way to stop the possibility of war. Scathingly real scenes between Henry and his father, his mother, and his peers make this book a brilliant examination of contemporary social problems.

L'Engle, Madeleine. **A Wind in the Door.** FS&G 1979.

> Charles Wallace, brilliant at age six, is misunderstood when he starts to school. His vocabulary is even beyond the teacher, and she scolds him the first day, accusing him of making up things and showing off. Charles Wallace must eventually learn to cope with his own uniqueness, but the main struggle is between good and evil.

Merrill, Jean. **Maria's House.** Illus. Frances Gruse Scott. Atheneum 1974.

> Maria is a talented artist, and takes lessons every Saturday at the museum. Her teacher's appreciation of Maria's drawing leads to a big step for Maria—she can admit without embarrassment her family's poverty.

Rainbolt, Richard. **Football's Clever Quarterbacks.** Lerner Pubns 1977.

> This book describes football's greatest pro quarterbacks. Included in it are Johnny Unitas, Bart Starr, Lenny Dawson, and Joe Namath,

among others. It briefly describes each person's boyhood through the present, discussing the highlights of their sports as well as their personal lives.

Rodgers, Mary. **A Billion for Boris.** Har-Row 1974.

Children who are bright and inventive have many adventures and misadventures in this entertaining story.

Sachs, Marilyn. **Marv.**

Tennant, Veronica. **On Stage, Please.** Illus. Rita Briansky. HR&W 1979.

After attending a ballet performance of "Cinderella," Jennifer Allen wants to be a ballerina. All the wonders and the hard realities of becoming a ballet dancer are skillfully told by Veronica Tennant, principal ballerina of the National Ballet of Canada. The story gives insight into the "joys and magic, hardships and sacrifices" that make up the world of ballet. The numerous etchings enhance the mood and charm of the story.

Ages 11 to 14

Conford, Ellen. **And This Is Laura.**

Cresswell, Helen. **Absolute Zero: Being the Second Part of the Bagthorpe Saga.** Macmillan 1978.

Mrs. Fosdyke, the Bagthorpe family's housekeeper, describes life with this eccentric, intellectual, highly competitive family as ". . . like one of them mad Dracula films on Friday telly." The family's efforts at slogan-writing, a slightly mad grandmother, and an irrepressible niece who writes profound statements on walls will keep the young reader amused.

Danziger, Paula. **The Cat Ate My Gymsuit.**

Hamilton, Virginia. **The Planet of Junior Brown.**

Hunter, Mollie. **A Sound of Chariots.** Har-Row 1972.

A teacher helps Bridie McShane, a young impoverished girl in Scotland, realize her gift of poetry. Bridie knows that writing will be her means to a satisfying life.

Konigsburg, E. L. **Father's Arcane Daughter.** Atheneum 1976.

Two children, handicapped by their parents' over-protection, are

Understanding the Gifted

helped to develop their considerable intellects by a woman who claims to be their long-lost half sister.

Levitin, Sonia. **Beyond Another Door.** Atheneum 1977.

A thirteen-year-old girl discovers that she has ESP and learns to cope with the kinds of psychic phenomena that are revealed to her. Her discovery opens a door that will enable her to develop another talent, the gift of artistic expression.

Mann, Peggy. **Whitney Young, Jr.: Crusader for Equality.** Illus. Victor Mays. Garrard 1972.

Born to a loving, happy, and exceptional family, Whitney Young, Jr. was destined to play a special role as an articulate advocate for blacks in business and the political arena. Young readers will relate to the human incidents in young Whitney's early years and appreciate the great influence this brilliant man had in the move toward "equal opportunity" in the job market.

Paterson, Katherine. **The Great Gilly Hopkins.**

Rodgers, Mary. **Freaky Friday.** Har-Row 1972.

Annabel, a rebellious thirteen-year-old, does not fully realize her own talents until a freaky Friday turns her into her mother for a day. In the course of following her mother's schedule, Annabel goes to a very enlightening school conference, where she gains a better understanding of herself and the school problems she had faced.

Smith, Alison. **Reserved for Mark Anthony Crowder.** Dutton 1978.

Mark Anthony Crowder is different from his peers. He is too tall, wears thick glasses, is unathletic and clumsy. His excellence in quiet scholarly pursuit of rocks, shells, and Indian artifacts is more embarrassing than rewarding to him. To make it worse, he gets good grades in school. There is no support for his differences from an athletic coach-father who cannot understand him. At the close of this story, Mark receives some recognition for his pursuits and develops a sense of his own worth.

Ages 14 and Up

Heide, Florence Parry. **Growing Anyway Up.**

Keyes, Daniel. **Flowers for Algernon.**

Madison, Winifred. **A Portrait of Myself.** Random 1979.

> Catherine d'Amato, sixteen and uncertain about the future, clings to the hope that her artistic talent is indeed a gift, as her first-grade teacher once claimed. She dreams and draws, idolizes a teacher who does not return the affection, and finally in desperation nearly takes her own life. She emerges with a new respect for her life, comes to terms with her heritage, and finds the courage to continue to develop her gift.

Mathis, Sharon Bell. **Teacup Full of Roses.**

Morgenroth, Barbara. **Tramps like Us.** Atheneum 1979.

> This is the story of two very creative and intellectually gifted young people. Nessa, who is not yet sixteen, is thoroughly repressed by her school, her small hometown, and her parents until she meets Daryl. The two of them fall in love at an off-limits dance. Neither of their respective parents will condone their relationship. There is finally nothing for Daryl and Nessa to do but run away. They are caught and returned to their parents. The book exemplifies problems encountered by the gifted.

Peyton, K. M. **Pennington's Last Term.** Illus. by author. T Y Crowell 1971.

> Patrick Pennington, a youth gifted in music, but unaware of the importance and implications of his gifts, sees no purpose in school or in his life. Often at cross-purposes with parents and teachers, he is viewed as a troublemaker, until he finds that his music can be an outlet for his emotions and that people value his ability.

Understanding Male and Female

Ages 1 to 5

Brightman, Alan. **Like Me.** Illus. by author. Little 1976.

> This picture book demonstrates the differences and uniqueness of one kindergartner who compares himself to a wide variety of others. In his own words, "The difference between us is different. That's all." The very young reader or sharer can gather insights into comparison and contrast and autonomy in discussion centered about *Like Me*.

de Paola, Tomie. **Oliver Button Is a Sissy.** Illus. by author. HarBraceJ 1979.

> Oliver Button is a boy who does not like the things boys are expected to like. He is poor at playing ball with his peers; his father chastises him and his friends tease him. Oliver likes to paint, to draw pictures, and to dance, and enters a talent show. Although he doesn't win, his parents and peers have the opportunity to see his talent and respect him for it. Teachers will be able to use this book to illustrate the many different kinds of abilities people have.

Heyward, Du Bose. **The Country Bunny and the Little Gold Shoes.** Illus. Marjorie Flack. HM 1974.

> Pre-schoolers will enjoy seeing the illustrations as well as listening to the story about a little girl cottontail who was able to overcome obstacles and prejudice through wisdom, kindness, and courage. This story provides a lighthearted way to introduce commendable virtues to young readers.

Hoban, Lillian. **Arthur's Pen Pal.**

Isadora, Rachel. **Max.** Illus. by author. Macmillan 1976.

> Max is a great baseball player. One Saturday, Max walks his sister Lisa to dance school and stays to watch for awhile. Then he decides to join the girls in all the fun, and, in so doing, finds that dancing isn't just for girls; dancing is good exercise for a baseball player.

Klein, Norma. **Girls Can Be Anything.** Illus. Roy Doty. Dutton 1973.

> In pictures and text, this humorous book explicates the argument between Marina and Adam about professional limitations set for women and girls. Marina, who is strongly supported by her mother, examines many of the new roles for females—surgeon, pilot, and president. The youngest readers will want to talk about these occupational possibilities as they see that today, "girls can be anything."

Lasky, Kathryn. **I Have Four Names for My Grandfather.**

Saul, Wendy. **Butcher, Baker, Cabinetmaker: Photographs of Women at Work.**

Vestly, Anne-Cath. **Hello, Aurora.**

Zolotow, Charlotte. **William's Doll.**

Ages 8 to 11

Barnes, Nancy. **The Wonderful Year.** Illus. Kate Seredy. Messner 1946.

> When Ellen and her parents move from a Kansas town to a Colorado ranch, Mother makes the move an adventure. Hard work and new neighbors make the year a memorable one. Set near the turn of the century, it is a family story concerned not only with adjustments to moving, but with Ellen's growing up, her romantic interests, and her increasing awareness of and ability to deal with her role as a young woman.

Brink, Carol Ryrie. **Caddie Woodlawn.** Macmillan 1970.

> Caddie's adventures on the Wisconsin frontier are very realistic and exciting (and glimpses of history appear also) as the Woodlawns rejoice at hearing that the Civil War has ended and later mourn the assassination of President Lincoln. Caddie is an adventurous tomboy who seems to resist accepting her sex role. However as she continues to understand the female role, one is certain that she will grow up to be a lovely young lady.

Brink, Carol Ryrie. **Two Are Better Than One.** Illus. Fermin Rocker. Macmillan 1968.

> The story tells in a realistic manner of problems that girls face as they are growing up. The book has a theme that young girls of today can identify with and understand.

Bulla, Clyde Robert. **Shoeshine Girl.**

Burleson, Elizabeth. **Middl'un.** Illus. Don Asumussen. Follett 1968.

A picture of the times and the people of Texas at the turn of the century, the story centers on tomboy Hannah's growing up and her search for cattle rustlers.

First, Julia. **Flat on My Face.**

Fukada, Hanako. **Wind in My Hand.** Illus. Lydia Cooley. Golden Gate. Childrens 1970.

Based on the autobiography of Issa, celebrated Japanese haiku poet, this story recreates his lonely childhood, his early life in Tokyo, his recognition as a poet after years of struggle, his wanderings across the length and breadth of Japan, and his final homecoming to his friends, the children. Poems included illustrate his deep love of nature and of the hearty, simple things of life, and they depict the love and reverence which the Japanese feel for their artists.

Gemme, Leila Boyle. **King on the Court: Billie Jean King.** Photographs by Bruce Curtis. Raintree Pubs Ltd 1976.

Billie Jean King, a great athlete, revolutionized tennis almost single-handedly. Only her consummate skill and persistence force the wealthy and male-dominated tennis tournament associations to equalize the sport for women and the working classes. This book portrays Billie Jean King as a human being with faults as well as victories. An unmistakable value for young readers is the book's clear presentation of the long, hard road that leads to being Number One.

Greene, Constance C. **The Unmaking of Rabbit.** Viking Pr 1972.

Paul, who lives with his grandmother, is called rabbit because of his unfortunately large and protruding ears. In this story the lonely boy must decide whether he can retain his own values or give in to those of his schoolmates to gain their friendship. Still another problem for Paul is his love for his mother who cannot accept the responsibility for her child. Paul learns that he has only himself and his grandmother. Young readers can learn to accept love where it is and to be true to themselves as Paul does in this story.

Jacobs, William Jay. **Mother, Aunt Susan and Me: The First Fight for Women's Rights.** Illus. Linda Sykes. Coward 1979.

This is the fictionalized diary of sixteen-year-old Harriot Stanton, daughter of Elizabeth Cady Stanton. Through her eyes we see the struggle for women's rights in the nineteenth century and the life of a free-thinking, liberal household active in the anti-slavery movement. The pictures and text will help young readers experience the early days of civil rights for blacks and for women.

Johnson, Annabel, and Edgar Johnson. **The Grizzly.**

Krumgold, Joseph. **And Now Miguel.** Illus. Jean Charlot. Apollo Eds 1970

Miguel, who is twelve, hopes to help the men in his family take the sheep to camp in the Sangre de Cristo Mountains. He desperately tries to prove that he is ready. In getting his wish, Miguel grows from boy to man and learns some valuable lessons about growing up and about giving and receiving.

Lampman, Evelyn Sibley. **Go up the Road.**

Lurie, Alison, retold by. **Clever Gretchen and Other Forgotten Folktales.**

McGovern, Ann. **The Secret Soldier: The Story of Deborah Sampson.** Illus. Ann Grifalconi. Four Winds. Schol Bk Serv 1975.

This is the intriguing story of possibly the first American woman in military service. Deborah Sampson, the impoverished daughter of an ailing mother, is required to work ten years to pay off her indentured bond. At eighteen, during the height of the Revolutionary War, she conceives a mad plan to enlist in Washington's Army as a soldier. Disguised as the foot soldier, Robert Shurtliff, she distinguishes herself before she is hospitalized and discovered. Young readers today will not easily accept the daringness of the scheme, but all will admire her courage.

Minard, Rosemary. **Womenfolk and Fairy Tales.**

Niemeyer, Marie. **The Moon Guitar.** Illus. Gustave E. Nebel. Watts 1969.

Twelve-year-old Su-Lin is American; she does not want to be sent to Taiwan to become "a proper Chinese girl." But Grandfather thinks she ought to be brought up in the old established ways—the ways of the family which once owned the long-lost and beautiful moon guitar. Su-Lin and her American friend Tracy search San Francisco's Chinatown for the family treasure. The result is exciting and changes the attitudes of both Grandfather and Su-Lin.

Peck, Robert Newton. **Trig.** Illus. Pamela Johnson. YB. Dell 1977.

Elizabeth Trigman, an incorrigible tomboy, after struggling for accep-

Understanding Male and Female

tance with the boys in her neighborhood, finally gets her wish. She gets a toy machine gun and the nickname "Trig." Only her grandfather understands the way she feels. In this rollicking tale of mischievous adventure, Trig gains understanding and self-acceptance. In this book for the late primary grades, boys and girls will come to find insights into male and female roles.

Robertson, Keith. **Henry Reed's Babysitting Service.** Illus. Robert McCloskey. YB. Dell 1974.

Fourteen-year-old Henry Reed, with the help of his friend Midge Glass, sets up a babysitting service and encounters all kinds of adventures.

Terris, Susan. **No Boys Allowed.**

Tobias, Tobi. **Arthur Mitchell.** Illus. Carole Byard. T Y Crowell 1975.

Arthur Mitchell was black and poor and lived in New York City. Astonishingly he wanted to become a classical dancer at a time when black people were not employed in ballet. Through his own genius and persistent hard work, the young man became a lead dancer with the New York City Ballet choreographed by Ballanchine. Following enormous success in that company, he wanted to help others. He now directs the world famous Dance Theatre of Harlem which he began so that he could fight with his art for black dancers.

Tolles, Martha. **Katie and Those Boys.**

Ages 11 to 14

Blume, Judy. **Then Again, Maybe I Won't.**

Branscum, Robbie. **Toby, Granny and George.**

Bridgers, Sue Ellen. **Home Before Dark.**

Burch, Robert. **Queenie Peavy.**

Byars, Betsy. **Good-Bye, Chicken Little.**

Byars, Betsy. **The 18th Emergency.** Illus. Robert Grossman. Viking Pr 1973.

Mouse is prepared for seventeen different emergencies which he will never face, but he needs a solution for the eighteenth emergency which is going to occur when Marv Hammerman, the school bully, catches up with him. After running for three days, Mouse faces the inevitable confrontation. Not only does he survive the blows, he is able to understand Marv's position, and both he and Marv are able to maintain their honor.

Cameron, Eleanor. **To the Green Mountains.**

Clapp, Patricia. **Constance: A Story of Early Plymouth.** Lothrop 1968.

Constance is a girl aboard the Mayflower who unwillingly must discover life in the New World. She is different from her peers and knows it. Her insights into herself and life in the early colony of Plymouth help all of us to recognize the strength and perseverance against hardship which is required for survival. In the character development of Constance, the burgeoning love and affection of a young woman is also portrayed.

Cleaver, Vera, and Bill Cleaver. **Trial Valley.** Bantam 1978.

Trial Valley is more a proving ground than a trial for Mary Call Luther. She is acutely conscious of the limitations of her life as a North Carolinian herb gatherer and wants more for herself. At the same time, Mary Call also appreciates the wisdom of the country and her responsibilities to support her orphaned brother and sister. Jack Parsons, a foundling, who desperately needs her love, tips the scales in favor of a continued life devoted to others. Readers come to appreciate the acceptance of mature choice and responsibility through Mary Call's decision.

Constant, Alberta Wilson. **Does Anybody Care About Lou Emma Miller?**

Cormier, Robert. **The Chocolate War.** Pantheon 1974.

This is the story of a young man in a private school who is different. He is more thinking, more sensitive, and more determined than his peers to establish his own, private identity. As a part of that privacy and self-actualization, he refuses to engage in the annual chocolate sale that earns money for the school. This story tells of the tremendous cost, both physically and emotionally, that must be paid by those who would be significantly different from their peers. Readers will come to recognize their own struggle for mature autonomy in this young man's story.

Donovan, John. **I'll Get There: It Better Be Worth the Trip.**

Engebrecht, P. A. **Under the Haystack.** Nelson 1974.

Sandy becomes a woman suddenly at age thirteen. When her mother abandons the fatherless children, Sandy must become the leader-mother-provider for her sisters. That summer she also discovers feelings for boys, physical changes, and wisdom about the hopelessness of life for rural women too early married. Best of all, there is no bitterness in Sandy's assumption of new responsibilities nor cynicism in considering her mother's choice. When the mother does return to the farm, each of the children presents the reader a chance to examine the variety of emotions possible toward a wandering mother.

Fitzhugh, Louise. **Nobody's Family Is Going to Change.**

Hall, Lynn. **Ride a Wild Dream.** Illus. George Roth. Camelot. Avon 1978.

In addition to being the youngest, Jon is the most sensitive of three boys. There is no doubt of his masculinity, but his responses to the animals and the earth of his farming life are somehow more aesthetic than most. In this novel he works to win the love and control of a magnificent horse; his attempts end disastrously. One of the truly significant aspects of this book for young readers is that they learn you do not have to win to become a hero. Jon matures and accepts, not without pain, a more realistic picture of his potential.

Holland, Barbara. **The Pony Problem.** Dutton 1977.

Jean Monroe is extraordinary. Against the backdrop of the most conventional suburban setting, Jean wins and tries to keep a horse. She has other differences, too. She cuts her own hair, dyes it a dreadful shade, and wears an ugly old hat. Her adventures are tragic, outlandish, and often desperately funny. This story spells out the cost of being different, winning recognition, and resisting the forces of socialization in the seventies.

Hopkins, Lee Bennett. **Wonder Wheels.**

Knudson, R. R. **Zanballer.** LFL. Dell 1978.

Suzanne Hagen wants to be called Zan. In addition to her dislike of cooking, sewing, and other supposedly feminine things, she has a passion for playing sports. In this story she organizes, practices, and leads her school's first girls' football team to victory against the boys. The story is told without apology and without the ruffles that would make Zan a stereotypic female with a love of sports. The struggle of young women for equality as well as the difficulty of anyone who would be different is clearly presented in this lively story.

Landau, Elaine. **Hidden Heroines: Women in American History.** Messner 1977.

role of women in early American history. How women participated in the settlement of colonies, moved westward to new frontiers, fought against injustices, and struggled to obtain their basic rights as citizens is told in a sparse, straightforward manner.

Lofts, Norah. **The Maude Reed Tale.** Illus. Anne Johnstone and Janet Grahame Johnstone. Nelson 1972.

Maude Reed, a member of the middle class in fifteenth-century England, does not care to become a lady. Maude wants to become a businesswoman, assuming responsibilities for her grandfather's woolen business. She is sent to a nearby castle to learn the things women are expected to know, runs away, and rescues her grandfather's business from a wicked apprentice. Maude Reed gives young readers a chance to explore differences of values as well as male-female roles in a new way.

Matthew, Scott. **The First Woman of Medicine: The Story of Elizabeth Blackwell.** Illus. Wayne Atkinson. Silver 1978.

This biography of Elizabeth Blackwell, the first woman doctor, chronicles her struggles against prejudice, loss of an eye, the necessity of leaving America to go to France in order to have a hospital in which to practice, and her ultimate return to America. This story could be used as motivation for discussion on careers for women.

Mazer, Harry. **The Dollar Man.**

Meltzer, Milton. **Tongue of Flame: The Life of Lydia Maria Child.** T Y Crowell 1965.

Lydia Maria Child, leading writer of the 1830s, was also one of the humanitarians in the abolitionist, later the civil rights, movement. She founded the first children's magazine, wrote a history of women, was an editor and syndicated newspaper columnist, and wrote the first book to attack slavery.

Miles, Betty. **The Real Me.**

Myers, Walter Dean. **Fast Sam, Cool Clyde, and Stuff.** Viking Pr 1975.

This story of a ghetto gang is more the tale of a group of boys and girls who care about each other than the tale of delinquency and anti-social behavior. The narrator, a young man who is not the stereotypic macho male, relates how kids in the ghetto are just like kids anywhere. The unusual part of this story is the formation of their gang, the "116th Street Good People," a mutual self-protection society. Their growing up portrays the narrow escapes many people have on the rocky, hazardous path to maturity.

Rabe, Berniece. **The Girl Who Had No Name.** Bantam 1979.

Papa had used up all his girl's names when the tenth child was born; she was simply named "Girlie." When mam died, all the girls were dispersed to live with relatives. Girlie Webster was different from the others; she had a will to succeed and to recapture the love of a father who would give her away. Intelligent and persistent, Girlie succeeds despite the turmoil of being placed in one home after another. She grows more mature than even her own father when she recognizes and accepts his foibles. The reader cannot help but admire this young woman as she struggles against seemingly impossible odds.

Rose, Karen. **There Is a Season.** Camelot. Avon 1969.

Katie Levin, a fifteen-year-old Jewish girl, is growing into womanhood with questions about herself and her religion. She meets James, almost eighteen and a devout Catholic. The relationship between them is confusing as feelings heretofore unknown are discovered. Jamey decides to fulfill his long-time ambition—to enter the priesthood. This decision and involvement in family problems help Katie develop into a mature woman.

Scott, John Anthony. **Woman Against Slavery: The Story of Harriet Beecher Stowe.** T Y Crowell 1978.

This biography of Harriet Beecher Stowe portrays a lady who is truly extraordinary. She is bright and educated when it was not popular for women to be so. She is strong and brave when those were considered unfeminine traits. Most important for her success was the support she received from her children, her parents, and her husband. The book will be an inspiration for those who understand the cost and the benefits of human difference.

Shreve, Susan. **The Nightmares of Geranium Street.** Avon 1979.

Elizabeth DuBois is the leader of the "Nightmares," a street gang whose professed purpose is to do good works. In trying to solve the mystery of Aunt Tess, a neighbor and exotic dancer, the club becomes involved in one of Philadelphia's biggest drug rings. The book is never without the realism of junior high age perceptions, but traditional roles for male and female are cast aside as these young people assume characters that fit their individual talents.

Simon, Marcia L. **A Special Gift.** HarBraceJ 1978.

> Peter has a special problem and a special gift. As a young athlete he never doubts his masculinity, but he also loves the ballet. His special problem is fear of ridicule should his schoolmates find out that he loves to dance. When they do, he learns the censure all male dancers experience. Peter discovers that the negation given the male dancer is not more powerful than his joy in the stage and ballet. This book clearly shows the struggle a young man has in finding his own way.

Smith, Alison. **Reserved for Mark Anthony Crowder.**

Sobol, Rose. **Woman Chief.** LFL. Dell 1979.

> Lonesome Star, a captive Gros Ventres Indian, did not want to grow up to do the things Indian women did. Instead, as she built her life among her new people, the Crow Indians, she wanted to do the things that men did: hunt, fish, and make war. In this story, Lonesome Star distinguishes herself through skill and bravery and is ultimately made a chief of the Crows. Perhaps the greatest value of this book, which is based on a true story, is in the natural, non-apologetic way it attacks stereotypes of gender.

Taylor, Mildred D. **Roll of Thunder, Hear My Cry.** Illus. Jerry Pinkney. Dial 1977.

> Three strong women, Cassie, Mama, and Big Ma, are the major forces in this story of blacks in the rural south following the Depression. Although their men are ever-present as this black family struggles to save their land and neighbors from poverty and landed whites, it is the women who, with indomitable strength and dignity, more vividly portray confrontation and negotiation. Teachers of social studies as well as English can use this book as a presentation of emotion and values in America's heartland during the first half of the twentieth century.

Thoger, Marie (translator Eileen Amos). **Shanta.** Illus. Marvin Friedman. Follett 1968.

> Shanta, who lives a life of extreme poverty in a small village in India, has the promise of comfort, security, and education when she is betrothed to a wealthy cousin. The plague changes Shanta's plans, but she courageously perseveres and proves that hardship can cause a girl to mature quickly into a woman able to take on the responsibility for her whole family.

Towne, Mary. **First Serve.** Illus. Ruth Sanderson. Atheneum 1976.

> This is the story of a young girl who wants to become a tennis pro. The tale is complicated because tennis is a career her parents had planned for an older sister. Dulcie's effort to use her athletic ability is made even more difficult by the plans of marriage and homemaking that are thought to be her great accomplishments. The book demonstrates to young readers that ultimately they must make their own life decisions.

Wayne, Bennett, editor. **Women Who Dared to Be Different.** Garrard 1973.

> This book portrays life stories of reporter Nellie Bly, sharp-shooter Annie Oakley, astronomer Maria Mitchell, and flyer Amelia Earhart. Also included are vignettes of other women who followed in their footsteps and "dared to be different." These easy-to-read, compelling, true stories will inspire and broaden understanding in young readers.

Wersba, Barbara. **Tunes for a Small Harmonica.** LFL. Dell 1977.

> J. F. McAllister is a wealthy student at a New York prep school. The fact that she wears only tattered boy's clothing is embarrassing to her parents, friends, and ultimately, herself. In this discovery of her first love, J. F. also finds herself. In comic and profound seriousness, this book describes the difficulty experienced by those who would be themselves if being most truly yourself is to be different from the ordinary.

Wojciechowska, Maia. **Shadow of a Bull.** Illus. Alvin Smith. Atheneum 1972.

> Manolo's father was a great bullfighter. The people of the village and his mother have decided that Manolo must follow in his father's footsteps. The boy's inner conflict as he tries to resolve the differences between his aspirations and the expectations of the community has been realistically and sympathetically described.

Wojciechowska, Maia. **A Single Light.** Bantam 1971.

> Her mother dies when she is born, and no one bothers to name her. Filled with shame for having a deaf daughter, her father ignores her. When the parish priest takes her in to help clean the church, she finds an old and extremely valuable statue. This event affects the lives of everyone in her village. Set in a tiny hamlet in southern Spain, *A Single Light* is concerned with the basic human need to love.

Ages 14 and Up

Angier, Bradford, and Barbara Corcoran. **Ask for Love and They Give You Rice Pudding.**

Arrick, Fran. **Steffie Can't Come Out to Play.** Bradbury Pr 1978.

> In this realistic story, a fourteen-year-old girl runs away from home to become a fashion model. What she becomes on the streets of New York is a prostitute. The lives of young women entrapped in the seedier side of life after unthought-out ambitions fail is well portrayed. Teachers of mature readers who want to understand value choices and attempts to escape reality may want to use this book with care.

Bach, Alice. **The Meat in the Sandwich.** Har-Row 1975.

> Mike is the meat in the sandwich between an older and a younger sister. He has always wanted to be a star athlete, but frankly he is not very good. When a superjock moves next door, Mike immediately adopts him as best friend and takes on the values of star competition as well. Finally the two boys are pitted against each other, Mike is injured, and in the painful weeks that follow he gets a chance to re-evaluate his priorities. This book would be excellent for use with boys and girls who see winning as all important.

Brown, Claude. **Manchild in the Promised Land.** Sig. NAL 1965.

> Autobiographical in approach, the book deals with ghetto life in Harlem. Claude Brown, former dope pusher completely enmeshed in ghetto misery, realizes that he is an example for no man. He finally extricates himself, becoming a law student at one of America's leading universities.

Buck, Pearl. **To My Daughter, with Love.** John Day 1967.

> From this shared talk with her seven daughters, Pearl Buck has distilled the articles and speeches that are collected in this volume. Personal values, love and marriage, woman's role, the sexual revolution are among the subjects which Miss Buck treats with candor, gentle understanding, and great wisdom.

Crompton, Anne Eliot. **A Woman's Place.** Illus. Ted Lewin. Little 1978.

> At fifty-year intervals, the story of five women who live in the same house is told. In each of the portraits from colonial to modern time, the difficulties as well as the source of their joys are described. The five women own and are owned by the house and life in rural New England. This book is not apologetic. The role women play in life is

often inordinately difficult to sustain. The last owner of the house, a modern woman, must destroy the house and its life, in order to save her own. Older adolescents, men as well as women, will come to appreciate of the meanings of "a woman's place" in American life.

Glaser, Dianne. **The Diary of Trilby Frost.** Holiday 1976.

At the turn of the century, Trilby Frost aspired to be something more than a woman in a log cabin. This story tells her most secret feelings as she struggles to change her life, to be something uncommonly different for a woman. Another strong part of Trilby is her insistence upon making her own decisions no matter how unpopular they might be. Her greatest maturation comes when a would-be lover, an orphaned half-breed, dies of tetanus. Junior-senior high school students will gain great insight into the harshness of rural American life at the turn of the century with the adventures of Trilby Frost.

Guy, Rosa. **Ruby.** Bantam 1979.

Ruby is a story about a high school love affair between two girls. Ruby is a recent immigrant from the West Indies. She is friendless and lonely partially due to her tyrannical and over-protective father who frightens away her friends. The object of Ruby's love in this story is Daphne, aloof, intelligent, and anti-social. The plot centers about the progression of their love affair, the secret meetings, the nights together, and the heartbreaking end when Daphne decides that Ruby is not right for her. This controversial story can stimulate discussion and composition about the differences people bring to life.

Hall, Lynn. **Gently Touch the Milkweed.** Follett 1970.

Janet Borofen, a young pioneer woman, has none of the petite, feminine characteristics all women seemed to want. She is big boned, awkward, plain-faced, and works as hard as a man. In this story she falls in love with the first man who causes her to feel womanly. Unfortunately, he is married. How Janet discovers her own inner beauty will give insight to all young women facing just such problems.

Hall, Lynn. **Sticks and Stones.** Follett 1972.

This short novel deals with the results of small town gossip. At seventeen, Tom is a brilliant pianist with a chance to win the state championship. His friendship with a discharged serviceman stirs up a hornet's nest of suspicion. No one, not even teachers, defends the young man who is wrongly accused. The book can be used to demonstrate and discuss the values and consequences of being different.

Hansberry, Lorraine. **Raisin in the Sun.** Sig. NAL 1961.

An insurance check for $10,000 is what World War II veteran Mr. Younger left for his wife and two children who live on Chicago's south side. Walter, the son, is eager to use the money to buy a business, but his wife and mother are more concerned about a house where they can live decently. Although he loses two-thirds of the money to an untrustworthy friend, Walter "comes into his manhood" when he faces the white man who tries to discourage the family from moving into a white neighborhood.

Heide, Florence Parry. **Growing Anyway Up.** Bantam 1978.

Florence Stirkel wrestles with being a unique and creative individual in the dull household of her mother. She learns to accept her own differences without fear through a special relationship with her aunt, an imaginative "Auntie Mame." Teachers will want to use this book to open discussions of what it is like to gain acceptance from supportive adults.

Hesse, Hermann. **Demian.** Har-Row 1965.

The story of a unique relationship between Emil Sinclair and Max Demian which has been described as "a primeval blood-tie among men of similar destiny" rather than a traditional friendship. The title is *Demian,* but Sinclair tells the story about his "trying to live in accord with the promptings which come from my true self."

Hill, Margaret. **Time to Quit Running.** Messner 1970.

How does an attractive, intelligent teenager from an impoverished home in the most run-down neighborhood in town overcome her environment? Valerie Leslie's valiant efforts to rise above her circumstances cause her to become enmeshed in a series of entangling falsehoods, and an exciting turn of events helps her to suddenly gain an insight into her perplexing problem. The author of this novel, a high school guidance counselor, writes with keen sympathy for this situation.

Kerr, M. E. **I'll Love You When You're More like Me.** LFL. Dell 1979.

This story tells of young people struggling to control their own destinies. Wallace Witherspoon, Jr., son of a funeral director, begins an affair with Sabra St. Amour, teenage television soap opera star. Their relationship causes them to change their lives in directions of their own choosing. The juxtaposed male and female narrators of the chapters (á la *Pigman*) help to develop a better understanding of different points of view.

Understanding Male and Female 131

Lader, Lawrence, and Milton Meltzer. **Margaret Sanger: Pioneer of Birth Control.** LFL. Dell 1974.

> This is the inspiring life story of a great woman whose ideas were far ahead of her time. Through her nursing experiences at the turn of the century, Margaret Sanger was moved to a then revolutionary and startling concept: the idea of birth control and family planning. A lovely, soft-spoken lady, she was ridiculed and jailed for crusading on behalf of birth control. Her work in founding International Planned Parenthood has affected the lives of millions.

LeRoy, Gen. **Cold Feet.**

Lyle, Katie Letcher. **The Golden Shores of Heaven.** Bantam 1978.

> This story tells of a young woman who leaves home in Baltimore to move to Nashville to become a country and western singer. The difficulties Mary Curlew McJunkie overcomes with men who pretend to help her are described in this fast moving novel. She encounters love of many types, accepting and rejecting the offers, in the rise of her career. Young readers will identify strongly with the sensible altruism of Mary as she attempts to succeed on her own.

Mauermann, Mary Anne. **Strangers into Friends.** Washburn 1969.

> Karen faces her senior year with dread. Shy and retiring with a fear of failing in anything, Karen has never belonged in the high school crowd. When her father becomes an exchange teacher to England, Karen is overjoyed to get away from Seattle. She finds, however, that she cannot escape the problem of finding herself.

Mazer, Norma Fox. **Dear Bill, Remember Me?** Delacorte 1977.

> This is a collection of stories about girls growing into womanhood. Situations may be typical, or not, but there are no stereotypes here.

Merriam, Eve, editor. **Growing Up Female in America: Ten Lives.** Illus. by editor. Dell 1973.

> Ten fascinating American women are introduced through excerpts from diaries, letters, journals, and autobiographies. This book supplies some of the missing history of women.

Potok, Chaim. **The Promise.**

Raucher, Herman. **Ode to Billy Joe.** Dell 1976.

> In this fast moving narrative of first love and the pressures put upon young lovers by their sexual feelings, Billy Joe, of the ballad, suffers impotence due to his own guilt feelings. Students will gain insight

into their own growing maturity and the difficulties society often places upon the open expression of differences.

Reit, Ann, editor. **The World Outside: Collected Short Fiction About Women at Work.** Illus. Lucy Martin Bitzer. Four Winds. Schol Bk Serv 1977.

This collection of short stories by authors such as Sarah Orne Jewett and Willa Cather presents women of the twentieth century in roles often ignored. The working women in this collection are not always "captains of industry" but they are always human, sometimes admirable. This collection could be used by social studies and English teachers to lend a better understanding of what it means to be a woman in America.

Ruby, Lois. **What Do You Do in Quicksand?** Viking Pr 1979.

A young man undertakes the care of his illegitimate daughter while working his way through high school. His next door neightbor, an emotionally disturbed sixteen-year-old, loves the baby and wants it for her own. Against the drama of the young people, their respective families represent eccentricities that are believable but not often found. This book vividly portrays the role reversal of a young man with a keen sense of responsibility and his struggle with role reversal.

Sergeant, Elizabeth. **Robert Frost: The Trial by Existence.** HR&W 1960.

This book about Robert Frost reveals the emergence of the poet and the man and shows a magnificent human being who dared to live differently from others, to think deeply, to feel keenly. In times of failure and personal tragedy, Frost somehow remained undestroyed by what might have broken lesser men. As teacher, as poet, as man, Frost discovered his own differences early and dedicated himself to finding out what they meant.

Stiller, Richard. **Queen of the Populists: The Story of Mary Elizabeth Lease.** LFL. Dell 1976.

Mary Elizabeth Lease, born in 1853, was the first important female politician in American history. Her early life on the Kansas prairie, first as a teacher, then as a housewife, mother, and lawyer, gave her an insight into the need for speaking out on behalf of the farmers, who were exploited by big business, especially the banks and railroads. Though she never ran for political office, her campaigns on behalf of the Populist Party advocated ideas that were far ahead of the times and since have become a reality.

Understanding Male and Female

Suhl, Yuri. **Eloquent Crusader—Ernestine Rose.** Messner 1970.

> This is the life story of one of the early crusaders for the emancipation of women. Born in a Polish ghetto in 1810, this daughter of a rabbi emigrated to the United States in 1836 and joined the early suffragist and abolitionist movements here. An eloquent but controversial crusader for social reform, she spoke widely of the evils of the time and helped change the thinking of an entire nation.

Tolan, Stephanie S. **The Last of Eden.**

Wong, Jade Snow. **Fifth Chinese Daughter.** Trophy. Har-Row 1950.

> Although Jade Snow and her family live in San Francisco, her strict parents demand that she conform to Chinese customs. Jade Snow's opinions are not highly regarded in her home until she goes away to college and learns the American way of life. As Jade Snow grows in independence, she earns the respect of her family, and is able to help them to cope with the problems arising from the conflict of cultures.

Woody, Regina J. **The Young Medics.** Messner 1968.

> Amanda Davis begins a nursing program but withdraws and enters an M.D. program even though her doctor grandfather had taught her that nursing is for women and medicine is for men. Convinced that there is a place for women she learns how to combine a demanding career with marriage.

Understanding Economic Differences

Ages 1 to 5

Harper, Anita. **How We Live.** Illus. Christine Roche. Har-Row 1977.
Along with describing the various kinds of living quarters for people—apartments, houses, trailers, boats—this book also describes the people who make up various types of families. In dealing with black and white families, single-parent families, and people who live alone, the book makes children aware of various life styles. Colorful illustrations give children an opportunity to talk and explain what's happening in the pictures.

Ages 5 to 8

Ardizzone, Edward. **Sarah and Simon and No Red Paint.** Delacorte 1966.
There is a painter who paints beautiful pictures, but no one buys them. He has a wife and three children, and although they are poor, they are very happy. When their povery is about to overcome them, Simon and Sarah, the older children, help restore their family's fortune without realizing what they are doing.

Hazen, Barbara Shook. **Tight Times.**

Hill, Elizabeth S. **Evan's Corner.**

Lexau, Joan. **Striped Ice Cream.** Illus. John Wilson. Schol Bk Serv 1971.
School means five pairs of shoes, an expense which calls for working and saving by all five children as well as Mama who works in a button factory and as a part-time domestic to avoid going on welfare. In spite of family squabbles, there is evidence of respect for one another and delight over sharing a goodwill bag.

Lisowski, Gabriel. **How Tevye Became a Milkman.** HR&W 1976.
This is a lovely old-world story of a poor Russian who received a suitable reward for his goodness.

Understanding Economic Differences

Rosen, Winifred. **Henrietta and the Day of the Iguana.** Illus. Kay Chorao. Four Winds. Schol Bk Serv 1978.

Henrietta goes on a shopping trip with her mother and sister and protests all the way. The department store has a wealth of dresses, shoes, and everything a little girl would need, but Henrietta is bored and decides she really needs an iguana. Her father takes her to a pet store, but meeting an iguana face to face is more than she bargained for. Her father observes that "it's pretty easy to get what you want.... That's why, if you're not careful, you end up not wanting what you get." A good observation of the affluent society, where even people who complain about not having enough, nonetheless, can indulge a few shopping whims.

Rosenberg, Janet. **Being Poor.** Illus. Nancy Inderieden. Carolrhoda Bks 1975.

Through stark black and white drawings and terse, straightforward prose, the bleakness of being poor is effectively projected by writer and artist. This book provides a good spring board for discussion regarding ordinary necessities (such as a warm coat for winter) that many children take for granted but poor children consider unattainable.

Viorst, Judith. **Alexander, Who Used to Be Rich Last Sunday.** Illus. Ray Cruz. Atheneum 1978.

An amusing story of how a boy and his money are soon parted. Grandparents give Alexander some spending money and he quickly loses it to bubble gum, bets, and other trifles. Children can be encouraged to tell how they would use the money.

Ages 8 to 11

Ancona, George. **Growing Older.**

Brink, Carol Ryrie. **Winter Cottage.** Illus. Fermin Rocker. Macmillan 1974.

Thirteen-year-old Minty Sparkes is intensely aware of the hardships which the Depression has placed on her dreamer father and younger sister. She becomes the acting leader of the family as first they decide to move into a vacant summer cottage and then include Joe, a runaway, in their plans. The chance of a new home rather than the constantly changing rented room gives Minty a new-found sense of responsibility and pride which the whole family shares. In an effort to win the money to pay rent for their "borrowed" cottage, the children plot together to discover Pop's secret recipe for pancakes in order to enter a contest. The family relationships and adjustments to change make this an enjoyable book.

Byars, Betsy. **The House of Wings.**

Clymer, Eleanor. **We Lived in the Almont.** Illus. David K. Stone. Dutton 1970.

Friends live in contrasting circumstances, and these, too, keep changing in a story that gives a realistic glimpse into life for youngsters in our mobile society.

Coatsworth, Elizabeth. **The Lucky Ones: Five Journeys Toward a Home.** Illus. Janet Doyle. Macmillan 1968.

These refugee children are called the "lucky ones" only because they survived the danger and hardship of escaping from the enemy and of adapting to a whole new culture and way of life. Even though the stories are brief, the reader is given a real feeling for the culture of the beloved homelands of China, Tibet, Hungary, Rwanda, and Algeria, as well as sympathy for the five distinctly different families as they relocate in alien lands. Together or singly, these stories should motivate good classroom discussion.

Estes, Eleanor. **The Hundred Dresses.**

Glasgow, Aline. **Pair of Shoes.** Illus. Symeon Shimin. Dial 1971.

Using the flavor and idiom of the folktale, Aline Glasgow tells the short story of a twelve-year-old boy's growth in understanding of the nature of pride. In this nineteenth-century Polish family, one pair of shoes is shared by three children. Jacob demands shoes of his own for his bar mitzvah, for how can he be a man without them. When his sister breaks her ankle and something must be sold to pay the doctor, Jacob sacrifices the shoes and gains understanding. His invalid father profits too by the lesson and decides to sell three of his beautifully bound books to buy shoes for the children.

Hamilton, Dorothy. **Linda's Rain Tree.** Illus. Ivan Moon. Herald Pr 1975.

Linda Powell is black and poor and Amory Clark is white and rich. They meet through a mutual interest in books and become friends. Through this relationship with Amory, Linda discovers that everyone has problems, rich or poor. Linda has an apprehensive summer when she learns she will be attending a mostly white school in the fall; however, through her friendship with Amory, Linda matures and actually looks forward to the fall and new experiences. This is a rather oversimplified story of little poor girl helped by older rich girl and vice versa.

Hopkins, Lee Bennett. **Mama.**

Karp, Naomi J. **Nothing Rhymes with April.** Illus. Pamela Johnson. HarBraceJ 1974.

Mollie, an eleven-year-old budding poetess, growing up during the Great Depression, wants a second-hand bike more than anything. Even though her father is a lawyer, the Stones are in economic straits because clients cannot pay. Mollie enters a poetry contest at school, hoping to win the ten dollar first prize so she can buy the bicycle of her dreams. She is accused of plagarism as the result of a "little white lie" and has to face up to the realities of growing up in hard times.

Little, Jean. **Look Through My Window.** Illus. Joan Sandin. Har-Row 1970.

Readers will get a look through a "window" at what it is like to live in a warm, extended family situation in an eighteen-room house.

McGovern, Ann. **The Secret Soldier: The Story of Deborah Sampson.**

Morse, Charles, and Ann Morse. **Evonne Goolagong.** Illus. Harold Henriksen. Amecus St 1974.

This book is about the life of Evonne Goolagong. Her background is not that of most tennis stars. She is a part-Aboriginal girl from Australia. To be an Aboriginal is to be from the lowest class, so some people classified Evonne. Even with these difficulties, she fought her way up the tennis ladder. She started as a five-year-old ball girl. At six, she received her first tennis racket. Eventually she becomes the Australian champion. From championship she gains world-wide fame. This will be an inspiring story for other young people who are starting out at an economic disadvantage.

Smith, Nancy Covert. **Josie's Handful of Quietness.** Illus. Ati Forberg. Abingdon 1975.

A twelve-year-old migrant girl's desire to have a home, close friends, and to go to school seems beyond her reach until Josie becomes friends with old Mr. Curtis. Through the mutual need of friendship, both Josie and Mr. Curtis are able to help one another. Josie's search for a "handful of quietness" is a good way to introduce young readers to the difficult life of migrant workers and the wisdom of an older person.

Snyder, Zilpha Keatley. **The Velvet Room.** Illus. Alton Raible. Aladdin. Atheneum 1977.

The Depression forces Robin's family to sell their dairy in central California and live a migratory life following the crops. In their circuitous travels, the old Model-T breaks down near the McCurdy ranch. Mr. Williams luckily finds immediate work in the surrounding apricot orchards, and eventually a permanent job. Robin escapes to a tranquil, book-lined "velvet room" in a nearby abandoned mansion to free herself from the harsh thoughts of schoolmates' attitudes and remarks about her and other farm labor children and from the realities of her noisy, crowded, poverty-stricken life. Ensuing events of a deep friendship and mystery compel Robin's acceptance of reality.

Taylor, Mildred D. **Song of the Trees.** Illus. Jerry Pinkney. Skylark. Bantam 1978.

During the Depression, Cassie's father goes to Louisiana to find work and leaves his family behind. They go to live with their grandmother who has a plot of land that contains a beautiful grove of giant trees. Trouble starts when Cassie's grandmother, in need of money, allows herself to be coerced by an unscrupulous lumberman into selling the trees. When it becomes apparent that the lumberman intends to cheat the family, Cassie and her brothers decide they have to stop the destruction of the grove of trees. What they attempt to do and how Papa comes home in time to help them is a story of strength and inner courage that young readers will admire.

Ages 11 to 14

Aaron, Chester. **Better Than Laughter.**

Alcock, Gudrun. **Turn the Next Corner.** Lothrop 1969.

Ritchie Osborne is hurt and angry when his father is convicted of embezzlement and sent to prison. Ritchie and his mother must move from the comfortable suburbs to the inner city. There they try to conceal their family shame and to adopt a more modest standard of living. Slugger, a black boy living in the same building, and Ritchie become friends. An accident made Slugger a cripple but he is fiercely independent. Together, Ritchie and Slugger learn to accept each other and the strengths and weaknesses they discover in themselves.

Blume, Judy. **Then Again, Maybe I Won't.** Dell 1973.

This is the story of a young man who leaves a comfortable blue collar neighborhood to start over with the upper middle class. His father's invention that accounts for the transformation is not so important as his mother's pretentiousness. Tony Miglione must deal with the sudden changes in his reality and value systems as he chooses what must truly be his own identity. The story portrays the falseness of those who pursue materialistic goals as well as problems common to all economic groups.

Branscum, Robbie. **Toby, Granny and George.** Illus. Glen Rounds. Avon 1977.

Toby, a mountain girl in Arkansas, has two missions in life. She must preserve the stability of her home with her adopted Granny and she must save the farm from destitution to provide a better life for her and Granny. Because she is so humanely sincere and so loves the land, she accomplishes her goals. Simultaneously, she finds her mother, her first love, and solves the mystery of two murders.

Bridgers, Sue Ellen. **Home Before Dark.** Illus. Charles Robinson. Knopf 1976.

The ever-present poverty of migrant farm workers is present in this novel, but poverty is not the point of it. This is the story of Stella, who has spent most of her fourteen years in the back seat of a stationwagon moving from town to town and job to job. The story is of her father, who comes to understand himself enough to return to his hometown farm and settle down. In his maturity, he allows Stella, who needs so desperately to find stability, to become a woman. Teachers will use this book to explicate social and personal values against a backdrop of poverty, transience, and despair.

Cameron, Eleanor. **To the Green Mountains.**

Cleaver, Vera, and Bill Cleaver. **Trial Valley.**

Crane, Caroline. **Don't Look at Me That Way.** Random 1970.

This is the story of Rosa Rivera, the oldest of seven fatherless children, living in the very poor section of New York's West Side. Situations arise which could end in a tragedy but are avoided through the kindness of the people involved.

Engebrecht, P. A. **Under the Haystack.**

Garfield, Leon. **The Apprentices.** Viking Pr 1978.

> Called "novels in miniature," these are, in fact, an interrelated collection of short stories about a group of boys and girls who are apprentices to a variety of trades in eighteenth-century London. Bound to their masters for seven years, these young people are learning to be lamplighters, morticians, ceramic sculptors, and mirror makers. The tales are told with humor and pathos, joy and sadness, as the apprentices go about their daily lives. Young people will come to understand themselves and the world of work from this book.

Gordy, Berry, Sr. **Movin' Up.**

Hall, Lynn. **The Siege of Silent Henry.**

Hayes, Sheila. **The Carousel Horse.**

Holman, Felice. **Slake's Limbo.**

Lee, Josephine. **The Fabulous Manticora.** John Day 1976.

> When George's older sister marries a wealthy, socially-prominent young man, the poverty of George's family becomes unbearable. Driven to extremes, twelve-year-old George steals a valuable artifact, a Manticora, in order to change their circumstances. He becomes deeply involved in intrigue, and only by sheer courage and determination can he extricate himself. In the end, George's only punishment for the theft comes from within, but he has matured enough to know that he no longer places so much importance on material wealth.

Levitin, Sonia. **Journey to America.**

Miles, Betty. **Just the Beginning.** Knopf 1976.

> Catherine Myers is a thirteen-year-old who lives in a wealthy neighborhood. In Camden Woods many people have cleaning ladies, but it is Catherine's mother who is soon to become one. In addition, Catherine lives in the shadow of a "perfect" older sister. As she grows, she learns to cope with the difficulties of her differences and enjoy being unique.

Ney, John. **Ox: The Story of a Kid at the Top.**

Oppenheimer, Joan. **It Isn't Easy Being a Teenage Millionaire.** Schol Bk Serv 1978.

Lissa Cunningham, bored with the ordinariness of her lower-middle-class high school life, dreams of the advantages of wealth. When she wins a million-dollar raffle, she gains all she has ever dreamed of, but she discovers in the process that her money has robbed her of everything she truly values—family, friends, and the challenges of the trials of ordinariness. Young readers will find a way to evaluate what they really have as they see through Lissa's eyes that the grass only appears greener across the fence.

Pinkwater, Daniel M. **The Last Guru.** Illus. by author. Skylark. Bantam 1980.

Harold Blatz persuaded his uncle to place a bet for him at the races, won big, and parlayed his winnings to the billions, making him the fifth richest person on earth. Harold does some surprising things with his money. A lighthearted book, more fantastic than realistic, it nonetheless gives insights into the world of wealth, power, and fanatic cults.

Rabe, Berniece. **The Girl Who Had No Name.**

Rivera, Geraldo. **A Special Kind of Courage.**

Wersba, Barbara. **Tunes for a Small Harmonica.**

Weston, John. **The Boy Who Sang the Birds.** Illus. Donna Diamond. Scribner 1976.

Beautiful descriptive phrases such as "a basket of pansy-faced kittens" and "the sky turned pale as beaten brass" are found throughout this unusual story of a strange little boy who speaks words but in a pattern that people cannot understand. He appears one day in a small town called Charley Crossing and is ignored by all the townspeople except one boy named Tobe. He takes the stranger home and names him "Dorkle" because of his odd bird-like and incomprehensible speech. The time Tobe and Dorkle spend together is an eloquent tale of the interdependency of nature as well as of human beings.

Wilkinson, Brenda. **Ludell.**

Yep, Laurence. **Child of the Owl.** Har-Row 1977.

When Casey, a twelve-year-old Chinese-American girl, goes to live with her grandmother in San Francisco's Chinatown, she learns not only about her Chinese heritage but also discovers the real values in life. She learns that there are certain riches that money cannot buy and that poverty of soul and mind is worse than not having money.

This moving, well-written story gives intimate glimpses of life as it really is in San Francisco's Chinatown.

Ages 14 and Up

Angier, Bradford, and Barbara Corcoran. **Ask for Love and They Give You Rice Pudding.** Bantam 1979.

Robbie Benson is rich. He has a Fiat, a sailboat, and a very generous monthly allowance. What Robbie does not have is love. His father deserted his mother, his grandfather is dying, and his grandmother doesn't believe that Robbie will ever succeed. Because of his insecurities, Robbie feels he must buy friends. In a final search for his missing father, a deep love for his girlfriend's mother, and the mature realization of what he has become, Robbie chooses to spend a year coming to terms with himself before going on to college. Teachers can use this book to help destroy the myth that money will solve problems.

Carlson, Dale. **A Wild Heart.** Illus. Chuck Freedman. Watts 1977.

Jona Kirkland is desperate to change her life from crude and illiterate poverty. She knows that her most stable love is with Danny, but Grega offers wealth and a view of the world that she has never known. Her family, a brutish mother and an alcoholic father, give her no support. In a surprising climax to this book, Jona is able to sort out values more clearly, but she still has "a wild heart."

Godden, Rumer. **An Episode of Sparrows.** Avon 1975.

The sparrows are the street children of a bombed section of London where the poor and the well-to-do touch but rarely meet. Thirteen-year-old Tim Malone is weaned away from his gang by Lovejoy Mason, an unusual eleven-year-old, when he aids her in creating a secret garden. They are discovered and brought to court for stealing soil from the square. The children find that "people need people."

Kerr, M. E. **Gentlehands.** Bantam 1979.

Buddy Boyle, a high school junior from an ordinary family, falls in love with an "upper-class" young lady. Conflict results due to the differences in social status and only Buddy's grandfather, the kindest and most sophisticated man he has ever known, seems to understand. Finally his grandfather is found to have been one of the most cruel of the Germans at Auschwitz. This gripping book will provide the opportunity to examine many of the values young adults wrestle with in growing up.

Kerr, M. E. **The Son of Someone Famous.**

Mathis, Sharon Bell. **Listen for the Fig Tree.**

Mayerson, Charlotte Leon. **Two Blocks Apart: Juan Gonzalez and Peter Quinn.** HR&W 1965.

Juan Gonzalez and Peter Quinn, both seventeen, live two blocks apart in New York City. Their lives are very different but their aspirations are surprisingly similar. The book is a compilation of edited tapes, but because of the selected details it seems more fiction than fact. The book delineates the problems of relating to family and peers in both worlds.

Miller, Arthur. **Death of a Salesman.**

Olsen, Tillie. **Yonnondio from the Thirties.** Delacorte 1974.

Not so much a novel as a sequence of touching vignettes is this book of poverty in America in the 1930s. Mazie, a young woman, observes her father go from coal mining, to sharecropping, to work in a packing plant. All the horrors, the ignorance, and the despair of poverty are described as they shape and mold this family. Teachers of social studies as well as English can use this book to explain a part of the human condition in American life.

Orwell, George. **Animal Farm.** Sig Classics. NAL 1974.

This frightening fable tells of the successful rebellion of the farm animals against their human masters. Although the animals set up a "classless" society, the pigs become the rulers, and the other animals find themselves in varying degrees of slavery. "Some are more equal than others," explain the pigs.

Peare, Catherine Owens. **The F.D.R. Story.** T Y Crowell 1962.

Franklin Delano Roosevelt grew up in an atmosphere of love and luxury. An adoring mother and father secured for him every privilege. His vibrant personality, great energy, and contagious enthusiasm soon established him as a leader in all schools he attended. Success seemed to attend every experience until he was stricken with polio. Struggling courageously to overcome this tremendous physical handicap, he rose to become one of the greatest leaders of the Western World. He also became a leader in the successful battle against polio. He did not give up and retreat into the shelter that his economic status would have provided.

Spencer, Elizabeth. **The Light in the Piazza.**

Steinbeck, John. **The Grapes of Wrath.** Penguin 1976.

A sharecropper family piles a few household goods onto its broken-down car and migrates from the dust bowl to California, where as migratory workers they experience deprivation and rejection.

Strachan, Margaret Pitcairn. **Trouble at Torrent Creek.** Washburn 1967.

A first-year teacher from the city goes to Appalachia to teach in a one-room schoolhouse. During the year, she succeeds in convincing the deprived families that school consolidation would benefit the entire community.

Professional References

Baskin, Barbara and Karen Harris. *Books for the Gifted Child.* New York: Bowker, 1979.

Baskin, Barbara and Karen Harris. *Notes from a Different Drummer: A Guide to Juvenile Fiction, Portraying the Handicapped.* New York: Bowker, 1977.

Bettelheim. Bruno. *The Uses of Enchantment: The Meaning and Importance of Fairy Tales.* New York: Alfred A. Knopf, 1976

Butler, Dorothy. *Cushla and Her Books.* Boston: The Horn Book, Inc., 1980.

Clapp, Ouida, ed. *Responses to Sexism: Classroom Practices in Teaching English 1976-77.* Urbana, Illinois: National Council of Teachers of English, 1976.

Cook, Sarah S. et al. *Children and Dying: An Exploration and Selective Bibliographies.* New York: Health Science Publishing Corporation, 1974.

Hendler, Marjorie R. "An Analysis of Sex Role Attributes, Behaviors, and Occupations in Contemporary Children's Picture Books." Doctoral Dissertation, New York University, 1976.

Rudman, Masha Kabakow. *Children's Literature: An Issues Approach.* Lexington, Massachusetts: D.C. Heath, 1976.

Stein, Sarah B. *About Dying.* New York: Walker and Co., 1974.

Ladder III

Interacting in Groups

Ladder III, "Interacting in Groups," is difficult to limit or define with any clear boundaries. Almost all books, whatever their strongest theme or message, involve interpersonal relationships. The inner growth or change discussed in Ladder I is very often the cause or result of these relationships; understanding individual differences explored in Ladder II and appreciating different cultures in Ladder IV also concern interpersonal relationships, as does coping in a changing world highlighted in Ladder V. In considering the indistinct perimeters of Ladder III, we selected books for this section that with all their universal applications and transfers still focus on interacting in groups in an especially strong or unique manner.

At the very center of group interaction is the relationship among members of a family. It is the first interaction for all individuals and one that continues in some form throughout life. The way these relationships are developed and the amount of security and self-respect they produce influence any other relationships developed at a later time.

While the family remains the basic unit in our society, the forms of family structure are in a state of flux. Not every child has the opportunity to grow up in a traditional family with two parents, with siblings, and with the influence of an extended family. Some do not even know their grandparents, aunts, uncles, and cousins. Many of today's children come from single-parent families, through divorce, the death of a parent, or the fact that their parent has chosen not to marry. Some children grow up with adopted families, or in foster homes, either temporarily or permanently. Still others are living in a home where there are stepparents, stepbrothers, and stepsisters, who add a new dimension to family relationships. Complex sibling relationships become even more so when the young people involved are related only by the marriage of their parents.

Just as there are many types of families, there are many ways to react to family life. Some children and adults feel stifled by too much family guidance and too many rules. Others, especially those who must sometimes prematurely assume adult roles, long for this protective family situation.

Outside the home environment the child uses the experiences already gained to form new relationships and to find a place in an ever-widening circle of people. The young person begins to function in the neighborhood, at school, in groups, clubs, camps, and other social organizations. All of these experiences contribute to the independence and maturity needed to function in the larger society.

Beyond the family, friendship is perhaps the next most intense relationship. Friendship is one of life's most rewarding relationships, and books about friendship number among them some of the most perceptive about human experience. These books illustrate an area where relationships are the result of choice rather than of circumstances. Friendships cross many barriers: culture, economic conditions, age, sex, and race; and thrive on two people needing and helping each other and sharing a significant part of their lives. Some of the books in this section are about those friendships that mature into a love relationship and result in marriage and thus the beginning of a new family and new primary relationships.

The section on peer relationships includes books that show just how powerful peer pressure can be. Books that illustrate both wholesome and disturbing influences have been chosen, but most of them emphasize the worth of the individual and show the courage needed to resist peer pressure.

Again, the boundaries are often indistinct between interactions with peers and interactions with other social groups. Books mentioned here usually deal with groups made up of individuals who are not necessarily peers, or with organized groups, such as clubs or gangs.

The books discussed in Ladder III were chosen for their interest and appeal to young people. We are cognizant of the power of books in children's lives, but know that books will not have any effect unless they are read. It is hoped that readers will enjoy or find satisfaction in the books listed here, and in that enjoyment come to new insights into their relationships with others.

Lucille Michael Hart

Family Relationships

Ages 1 to 5

Arnstein, Helene S. **Billy and Our New Baby.**

Asch, Frank. **Monkey Face.**

Barrett, Judi. **I Hate to Go to Bed.**

Berger, Terry. **A New Baby.** Illus. Heinz Kluetmeier. Raintree Pubs Ltd 1975.

>To the mind of a young boy, having a new baby in the family raises many questions as to how he, himself, will fit into the family. Will he still be loved as much? Much love and understanding help see this child through a difficult period in his life.

Bible, Charles. **Jennifer's New Chair.** Illus. by author. HR&W 1978.

>Jennifer is secure in her world with a chair that is especially hers and a sixth birthday party coming up. A fire just before the celebration destroys all the family's household items, including the chair and party favors. Gammy softens the blow by finding another chair for Jennifer and by seeing that the birthday celebration takes place.

Borack, Barbara. **Grandpa.** Illus. Ben Shecter. Har-Row 1968.

>This book tells the story of the way a little girl sees her grandfather. The two have so much in common: when Marilyn dresses up in grandpa's shirt, her grandmother can't tell them apart. When company comes, they both hate it, but they sit quietly in the corner where the candy is—and eat it up!

Buckley, Helen E. **Grandfather and I.** Illus. Paul Galdone. Lothrop 1959.

>A young boy delights in taking walks with his grandfather because neither has to hurry, and they can stop and look at anything which interests them. It is a special relationship between two people who have the time to truly enjoy one another's company.

Buckley, Helen E. **Grandmother and I.** Illus. Paul Galdone. Lothrop 1961.

> In childlike terms, the book tells of a youngster's comfort in sitting on grandmother's lap as she rocks back and forth, humming a tune. The concept of a special love between grandmother and child is simply, yet fully, developed.

Burningham, John. **The Baby.** Illus. by author. T Y Crowell 1975.

> A young child describes his feelings about the new baby at his house. He hopes the baby grows up soon so he will have someone to play with. An honest portrayal: sometimes he likes the baby; sometimes he doesn't.

Caines, Jeannette Franklin. **Abby.** Illus. Steven Kellog. Har-Row 1973.

> "Ugh, a girl," says Kevin when newly adopted eleven-month-old Abby is brought home. In time, he asks to bring Abby to school for show-and-tell, to share the news that they get to keep her forever.

Corey, Dorothy. **You Go Away.** Illus. Lois Axeman. A Whitman 1976.

> This story illustrates a very young child's reactions to a parent's leaving. The child is relieved to learn that whenever parents go away, whether just out of the room or on a long trip, they will return.

Delton, Judy, and Elaine Knox-Wagner. **The Best Mom in the World.**

Flack, Marjorie. **Ask Mr. Bear.** Illus. by author. Macmillan 1971.

> Danny wants to give his mother a present for her birthday but does not accept the suggestions of a succession of animals whom he meets. Mr. Bear, however, provides the solution to Danny's problem—a Big Birthday Bear Hug. The simple repetitive plot and satisfying ending are appropriate for the young child.

Flournoy, Valerie. **The Best Time of the Day.** Illus. George Ford. Random 1979.

> As William, a little black boy, goes through his busy day he knows the time he likes best. It is when Daddy comes home. William sits and listens for the car to enter the driveway. His daddy plays with him until suppertime and at bedtime William usually calls for one more drink of water, but what he really wants is a big hug—the perfect end for a busy day.

Greenfield, Eloise. **First Pink Light.** Illus. Moneta Barnett. T Y Crowell 1976.

> A little boy wants to stay up until his daddy gets home from a trip,

Family Relationships 151

but his mother says that his father will not be there until the day's first pink light. The little boy thinks he has won this argument about staying up late when his mother lets him wait in the big arm chair. When sleep overcomes him, he knows his mother has won, but he feels comfortable and loved, and smiles as he falls asleep.

Johnston, Johanna. **Edie Changes Her Mind.** Illus. Paul Galdone. Putnam 1964.

Edie is a little girl who hates to go to bed. Every night when her mother says, "Time now," Edie opens her mouth and yells. One night her mother says: "We'll forget about bed." Mother takes away the bedclothes and Daddy takes the bed apart and carries it away piece by piece. After a while Edie changes her mind about bedtime.

Lapsley, Susan. **I Am Adopted.** Illus. Michael Charlton. Bradbury Pr 1975.

This book tells of two children, Charles and Sophie, who enjoy working with and helping their parents. And every night they share a bedtime story before going to sleep. Charles and Sophie are adopted, and Charles says adoption means belonging.

MacLachlan, Patricia. **Through Grandpa's Eyes.**

Scott, Ann Herbert. **On Mother's Lap.**

Skorpen, Liesel Moak. **Mandy's Grandmother.**

Skorpen, Liesel Moak. **Michael.**

Watson, Wendy. **Moving.**

Yolen, Jane. **No Bath Tonight.** Illus. Nancy Winslow Parker. T Y Crowell 1978.

Small aches and pains cause Jeremy to avoid bath time. "No bath tonight!" says Jeremy throughout the week. On Sunday, Jeremy's grandmother comes to visit. She listens to his week's adventures and takes a good look. Jeremy has met his match. Cleverly, Grandmother steers him into the long-postponed bath.

Ages 5 to 8

Adoff, Arnold. **Black Is Brown Is Tan.** Illus. Emily Arnold McCully. Har-Row 1973.

The fun and love a family shares are eloquently expressed in this story of an interracial family. Additionally, the father and mother are depicted in nonsexist roles. A biracial heritage is seen with joy in this timely book.

Bach, Alice. **Grouchy Uncle Otto.**

Berger, Terry. **Big Sister, Little Brother.** Illus. Heinz Kluetmeier. Raintree Pubs Ltd 1975.

A young boy tells about his relationship with an older sister. He appreciates the times they share and he knows he learns things when he is in her company. However, his sister's concern for him can be a burden. Realizing that she too gains from these experiences, he adjusts his feelings.

Bond, Gladys Baker. **Boy in the Middle.**

Bronin, Andrew. **Gus and Buster Work Things Out.** Illus. Cyndy Szekeres. YB. Dell 1977.

Gus and Buster are brother raccoons. Gus is a smart little raccoon and is always trying to trick his brother Buster. Somehow Buster has a way of making the tricks backfire on his brother without realizing that he is doing it. In the end each brother does something nice for the other and they find that they can get along.

Brooks, Ron. **Timothy and Gramps.** Illus. by author. Bradbury Pr 1978.

Timothy has no sisters or brothers and his best friend is Gramps. They share hours of wild, made-up stories of adventure and far-off lands. At school, Timothy is quiet and shy. He doesn't contribute to show-and-tell and plays alone. Then one day Gramps appears at school and tells the children one of his stories. Afterwards the children want to know more about Timothy and Gramps, and Timothy begins to enjoy school more.

Brown, Margaret Wise. **The Runaway Bunny.** Illus. Clement Hurd. Trophy. Har-Row 1977.

This is a repetitive tale of a bunny who threatens to run away. Each time he tells his mother what he will become, she answers with what she will become so that she can be near and care for him. Finally he decides he might as well stay home. The theme of a mother's love for her child becomes even more explicit in the "Song of the Runaway Bunny" at the close of the book.

Bulla, Clyde Robert. **Keep Running, Allen!**

Family Relationships

Bunting, Eve. **The Big Red Barn.**

Caudill, Rebecca. **Did You Carry the Flag Today, Charley?** Illus. Nancy Grossman. HR&W 1971.

> That Charley carry the flag, the reward for best behavior at school, becomes the daily concern of Charley's parents. However, Charley's intense imagination and curiosity seem always to get in the way of "good behavior." A number of comic episodes lead to the day Charley finally does carry the flag.

Charlip, Remy, and Lilian Moore. **Hooray for Me!**

Clifton, Lucille. **Amifika.** Illus. Thomas DiGrazia. Dutton 1977.

> Little Amifika overheard his mother and cousin talking about his father coming home from the army. His cousin could not imagine how they would all fit in the two-room apartment, and when his mother responded, "We'll just get rid of something he won't miss. Lot of stuff around here he won't even remember," Amifika grew positive that his father would not remember him and tried to find a hiding place. His father's warm greeting, upon returning home, sets Amifika's fears at ease.

Clifton, Lucille. **My Brother Fine with Me.** Illus. Moneta Barnett. HR&W 1975.

> Baggy is a little boy who decides to run away from home. His older sister, Johnetta, is more than pleased because she has to look after him while Mom and Dad work. Johnetta makes many discoveries after Baggy leaves—there are no mini-bike pictures to pick up; there are no motor sounds to keep the house from being quiet; and there is no one to eat all the peanut butter and jelly. Johnetta learns at an early age it may not be easy having a kid brother around, but it is not fun without one either.

Coville, Bruce. **Sarah's Unicorn.** Illus. Katherine Coville. Lippincott 1979.

> Sarah lives in the forest with her Aunt Meg who is a wicked witch. Aunt Meg, once a good person, has been turned into a witch by a spell that was cast upon her. In the forest, Sarah meets a unicorn who teaches her to talk to the animals. The unicorn is Sarah's friend and companion. Aunt Meg's jealousy brings her to the forest in hopes of capturing the unicorn, but the animals gang up and save the unicorn. When the unicorn touches Aunt Meg with his horn, she turns into a good person again.

Delton, Judy. **It Happened on Thursday.** Illus. June Goldsborough. A Whitman 1978.

> Jamie has noticed that Thursday seems to be a good day. Special things seem to happen to him that day—even his birthday. He pastes a blue star on every Thursday on his calendar. Then real disaster strikes. Jamie's mother becomes so sick she has to go to the hospital. Jamie is severely shaken when she has not improved by his favorite day. In the end, Jamie decides he can still believe in Thursdays but he learns good things can happen on other days, too.

de Paola, Tomie. **Watch Out for the Chicken Feet in Your Soup.** Illus. by author. P-H 1974.

> Joey brings his friend Eugene to meet his grandma, and he begins to see his grandmother in a new light as he realizes how Eugene is enjoying himself. Joey sees how special Grandma really is.

Duncan, Lois. **Giving Away Suzanne.** Illus. Leonard Weisgard. Dodd 1963.

> Mary Kay trades her troublesome little sister for a goldfish. She soon realizes, however, that although Suzanne was troublesome at times, she was much more enjoyable and entertaining than a fish.

Eisenberg, Phyllis Rose. **A Mitzvah Is Something Special.**

Fisher, Aileen L. **My Mother and I.** Illus. Kazue Mizumura. T Y Crowell 1967.

> A little girl comes home from school to find that her mother has been called to care for "Gran" for two weeks. During this period she thinks about creatures such as frogs and butterflies who have no mothers to love them. When her mother returns, she expresses her feelings with a hug and a comment that she is glad she is not a frog or a bug.

Fox, Paula. **Maurice's Room.** Illus. Ingrid Fetz. Macmillan 1972.

> As a "collector," Maurice has a problem in his small room keeping things in order. His problem is solved when his family moves to the country where he will have a barn to keep his treasures.

Gackenbach, Dick. **Hattie Be Quiet, Hattie Be Good.** Har-Row 1977.

> Hattie Rabbit wants to do something nice for her mother so she sits still for one hour. Her mother wonders if she is sick. Children will enjoy the funny but loving thoughts and actions of Hattie Rabbit.

Family Relationships

Gill, Joan. **Hush, Jon.** Illus. Tracy Sugarman. Doubleday 1968.

> Jon is resentful of his baby sister, basically because her presence requires his silence, and there are only so many quiet activities one can pursue in a small apartment. However, he decides that she is growing up when he discovers that he can make her laugh.

Goldman, Susan. **Cousins Are Special.** Illus. by author. A Whitman 1978.

> This is Sarah's first visit to Carol Sue's house. Right away, they are best friends. They bounce down the stairs together, watch clothes go down the laundry chute, jump on beds, play with finger paints, and ride bikes. Sarah and Carol Sue look through a photograph album and notice that they each have the same grandmother! They then realize that their relationship is extra special.

Greene, Laura. **I Am an Orthodox Jew.**

Greenfield, Eloise. **She Come Bringing Me That Little Baby Girl.**

Hallinan, P. K. **We're Very Good Friends, My Brother and I.** Illus. by author. Childrens 1973.

> A boy explains the friendship he shares with his brother. He tells of the happy times, the sad times, and the "we don't see eye to eye" times. Rhymes with illustrations portray their special relationship.

Hazen, Barbara Shook. **Tight Times.** Illus. Trina Schart Hyman. Viking Pr 1979.

> Tight times are times when everything keeps going up, explains Dad. Tight times are times the family eats Mr. Bulk instead of cereals in little boxes. They are times the family goes to the sprinkler instead of the lake. They are times Dad is without work and cannot afford extras. However, tight times do not stop a boy from wanting a dog. He finds a cat and is permitted to keep it; he names the cat Dog.

Hill, Elizabeth S. **Evan's Corner.** Illus. Nancy Grossman. HR&W 1967.

> Evan longs for a place to be alone, but as one member of a family of eight living in a two-room apartment, this is nearly impossible. When his mother gives him a corner of the living room, he decorates it, sits there, yet feels vaguely dissatisfied. Only when he begins to help his younger brother fix up another corner does he feel truly happy.

Hoban, Lillian. **Arthur's Pen Pal.** Illus. by author. Har-Row 1976.

> Arthur wishes for a baby brother instead of a baby sister. He envies

the relationship of his pen pal, Sandy, with an older brother. Sandy plays drums and does karate with "his" older brother. Then Arthur discovers that Sandy is a girl and realizes that a little sister may not be so bad, after all.

Hoban, Russell. **A Baby Sister for Frances.** Illus. Lillian Hoban. Trophy. Har-Row 1976.

Frances, a badger who acts like a little girl, has a baby sister who gets an inordinate amount of attention. Frances decides to run away under the dining room table, but is enticed back because "everyone misses her and wants to hug and kiss her." A gentle story is interspersed with Frances' original poems.

Hoban, Russell. **Bedtime for Frances.** Illus. Garth Williams. Trophy. Har-Row 1976.

Frances, a badger with all the characteristics of a young child, uses many well-known ploys to keep from going to bed and staying there. Her understanding parents allow Frances several trips to their bedroom before father finally suggests the possibility of a spanking. This seems to be an effective sleep-inducer.

Hoban, Russell. **A Birthday for Frances.** Illus. Lillian Hoban. Trophy. Har-Row 1976.

Frances, a humanlike badger, suffers from an acute case of jealousy when her little sister Gloria has a birthday. Her parents demonstrate love and understanding as they adeptly cope with the situation.

Hoban, Russell. **Bread and Jam for Frances.** Illus. Lillian Hoban. Schol Bk Serv 1969.

Frances' philosophy of eating is that many different foods taste many different ways, but if she always has bread and jam, then she always knows what she is getting. Her parents cooperate by giving her only bread and jam. As expected, she tires of this menu and decides that she would rather eat a greater variety of foods.

Jeschke, Susan. **Mia, Grandma and the Genie.**

Jordan, June. **New Life: New Room.** Illus. Ray Cruz. T Y Crowell 1975.

A family living in a small apartment in a housing project finds a creative solution to the need for more space. When a new baby arrives, the parents trade rooms with the children and make their larger bedroom into a kind of dormitory for the children, who find the new arrangement as exciting as a new house.

Family Relationships

Kellogg, Steven. **Much Bigger Than Martin.**

Kerr, Judith. **Mog's Christmas.** Illus. by author. Collins Pubs 1976.

> Mog, the family cat, does not understand anything about Christmas. He feels uneasy with so many relatives in his house. He is especially frightened when a tree appears to be walking into his house and talking to him! This is a delightful view of a family's preparation for a holiday. The brightly colored illustrations add to the humor.

Kraus, Robert. **Big Brother.** Illus. by author. Parents 1973.

> A little boy feels as if he is always "in the shadow" of his big brother. He feels bad because he will always be smaller than his older brother. To make matters worse he must follow his brother's orders while their mother is in the hospital. His dismay turns to happiness when she returns with a new little brother.

Lasker, Joe. **He's My Brother.**

Lasky, Kathryn. **My Island Grandma.** Illus. Emily McCully. Warne 1979.

> Abbey and her grandmother share a wonderful friendship. Abbey is very happy because her grandmother lives near her parents' summer cabin on an island. Grandmother and Abbey go swimming and sailing together; they pick sea herbs, sea snails, and blueberries; they watch and talk about things; and they make moss gardens and moon cookies. When the summer is over, Abbey is left with pleasant memories.

Leech, Jay, and Zane Spencer. **Bright Fawn and Me.**

Lexau, Joan. **Benjie.** Illus. Don Bolognese. Dial 1964.

> Benjie is a very shy youngster who refuses to speak to people. When his grandmother loses an earring which she has cherished for years, Benjie slips out to look for it. In the course of his search, he must speak to several people and thus overcome his shyness.

Lexau, Joan. **Me Day.**

Little, Lessie Jones, and Eloise Greenfield. **I Can Do It by Myself.**

Lloyd, Errol. **Nini at Carnival.**

Lundgren, Max. **Matt's Grandfather.**

Marzollo, Jean. **Close Your Eyes.** Illus. Susan Jeffers. Dial 1978.

> This beautifully illustrated book shows a gentle relationship between a father and his child.

Miles, Miska. **Aaron's Door.** Illus. Alan E. Cober. Little 1977.

> Aaron shuts himself off from memories of his mother and foster homes; he shuts himself off from his sister, and from the people who have offered him a home. He just huddles on his bed. He feels he can trust no one, until his new father breaks through the shell Aaron has made for himself.

Minarik, Else H. **Little Bear.** Illus. Maurice Sendak. Trophy. Har-Row 1978.

> This easy-to-read book has four chapters in which Little Bear plays in the snow, makes "birthday soup" when he fears he may not get a cake, pretends to go to the moon, and talks with Mother at bedtime. The mother is warm and very understanding, and Little Bear expresses his feeling for her when he says, "You always make me happy."

Noble, June. **Two Homes for Lynn.** Illus. Yuri Salzman. HR&W 1979.

> Lynn had heard the word "divorce," but what does it mean for her? When her parents divorce, a little girl finds that it means a home with Dad where she cooks, makes her bed, and keeps her dollhouse; and a home with Mom where she throws toys and rips her room apart when she is angry—until she develops an imaginary friend, Janelle. Lynn now has someone to play with when she is with Mom, and her disposition changes. Janelle is permitted to stay at Dad's, too, when Lynn is there, after Dad hears about her. Lynn is beginning to cope with, and even appreciate, having two homes.

Pinkwater, Daniel M. **The Wuggie Norple Story.** Illus. Tomie de Paola. Four Winds. Schol Bk Serv 1980.

> This humorous story of family squabbles is enhanced by exciting and lively illustrations.

Power, Barbara. **I Wish Laura's Mommy Was My Mommy.**

Raynor, Dorka. **This Is My Father and Me.**

Reyher, Becky. **My Mother Is the Most Beautiful Woman in the World.** Illus. Ruth Gannett. Lothrop 1945.

> This Russian folktale is about a little lost girl who describes her mother as "the most beautiful woman in the world." To the children, "beautiful" means "much loved."

Sendak, Maurice. **Where the Wild Things Are.** Illus. by author. Har-Row 1963.

Family Relationships 159

Max is sent to his room without his supper because he has been misbehaving. He sails off in his own imaginary boat, through night and day, to where the wild things are, and becomes their king. Lonely, he decides to go back to where "someone loved him best of all." When he returns home, supper, still hot, is waiting for him.

Simon, Norma. **All Kinds of Families.** Illus. Joe Lasker. A Whitman 1976.

This book stresses the many patterns of family life, displays the supportive family which guides the child into a happy, healthy life, and also expresses the importance of a child's special place in the family. Illustrations show the "happy family" in many cultures as parents and their children, whether they live together or not.

Smith, Lucia B. **My Mom Got a Job.** Illus. C. Christina Johanson. HR&W 1979.

A little girl remembers the things she and her mother used to do together before Mom got a job. However, as a result of her mother working, she gets to do some new things she hadn't done before. She realizes that instead of Mom taking care of her and Dad, they all take care of each other.

Stren, Patti. **There's a Rainbow in My Closet.**

Tester, Sylvia Root. **Feeling Angry.** Illus. Peg Roth Haag. Childrens 1976.

Paula Jean is angry when Mother brings Baby Carl home from the hospital. Mother has to give the new baby a lot of attention. Paula pretends to send him away, but when she checks his room he is still there. She reaches into the crib to touch him, but it ends in a pinch. She feels very angry again, until Mother develops a plan to make Paula Jean feel better.

Thompson, Jean. **I'm Going to Run Away!** Illus. Bill Myers. Abingdon 1975.

Jimmy's day starts out wrong and he decides to run away "forever." He looks for a new home on his block, but has no luck. Jimmy decides running away isn't as easy as it sounds. He finally finds a house where he is wanted and he is glad to be back home with his mother and father.

Turkle, Brinton. **Obadiah the Bold.** Illus. by author. Puffin 1977.

This story, with its setting in Nantucket about one hundred years ago, shows young Obadiah in the midst of a happy Quaker family. Brothers will tease, however, and when Obadiah wants to "play pirate" (in hopes of someday being one), he is not spared a little fright. An understanding father helps his son think about following in the footsteps of another kind of seafarer, his grandfather, Captain Obadiah Starbuck.

Vestly, Anne-Cath. **Hello, Aurora.** Ilus. Leonard Kessler. T Y Crowell 1974.

Every morning Aurora's mother goes to work while Aurora's father stays home taking care of her and her baby brother, Socrates. This arrangement suits Aurora's family just fine, but the neighbors think it very strange. Aurora is hurt and puzzled by this attitude until her mother explains that their family is a group on their own and they may take care of each other however they choose.

Waber, Bernard. **But Names Will Never Hurt Me.**

Wahl, Jan. **Old Hippo's Easter Egg.** Illus. Lorinda Bryan Cauley. Har-BraceJ 1980.

Old Hippo longs to have a child of his own to paint Easter eggs with. When an egg is left on Hippo's doorstep, he is pleased when it hatches into Small Quack, a yellow duck. They share a wonderful summer together until Small Quack hears his call to fly South. Hippo resigns himself to a lonely winter until it is Easter again and his now married son, Big Quack, sends a special gift for Hippo to love and nurture.

Williams, Barbara. **If He's My Brother.**

Young, Miriam. **Miss Suzy's Birthday.** Illus. Arnold Lobel. Parents 1974.

Miss Suzy worries about her adopted children growing up and leaving home. Meanwhile her children and friends plan a surprise birthday party for her. The youngest child gives the surprise away, and the child's inability to keep a secret reassures Miss Suzy that the children are still young and will be around for some time.

Zolotow, Charlotte. **If It Weren't for You.** Illus. Ben Shecter. Har-Row 1966.

An older brother thinks of all the advantages of not having a younger brother; for example, he could "cry without anyone knowing." On the final pages he remembers that, "if it weren't for you, I'd have to be alone with the grownups" and this seems to outweigh all the disadvantages.

Zolotow, Charlotte. **Mr. Rabbit and the Lovely Present.** Illus. Maurice Sendak. Trophy. Har-Row 1977.

> The little girl wants to give her mother a nice birthday present but says she has nothing to give her. Mr. Rabbit helps her to see that even though her mother would like emeralds or a blue lake, she will be most happy with the basket of fruit in colors of the rainbow because it is something the little girl can give.

Zolotow, Charlotte. **The Quarreling Book.** Illus. Arnold Lobel. Har-Row 1963.

> Mr. James' forgetfulness makes Mrs. James cross; her crossness irritates Jonathan; and so the plot continues. The trend is finally reversed by a friendly dog.

Zolotow, Charlotte. **William's Doll.** Illus. William Pene du Bois. Har-Row 1972.

> William wanted a doll to love and take care of more than anything he could think of. His father, upset by this, bought William first a basketball and then an electric train, but William still wanted a doll. Finally his understanding grandmother bought him one because she realized how important this was to fill a small boy's needs, a boy who someday might become a loving father.

Ages 8 to 11

Armstrong, William H. **Sounder.** Illus. James Barkley. Trophy. Har-Row 1972.

> A strong and forcefully written tale of the alienation of the black sharecropper of a century ago, *Sounder* is also the story of an enduring family relationship of father, mother, and son: the father who steals food for his hungry family and is imprisoned; the mother who toils quietly on to provide for her son; and the boy who searches constantly and maintains his hope for his father's return.

Bates, Betty. **My Mom, the Money Nut.** Holiday 1979.

> Fritzi and her mother have such different values that they have trouble understanding each other. Fritzi loves singing and people while her mother is more interested in money and material possessions. A visit to her grandfather helps Fritzi understand that her mother is compensating for a childhood she never had.

Blume, Judy. **Tales of a Fourth Grade Nothing.**

Bourne, Miriam Anne. **Nabby Adams' Diary.**

Bulla, Clyde Robert. **Shoeshine Girl.**

Bunting, Eve. **Magic and the Night River.**

Burch, Robert. **D.J.'s Worst Enemy.** Viking Pr 1965.

> D.J. constantly makes trouble for everyone in his family—especially his little brother Renfroe. Through the steady love and understanding of his family, D.J. begins to see that he is his own worst enemy. This humorous and sensitive book makes good use of the regional language of Georgia.

Burch, Robert. **Renfroe's Christmas.** Illus. Rocco Negri. Viking Pr 1968.

> Renfroe doesn't like being told he has a "selfish streak," but the remembrance of buying a more expensive pocketknife for himself than for his brother nags at his conscience. Finally he spontaneously gives away his watch, "the finest thing he'd ever owned," and experiences the deep satisfaction of bringing pleasure to another individual.

Byars, Betsy. **The Cartoonist.** Illus. Richard Cuffari. Viking Pr 1978.

> Alfie's attic and the cartoons he draws there keep him going when he needs an escape. When he learns his mother is planning to give his attic room to his older brother and his wife, Alfie climbs into the attic and refuses to talk or to come down. After the threat is removed, Alfie comes down mature enough to view his situation with insight, humor, and hope.

Byars, Betsy. **The House of Wings.** Illus. Daniel Schwartz. YB. Dell 1973.

> Sammy is left with his grandfather while his parents go on to Detroit to look for a new home. He resents being left and runs away. His grandfather follows him and they come upon a blind crane and try to help it survive. Grandfather can't keep his own children straight in his mind, but he remembers every bird he has nursed back to health. Sammy decides he wants his grandfather to remember him when his visit is over just as well as he does his birds.

Byars, Betsy. **Summer of the Swans.**

Byars, Betsy. **Trouble River.**

Carlson, Natalie Savage. **The Family Under the Bridge.** Illus. Garth Williams. Schol Bk Serv 1972.

An old Parisian hobo, Armand, finds that his special place under a bridge has been appropriated by three children. They convince him that he should stay there too and be their grandfather. He finds it impossible to continue his facade of gruffness, and a deep relationship develops between Armand, the children, and their mother.

Carlson, Natalie Savage. **The Half Sisters.** Illus. Thomas di Grazia. Trophy. Har-Row 1974.

Luvena Savage longs to be accepted as "one of the girls." Luvvy finally achieves her desire by winning the respect of the older girls. This spirited, satisfying story of family life and growing up in Maryland in 1915 was drawn from the author's own childhood and has the ring of truth.

Cleary, Beverly. **Beezus and Ramona.** Illus. Louis Darling. YB. Dell 1979.

Beezus is continually exasperated by the antics of her younger sister Ramona, who somehow always manages to get her own way. However, Beezus begins to understand her feelings and accept them when her mother and aunt tell her of arguments they had as children, and that there were times when they did not love each other. Written in a light and humorous style, the book nonetheless has a deeper theme of family relationships.

Cleary, Beverly. **Ramona and Her Father.** Illus. Alan Tiegreen. YB. Dell 1979.

When her father loses his job, Ramona wants to help. She means well, but sometimes her actions place an additional strain on her family. Ramona practices for a career in television commercials, begins a no-smoking campaign for her father, and puts a new twist into the Christmas pageant. Fortunately, theirs is a warm, close family who can survive even Ramona's good intentions.

Cleary, Beverly. **Ramona and Her Mother.** Illus. Alan Tiegreen. Morrow 1979.

A little bit of sibling rivalry, a large dose of self-pity, and some very ordinary family tensions combine to make Ramona feel unloved—especially by her mother. When Ramona threatens to run away, her mother picks a unique way to show Ramona just how much she really does love her.

Cleary, Beverly. **Ramona the Brave.**

Cleary, Beverly. **Ramona the Pest.** Illus. Louis Darling. Schol Bk Serv 1976.

Ramona, the pesty kid sister of the *Beezus and Ramona* book, is going to kindergarten. Even more of a trial to her older sister than she had been earlier, Ramona keeps the reader delightfully entertained with her escapades.

Cleaver, Vera, and Bill Cleaver. **Grover.** Illus. Frederic Marvin. Lippincott 1970.

No one tells Grover anything during the time of his mother's emergency surgery. No one even hints that she might not recover. Following her suicide and funeral there is a long, empty summer during which neither his grieving father nor the clergyman who fails to answer his questions about life and death can comfort him. Despite the grim situation, the book is not wholly depressing. Comic incidents and dialogue serve to heighten and lighten the story somewhat. And eventually Grover comes to a new understanding of his father.

Cleaver, Vera, and Bill Cleaver. **Lady Ellen Grae.** Illus. Ellen Raskin. Lippincott 1968.

Ellen Grae's love for disarray and telling wild stories prompts Jeff, her divorced father, to send her to Aunt Eleanor's comfortable home in Seattle to learn the "big values." Ellen Grae plots not to leave the small Florida town she loves; once in Seattle, her homesickness nearly brings disaster. At last Jeff sends for her; he has decided that Ellen Grae belongs at home whether she learns to be ladylike or not. Humor and insight into unique child-adult relationships make this a memorable book.

Clifton, Lucille. **Everett Anderson's 1.2.3.** Illus. Ann Grifalconi. HR&W 1977.

Everett Anderson thinks there are many things one can enjoy doing alone, but Mama thinks that one can sometimes be lonely. When Mr. Perry moves nearby and begins to spend a lot of time with Everett's Mama, he tries to understand. It is not easy at first. This is a warm story of the development of a new family.

Clymer, Eleanor. **My Brother Stevie.** Illus. Estal Nesbitt. HR&W 1967.

Annie and Stevie's mother leaves them with their grandmother after the children's father dies. Annie's mother says: "Take care of your brother." But at age eight Stevie throws stones at trains and breaks into candy machines. Grandmother is particularly impatient with Stevie, and whether this is the result of Stevie's behavior or whether his behavior resulted from harsh treatment remains a mystery to Annie. A new teacher at school, Miss Stover, shows Stevie love and understanding which change his life.

Family Relationships 165

Conta, Marcia Maher, and Maureen Reardon. **Feelings Between Kids and Parents.** Illus. Jules M. Rosenthal. Raintree Pubs Ltd 1975.

>In the mind of a child many things in life do not seem fair and are hard to understand. This book explores the emotions involved in relationships between parents and their children and brings about an opportunity for the child to discuss with parents why they act in certain ways and say certain things.

Conta, Marcia Maher, and Maureen Reardon. **Feelings Between Brothers and Sisters.** Illus. Jules M. Rosenthal. Raintree Pubs Ltd 1975.

>In various situations, brothers and sisters share experiences involving play, loneliness, fantasy, illness, and sibling rivalry. Each episode portrays the emotions present when brothers and sisters are interacting.

Dionetti, Michelle. **Thalia Brown and the Blue Bug.**

Estes, Eleanor. **The Moffats.** Illus. Louis Slobodkin. HarBraceJ 1968.

>An episodic plot has been used in developing the warm family relationship of the Moffats—Janey, Joey, Sylvie, and Rufus. The Moffats live with their mother in a yellow house on New Dollar Street in Cranbury, Connecticut, when trolleys and oil lamps are still common. A dance recital, an unexpected train ride, and a Halloween ghost are three of the humorous experiences shared by the four children.

Fox, Paula. **The Stone-Faced Boy.** Illus. Donald A. Mackay. Bradbury Pr 1968.

>At first, Gus assumed the stone-face to shut out unpleasant questions and remarks, but now the stone-face is stuck. He isn't able to react even to pleasant things. He feels more and more removed from other people until he attempts to rescue his sister's dog. His success in this cold, frightening mission gives him confidence to remove the protective "stone-face."

Gates, Doris. **Blue Willow.**

Gordon, Shirley. **The Boy Who Wanted a Family.** Illus. Charles Robinson. Har-Row 1980.

>Michael, who has moved from one foster home to another, is finally adopted, but not into a big family with mother and father and brothers and sisters, as he has always dreamed. Rather, a single woman adopts him. Michael finds that life with his new mom is full of surprises, love, and adventure as the two develop their own special kind of family unit.

Greenfield, Eloise. **Talk About a Family.** Illus. James Calvin. Lippincott 1978.

>A little girl wants to keep her family from breaking up, but finally has to accept the fact that her parents are going to separate. Other children from broken homes will identify with Ginny's feelings.

Harrison, Deloris. **The Bannekers of Bannaky Springs.** Illus. David Hodges. Hawthorn 1970.

>This is more a story of Benjamin Banneker's parents and his grandparents than it is of the great self-taught scientist, astronomer, and mathematician himself. His white grandmother, having completed her seven-year indenture, bought Bannaky, a proud African prince whom she later married. The relationship between Benny and the tiny brave grandmother he called "Big Ma-Ma" is one to be remembered.

Hays, Wilma Pitchford. **Trouble at Otter Creek.**

Herman, Charlotte. **Our Snowman Had Olive Eyes.**

Hirsch, Karen. **My Sister.** Illus. Nancy Inderieden. Carolrhoda Bks 1977.

>This is a warm story told by a child about his sister. His sister is special, and some people don't understand her. Their mother says she is retarded; that her brain was hurt when she was born. This story shows a family's love and understanding for a member who is different.

Holland, Marion. **The Christmas Tree Crisis.** Illus. Leigh Grant. Schol Bk Serv 1977.

>Teddy's great-aunt Abby is spending Christmas with his family. Teddy's Christmas excitement is soon stifled by Aunt Abby who feels that everything should be done the way it was when she was a girl. Unable to find a Christmas tree to suit Aunt Abby, Teddy sets out to find one for himself. After becoming lost, being caught in a storm, and catching a thief, he does manage to enjoy an "old-fashioned" Christmas after all.

Hopkins, Lee Bennett. **Mama.**

Johnson, Annabel, and Edgar Johnson. **The Grizzly.** Schol Bk Serv 1972.

>David's parents have been separated and David fears his father with an unreasoning fear. David remembers his parents fighting over the possibility of his becoming a sissy and he has a premonition that a weekend fishing trip has been planned to be some sort of test for him. On the trip father and son encounter a bear. They become

tentatively close, and David comes to realize how important having a son is to his father.

Klein, Norma. **Confessions of an Only Child.** Illus. Richard Cuffari. Pantheon 1974.

Unhappy about the prospects of losing her status as an only child, a little girl has to cope with new feelings when the baby does not live. By the time another baby arrives, a healthy baby boy, the girl is accepting and actually pleased. The range of emotions of this nine-year-old girl is treated frankly and sensitively.

Lattimore, Eleanor Frances. **Which Way, Black Cat?** Illus. Beatrice Darwin. Schol Bk Serv 1978.

Phoebe's father and brother have moved to the city where her father has a new job. Fearing that he will not send for her, Phoebe decides to try to find her father. A small black cat helps her find her way.

L'Engle, Madeleine. **Meet the Austins.** Vanguard 1960.

The children in the Austin family are four individualists: John wants to be a scientist and is very logical; Vicky is writing a book and wishing she were prettier; Suzy is a sweet, but easily influenced imp; and Rob includes mashed potatoes and dogs in his prayers. When a tragic accident makes her an orphan, Maggy makes five. Not only does the grapefruit not divide evenly into halves with five children, but Maggy is a completely spoiled, inconsiderate child. Mother insists that if one ten-year-old can upset the family solidarity, they aren't as unique a family as they thought they were. After trying (and interesting) episodes, Maggy does become a part of the family.

L'Engle, Madeleine. **A Wrinkle in Time.** YB. Dell 1973.

This unusual story describes the adventures of Meg, brother Charles, and friend Calvin as they experience a tesseract, or wrinkle in time, in their search for Meg's father. The story shows warm family relationships.

Little, Jean. **Home from Far.** Illus. Jerry Lazare. Little 1965.

Jenny's twin brother is killed in an automobile accident and Jenny has the secret feeling that she alone really misses him, that her parents and two younger brothers don't feel the same way. The family takes in two foster children who have an equally difficult time facing the loss of their mother. The normal cycle of family events brings out each child's individual problems in adjustment to a new family pattern.

Lowry, Lois. **Anastasia Krupnik.**

Mann, Peggy. **My Dad Lives in a Downtown Hotel.** Illus. Richard Cuffari. Doubleday 1973.

> Joey feels, as many children do, that it is his fault that his parents are separating even though they try to reassure him that this is not the case. It is painful for him to face the fact that his dad lives somewhere else, but Joey finds that other children in the city also live in single-parent homes and he decides to form a club.

Mann, Peggy. **There Are Two Kinds of Terrible.**

Mathis, Sharon Bell. **The Hundred Penny Box.**

Rawls, Wilson. **Summer of the Monkeys.** LFL. Dell 1977.

> In the late 1800s, Jay Berry Lee leaves Missouri for Oklahoma with his parents and crippled twin sister, Daisy. A poor family, they welcome their grandfather's offer of land. Fourteen-year-old Jay Berry and his dog, Rowdy, like to explore the river bottoms. Seeing a monkey one day sets in motion a series of exciting adventures. A reward that will buy what Jay Berry wants most in his life is the incentive he needs to work hard to capture the elusive monkeys. A generous, loving family helps Jay Berry put his "wants" in perspective.

Rawls, Wilson. **Where the Red Fern Grows.** Bantam 1974.

> Billy Colan, who lives on Cherokee land in the heart of the Ozarks, wants a dog more than anything. He finally is able to buy two coon dogs, Old Dan and Little Ann. By training the brawn of Old Dan and the brains of Little Ann to work as one, he wins the coveted gold cup in the annual coon contest. More important, the three of them, boy and dogs, show a rare love for each other.

Silman, Roberta. **Somebody Else's Child.**

Smith, Robert Kimmel. **Chocolate Fever.**

Steele, William O. **The Perilous Road.** Illus. Paul Galdone. VoyB. HarBraceJ 1965.

> Eleven-year-old Chris Brabson thinks all Yankees are inhuman. He is torn with conflicts when his older brother joins the Union army and his parents seem to approve. Then he hears of a planned Confederate attack on a Union wagon train and his fear of the Yankees

Family Relationships 169

is overshadowed by his loyalty to and his concern for his brother who might be with the supply wagons. Family relationships and loyalties are realistically described.

Steptoe, John. **Stevie.** Illus. by author. Har-Row 1969.

Robert's mother takes care of Stevie while the younger child's mother works. Stevie demands and gets lots of attention, much to Robert's displeasure. Despite the fact that he resents Stevie's intrusion into his life, Robert misses him a great deal when Stevie's family moves away. The impact of the book is very strong and should appeal to any older child who has mixed feelings about sharing love with a younger one.

Taylor, Sydney. **All-of-a-Kind Family.** Illus. Helen John. YB. Dell 1966.

Although they have little money, five little Jewish girls and their parents find life rich and satisfying in New York's Lower East Side.

Watson, Pauline. **A Surprise for Mother.** Illus. Joanne Scribner. P-H 1976.

Ann and Paul must work together and keep the household running when their mother becomes ill. Initially prodded by their father, they begin to do the household tasks and, inspired by their newly acquired responsibility, they begin to think of more things to do, realizing satisfaction in tasks well done.

Wilder, Laura Ingalls. **The Little House** (series). Illus. Garth Williams. Trophy. Har-Row 1973.

These universally loved stories picture the bravery, the hardships, and the joys of pioneer family life in the middle of the nineteenth century. Four of these are *Farmer Boy, Little House in the Big Woods, Little House on the Prairie,* and *On the Banks of Plum Creek.*

Yarbrough, Camille. **Cornrows.**

Yates, Elizabeth. **A Place for Peter.** Illus. Nora S. Unwin. Coward 1952.

Sensing his father's attitude that he is too young to do any of the important tasks on their New Hampshire farm, young Peter works hard to prove his value and earn his father's comradeship. The growth of the new father-son relationship as the boy slowly matures under the challenge is well developed.

Ages 11 to 14

Aaron, Chester. **Better Than Laughter.**

Ames, Mildred. **Without Hats, Who Can Tell the Good Guys?**

Angell, Judie. **Ronnie and Rosey.** Bradbury Pr 1977.

> Veronica "Ronnie" Rachman and Robert Rose are drawn together by a mutual interest in music and drama. When their friendship deepens, their situation is complicated as Ronnie's mother, reacting to her husband's sudden death, sets up rigid rules that are impossible to follow. When Ronnie in desperation runs away from home, her mother realizes Ronnie's need for trust and independence.

Blos, Joan W. **A Gathering of Days: A New England Girl's Journal, 1830-32.**

Blume, Judy. **It's Not the End of the World.** Bradbury Pr 1972.

> Karen loves both her parents very much and cannot understand why they are getting a divorce. She plots to get them together, sure that if they could talk everything would be all right. Eventually she realizes the divorce is inevitable, that both her parents still love her, and that her life is not ruined.

Bridgers, Sue Ellen. **Home Before Dark.**

Clark, Ann Nolan. **All This Wild Land.**

Cleaver, Vera, and Bill Cleaver. **Queen of Hearts.**

Cleaver, Vera, and Bill Cleaver. **Where the Lilies Bloom.** Lippincott 1969.

> When Roy Luther dies it is Mary Call, his fourteen-year-old daughter, who must assume the responsibility for the lives of her brother and two sisters in a broken-down house in the Appalachian Mountains.

Clifton, Lucille. **The Times They Used to Be.**

Conford, Ellen. **And This Is Laura.** Little 1977.

> Laura is thrilled to discover she seems to be able to foresee the future. Now her family, a group of talented overachievers, will be proud of her. When she confesses her feelings, they assure her they are very proud of her, not for her psychic powers, but for her many accomplishments and because she is growing up to be such a fine person.

Family Relationships

Cooper, Gordon. **A Second Springtime.**

Corcoran, Barbara. **The Watching Eyes.** Illus. Bob Dacey. Schol Bk Serv 1974.
> When her mother goes to the mental hospital again, a young girl is left to the mercy of an uncle with a court order for her custody. She fears his abusive ways and manages to run away. She is given refuge by an old woman, her crippled son, and a grandson. At first she distrusts this family, too, but learns to accept them as they care for her.

Crane, Caroline. **Don't Look at Me That Way.**

Danziger, Paula. **Can You Sue Your Parents for Malpractice?** Delacorte 1979.
> Growing up is hard for Lauren Allen. Her older sister is beautiful; her younger sister is a pest. Her teachers seem uncaring and unfair; her classmates tease her. Her parents don't seem to realize she is almost an adult. One gifted teacher, several good friends, and her understanding older sister help her to handle these problems. As she does, she gains maturity and confidence.

Danziger, Paula. **The Cat Ate My Gymsuit.**

Danziger, Paula. **The Pistachio Prescription.** Delacorte 1978.
> Cassie's life is so filled with unbearable situations that she looks for an escape. Sometimes she eats pistachio nuts, at other times she hides behind her asthma. When her parents divorce, she realizes some things can't be changed or escaped and must be accepted as they are.

Doss, Helen. **The Family Nobody Wanted.** Schol Bk Serv 1954.
> This is a true story of a minister's wife who became mother to twelve adopted children—eleven of whom were considered unadoptable because of their mixed parentage: Oriental, American Indian, Spanish American, etc. A theme of accepting each person for his or her personal worth, regardless of background, is inherent in this story of a large, loving family.

Dunlop, Eileen. **Fox Farm.** HR&W 1979.
> Motherless and rejected by his father, Adam resists caring too much for his loving foster family. When he finds an abandoned fox cub he enlists the help of his foster brother, Richard, to help him secretly keep the pet. As they care for the animal, Adam finds himself becoming very attached to Foxy, as well as to Richard and his foster

family. Forced to confide in their parents, the boys are amazed to find that Foxy is a dog, and a welcome addition to their farm.

Engebrecht, P. A. **Under the Haystack.**

Farley, Carol. **The Garden Is Doing Fine.** Illus. Lynn Sweat. Atheneum 1978.

Corrie refuses to accept the fact that her father is dying. She cannot understand how one who loves life so much can leave it. She finally realizes his many questions about how the garden is doing do not refer to the wasted patch in their yard, but to herself and how she will nurture the love and ideas he has "planted" in her.

Fitzhugh, Louise. **Nobody's Family Is Going to Change.**

George, Jean Craighead. **The Cry of the Crow.**

Gerson, Corinne. **Tread Softly.** Dial 1979.

After her parents are killed, eleven-year-old Kitten creates a secret, imaginary family of her own. When she tells a prospective employer about this family, she is caught in a long series of lies. Exposure of these lies results in the loss of her babysitting job, but also brings complete acceptance and understanding of her needs by the grandparents with whom she lives.

Graber, Richard. **A Little Breathing Room.** Har-Row 1978.

Thirteen-year-old Ray Decker feels his family is smothering him. His father is impossible to please and is constantly humiliating him. His little brother, Bud, is solely his responsibility, and his mother is quick to share her unhappiness with him. When Ray and his father have a frightening verbal and physical confrontation, his mother acts to defend her older son and sends him to his grandparents for a "little breathing room."

Greene, Constance C. **Beat the Turtle Drum.** Illus. Donna Diamond. Viking Pr 1976.

With great love, twelve-year-old Kate tells of the last few weeks in the life of her younger sister, Joss, and of the sudden accident which took her life. She tells, also, of the family's attempts to accept Joss' death, both as a group and individually.

Greene, Constance C. **Getting Nowhere.** Viking Pr 1977.

Mark has a lot of anger; enough for the boys at school plus plenty

Family Relationships

for his father and Pat, his new stepmother. There is even anger left for Mark to be mad at himself when he mistreats his brother, Tony, or deliberately defaces Pat's car. All this anger strains relationships among the whole family until an accident helps Mark decide to direct his energy in a more positive way and to quit fighting his loving family.

Greenfield, Eloise. **Sister.** Illus. Moneta Barnett. T Y Crowell 1974.

Sister finds many things in her memory book. She recalls a happier family when her father was alive. She strengthens her black pride by remembering stories told by her grandfather and values learned at her school. The most important thing she discovers is a sense of her own identity which helps to alleviate her fears that she will grow up like her sister, Alberta, whose actions bring so much grief to their mother and whose own eyes cry deep, hidden tears.

Hamilton, Virginia. **Arilla Sun Down.**

Hunt, Irene. **Across Five Aprils.**

Hunt, Irene. **William: A Novel.** Scribner 1977.

Warmth and love keep this unusual family together and help them through some difficult times. When three young black children lose their mother, they join with a young, white, unmarried mother and her baby to form a new and very determined family. Growing up together, they face the challenges of making ends meet, too much work, sickness, and getting along with each other.

Hunter, Mollie. **The Third Eye.**

Hurmence, Belinda. **Tough Tiffany.** Doubleday 1980.

Eleven-year-old Tiffany is the youngest member of her poor, black family, but she is also the toughest and the smartest. She is smart enough to find a way to keep their new bunk beds from being repossessed, and tough enough to help her sister, Dawn, when she is in labor. Tiffany is tough enough to endure the barbs and whims of their granny, and smart enough to get the old lady to accept her help.

Kaplan, Bess. **The Empty Chair.** Har-Row 1978.

Ten-year-old Becky has a hard time accepting the recent death of her mother. She feels her mother's presence so strongly that she feels guilty about her growing love for Sylvia, her new stepmother. When

Kingman, Lee. **The Year of the Raccoon.** Illus. David Grose. HM 1966.

> Joel, fifteen, is the "normal, average" boy in a family with a nine-year-old scientific genius and a brilliant eighteen-year-old pianist. Joel's father, an aggressive, world-traveling businessman, tries to run the lives of his family with the efficiency of a factory. When conflict develops in the family, Joel's "normal" behavior is the responsible force that takes command.

Klein, Norma. **Mom, the Wolf Man and Me.** Pantheon 1972.

> Despite the fact she has never married, Brett's mom is a very satisfactory parent. The two of them have a loving relationship and enjoy their unconventional life until Brett's mom decides to marry. Brett feels her security is threatened but she soon recovers to enjoy her new family.

LeShan, Eda. **What's Going to Happen to Me? When Parents Separate or Divorce.**

Lowry, Lois. **A Summer to Die.**

Mazer, Harry. **The Dollar Man.** Delacorte 1975.

> Marcus finds it easier to idolize his unknown father than to respect the wishes of his single mother with whom he lives and who assumes all responsibility for him. He becomes obsessed with finding and meeting his father. When their meeting occurs, Marcus is forced to re-examine his exaggerated dreams about both his father and himself.

Mazer, Harry. **The War on Villa Street.** Delacorte 1978.

> Willis is always running; he runs as an athlete who loves the sport, he runs from the bully, Robbit Slavin, and his gang, and he runs from an abusive, alcoholic father. After a public humiliation and a severe beating from his father, Willis runs away from home. When he returns, he realizes that he can only stop running by accepting the truth and by using his own strengths to gain independence and freedom.

Mazer, Norma Fox. **A Figure of Speech.**

Meyer, Carolyn. **Amish People: Plain Living in a Complex World.**

Sylvia learns of Becky's fears, she helps her to understand and cope with her emotions. Jewish customs and expressions are a natural part of this story of family life.

Family Relationships 175

Myers, Walter Dean. **It Ain't All for Nothin'.** Viking Pr 1978.

When his grandmother enters a nursing home, Tippy goes to live with Lonnie, his father. Lonnie is unwilling and unable to accept the responsibility of a twelve-year-old son. He continues his life of drugs, alcohol, and crime. Tippy, too, turns to alcohol as his loneliness and fears grow. In an act of emotional self-preservation he reports his father to the police after a robbery. Even so, Tippy continues to hope for a father-son relationship while realizing it can never happen.

Neufeld, John. **Edgar Allen.** S G Phillips 1968.

Told from the viewpoint of a twelve-year-old, this is the story of a white, suburban minister's family that adopts a black baby. The large family is torn apart, faith in the father is jeopardized, and only a shaky truce is finally reached between father and son.

Ney, John. **Ox: The Story of a Kid at the Top.** Little 1970.

Ox is truly a poor little rich kid. Not only is he completely neglected at home, he is smart enough to realize how phony and desperate the people and situations surrounding him really are. His statement: "I'm supposed to be the kid at the top, and if I feel that lousy, how do the kids at the bottom feel? And the kids in the middle? You can hardly think about it," sums up his growing awareness that his life lacks some basic values.

Pascal, Francine. **The Hand-Me-Down Kid.** Viking Pr 1980.

Eleven-year-old Ari is convinced that her family only wants her around to use the clothes, books, toys, etc. outgrown by her older siblings until she learns that youngest children have rights, too. From her new friend Jane, she picks up a few pointers on self-assertiveness and the survival of the youngest.

Peck, Robert Newton. **A Day No Pigs Would Die.** Knopf 1972.

The wisdom and love of his Shaker father guide Rob as he learns the truths of birth, life, and death. Drawing upon these resources he is able to accept the responsibilities of growing up with courage and dignity. Rob sacrifices his pig for the family's food, and realizes this loss is really a stepping stone to accepting the death of his father.

Perl, Lila. **Pieface and Daphne.** Clarion. HM 1980.

Pamela enjoys her position as an only child, and is jealous when her mother invites her troubled, unwanted cousin, Daphne, for an extended stay. Pamela resents sharing her schoolmates and her family with Daphne, but most of all she resents sharing the friendship of Shirley Brummage, a lonely, impoverished old woman. When Shirley suffers a stroke, it is Daphne who knows how to help her, but it is Pamela she wants to see. This crisis helps Pamela to appreciate Daphne and to understand her unfortunate situation.

Pevsner, Stella. **And You Give Me a Pain, Elaine.** Clarion Bk. Seabury 1978.

Andrea's older sister, Elaine, keeps the family in turmoil. Her disruptive behavior steals parental attention from Andrea who feels excluded. Andrea finds the love and support she needs from her brother, Joe. However, when Joe is killed, she is forced to turn to her own inner strength and courage.

Pevsner, Stella. **A Smart Kid like You.** Clarion Bk. Seabury 1975.

Just as Nina is getting used to her parents' divorce, she discovers her father's new wife is her seventh-grade math teacher. When her friends come up with a plan to harass Dolores Beckwith, the other woman, Nina joins in. As she sees her mother happier now, absorbed in a new job, and gets acquainted with her dad's new family, she sees they are both enjoying their new lives. She finally learns to accept things as they are.

Rabe, Berniece. **The Orphans.** Dutton 1978.

When they are orphaned for the second time, Adam knows he must find a permanent home for his twin sister, Little Eva. Some of his plans go astray before he is aided by several courageous women whose strength and determination triumph over their poverty and hard times.

Rodgers, Mary. **Freaky Friday.**

Rogers, Pamela. **The Rare One.**

Sebestyen, Ouida. **Words by Heart.**

Seixas, Judith S. **Living with a Parent Who Drinks Too Much.** Greenwillow 1979.

By helping to identify and clarify the family situation that exists when a parent drinks too much, this book offers encouragement to children living with alcoholics. It tells how others have handled similar situations, suggests possible actions, and tells where to get help.

Sherburne, Zoa. **Stranger in the House.** Morrow 1963.

Family Relationships 177

> Kathleen's comfortable life with her father, brother, and devoted housekeeper is disrupted when her mother returns from a mental hospital after an eight-year absence. The whole family faces the tensions of mixed feelings and uncertain roles; slowly they learn more about the ties that make a group into a family.

Shyer, Marlene Fanta. **Welcome Home, Jellybean.**

Stolz, Mary. **Go and Catch a Flying Fish.** Har-Row 1979.

> Thirteen-year-old Taylor and her brother, Jem, are intelligent and perceptive enough to know their parents' marriage is in trouble. When their mother leaves, Taylor tries unsuccessfully to compensate by concentrating on her interest in birds while Jem collects marine animals. Their personal loss does not keep them from being sensitive to the overwhelming needs of their small brother, B.J., who has no resources for handling the loss of his mother.

Strait, Treva Adams. **The Price of Free Land.**

Taylor, Mildred. **Roll of Thunder, Hear My Cry.**

Wolitzer, Hilma. **Toby Lived Here.** FS&G 1978.

> Toby and Anne are placed in a foster home when their widowed mother is hospitalized. At first, Toby is reluctant to accept their situation and worries about inheriting her mother's mental illness. Later, her joys over her mother's recovery are clouded by thoughts of how much she will miss her new friends and family.

Yep, Laurence. **Child of the Owl.**

Yep, Laurence. **Dragonwings.**

Yep, Laurence. **Sea Glass.**

Ages 14 and Up

Agee, James. **A Death in the Family.** Bantam 1971.

> The father's death shatters the world of the close-knit Follet family. As the point of view shifts the reader sees the tragedy through the eyes of the loving, religious mother, the eyes of the relatives, and the eyes of young Catherine. Most often, however, it is six-year-old Rufus' troubled mind through which we look.

Bond, Nancy. **Country of Broken Stone.**

Bradbury, Bianca. **Where's Jim Now?** HM 1978.

Out of loyalty to her deceased husband, Mrs. Harrison agrees to accept responsibility for her stepson, Jim, when he is released from prison. She and her son, Dave, struggle with this loyalty and their emotions as their attempts to rehabilitate Jim fail and he is again imprisoned and finally killed.

Butterworth, W. E. **LeRoy and the Old Man.** Four Winds. Schol Bk Serv 1980.

To avoid testifying as a material witness, LeRoy leaves Chicago for a home with his grandfather in Mississippi. While there he helps the old man with his shrimp fishing, watches him build a house, and observes the great respect the old black man receives from his southern community. When LeRoy is called back to Chicago, his respect for his grandfather and for his principles helps him find the courage he needs to testify.

Campbell, R. Wright. **Where Pigeons Go to Die.** Rawson Wade 1978.

Hugh and his grandfather share their hobby of racing homing pigeons. Through his teachings about the care and training of the birds, the grandfather shares his philosophy of life with the boy. On the day Hugh releases his first pigeon, his grandfather suffers a massive stroke. Ten-year-old Hugh understands that just as the birds must come home, so must his grandfather. He sneaks the old man out of the hospital in his wagon and takes him home to die.

Capote, Truman. **A Christmas Memory.** Random 1966.

Each year Buddy and Miss Sook bake pecan-rich fruitcakes which they give to their friends. Through the Christmas rituals of cake baking, tree cutting and trimming, gift making and giving, emerges the wonderful relationship which exists between a lonely boy and his elderly cousin.

Collier, James Lincoln. **Give Dad My Best.** Four Winds. Schol Bk Serv 1976.

Fourteen-year-old Jack is forced to assume the responsibility of keeping his family together. His mother is in a mental institution, and his father is an unemployed musician who lacks the maturity to put his family's welfare before his own interests. Although basically honest, Jack steals from his employer to pay the rent. When he overhears his father's plans to dissolve the family, Jack realizes the extent of his father's irresponsibility and the futility of his own actions.

Colman, Hila. **Sometimes I Don't Love My Mother.** Morrow 1977.

> After her father's death, Dallas finds that her mother expects to be her constant companion and to be included in all her social activities. Dallas struggles to cope with grief, with her mother's dependence, and with growing feelings of resentment. Her friend Victor helps Dallas to find the strength to tell her mother that each of them must live her own life.

Cormier, Robert. **After the First Death.** Pantheon 1979.

> When a group of terrorists hijack a bus of children, an Army general is called in to help with the rescue. Using his son, Ben, as a messenger, the general executes a rescue operation and recaptures the bus. When Ben realizes his father had been so sure of his son's breaking point that he planned the maneuver around it, he is completely devastated and commits suicide.

Elfman, Blossom. **The Sister Act.** HM 1978.

> Eighteen-year-old Molly wants to leave home, to live with Jason, her boyfriend, to travel abroad, to be on her own. However, each time she tries to leave she is trapped by a selfish mother who is afraid of life, and by Shera, her younger sister, whose life is a series of crises. Molly struggles to handle their problems and their love, to show her own love for them, and to learn when and how to let go.

Ferry, Charles. **O Zebron Falls!** HM 1977.

> During her senior year, Lukie Bishop works to resolve conflicts in her past, present, and future. She is concerned about her relationship with her father—and about his with her beloved Uncle Farnie. She struggles with her romantic feelings for Harvey and for Billy, the only black in her school. As she understands her past, she is able to make sound choices for the future.

Forbes, Kathryn. **Mama's Bank Account.** Schol Bk Serv 1975.

> Mama, the lovable and resourceful mother of a large Scandinavian family in San Francisco, gives her children a sense of values and a feeling of security. She helps them adjust to new ways while maintaining the old.

Girion, Barbara. **A Tangle of Roots.** Scribner 1979.

> After her mother's sudden death, Beth must learn to cope with her own grief, with her father's new interests, and with her grandmother's hovering attentions. She also has to adjust to her friends' insensitivity

and lack of understanding about her problems. With her father's guidance she gains the strength she needs to adjust to her loss.

Guest, Judith. **Ordinary People.** Viking Pr 1976.

Just back from eight months in a mental hospital following an attempted suicide, Conrad wonders if he is really able to adjust to life at home. His parents also struggle with their emotions as the three of them watch their family disintegrate. His mother leaves, but Conrad and his father, with the aid of a psychiatrist who helps them identify and face their problems, are able to look backward with understanding and forward with confidence.

Guy, Rosa. **Edith Jackson.** Viking Pr 1978.

Orphaned and poverty-stricken, eighteen-year-old Edith tries desperately to keep her family together. One by one they are separated until Edith is left alone. Looking for love, she becomes pregnant by a young drifter who cares nothing for her. Hurt by the many people who think her unimportant, she resolves to make something of herself and to rise above her situation.

Hayes, Kent, and Alex Lazzarino. **Broken Promise.** Putnam 1978.

When Patty is eleven, she and her four younger siblings are abandoned. Homeless and penniless, the five are determined to stay together. They become victims of a bureaucratic society that is equally determined to separate them. For four years the children endure unbelievable hardships before they are permanently reunited and permitted to live as a family.

Hinton, S. E. **Tex.** Delacorte 1979.

Fifteen-year-old Tex knows "love ought to be a simple thing," but his emotions are mixed concerning his over-protective, older brother, Mason; his easy-going, usually absent Pop; and his first girlfriend, Jamie. Learning that Pop is not his real father forces Tex to grow up quickly and helps him to understand the love he and Mason share.

Holland, Isabelle. **Of Love and Death and Other Journeys.** Lippincott 1975.

Meg's life until she was fifteen had been unorthodox but delightful and exciting. She enjoyed traveling around Europe with her mother and her companions. When her unknown father appears in her life, Meg is frightened by the changes she suspects will come. When her mother dies, Meg is devastated until her father helps her to see that the choices in her life can only be hers.

Family Relationships

Johnston, Norma. **The Keeping Days.** Atheneum 1973.

    The members of Tish Sterling's family are a trial to her patience during her fourteenth year. As she struggles to understand them, she begins to respect them as individuals. Coping with her mother's unwelcome pregnancy, her father's worries about finances, her sister Bron's choice of a husband, and her brother's growing rebellion all help Tish to mature and to make some decisions about her own values.

Kerr, M. E. **Dinky Hocker Shoots Smack!** Har-Row 1972.

    Despite all Dinky's attempts to gain her mother's attention, including dressing sloppily, using gross eating habits, and deliberately getting obese, she has to make a desperate and public negative statement to get the love and recognition she is seeking.

Kerr, M. E. **Gentlehands.**

Kerr, M. E. **The Son of Someone Famous.** Har-Row 1974.

    Adam, living in the shadow of a very successful, famous father, feels himself to be of little value. Brenda Belle has doubts about her femininity. These doubts are caused by her low voice and facial hair, and reinforced by her mother's constantly trying to impose her own standards of ladylike conduct on Brenda Belle. These two form a club based on "nothing power" and are amazed at their positive results.

Lee, Harper. **To Kill a Mockingbird.** Popular Lib. 1977.

    A young brother and sister in a small town in Alabama find themselves involved in adults' conflicting values. When their father, a lawyer, defends a black man who has been charged with rape, they are forced to hold their tongues and their fists when taunted by the townspeople and their peers. During the trial, they discover that their father is braver than any other man they know and also much wiser.

Lowry, Lois. **Find a Stranger, Say Goodbye.** HM 1978.

    Natalie Armstrong has a loving adoptive family including her father, mother, younger sister, and grandmother. However, she feels compelled to search for her biological parents. During this search she meets her uncaring mother and her dying grandfather. She also finds answers to many questions about the special relationship between parent and child, and about true familial love.

Mathis, Sharon Bell. **Teacup Full of Roses.** Viking Pr 1972.

Making up stories is Joe's gift, but he is realistic enough to see that his mother's blind love for his drug-wasted brother, Paul, has shut out his talented younger brother, Davy. Joe sacrifices his own plans to help Davy, but tragedy strikes this black family when Davy is killed in a fight caused by Paul.

Murray, Michele. **The Crystal Nights.** Seabury 1973.

Ellie's world is filled with daydreams about moving to town and becoming a famous actress. Her real life is filled with a loving family facing illness, economic pressures, and World War II. When their Jewish relatives arrive from Europe to stay with them, and the two families must learn to live together, Ellie struggles to face reality without losing her dreams.

Peck, Richard. **Father Figure.** Viking Pr 1978.

Since his parents' divorce, seventeen-year-old Jim Atwater has been a father to Byron, his younger brother. They live in New York with a strong matriarchal grandmother and a disturbed mother. When their mother dies, they go to Florida to spend a summer with their father. Byron's adjustment is easy, but the others must re-examine their roles. Mr. Atwater learns to assume the parental role which Jim grudgingly relinquishes while learning to be a son.

Potok, Chaim. **The Chosen.**

Richards, Arlene Kramer, and Irene Willis. **How to Get It Together When Your Parents Are Coming Apart.** McKay 1976.

As a guide for adolescents living through their parents' divorce, this book helps identify problems and offers solutions. Readers are assured their feelings are normal, and given guidance on how to handle their situations. Many helpful suggestions include how to adjust to changing family members, how not to be manipulated, and when and where to get help.

Samuels, Gertrude. **Adam's Daughter.** T Y Crowell 1977.

When Robyn's father is released from prison, she is determined to share his life. To do so she severs her relationships with her mother, stepfather, and boyfriend. Soon after she moves in with her father he violates his parole and is sent back to prison, but Robyn's faith in him is strong as she plans to help him even more when he returns.

Schwartz, Sheila. **Like Mother like Me.** Pantheon 1978.

After her father runs away with one of his students, sixteen-year-old

Jen and her mother face many adjustments. Jen oftens finds herself in the role as the more mature of the two as they help each other with new relationships and with becoming independent people.

Stolz, Mary. **The Edge of Next Year.** Har-Row 1974.

When Orin's mother dies, each member of the family reacts differently. His father turns to alcohol while young Victor spends his time studying animal life. Only fourteen, Orin struggles to hold the family together as he tries to cope with his own grief while resenting the others' adjustment. Eventually he gains some emotional balance in his life and is able to face the future with hope.

Wersba, Barbara. **Run Softly, Go Fast.** Atheneum 1972.

Not just a generation gap but their own interests and values keep Davy and his father apart. Their great love and high expectations for each other interfere with every aspect of their relationship. After his father's death, Davy examines his own grief and guilt and is able to better understand both his father and himself.

West, Jessamyn. **Friendly Persuasion.** Penguin 1981.

The Birdwells, a family of Irish Quakers living in Indiana at the time of the Civil War, typify the gentle ways of Friends. These sketches, with gentle humor, make real the inner tensions, the idiosyncrasies of members of the family, and the strain of going against conventions imposed by the community.

Wilder, Thornton. **Our Town** (in **Three Plays**). Avon 1975.

Life in Grover's Corners, New Hampshire, in the early 1900s is portrayed through the routine daily events and the major moments in the lives of George Gibbs, Emily Webb, and their families. Through them the priceless value of even the most common and routine event becomes clear.

Winthrop, Elizabeth. **Knock, Knock, Who's There?** Holiday 1978.

After Dr. Everett's death, each member of the family mourns in a personal way. Sam finds comfort in memories of his Pa; Michael escapes through outside activities. Ma's grief takes the most disastrous form of all as she retreats into the world of alcohol. Complete honesty among the three of them plus outside help offer guarded hope for the future.

Friendships

Ages 1 to 5

Carle, Eric. **Do You Want to Be My Friend?** Illus. by author. T Y Crowell 1971.

The only words in this picture book are little Mouse's question, "Do you want to be my friend?" After that, every child will create his own story based upon the striking and imaginative pictures.

Emberly, Ed. **A Birthday Wish.** Illus. by author. Little 1977.

A printless book with only pictures tells of a little mouse making a wish for ice cream on his birthday. One can follow the many transactions with others that bring the little mouse his wish for ice cream.

Ages 5 to 8

Anglund, Joan Walsh. **A Friend Is Someone Who Likes You.** Illus. by author. HarBraceJ 1958.

A friend can be a boy or a girl, a cat or a dog. It can be a brook that "lets you sit quietly beside it" when you don't feel like speaking.

Armstrong, William H. **The Tale of Tawny and Dingo.** Illus. Charles Mikolaycak. Har-Row 1979.

Tawny, a strange-looking lamb, is rejected by the flock. Lonely and frightened, he develops a friendship with Dingo, the shepherd's dog. Dingo teaches Tawny that the world is fresh and exciting. During a crisis at the sheepfold, Tawny discovers an unusual courage and leadership that he has learned from Dingo.

Berger, Terry. **Special Friends.**

Calhoun, Mary. **The Witch Who Lost Her Shadow.** Illus. Trinka Hakes Noble. Har-Row 1979.

Shadow, a sleek black cat, is Falinda's closest companion. Falinda is a healing witch, and her black cat follows her everywhere she goes.

Friendships

Then one day Shadow does not come home and Falinda is lonely. When a gray-striped cat appears at the doorstep, Falinda shouts, "I don't want a new friend," but the cat stays there. Finally Falinda makes friends with the cat and decides to call her Homebody. This story can help children see that there is room in life for more than one friend.

Child Study Children's Book Committee at Bank Street, editor. **Friends Are like That! Stories to Read to Yourself.** Illus. Leigh Grant. T Y Crowell 1979.

Experiences common to childhood are told as a child would tell them in this book of stories and poetry by authors like Charlotte Zolotow and John Steptoe.

Clifton, Lucille. **The Boy Who Didn't Believe in Spring.** Illus. Brinton Turkle. Dutton 1973.

King Shabazz and Tony Polito go looking for spring. King has heard that it is just around the corner. They set off down their street and far from home come to a vacant lot where they find spring. A gentle story of friendship between two boys, one Italian and one black who feel the universal lure of spring, is presented.

Cohen, Miriam. **Will I Have a Friend?** Illus. Lillian Hoban. Macmillan 1971.

While Pa is taking him to school for the first time, Jim asks if he will have a friend. Jim goes through the day watching other children playing with their friends until Paul shows him a toy car with doors that really open. Jim promises he will bring his gas pump the next day and goes home secure in the knowledge that he has a friend. The charming illustrations include black and white children and a black teacher.

Croll, Carolyn. **Too Many Babas.** Illus. by author. Har-Row 1979.

Baba is going to make some soup. The neighbors begin dropping by and she asks them to stay for soup. Each neighbor tastes the soup and decides it needs something more. When they finally eat the soup, they discover it tastes terrible. It is an account of four friendly cooks that spoil the meal and how they work the problem out without losing their friendship.

Dauer, Rosamond. **Bullfrog Builds a House.** Illus. Byron Barton. Greenwillow 1977.

Bullfrog and Gertrude find the perfect spot to build a new house.

Gertrude has many ideas to help Bullfrog build a nice house and they furnish it with fine things. But when the house is finished and Gertrude leaves, Bullfrog is not the same. Nothing is the same or as much fun without Gertrude. When he finally realizes this, Bullfrog runs after Gertrude and brings her back to the house they had built together.

Delton, Judy. **Two Good Friends.**

Delton, Judy. **Two Is Company.** Illus. Giulio Maestro. Xerox Ed Pubns 1976.

Bear and Duck are very close friends. Their friendship is interrupted by Chipmunk, who has recently moved into the neighborhood. The two friends react differently to Chipmunk's arrival. Duck wants to include him, and Bear feels his arrival is an intrusion. The dilemma will provoke good discussion.

Fisher, Aileen. **Once We Went on a Picnic.** Illus. Tony Chen. T Y Crowell 1975.

Four friends go to the park for a picnic and find many insects and animals along the way. As they see the different creatures, they feed them, imagining themselves to be insects and animals. When noon comes they realize that they have very little lunch left and one of them asks how they could go on a picnic with crumbs to eat. This beautiful poem sparks the imagination.

Freeman, Don. **Corduroy.** Illus. by author. Puffin 1976.

One day Corduroy, a toy bear who lives in a big department store, discovers he has lost a button. That night he goes to look for it and in his search he sees many strange and wonderful things. He does not find his button, but the following morning he finds what he has always wanted—a friend, Lisa.

Fregosi, Claudia. **Snow Maiden.**

Goffstein, M. B. **Neighbors.** Illus. by author. Har-Row 1979.

When a new neighbor moves in next door, a woman wants to be friends, but every time she intends to ask her neighbor over, she is afraid her house isn't clean enough, or she thinks she must have something special prepared. As a result of her shyness, a whole year passes before they finally really get together.

Gordon, Shirley. **Crystal Is My Friend.** Illus. Edward Frascino. Har-Row 1978.

When Susan's friend Crystal comes to spend the night, Mother suggests to Susan that she must be nice to Crystal because she is a guest. However, Susan discovers that Crystal prefers to play Yahtzee instead of Monopoly and makes brownies with raisins in them. The last straw is when Crystal decides to sleep in Susan's bed. As the girls engage in a midnight talk and decide just because Crystal is a guest is no reason for her to choose what to do, they both learn the meaning of friendship.

Gordon, Shirley. **Crystal Is the New Girl.** Illus. Edward Frascino. Har-Row 1976.

Susan is disappointed when she has to sit next to the new girl in class. She does not want to become friends with this girl Crystal, who repeatedly gets her into trouble for talking in class. Crystal's interesting sense of humor changes Susan's attitude and a new friendship grows.

Hall, Adelaide. **Small Bear Builds a Playhouse.** Illus. Cyndy Szekeres. Garrard 1978.

An easy reading book about Small Bear who decides to build a playhouse. He consults his friends Robin, Woodchuck, Beaver, and Turtle. The kinds of houses they suggest do not appeal to Small Bear. Small Bear builds a lovely house on soft grass under a tree, but he is lonely by himself. Mother Bear points out that his friends are missing. Small Bear learns that it doesn't matter where you build a house as long as there are friends to come and visit.

Hallinan, P. K. **That's What a Friend Is.** Illus. by author. Childrens 1977.

This rhyme about friendship tells what friendship is, what friends do together and for each other, and that to be a friend is very special.

Hickman, Martha Whitmore. **My Friend William Moved Away.** Illus. Bill Myers. Abingdon 1979.

Jimmy's best friend William is moving away. The day after William leaves, Jimmy is sad and lonely. He does not know what to do; he walks to William's old house and sees the empty windows. When he walks to Mary Ellen's house and asks if she can come out to play, he discovers Mary Ellen may be a good friend, too.

Holt, Deloris L. **Good Friends Come in Many Shapes.** Illus. Jay Rivkin. Childrens 1973.

The Geos spend most of their time hating each other. Their shapes are different and they often make fun of each other's looks. But the young Geos have not learned to hate; they enjoy playing together which upsets the parents. The young Geos invite the parents to a field to see the different things that they make by getting together, and soon all differences are forgotten.

Keats, Ezra Jack. **Goggles!** Illus. by author. Macmillan 1971.

This story shows the relationship between Archie and Peter, and the helpfulness of the dog Willie. The pictures themselves could readily tell the story and because there is little narration, a child can progress rather rapidly through the story of the peril of the young boys. Keats' characters are black and the inner city setting provides young readers with a broadening experience.

Keats, Ezra Jack. **A Letter to Amy.** Illus. by author. Har-Row 1968.

Peter is planning a birthday party that at the moment is an "all-boy" party. When he expresses a desire to invite another friend, Amy, he is encouraged to do so by his mother; however, he isn't quite sure the fellows will understand his wanting a girl at the party. Peter begins to build some personal values of his own when he makes a decision, sticks by it, and is very pleased that he did.

Keats, Ezra Jack. **Louie.** Illus. by author. Schol Bk Serv 1975.

Susie and Roberto are putting on a puppet show for the other children. One of the children, Louie, is shy and quiet and has no friends. He becomes very excited over a puppet named Gussie, feels that Gussie is his friend, and speaks for the first time in front of Susie and Roberto. Other shy children may be helped by making puppets about this story.

Keats, Ezra Jack. **Skates!** Illus. by author. Watts 1973.

Two dog friends discover skates in a garbage can. The skates gives the friends a "start" as their legs slip out from under them, and they are propelled uncontrollably down the street, directly into the path of a family of kittens. The dogs rescue the kittens and proceed to skate, giving all the kittens a ride. A feeling of cooperation is stressed. Most of the story is told with pictures, enabling young children to develop their own version.

Klein, Norma. **Visiting Pamela.** Illus. Kay Chorao. Dial 1979.

When Carrie turns five, Mother puts her foot down—"No more visitors if you won't go to their house." So when Pamela invites her on Tuesday, she says yes. They have to ride the crowded school bus to get there and Pamela has a smelly baby brother and a growling dog. Carrie wants to go back home but, by the time Mother arrives, things are taking a turn for the better. Carrie is learning the "give and take" of friendship.

Lobel, Arnold. **Frog and Toad All Year.** Illus. by author. Har-Row 1976.

This book tells of the adventures of two close friends, Frog and Toad. It portrays their love and concern through humorous stories for each season of the year and one story for Christmas. Frog and Toad go sledding together in the winter, watch the spring come in together, eat ice cream together in the summer, rake each other's lawns in the fall, and, of course, want to spend Christmas with each other.

Lobel, Arnold. **Frog and Toad Are Friends.** Illus. by author. Trophy. Har-Row 1979.

The continuing story of the unlikely twosome centers around five tales that show the very caring kind of friendship Frog and Toad possess and that make clear why the two get along so well.

Lobel, Arnold. **Frog and Toad Together.** Illus. by author. Trophy. Har-Row 1979.

Continuing the saga of this rib-tickling twosome are five tales. In one of them, Toad makes a list of things to do. Number one on the list is "wake up." This book should wake up the reluctant reader.

McNulty, Faith. **Mouse and Tim.** Illus. Marc Simont. Har-Row 1978.

This is a warm story of a boy and his pet. Mouse is a baby when Tim rescues him. For four months they are together. The book is an account of how each perceives the other—in different ways.

Milord, Sue, and Jerry Milord. **Maggie and the Goodbye Gift.** Illus. by authors. Lothrop 1979.

At first Maggie did not know what transferred meant, but it didn't take long to find out transferred means leaving your friends and moving to a faraway place where there are only strangers. The family is lonely in their new home among strangers until Maggie opens the goodbye gift. The gift is an electric can opener. She opens can after can of food and the only way to get rid of all the food is to invite the neighbors over. After the dinner party the family is no longer lonely in the new place.

Sharmat, Marjorie Weinman. **Thornton the Worrier.** Illus. Kay Chorao. Holiday 1978.

Thornton, the rabbit, worries about everything—toothaches, bad weather, mosquito bites, hunger, enemies, and fleas. He doesn't even have time to watch his favorite television program for worrying. One day he meets an old man whose house is leaning over the edge of a mountain. The house makes threatening noises, and Thornton becomes more and more anxious until the old man shows him another way of viewing things.

Steig, William. **Amos and Boris.** Illus. by author. Puffin 1977.

Amos, a mouse, and Boris, a whale, become great friends when Boris rescues Amos from drowning. As Boris rides Amos toward shore on his back, they share their innermost secrets. They part promising never to forget each other and vowing to come to each other's aid should the need arise. Many years later Amos is able to repay Boris's kindness when the latter is tossed on shore by a tidal wave and stranded on a beach. The book points up the value of true and lasting friendship.

Stren, Patti. **Hug Me.** Illus. by author. Har-Row 1977.

Elliot Kravitz is lonely and wants one thing—a hug from a friend. A hug is a special thing, particularly when one happens to be a porcupine. During his search for a friend to hug, Elliot tries to hug telephone poles, parking meters, and even traffic lights, but none of those things can hug back and be a friend. Finally Elliot meets another porcupine who is in search of a hug too.

Thomas, Ianthe. **Hi, Mrs. Mallory!**

Turkle, Brinton. **Thy Friend, Obadiah.** Illus. by author. Viking Pr 1969.

Who wants a sea gull following him around like a pet? A boy named Obadiah who lives in Old Nantucket has just such a problem. The silly bird annoys Obadiah every day, and at night the gull roosts outside his bedroom window. One very cold day when Obadiah needs a friend, the bird is gone and the boy misses it. The gull shows up later with a fish hook caught in its beak. After Obadiah has removed the hook, he discovers it is pleasant to make a real friend, and both the boy and the gull are happy. The story can help children to realize that we all need friends.

Udry, Janice M. **Let's Be Enemies.** Illus. Maurice Sendak. Schol Bk Serv 1969.

Friendships 191

James and John have a rather superficial argument because, as John says, "James always wants to be the boss." The quarrel is resolved simply, and they continue their friendship. Sendak's illustrations are especially effective in portraying the emotions of the two boys, and one notes a change in the weather which corresponds to the change in the feelings of James and John.

Vigna, Judith. **The Hiding House.** Illus. by author. A Whitman 1979.

Friendship is challenged when Mary Beth's best friend, Barbara, befriends the new girl in the neighborhood. Mary Beth has difficulty dealing with Barbara's new friendship and seeks ways of hurting Barbara. It's not until Mary Beth hears Barbara telling her new friend that she thought she was Mary Beth's best friend that Mary Beth realizes that friendships aren't exclusive, they grow to include others.

Watts, Marjorie Ann. **Crocodile Medicine.** Illus. by author. Warne 1978.

Crocodile is always complaining about a pain, but no one takes him seriously. He lives next door to the hospital where Julie has been for some time. One day Julie tells Giraffe, Crocodile's friend, that all the people in the hospital have pains and suggests that Crocodile join them. He makes life on the children's ward more fun, and Julie loves having him there.

Weil, Lisl. **Walt and Pepper.** Illus. by author. Parents 1974.

Walt, a dog, and Pepper, a cat, are enemies. They say mean things to each other, growling and snarling at each other. However, when Walt goes away, Pepper misses him and is glad when he comes back.

Zolotow, Charlotte. **The Hating Book.** Illus. Ben Shecter. Har-Row 1969.

A little girl tells of several instances of being rebuffed by her friend, ending with the comment, "I hated my friend." Finally, at the urging of her mother, she goes to see the friend and asks her why she's been so "rotten." The answer is that "Sue said Jane said you said I looked like a freak." The actual remark had been that she looked "neat." The point of the book is clear as the two friends make plans to play together the following day.

Zolotow, Charlotte. **My Friend John.** Illus. Ben Shecter. Har-Row 1968.

A brief but basic explanation of the friendship of two young boys is presented. Their knowledge of each other's strengths and weaknesses is stressed, and the book concludes with the idea that they like "everything that's important" about each other.

Ages 8 to 11

Ames, Mildred. **What Are Friends For?** Scribner 1978.

> Amy's first friend in her new school is Michelle with whom she shares the problems of having recently divorced parents. Later Amy is upset by Michelle's bitterness, by her selfishness, and by her dishonesty. When Michelle steals a valuable antique doll for Amy's collection, Amy realizes that true friendship demands that she help Michelle by telling those adults who can guide her.

Bawden, Nina. **The Runaway Summer.** Puffin 1976.

> Mary, whose parents are getting a divorce, is sent to live with Grandfather and Aunt Alice in their English seaside home. Though resentful and determined to act hateful, Mary can't help being friends with Simon, who seems to believe her elaborate lies about her family. The arrival of Krishna, an Indian boy brought illegally into the country, leads Mary and Simon to cement their friendship in their efforts to hide him from the police. When Krishna's sudden illness forces them to get help, Mary begins to see that the only way to handle problems is to face them.

Berger, Terry. **A Friend Can Help.**

Blume, Judy. **Otherwise Known as Sheila the Great.**

Bradbury, Bianca. **The Young Loner.**

Bulla, Clyde Robert. **Last Look.** Illus. Emily Arnold McCully. T Y Crowell 1979.

> Rhoda is eager to become friends with Fran, Audrey, and Monica. Fran and Audrey openly rebuff Rhoda, but Monica acts friendly without truly accepting her. Rhoda senses this and draws Monica into a dangerous midnight meeting. When Rhoda is sent away, Monica realizes she failed to understand Rhoda's need for friendship, and resolves to be more open in the future.

Byars, Betsy. **After the Goat Man.**

Calhoun, Mary. **Honestly, Katie John.** Illus. Paul Frame. Har-Row 1963.

> Katie John, a tomboyish sixth grader, announces that she hates boys after being teased about them by some of her girl friends. Edwin, her special friend, overhears her and terminates their friendship. Katie John has several unhappy experiences as she attempts to understand

Friendships 193

her own feelings. At last she grows in maturity and once again establishes a friendship with Edwin.

Clymer, Eleanor. **My Brother Stevie.**

Conta, Marcia Maher, and Maureen Reardon. **Feelings Between Friends.** Illus. Jules M. Rosenthal. Raintree Pubs Ltd 1974.

Children experiencing mistakes, fights, disappointments, displays of anger, or apprehension express their feelings in given situations. Each time, a friend gives some comforting words to make the situation look brighter. Readers discover that friends, adults or children, are helpful when we feel disgruntled or unhappy.

Delton, Judy. **Lee Henry's Best Friend.** Illus. John Faulkner. A Whitman 1980.

This story offers a brief but simple explanation of how a young boy views friendship. Lee Henry believes you can only have one best friend, which to him is the only kind of friend to have. When Lee Henry's best friend moves away and a new boy moves in, Lee Henry begins to realize that it is possible to have more than one friend.

Ewing, Kathryn. **A Private Matter.** Illus. Joan Sandin. Schol Bk Serv 1975.

Marcy's parents are divorced and she is a very lonely nine-year-old. When the Endicotts, a retired couple, move in next door, Marcy finds a very special friend in Mr. Endicott; she finds strength in their friendship. When much sadness comes to the Endicott home and Mr. Endicott moves away, Marcy must learn to go on alone without her special friend.

Greene, Constance C. **A Girl Called Al.** Illus. Byron Barton. YB. Dell 1977.

Written in an amusing first-person style, this is the story of a friendship between two seventh-grade girls. Al (short for Alexandra) and the unnamed narrator of the story learn much from Mr. Richards, the elderly assistant superintendent of their apartment house, as he helps build their self-confidence and reveals his own ability to accept life's problems as well as its joys.

Hansen, Joyce. **The Gift-Giver.** Clarion. HM 1980.

Ten-year-old Doris lives in the ghetto, but has a loving family and teachers and parents who set forth important values in her life. In fact, Doris believes her life is too protected and restricted until Amir moves into the neighborhood. Amir shows her that she does not have to be exactly like everyone else and helps Doris and others in their class to develop their own special talents. The author gives a non-stereotypical view of life in a ghetto.

Konigsburg, E. L. **Jennifer, Hecate, Macbeth, William McKinley, and Me, Elizabeth.** Illus. by author. Atheneum 1967.

When you're lonely and bored as Elizabeth is, feet clad in Pilgrim shoes dangling from a tree and attached to a strange girl can mean the beginning of a friendship. Jennifer claims to be a witch and accepts Elizabeth as an apprentice. Secret meetings on Saturday, forbidden foods, watermelon on New Year's Day, and a very special toad acquired in the middle of winter are a few of the unusual elements in this story of a growing friendship. Both Elizabeth and Jenny grow into maturity when they put off the pretense of being witches and accept each other for what they are.

Krumgold, Joseph. **Onion John.** Illus. Symeon Shimin. Apollo Eds 1970.

Andy, twelve, and his father, a small town hardware dealer, are in conflict about Andy's vocational and educational plans and about his friendship with Onion John, the town's odd-job man. Onion John, a middle-European immigrant who has never learned English, lives close to nature and finds in the supernatural answers to all his questions. A high spot comes when the two Andy loves best, his father and Onion John, begin to understand each other.

Little, Jean. **Take Wing.** Illus. Jerry Lazar. Little 1968.

Shy, sensitive Laurel is unable to make friends because of the demands made on her time by her seven-year-old retarded brother James. When her mother is hospitalized and an aunt comes to run the household, the family acknowledges for the first time that James is "different." The family rallies and demonstrates that love and courage can help the handicapped boy while Laurie's determination wins her a friend.

Orgel, Doris. **Next Door to Xanadu.** Illus. Dale Payson. Har-Row 1969.

Patricia Malone is going to be ten years old soon, but she still has no special friend. Her two great wishes are that she find a friend and that she be thin so that Bill Wexler and Charlie Kriefer won't call her Fatsy Patsy any more. One day when Patricia comes home from school she finds that a family has moved in next door with a girl her own age. Friendship with Dorothy begins to change Patricia's life.

Friendships

Paterson, Katherine. **Bridge to Terabithia.** Illus. Donna Diamond. T Y Crowell 1977.

After practicing all summer to be the fastest runner in school, Jesse is beaten by the new girl, Leslie Burke. As Leslie and Jesse develop a beautiful friendship, she broadens his world and they share an imaginary kingdom, Terabithia. When Leslie is accidentally drowned, Jesse's growth continues as he copes with this tragedy by drawing on the resources Leslie has helped him to develop.

Sachs, Marilyn. **A Secret Friend.** Doubleday 1978.

After years of being best friends, Wendy suddenly wants nothing to do with Jessica. Hurt and desperate, Jessica contrives a plan to make Wendy jealous. She writes a series of notes to herself signing them "A. S. F." for a secret friend. Jessica is almost too busy trying to regain Wendy's friendship to recognize the overtures of Barbara who really wants to be her friend and who signs her notes "A. R. F." for a real friend.

Sivers, Brenda. **The Snailman.** Illus. Shirley Hughes. Little 1978.

To the villagers the snailman is an eccentric outcast; to eleven-year-old Timothy he is a friend who aids him when the other boys tease him or when his parents quarrel. When the snailman and his dog are falsely accused of chasing cattle, Timothy is able to repay his friendship by exposing the real culprit.

Stolz, Mary. **Cider Days.** Har-Row 1978.

When her best friend moves away, Polly is too preoccupied with her loneliness to offer more than very slight attempts to make Consuelo, the new girl in the fifth grade, feel welcome. With the help of Polly's loving family and Consuelo's dynamic mother, the two girls develop a special friendship.

Stolz, Mary. **A Dog on Barkham Street.** Illus. Leonard Shortall. YB. Dell 1968.

Edward Frost's life has one constant irritation—his neighbor, Martin. To Edward, Martin is simply a bully to be alternately avoided and teased. With his father's "encouragement," Edward is made aware of Martin's needs and begins to understand another person's problems.

Stolz, Mary. **Ferris Wheel.**

White, E. B. **Charlotte's Web.** Illus. Garth Williams. Har-Row 1952.

> Fern, a little girl; Wilbur, a runt pig; and Charlotte, a spider, form a fast friendship. Wilbur becomes distraught when he discovers he is to be killed. The devoted spider spins messages about Wilbur into her web in order to save his life. People come to see the messages and marvel at Wilbur. As a final act of love and friendship, Charlotte accompanies Wilbur to the fair even though she knows her own life is nearly over. Her final message and Wilbur's ribbon assures his living. Wilbur's final act of love and friendship is to care for Charlotte's egg sac so her children can survive.

Wrightson, Patricia. **A Racecourse for Andy.** Illus. Margaret Horder. HarBraceJ 1968.

> The boys in the neighborhood play with Andy and protect him even though he is not able to keep up with them intellectually. They are furious with an old tramp who takes Andy's money and pretends he has "sold" him the racetrack. The protective allegiance of a group of friends distinguishes this story of a slow-learning child.

Yolen, Jane. **The Transfigured Hart.**

Ages 11 to 14

Bosse, Malcolm J. **The 79 Squares.**

Bridgers, Sue Ellen. **All Together Now.** Knopf 1979.

> When Casey Flanagan comes to stay with her grandparents her special friend is Dwayne Pickens, a man whose mind is still that of a boy. As they share a summer of baseball, stock car races, and bicycle rides, Casey comes to understand Dwayne, to appreciate him, and to protect him. When Dwayne's happiness is threatened by being institutionalized, Casey works with her family and her town to save him.

Burch, Robert. **Wilkin's Ghost.** Illus. Lloyd Bloom. Viking Pr 1978.

> Wilkin is not really unhappy with his life on the farm, he is just restless and longs to visit other places. He sees his chance to run away with Alex, an older boy, whom he befriends and defends when Alex is accused of stealing. At the very last moment, Wilkin finds that Alex has used him and betrayed his friendship, but does not abandon his dreams of travel, he just postpones them.

Burnford, Sheila. **The Incredible Journey.** Illus. Carl Burger. Bantam 1977.

Friendships 197

A very old bull terrier, a young Labrador retriever, and a Siamese cat make an incredible journey through 400 miles of Canadian wilderness to return to their old home. This remarkably well-written and absorbing story is told with great simplicity and understanding. The friendship and group feeling enjoyed by the three is a rare experience for children and young adults to share.

Callen, Larry. **Sorrow's Song.** Illus. Marvin Friedman. Little 1979.

Sorrow is a young mute girl who communicates clearly with her expressive eyes and with her actions. When she finds an injured crane, Sorrow knows that the beautiful bird must be protected while it heals and then set free. The many people who want to catch the crane for their various selfish reasons are no match for this determined girl and her friend, Pinch, who develop a close relationship with the bird.

Cunningham, Julia. **Come to the Edge.**

Distad, Audree. **Dakota Sons.**

Engel, Beth Bland. **Ride the Pine Sapling.** Har-Row 1978.

It is Hallie, their family's housekeeper, who is Ann's best friend during the Depression summer when her daddy loses his job, her mother experiences a difficult pregnancy, and her grandmother dies of cancer. These trials, plus a scare from an evil, itinerant preacher and the burning of the homes in the black community, strengthen the love between a young, white girl and an old, black woman.

Garrigue, Sheila. **Between Friends.**

Gilbert, Harriett. **Running Away.**

Greene, Constance C. **I Know You, Al.** Illus. Byron Barton. Viking Pr 1975.

Al and her friend, who narrates the story, share the joys and trials of growing up. Together they worry about their physical development, about Al's mother's new boyfriend, and about her father's plan to remarry. Their personalities complement each other perfectly as the calm narrator enjoys and stabilizes the more exuberant Al.

Greene, Constance C. **Your Old Pal, Al.** Viking Pr 1979.

Al has a hard time as she anxiously awaits two letters, an invitation from her father and a personal letter from a boy. Also, she is jealous of Polly who has been invited for an extended stay by Al's best friend. All these pressures strain the relationship between Al and her friend, but when reconciliation comes it brings expressions of appreciation for true friendship.

Hayes, Sheila. **The Carousel Horse.** Nelson 1978.

Fran Davis is upset when she learns her mother has accepted a summer position as cook for the wealthy Fairchilds. She sees a wide gap between herself, the servant's child, and Andrea Fairchild. During the summer she learns that Andrea's many material possessions, including the carousel horse, do not keep her from being a lonely girl who wants and needs Fran to be her friend.

Hunt, Irene. **No Promises in the Wind.** Tempo. G&D 1973.

At the height of the Depression, fifteen-year-old Josh Grondowski leaves home to escape a harsh, irritable father. His travels looking for work force him to assume adult responsibilities. When he finally returns home, he has come to understand the other people better and has even learned to love his father.

Kidd, Ronald. **That's What Friends Are For.** Nelson 1978.

Gary and Scott share some terrific times during their thirteenth year. Both of them are interested in chess, folk music, and science. When Scott develops leukemia, Gary reacts by withdrawing from a situation he cannot accept. After Scott's death, Gary searches for the deficiency in himself which made him fail Scott when he needed him the most.

Mark, Jan. **Thunder and Lightnings.** Illus. Jim Russell. T Y Crowell 1976.

Andrew is interested in racing cars; Victor likes airplanes. Andrew's family is cheerful and loving; Victor's is tense and cold. Yet these two develop a close friendship raising guinea pigs and watching the Lightning airplanes at a nearby base.

Neufeld, John. **Lisa, Bright and Dark.** S G Phillips 1969.

An unusual story of how three teenage girls attempt to help their friend Lisa, whose parents cannot be convinced that she needs psychiatric treatment. Tangled relationships and mounting frustrations finally frighten the parents into taking action.

Swearingen, Martha. **If Anything.** Elsevier-Nelson 1980.

An intriguing ghost story, this is actually a love story about two young spirits whose untimely deaths cannot quite quell their driving energy. Poignant, but also amusing episodes are portrayed.

Taylor, Theodore. **The Cay.** Avon 1970.

> When Phillip and his mother are on their way from Curacao to the United States, their ship is torpedoed. Phillip is washed upon a cay with only one other survivor, Timothy, an old West Indian. Phillip, who has been prejudiced against blacks, now finds himself blinded and completely dependent upon Timothy. They develop a beautiful relationship as Timothy not only takes care of Phillip, but prepares him to survive alone after Timothy's death. The teachings of Timothy continue to guide Phillip after his rescue.

Wersba, Barbara. **The Dream Watcher.** Atheneum 1968.

> Anti-hero Albert Scully doesn't seem to fit in anywhere, either at home or at school. Thoroughly convinced that he is destined for failure in life, he meets an eccentric, aging actress who teaches him that there is nothing wrong with being different.

Weston, John. **The Boy Who Sang the Birds.**

Winthrop, Elizabeth. **Marathon Miranda.**

Ages 14 and Up

Baker, Will. **Chip.** HarBraceJ 1979.

> As soon as Chip drifts into town, Mutt knows they are going to be friends. The boy and the man learn from each other as their friendship develops. When Chip is accused of murder, Mutt sets out to prove his friend's innocence by exposing the real murderer.

Butterworth, W. E. **Under the Influence.** Four Winds. Schol Bk Serv 1979.

> During their senior year, Allen and Keith are drawn together when they are unjustly thrown off the football team. As their friendship progresses, Allen grows more and more alarmed about Keith's drinking. Keith's reaction to all pressures is to drink even more heavily. After several tragic auto accidents and a legal battle, Keith is so broken he retreats psychologically and is placed in a mental hospital. Allen is powerless to help his friend.

Glass, Frankcina. **Marvin and Tige.** St. Martin 1977.

> Middle-aged, white, alcoholic Marvin Stewart and eleven-year-old, black, orphaned Tige Jackson are drawn into a close relationship almost against their wills. Each knows better than to care too much for someone else; yet each knows the needs of a terrible loneliness. As they help each other survive physically, they grow emotionally

dependent upon each other. Together they share the problems of daily life, illness, and separation, as well as the joys of true friendship.

Greene, Bette. **Summer of My German Soldier.** Bantam 1978.

Completely rejected by her parents and peers, Patty Bergen, a young Jewish girl, is desperate for acceptance from others. Only her grandparents and Ruth, the family's black housekeeper, give her the love she needs. When she aids an escaped German P.O.W. the consequences are disastrous. From these experiences Patty gains a sense of self-worth by identifying and following her own values.

Guy, Rosa. **The Friends.**

Hanlon, Emily. **It's Too Late for Sorry.** Bradbury Pr 1978.

Influenced by his old friend Phil, Kenny is deliberately cruel to Harold, a retarded boy who values his friendship. This action causes Kenny to lose Rachel, the girl he loves, his self-respect, and the respect of others. His guilt is compounded by his knowledge that he and Phil had long ago lost the bonds of friendship.

Holland, Isabelle. **The Man Without a Face.** Lippincott 1972.

Oppressed by life as the only male in the household, fourteen-year-old Charles decides to spend his summer cramming to pass the entrance exams for boarding school. Justin, a badly scarred recluse, reluctantly agrees to tutor Charles, but only on his own terms. He proves a hard taskmaster who helps Charles with far more than his lessons—he teaches Charles about courage and responsibility, about compassion and friendship, and about love.

Johnston, Norma. **If You Love Me, Let Me Go.** Atheneum 1979.

When her friend Lisa moves to Glenwood, Allison is thrilled. She and Lisa have so much to share—their family problems, their worries about boys, and their school activities. Their close friendship is so comforting and so consuming to Allison that she is hurt and surprised when Lisa begins to pull away, until Lisa shows her that love sometimes means letting go.

Lee, Mildred. **Sycamore Year.** Lothrop 1974.

Anna's friendship is particularly important to Wren because she is her best friend in a new town. Wren is distressed when Anna begins to prefer the company of her boyfriend Tony. When Anna becomes pregnant, she is deserted by Tony and again turns to Wren who proves her friendship as she suffers with Anna and agonizes when she feels her actions have betrayed Anna by exposing her condition.

LeGuin, Ursula K. **Very Far Away from Anywhere Else.** Atheneum 1978.

Seventeen-year-old Owen is bright, sensitive, and knows what he wants from life—college at Massachusetts Institute of Technology, a scientific career, and a friend with whom to share ideas. That special friend is Natalie, who is also intelligent and dedicated to becoming a composer. Their intellectual relationship progresses to one that includes emotional and physical attractions. They react individually, ultimately retaining their goals and their perspective.

Orgel, Doris. **The Devil in Vienna.** Dial 1978.

In Vienna in 1938, Inge Dornenwald, a young Jewish girl, and Lieselotte Vessely, a member of the Hitler Youth, find their long friendship threatened by the wartime climate. Yet outside pressures, parental objections, separation, and even danger cannot diminish the special relationship between these two friends. In the end, Lieselotte is able to help Inge and her family escape to Yugoslavia.

Richards, Arlene Kramer, and Irene Willis. **Boy Friends, Girl Friends, Just Friends.** Atheneum 1979.

Where to find friends, how to make friends, and how to keep them are all discussed in this guide for teenagers concerned about their relationships with others. Fictionalized scenes are used to illustrate possible situations and solutions. No specific advice is offered, just suggestions and possibilities.

Steinbeck, John. **Of Mice and Men.** Bantam 1970.

The painful responsibilities of friendship are explored in this tragic story of the relationship between two migratory workers: George and Lennie. Lennie is a huge man of great strength and simple mind. Caring for Lennie becomes increasingly difficult for George. Lennie loves small animals, but because he is unable to control his strength, he often maims or kills them. When it is the matter of a girl's death rather than an animal's, George mercifully kills Lennie to save him from a mob. The book is also available as a play.

Thiele, Colin. **Fire in the Stone.**

Tolan, Stephanie S. **The Last of Eden.** Warne 1980.

Unhappy at home, Michelle considers her boarding school an Eden. She is especially dependent upon her friendship with her roommate

Marty. When a jealous classmate spreads rumors about a homosexual relationship between Marty and her art teacher, Michelle defends Marty only to find that Marty is indeed having such a relationship with another student. Michelle struggles to maintain her equilibrium as she copes with disillusionment, the loss of her friend, and coming to terms with her own feelings.

Walsh, Jill P. **Fireweed.** Avon 1972.

In London, during the blitz of 1940, a fifteen-year-old runaway who calls himself Bill meets Julie, another runaway. They cast their lot together and are so jubilant about being on their own that their friendship is a happy one, nearly untouched by the grim details of war around them. To escape detection, they move into a bombed-out cellar, where Julie is buried alive in fallen rubble. She survives, and Bill finally sees her reunited with her family. He realizes that their special feeling for one another, born of crisis, must inevitably end.

Wangerin, Walter, Jr. **The Book of the Dun Cow.**

Westheimer, David. **My Sweet Charlie.** Sig Classics. NAL 1965.

Marlene Chambers, seventeen, is the epitome of a southern bigot. Forced to leave home when her father discovers she is pregnant, Marlene seeks sanctuary in a deserted summer house. This haven is soon invaded by Charles Roberts, an educated northern black man who is fleeing the law after killing a man in a fight. Slowly their antagonism turns to mutual liking and respect, and Marlene comes to view Charles as a friend.

Wilkinson, Brenda. **Ludell and Willie.**

Peer Relationships

Ages 1 to 5

Burningham, John. **The Friend.** Illus. by author. T Y Crowell 1976.

A young child describes his relationship with his friend Arthur. Sometimes he doesn't like Arthur, so Arthur goes home. Although he has other friends, Arthur is his best friend.

Stubbs, Joanna. **Happy Bear's Day.** Illus. by author. Sackville Pr 1978.

Baby Bear's mother wanted Baby Bear to be like all the other bears: to love going to parties, to enjoy school and playing with friends. But Baby Bear doesn't enjoy being with others; he enjoys being alone. His mother plans a party, which works in a surprising way to bring Baby Bear and the other little bears together in friendship.

Ages 5 to 8

Amoss, Berthe. **The Very Worst Thing.** Illus. by author. Parents 1972.

Thomas is the new boy in school. All the other kids know each other and have the right book, while Thomas has to share with a girl! All the kids have sandwiches for lunch, while Thomas has a hard boiled egg. At recess, the popular game is football—Thomas is good at baseball. Finally Thomas discovers another new boy and they become friends. Most children want to belong and be part of the group. Thomas' survival of this difficult situation will be a comfort to children.

Bemelmans, Ludwig. **Madeline.** Illus. by author. Puffin 1977.

The story of Madeline's individuality comes through the rhythmic verse in a steady beat. A scar from an appendectomy makes her the envy of all her peers.

Clifton, Lucille. **Everett Anderson's Friend.** Illus. Ann Grifalconi. HR&W 1976.

Everett Anderson wonders who is going to move into Apartment

13A. The new neighbor turns out to be Maria and a family of girls. Everett is disappointed, but he finds that Maria can run and win at ball. He also learns, when he loses a key and wins a friend, that things have a way of balancing out.

Conaway, Judith. **I'll Get Even.**

Duvoisin, Roger. **Petunia's Treasure.**

Fremlin, Robert. **Three Friends.** Illus. Wallace Tripp. YB. Dell 1977.

Three friends, Pig, Squirrel, and Cat, are all different. Pig decides to move but Cat and Squirrel come to the rescue and show Pig that things aren't so bad and convince Pig to stay. The three friends prove that you can overlook the bad things if you love each other.

Hallinan, P. K. **Where's Michael?**

Hoff, Syd. **The Littlest Leaguer.** Illus. by author. Schol Bk Serv 1976.

Harold is the smallest player in the little league. He unsuccessfully tries out for various positions and becomes very discouraged when he must sit on the bench at each game and endure the teasing of his peers. During the championship game, the star player injures his foot and is unable to play. Harold is called to bat, and he devises a scheme to make his small size an asset for his team.

Mack, Nancy. **Tracy.**

Moncure, Jane Belk. **A New Boy in Kindergarten.** Illus. by Dan Siculan. Childs World 1976.

David enters a new classroom with strange faces. He tries to become involved in the different activities, but his attempts at being accepted are ignored until he helps a classmate who is having difficulty. Now he has a friend, and together they are able to devise a plan which assures them of everyone's acceptance.

Riley, Susan. **Angry: What Does It Mean?**

Vigna, Judith. **Anyhow, I'm Glad I Tried.** Illus. by author. A Whitman 1978.

A little girl tries to figure out why classmate Irma Jane is so mean. With the help of her mother, she tries to be nice to Irma Jane by giving her a small birthday cake. Irma Jane sarcastically accepts it, but the little girl leaves before she knows if Irma Jane even cares. She leaves, though, feeling good about herself, knowing that at least she tried.

Peer Relationships 205

Waber, Bernard. **Ira Sleeps Over.**

Yashima, Taro. **Youngest One.** Illus. by author. Viking Pr 1962.

> It's not always easy to make new friends. Bobby tries many times to see who lives on the other side of the large hedge growing by his house, but when Momo comes near to speak, Bobby backs away and closes his eyes. Only after many tries does Bobby open his eyes to meet the smiling face of a new friend.

Ages 8 to 11

Allen, Alex B. **Basketball Toss-Up.**

Berger, Terry. **Being Alone, Being Together.** Photographs by Heinz Kluetmeier. Raintree Pubs Ltd 1975.

> When a boy is by himself, he can pretend, explore, and think without having to share experiences with others. Sometimes though, he does not want to be alone, so he seeks company. He and his friend play games, exchange ideas, and are with other friends. Being alone and being with friends both can be satisfying and rewarding experiences.

Biesterveld, Betty. **Run, Reddy, Run.** Illus. E. Harper Johnson. Nelson 1962.

> Eleven-year-old Henrilee Fenton, daughter of a migrant worker in Ohio, finds Reddy, a baby fox that she wants desperately to domesticate and keep as a pet. She has numerous conflicts with Jiggers, a boy from a neighboring farm, who belittles her because her father is a migrant worker. Jiggers also threatens to kill Reddy because he thinks the fox is killing his family's chickens. The two children eventually learn to get along, the fox is released, and all ends well.

Blume, Judy. **Blubber.** Bradbury Pr 1974.

> This story is about peer group cruelty. As Linda is giving an oral report on whales to her fifth-grade class, Caroline sends a note to Jill stating that "Blubber" is a good nickname for Linda because of her size. The note accidentally gets passed around. This causes several classmates to see how far they can go in doing cruel things to Linda. Suddenly, the tide is turned, and Jill is the target. Her mother's advice to know when to "laugh at herself" helps her resolve the situation.

Byars, Betsy. **The 18th Emergency.**

Christopher, Matt. **Glue Fingers.**

Christopher, Matt. **Power Play.**

Cleary, Beverly. **Otis Spofford.** Illus. Louis Darling. Morrow 1953.

> This humorous book is an excellent one for reading aloud. Otis, a mischievous, fun loving boy, is always getting in and out of trouble. His mother, a dancing teacher, is busy and often leaves Otis on his own. This book tells of several episodes in Otis's life—from his sneaking vitamins to a white rat to "disprove" a diet experiment, to getting his final "come-uppance" when a trick on Ellen Tebbits backfires.

Colman, Hila. **Classmates by Request.** Morrow 1964.

> Carla, a white girl, is one of ten teenagers who decide to request a transfer to an all black school and thus help to integrate a city school. To Ellen, who is black, this is only a "token step." Many human problems and understandings of a complex nature arise for impatient Carla and angry Ellen as they struggle to learn to live with others and finally realize that all goals cannot be reached directly.

Conford, Ellen. **Felicia the Critic.** Illus. Arvis Stewart. Little 1973.

> Not only does Felicia have great respect for the truth, she is forever broadcasting her beliefs and insights. When her offerings are not always appreciated, Felicia's mother explains the value of constructive criticism to her. After several disastrous episodes, Felicia learns that people accept even constructive criticism only when it is offered in a positive manner at the right time.

Conford, Ellen. **Me and the Terrible Two.** Illus. Charles Carroll. Little 1974.

> When Dorrie's best friend, Marlene, moves to Australia, it is a big adjustment for Dorrie to make new friends since Dorrie had been used to doing everything with Marlene. Then Haskell and Conrad, twins without a father, move next door. The "terrible two" are mischievous and frequently like to bother Dorrie. As the story progresses, a friendship is eventually built between Dorrie and the twins.

Estes, Eleanor. **The Hundred Dresses.** Illus. Louis Slobodkin. VoyB. HarBraceJ 1977.

> A little Polish girl in an American school wants to win the acceptance of her classmates. Through her skill in art, shabby Wanda makes

good her boast of having one hundred dresses and wins the art contest, to the surprise of the children who have rejected her. At least one child does some soul-searching about their treatment of Wanda.

Fitzhugh, Louise. **Harriet the Spy.** Illus. by author. YB. Dell 1975.

Harriet records in a notebook her reactions to and observations of various people who live in her New York neighborhood because she wants to become a writer and writers must be good observers. When Janey and Sport, her best friends, discover the candor with which she has been writing, she is ostracized. Harriet then evaluates her friendships and develops some insight into the feelings and needs of herself and others.

Girion, Barbara. **Joshua, the Czar, and the Chicken Bone Wish.**

Green, Phyllis. **The Fastest Quitter in Town.**

Grisé, Jeannette. **Robert Benjamin and the Great Blue Dog Joke.**

Hoff, Syd. **The Littlest Leaguer.**

Kennedy, Richard. **The Dark Princess.** Illus. Donna Diamond. Holiday 1978.

This is the story of a princess so beautiful that no one could bear to look at her. When she is ready for marriage, no one can look into her face without being blinded. The princess is herself totally blind. Many princes ask for her hand in marriage, but the princess doubts their love. She believes she is loved for her beauty and not for herself. One day she comes upon the Court Fool and learns more about love than she has ever before realized.

Konigsburg, E. L. **About the B'Nai Bagels.** Illus. by author. Aladdin. Atheneum 1973.

This is a warm and humorous story of a Jewish little league team. Twelve-year-old Mark Setzer has problems: his mother is manager of the team; his brother is coach. This makes some sticky situations and "overlaps" in his life. And he has worries about losing his best friend. Mark matures, having to make some difficult decisions on his own.

Mack, Nancy. **Why Me?** Photographs by Heinz Kluetmeier. Raintree Pubs Ltd 1976.

Young children tell about their feelings of rejection and inferiority. Each episode depicts the individual's feeling toward social interaction.

This book discusses problems but does not offer "easy" solutions. It would be good to stimulate class discussion of possible solutions.

Robinson, Barbara. **The Best Christmas Pageant Ever.**

Sachs, Marilyn. **Veronica Ganz.** Illus. Louis Glanzman. YB. Dell 1977.

Thirteen-year-old Veronica's automatic response to being teased about her height is to bully the teaser. One day she realizes that Peter actually admires her and instead of bullying him, she giggles. The enmity is over.

Snyder, Zilpha Keatley. **The Egypt Game.** Illus. Alton Raible. Aladdin, Atheneum 1972.

Melanie and April discover a common interest in reading and imaginative games. So begins the "Egypt game"—a re-creation of ancient rituals which comes to include Melanie's little brother, a new neighbor, and two sixth-grade boys. A murder in the neighborhood creates suspense for the exciting climax.

Stolz, Mary. **The Bully of Barkham Street.** Illus. Leonard Shortall. YB. Dell 1968.

Eleven-year-old Martin Hastings, large for his age, unattractive, and a bully, has trouble getting along with other young people. Several unpleasant incidents occur before he begins to realize that he may be at fault and that there are two sides to every issue. The story provides a perceptive study of a typical phase of growing up—feeling misunderstood.

Stolz, Mary. **A Dog on Barkham Street.**

Tolles, Martha. **Katie and Those Boys.**

Wallace, Barbara Brooks. **The Secret Summer of L.E.B.**

Yashima, Taro. **Crow Boy.** Illus. by author. Puffin 1976.

This warm and sensitive story centers on the problems of a frightened, introverted country boy who is ridiculed by his classmates. A new teacher finds his special talents and brings them to the attention of the other children. Although Chibi never becomes part of the group, the children realize the wrong they have done him and regret it. A picture book in format, it will be most appreciated by eight- to ten-year-olds.

Young, Scott. **Learning to Be Captain.** Illus. Kenneth M. Shields. EMC 1973.

Billy Amherst is captain of a hockey team. Norm Dennison, a new player on the team, is the best player by far, but the teammates do not give Norm any encouragement at all. He is never included in any of the other activities that the boys have. Billy must make a decision to include Norm in their fun or not.

Ages 11 to 14

Angell, Judie. **Secret Selves.** Bradbury Pr 1979.

Julie likes Rusty, but she is too shy to let him know she does. She calls him pretending she is Barbara calling Wendall. During many telephone converstions Barbara and Wendall find they have much in common; at school Julie and Rusty find they do not. Julie's grandmother intervenes, helping them to see that their shyness and self-conciousness are inhibiting their relationship, and that they do share many interests.

Blume, Judy. **Deenie.**

Bonham, Frank. **Durango Street.** Dutton 1965.

In order to survive, Rufus Henry violates the terms of his parole and joins the Moors, one of the rival gangs in the Durango Housing Project. Rufus fights his way to leadership and establishes a territory that no one dares challenge. This book gives insight into the lives of teenagers who must resort to violence in order to survive and tells of the frustrations of those who try to help them.

Branscum, Robbie. **The Ugliest Boy.**

Bunting, Eve. **The Wild One.**

Burch, Robert. **Queenie Peavy.** Illus. Jerry Lazare. Viking Pr 1966.

"I don't care" is tomboy Queenie's outward reaction as she contends with the taunts of her rural Georgia classmates about her father, who is in the penitentiary. Faced with a sheriff's investigation and the possibility of the reformatory when wrongly accused of breaking some windows, Queenie decides truth and reality are more important than toughness and pretense.

Constant, Alberta Wilson. **Does Anybody Care About Lou Emma Miller?**

Gauch, Patricia Lee. **Fridays.** Putnam 1979.

There are plenty of warnings that Corey's junior high crowd, The

Eight, is moving too fast and in the wrong direction. These warnings come from worried parents and concerned teachers and friends. Gradually, the Friday night parties get more and more out of control. When an ostracized group member, Terry, becomes involved in serious trouble, Corey must examine her values, goals, and friends.

Golding, William. **Lord of the Flies.** Coward 1978.

A group of English schoolboys marooned on a tropical island regress to ritual and savagery in their attempt to establish social order among themselves.

Hanlon, Emily. **The Swing.** Bradbury Pr 1979.

Both Beth and Danny consider a swing to be their own private refuge from their problems at home. Beth, who is deaf, wants to assert her independence; Danny resents his stepfather's attempts to replace his dead father. Tension grows between Beth and Danny until Danny's lie about a hunting accident brings disastrous results. As Danny attempts to explain his position to Beth, each gains insight into the other's needs, and they are able to share feelings as well as the swing.

Hentoff, Nat. **This School Is Driving Me Crazy.**

Hopkins, Lee Bennett. **Wonder Wheels.**

Lee, Mildred. **The Skating Rink.** Clarion Bk. Seabury 1969.

Tuck Faraday is a shy fifteen-year-old farm boy who, because of his awkwardness and stuttering, is accepted neither by his peers nor by his family. He becomes interested in a new skating rink being built near his home and is trained by the owner to be the star skater on opening night. His success brings courage, self-confidence, and self-respect, which lead not only to an improvement in his speech, but also in his relations with others.

Perl, Lila. **Don't Ask Miranda.** Clarion Bk. Seabury 1979.

Her unstable home life causes Miranda to change schools frequently and she is never in one place long enough to develop relationships with her peers. When she is finally asked to join a group, she learns they expect her to steal and cheat for them. One true friend and her own good sense help her to decide just how far she should go to be part of a group.

Pevsner, Stella. **Cute Is a Four-Letter Word.** Clarion. HM 1980.

Clara has great plans for being popular during her eighth-grade

Peer Relationships

year. These plans are hampered by an overbearing houseguest, by a wise and strict mother, and by the discovery that she is being used by some of the members of the "in crowd." These problems help her decide to re-examine her values, and to change not her goals, but her methods of achieving popularity.

Rabinowich, Ellen. **Toni's Crowd.** Photographs by G. Richardson Cook. Watts 1978.

Sandi quickly selects a crowd when she arrives at a new school. She wants to belong to Toni's crowd enough to try cutting classes, shoplifting, and inviting a boy to a party. When Toni is deliberately cruel to another girl at the party, Sandi resists peer pressure and speaks out for what she knows is right.

Smith, Doris Buchanan. **Kick a Stone Home.** T Y Crowell 1974.

Sara doesn't want to give up the childish pursuits and sports that have been her refuge since her parents' divorce but she would like to have more friends and even more dates. Sara is pulled from her shell by coping with new situations. When she finds her position is not unique, she is able to make decisions and make friends.

Van Leeuwen, Jean. **I Was a 98-Pound Duckling.**

Waldron, Ann. **The Integration of Mary-Larkin Thornhill.** Dutton 1975.

Mary-Larkin respects and shares her parents' liberal views, but she has misgivings about being the only white girl in a black junior high school. She experiences some rejection, but she has some good times, too, and as she makes new friends, she comes to understand the real meaning of integration.

Zindel, Paul. **The Pigman.**

Ages 14 and Up

Butterworth, W. E. **The Narc.**

Cartman, Shirley. **The Stolen Key.** Photographs by Mike Mitchell. McCormick-Mathers 1975.

Richard Briggs, the senior class clown, is expelled from school for two weeks. As punishment, his dad makes him work at hard labor. When he gets back to school, his attitude has changed and he wants to graduate. Kevin, an outstanding student, offers to help him study and they both have perfect papers, but when the teacher discovers her answer key is missing, Richard is blamed. By persuading Kevin to admit that he had tutored him, Richard is able to save himself and finally graduate.

Crawford, Charles P. **Bad Fall.** Har-Row 1972.

When Wade Sabbat chooses him for a friend, lonely Sean Richardson is flattered. He allows Wade to charm and persuade him to do things that he knows are wrong. They smoke pot, ride around in a stolen car, and play cruel tricks on schoolmates. On Halloween, they involve a young girl in a terrifying episode. Sean objects and the boys have a confrontation. Against his better judgment Sean again accepts Wade's friendly overtures only to "fall" one more time.

Crawford, Charles P. **Letter Perfect.** Dutton 1977.

Chad was enjoying their practical jokes as much as B. J. and Toad until they went too far and caused their teacher, Mr. Patterson, real mental anguish and the loss of his job. Chad draws on his basic sense of morality to find the strength to confess to Mr. Patterson, sense of morality to find the strength to confess to Mr. Patterson and to resist peer pressure enough to break away from his former friends.

Crawford, Charles P. **Three-Legged Race.** Har-Row 1974.

Drawn together during their extended hospitalizations, Kirk, Brent, and Amy become close friends. They share problems, exchange past experiences, and come up with some wild pranks to relieve their boredom. When Amy dies as an indirect consequence of one of these pranks, Brent and Kirk are shattered. They part knowing that what they had together is also gone.

Gerson, Corinne. **Passing Through.** Dial 1978.

Liz is struggling with her feelings against her parents' values and with the pain of her brother's recent suicide. Sam is struggling with his physical handicap, cerebral palsy. Both are struggling with being fifteen years old. Theirs is a special relationship in which they share troubles and encouragement while "passing through" each other's lives.

Kent, Deborah. **Belonging.** Dial 1978.

Despite her blindness, fifteen-year-old Meg is determined to be accepted as a "normal" teenager. Attending a public school for the first time, she confuses acceptance with friendship and almost loses her individuality as well as her perspective.

Knowles, John. **A Separate Peace.**

Lee, Mildred. **Fog.** Seabury 1972.

> Fog is a good word to describe not only the weather, but also the confusion in Luke Sawyer's mind. During his seventeenth year, he attempts to cope with his love for pretty Milo Tarrant, his father's sudden death and his mother's grief, a fire which destroys his club, and his plans for the future.

Peck, Richard. **Representing Super Doll.** Viking Pr 1974.

> Each of the girls in the group has her own personality—Berniece has a social conscience, Moon is a liberal, Ludmilla is an intellectual, Darlene is a beauty, and Verna is a level-headed girl from the country. When Verna accompanies Darlene to a beauty contest, she is mistaken for the contestant. Her reactions include a wish to protect Darlene and an appreciation of her own solid values.

Skármeta, Antonio. **Chileno!**

Wilkinson, Brenda. **Ludell's New York Time.**

Other Social Groups

Ages 1 to 5

Burningham, John. **Mr. Grumpy's Motor Car.** Illus. by author. T Y Crowell 1976.

> When Mr. Grumpy goes for a ride in his car, he takes with him the children, the rabbit, the cat, the dog, the pig, the sheep, the chickens, and the goat. They drive along happily until it begins to rain and they get stuck on the muddy road. Someone has to get out and push; so, they all get out and push. Cooperation proves to be beneficial to all.

Seuss, Dr. (Theodor Geisel). **Horton Hears a Who!** Random 1954.

> Big Horton the elephant tries to protect the settlement of small Whos that he discovers. Horton espouses the theme that "a person's a person, no matter how small."

Ages 5 to 8

Barkin, Carol, and Elizabeth James. **Sometimes I Hate School.** Photographs by Heinz Kluetmeier. Raintree Pubs Ltd 1975.

> Danny enjoys school until the day Mr. Coleman, the substitute teacher, comes. Mr. Coleman doesn't do things the way the regular teacher does. In fact, nothing seems the same at school anymore. Danny doesn't like Mr. Coleman or school. After a few days and some good talks, Mr. Coleman and Danny become friends. Danny even feels that he will miss Mr. Coleman when it's time for the regular teacher to come back.

Christian, Mary Blount. **The Sand Lot.** Illus. Dennis Kendrick. Harvey 1978.

> Walt and his friends form a baseball team. They have to make do with however many players they have and old and discarded equipment, but still it is their team. When some men in the community

Other Social Groups

take an interest in the team, they buy new equipment and uniforms and tell how the game should be played. Soon older children take over, and Walt and his friends are only allowed to watch the games. So the children find another place to play and start over again with discarded junk, but at least it is their own.

Molarsky, Osmond. **Song of the Empty Bottles.**

Sauer, Julia. **Mike's House.** Illus. Don Freeman. Viking Pr 1954.

Robert attends story hour at the public library and hears *Mike Mulligan and His Steam Shovel,* which becomes his favorite book. His sense of belonging at the library helps him in a time of need.

Ages 8 to 11

Carlson, Natalie Savage. **A Brother for the Orphelines.** Illus. Garth Williams. Har-Row 1959.

Twenty orphan girls living in a village near Paris want to keep an infant boy who was left at their orphanage. Just when he is about to be sent to the boys' orphanage, a photographer and newsreporter print the story, including details of the deplorable condition of the building. As a result, the two orphanages are to be combined and the children may stay together.

Chaikin, Miriam. **I Should Worry, I Should Care.**

Conta, Marcia Maher, and Maureen Reardon. **Feelings Between Kids and Grownups.** Photographs by Jules M. Rosenthal. Raintree Pubs Ltd 1975.

Children experience uncertainties with adults when interacting in daily living. Each episode depicts a situation in which children judge the actions of the adults. The children are able to accept some of the interactions in a positive manner. However, they have a difficult time understanding every interaction. Through discussing these experiences, other children should be better able to understand adults.

Erickson, Russell E. **Warton and Morton.** Illus. Lawrence Di Fiori. YB. Dell 1978.

Warton and Morton are brother toads that decide to go on a trip. On their way they are separated by a flood and set off to look for each other. Warton engages the muskrats to help him find

Morton. While with the muskrats, Warton finds that they are going to war with the beavers. From the turtle he finds out that his brother may be living with the beavers just as the muskrats are about to attack. The two brothers find each other just in time to prevent a war between the muskrats and beavers who really didn't understand each other.

Foreman, Michael. **War and Peas.**

Fox, Paula. **How Many Miles to Babylon?** Illus. Paul Giovanopoulos. D White 1967.

James Douglas lives in Brooklyn with his three great-aunts. He runs away from school one day in search of his mother. A gang of boys decide that they can use him in their racket of stealing dogs. James finally escapes and finds his mother sitting on his bed when he returns home. Although there is little hope at the end of this story for a better life for Jim, the reader will not soon forget him.

Fox, Paula. **Portrait of Ivan.** Illus. Saul Lambert. Bradbury Pr 1969.

Ivan, a lonely boy whose mother has died and whose father is too busy for him, comes to a series of sittings while he has his portrait painted. The young painter and Mrs. Manderby, the old woman the painter has hired to read to his restless subjects, open up a whole new world for Ivan—helping him make and explore new relationships as well as talk about his mother whom he never knew.

Griese, Arnold. **At the Mouth of the Luckiest River.**

Griese, Arnold. **The Way of Our People.**

Hodges, Margaret. **The Hatching of Joshua Cobb.** Illus. W. T. Mars. FS&G 1967.

A camp counselor bullies the boys in Cabin 13 and gives them all nicknames they hate. As the boys stick together, they turn the summer vacation into a memorable, happy experience.

Kendall, Carol. **The Gammage Cup.** Illus. Eric Blegood. VoyB. HarBraceJ 1966.

This excellent fantasy of the nonconforming minnipins versus the Establishment seems to be particularly appropriate now. The understated commentary on the false values of society and on the need for both tradition and innovation is timeless.

Neville, Emily Cheney. **The Seventeenth-Street Gang.** Illus. Emily McCully. Har-Row 1966.

> When Hollis moves into their block, the six children who play together in the Seventeenth-Street Gang label him a "flot"—imaginative Minnow's word for a stuffy adult—and lay plans for making him miserable. One scheme results in Minnow's fall into the East River, and it is Hollis who swims to her aid, making possible the first real overtures of friendship. The story explores the shifting loyalties within the group and reveals contrasts between group attitudes and individual feelings.

Rinkoff, Barbara. **Member of the Gang.** Illus. Harold James. Crown 1968.

> Because he wants to be a respected member of Leroy's gang, Woodie agrees to play hooky and to "front" for the gang in a store stickup. When one boy is knifed in the fracas, Woodie stays with him, is "busted," tried, and put on probation. An honest and realistic treatment of boys seeking easy prestige and of their handling by understanding personnel representing authority is presented.

Smith, Nancy Covert. **Josie's Handful of Quietness.**

Steele, William O. **The Magic Amulet.**

Ages 11 to 14

Baker, Betty. **Walk the World's Rim.** Har-Row 1965.

> Fourteen-year-old Chakoh, an Indian, travels with four Spanish survivors of an exploring party to Mexico. He becomes a close friend of the black slave Esteban, a man who displays great courage on the expedition through Indian territories. Chakoh discovers that Esteban is a slave, but the Indian learns, through his friendship with Esteban, that the institution of slavery, not the slave himself, is to be despised.

Byars, Betsy. **The Pinballs.** Har-Row 1977.

> Harvey's father had run over him with the car and broken both his legs; Carlie couldn't get along with her new stepfather; and Thomas J. didn't really know who he was or where he belonged. They all felt like pinballs until the summer they came to live with the Masons. While staying in this warm foster home, they learn their own worth, find their own identities, and most important of all, they learn how to give and accept love.

Cormier, Robert. **The Chocolate War.**

Hamilton, Virginia. **The Planet of Junior Brown.** Illus. by author. Macmillan 1974.

> This is the story of a crucial week in the lives of two black, eighth-grade dropouts who have been spending their time with the school janitor. Each boy is presented as a distinct individual. Jr. is a three-hundred-pound musical prodigy as neurotic as his overprotective mother. Buddy has learned to live by his wits in a world of homeless children. Buddy becomes Jr. Brown's protector and says to the other boys, "We are together because we have to learn to live for each other."

Holman, Felice. **Slake's Limbo.** Scribner 1974.

> Slake is lacking an essential ingredient necessary for getting along with others—he has no sense of self-worth or even of identity. In a desperate search for survival, Slake finds a crack in the subway wall where he stays for four months. He slowly experiences some positive contacts with others and gains confidence in his own abilities as well as hope for the future.

L'Engle, Madeleine. **The Young Unicorns.** Dell 1980.

> Josiah Davidson, seventeen, is seen in relation to many others—Emily, the blind piano prodigy; the Austins, who are his only real family; the Alphabats, a teenage gang whose power he is trying to escape; and the dean of the great cathedral where much of the action is set. An exciting climax emphasizes the theme of the importance of free will; even good cannot be forced on others.

Myers, Walter Dean. **Fast Sam, Cool Clyde, and Stuff.**

Paterson, Katherine. **The Great Gilly Hopkins.** T Y Crowell 1978.

> Though bright and fiercely independent, Gilly realizes too late that her compulsion to be with her natural mother made her overlook the real love in her foster home with Trotter, Mr. Robinson, and William Ernest. It is warm, motherly Trotter, though, who helps Gilly by teaching her that, "life is tough—but there is nothing to make you happy like doing good on a tough job."

Ages 14 and Up

Barrett, William E. **Lilies of the Field.** Doubleday 1962.

> Homer Smith, an easy-going yet hard-working black man, is "trapped"

Other Social Groups

by Mother Marie Marthe into building a chapel for the convent. Mother Marie Marthe thinks that God sent Homer to do the job. Despite initial conflicts and obstacles, he agrees to do the work and the chapel is constructed, followed by reconciliation between Homer and the nuns.

Brancato, Robin F. **Blinded by the Light.** Bantam 1979.

When her brother Jim cuts all family ties to join the Light of the World, a religious cult, Gail poses as a possible recruit in order to see him. She finds she needs all her own strength to resist being brainwashed herself. When Gail does see Jim, she must decide if she has the right to try to influence his decision to stay.

Britton, Anna. **Fike's Point.** Coward 1979.

Catherine, a fourteen-year-old girl, tells of her struggles as she roams with her parents, whom she describes as "lousy, long-haired bums," from one commune in England to another. Dimsy, her mentally slow brother, born a drug addict, is her only companion. Other children taunt her ragged appearance and odd life. The book and its shocking conclusion will give stimulus to thought about the effects of counterculture life on children. (Language and behavior may be offensive to many readers.)

Cather, Willa. **Death Comes for the Archbishop.** Vin. Random 1971.

Two French priests come with faith and zeal to the Indians of New Mexico. While influencing many to accept the Christian way of life, they must themselves adjust to the people they meet.

Guy, Rosa. **The Disappearance.**

Haskins, James. **Street Gangs: Yesterday and Today.** Hastings 1978.

This historical study of street gangs in America includes interesting portraits of individual gang members and discusses topics such as secret rules, initiation, and costumes. The use of newspaper accounts, sociological studies, photographs, and oral accounts help to create a vivid picture of the world of gangs.

Hesse, Hermann. **Demian.**

Hurwood, Bernhardt J. **Born Innocent.**

LeRoy, Gen. **Cold Feet.**

McCullers, Carson. **Member of the Wedding.** Bantam 1969.

Frankie Adams, a tall thirteen-year-old girl, is a loner in a small southern town. The only balm to her loneliness is six-year-old John Henry. When her brother comes home from the army, Frankie at last has someone to belong to, but when he marries and doesn't take her on the honeymoon, she is forced to grow up. After floundering, she manages to accept the situation and herself.

O'Dell, Scott. **Child of Fire.**

Peck, Richard. **Representing Super Doll.**

Schmidt, J. H. **Getting Along: How to Be Happy with Yourself and Others.** Putnam 1979.

To get along well with others, one must first get along with oneself. Using fictionalized characters and situations, the author gives practical suggestions and examples of ways to accomplish these goals.

Wharton, Edith. **Ethan Frome.**

Young, Alida E. **Land of the Iron Dragon.**

Professional References

Cleary, Florence Damon. "A Total School Approach to Reading Guidance." From *Blueprints for Better Reading.* New York: H. W. Wilson and Co., 1972.

Ginott, Haim. *Between Parent and Child.* New York: Avon, 1973.

Ginott, Haim. *Between Parent and Teenager.* New York: Avon, 1973.

Ginott, Haim. *Teacher and Child.* New York: Macmillan, 1972.

Larrick, Nancy. *A Parent's Guide to Children's Reading.* 4th rev. ed. New York: Doubleday, 1975.

Ladder IV

Appreciating Different Cultures

Over the years, both practicing and prospective teachers have relied heavily upon forms of the word *appreciate* when writing learning objectives for lesson plans. Remember: "The children will appreciate the lives of certain world and national leaders"; and "The class will have an appreciation for the problems of racial integration during various historical eras of the United States"; and "The students will read and discuss stories about various social groups throughout the world and, thereby, will be appreciating cultures different from their own."

It would appear that such objectives can continue to be cranked out easily, but what is intended when one calls upon the infinitive, *to appreciate*? The answer must necessarily be varied, for it is as broadly interpreted as there are professionals using that verb form. Yet it is the hope of the compilers of this particular Ladder that *appreciating* will include 1) increasing one's knowledge of peoples, places, and events; 2) maintaining a positive mind-set which allows and encourages genuine acceptance of other expressions and interpretations of the human condition; and 3) a nurturing of the gnawing need to find out, to become more fully informed, and perhaps, even, to understand as much as possible about peoples and places both in the present and the past.

In his introduction to *Many Smokes, Many Moons: A Chronology of American Indian History Through Indian Art* (J. B. Lippincott, 1978), Jamake Highwater, of Blackfeet/Cherokee heritage, author, and scholar of cultural anthropology, makes a number of points pertinent to our needs as we consider this particular Ladder. He indicates that, at times, he felt

> alienated by the way ideas find their way into English words. For instance, when an English word is descriptive—like the word "wilderness"—I am often appalled by what is implied by the description. After all, the forest is not "wild" in the sense that it is something that needs to be tamed. For Blackfeet Indians, the forest is the natural state of the world. It is the cities that are wild and need "taming." (p. 10)

Highwater continues by suggesting an even more complex problem when he discusses the English word "universe."

> Indians do not believe in a "*uni*-verse," but in a "*multi*-verse." Indians don't belive that there is only *one* truth, but think there are many truths." (p. 10)

Highwater grew up in a dual environment, a Native American home and an English speaking school, and he tells of the lesson learned many times in his childhood when the home word for something was absolutely not acceptable and he was expected to substitute the school word. "The people of white America don't *see* the same things that Indians see. America is one land, but it is two worlds." (p. 9) Yes, and more worlds, too. In suggesting "that there is not one truth, but many; not one *real* experience, but many realities; not one history but many different ways of looking at events," Highwater is urging us to value the "paradox that the real humanity of people is understood through cultural *differences* rather than cultural similarities . . . ." (p. 10)

The four cultural categories in this Ladder would suggest at least four basic "worlds" out of which individuals have their roots. A few brief comments follow, but it should be noted that neither the categories nor the comments are meant to be inclusive. They do represent the viewpoints of the writers, but they are intended to *assist* the reader, not lead.

The cultural categories are, "Ethnic," "Religious," "Regional," and "World." It is often difficult to differentiate among the categories; for example, a story of the Passover might appropriately be placed in either "Religious" or "Ethnic"; and a story of Chinese Americans living in San Francisco's Chinatown might well be considered for either "Ethnic" or "Regional." With regard to the "World" and "Regional" categories, we have presumed to include folklore, for such traditional literature is found in every culture. In *Children's Literature in the Elementary School* (HR&W, 1979) Charlotte Huck suggests:

> A study of the folktales of Africa, Russia, or the American Indian will provide insights into the beliefs of these peoples, their values, their jokes, their life styles, their histories. A cross-cultural study of folk literature will help children discover the universal qualities of humankind. (p. 160)

Also, the inclusion of poetry, wherever possible, seemed essential in this Ladder as it often is a very personal expression of some aspect of a culture, and it is a unique use of language often neglected when it comes to choosing "something to read." According to Huck,

> Poetry may broaden and intensify experience, or it may present a range of experiences beyond the realm of personal possibility for the individual listener. . . . Poetry does more than mirror life; it reveals life in new dimensions. (p. 306)

Surely our efforts to appreciate different cultures will be enriched by sharing the haunting chants and soothing lullabies of the North American Indian in *The Trees Stand Shining* (ed. by Hettie Jones, Dial Press, 1971)

Appreciating Different Cultures 225

and by experiencing the "heart-stopping" moment when both poet and reader fleetingly spot a deer in the Allegheny Mountain country through Lilian Moore's "Encounter" in her *Sam's Place: Poems from the Country* (Atheneum, 1973).

Difficulties arose in developing this Ladder, and they were never as satisfactorily resolved as would have been desired. One had to be careful not to let this list turn into a social studies resource, though certainly many books here provide useful, accurate information along with their insight and potential for appreciation. Another concern has been for selecting books that do not negatively nor inaccurately stereotype individuals or groups. Not all who use this resource will agree that every entry succeeds, for it is not always easy to determine whether an inappropriate stereotype exists in a given book, for we each attend to that issue from a different perspective. A final, disturbing problem has been that many titles that should be here are missing due to the time and quantity limitations. Even more frustrating for the compilers of this Ladder (and the entire book, we are sure) will be all those times in the future when they come across titles that could have been and should have been included, but weren't!

Here are a few brief suggestions that may aid you in overcoming most of the difficulties described:

1. Continue to seek out other books by authors and illustrators contained in this resource. They frequently will have other suitable material for your needs.

2. Become aware of possible topics that appear quite useful to you. They may be explicit or implied in the annotations, but either way, your awareness will aid you in now seeking further such material by consulting a librarian, teacher, or reviewing journal.

3. When you discover what you consider to be an inappropriate stereotype in a book you selected from this list, please assume this two-fold responsibility: (a) discuss in depth the issue with those who are reading the particular book; and (b) locate, yourself, books you believe must be made available in order to provide a balance to the view you are questioning.

In closing, let Jamake Highwater guide you as you turn to this Ladder for ideas and material:

> Today we are learning that people are not the same, and that we cannot evaluate all experience the same way. We are also learning that everybody doesn't have to be the same in order to be equal. It is no longer realistic for dominant cultures to send out missionaries to convert everyone to their ideas of the "truth." Today we are beginning

to look into the ideas of groups outside the dominant culture, and we are finding different kinds of "truth" that make the world we live in far bigger than we ever dreamed it could be—for the greatest distance between people is not geographical space, but culture. (p. 14)

Roy Wilson and Darlene Hughes

Ethnic Cultures

Ages 1 to 5

Corey, Dorothy. **Pepe's Private Christmas.** Illus. John Wallner. Parents 1978.

Pepe worries about how Santa will get into his home since there is no chimney or fireplace. After everyone goes to bed, he opens the door. During the night all the family members become so cold that they must find something as extra cover—a shaggy rug, a big bath towel, and the large straw hat that Uncle Carlos brought from Mexico. In the morning, Pepe finds a little kitten that had wandered in and he is sure it is from Santa.

Giovanni, Nikki. **Spin a Soft Black Song.** Illus. Charles Bible. Hill & Wang 1971.

A beautifully illustrated book of poems about black children tells what childhood and growing up are all about as seen through the eyes of the very young. There are poems about mommies and daddies, going to bed and out to play and to the supermarket, having friends, being afraid, and just wanting a chance to grow up and meet the world. Simple in theme, it is a very moving collection for all ages.

Houston, James. **Kiviok's Magic Journey: An Eskimo Legend.** Illus. James Houston. Atheneum 1973.

Kiviok is a character well-known in many Eskimo legends. He marries a beautiful girl who is a snow-goose whose coat was stolen by a raven. The snow-goose was cursed and flew away. The story tells of Kiviok's adventures as he travels to find his family. Many Eskimo beliefs and customs are portrayed.

Scott, Ann Herbert. **On Mother's Lap.**

Ages 5 to 8

Adoff, Arnold. **Big Sister Tells Me That I'm Black.**

Baker, Betty. **Killer-of-Death.** YB. Dell 1974.

> Killer-of-Death, son of an Apache chief growing to manhood toward the close of his tribe's freedom, knows that the ever-increasing demands of the white man will bring war. As friction increases between the Apaches and the whites, so does the tension between Killer-of-Death and his rival. They appease their hatred for one another to stand together for their tribe. The author's knowledge of Apache customs and lore is evident in this story of a fierce, proud, and doomed world.

Benchley, Nathaniel. **Running Owl the Hunter.** Illus. Mamoru Funai. Har-Row 1979.

> In this fanciful tale, youthful Running Owl goes on his own hunting exploration after his father says he is too young to join the men of the tribe. He encounters various animals and finally a rabbit who advises aiming his arrows at something big and slow. Running Owl then decides to get a feather for his hair and sets out to capture an eagle. Instead he is carried away by the eagle to the nest where he earnestly must explain his need for a feather.

Bernstein, Margery, and Janet Kobrin. **How the Sun Made a Promise and Kept It: A Canadian Indian Myth.** Illus. Ed Heffernan. Scribner 1974.

> This myth from the Bungee tribe tells of the god Weese-ke-jak who captures the sun in a net because in those days it went wherever it wanted to go. Once caught, though, the sun was too close and everything was becoming hotter and hotter. The sun was eager to be free and after promising to come close to the edges of the earth only in the morning and evening, it was released.

Blue, Rose. **I Am Here, Yo Estoy Aqui.** Watts 1971.

> Luz, who speaks no English, is lonely and frightened in kindergarten, until a Spanish-speaking aide and her teacher help her to understand how to exchange words with the other children.

Brenner, Barbara. **Wagon Wheels.**

Clifton, Lucille. **Amifika.**

Clifton, Lucille. **The Black BC's.** Illus. Don Miller. Dutton 1970.

> A short poem and a page of prose for each letter of the alphabet set forth the ways in which black people and black culture have con-

tributed to our American heritage. The book talks of soldiers and politicians, teachers and writers, scientists and sportsmen—such people as Frederick Douglass, Harriet Tubman, Malcolm X, Martin Luther King, Jr., Mohammed Ali, Julian Bond, and Edward Brooke. Tempera drawings enhance the text.

Clifton, Lucille. **My Brother Fine with Me.**

de Paola, Tomie. **Watch Out for the Chicken Feet in Your Soup.**

Gray, Genevieve. **How Far, Felipe?** Illus. Ann Grifalconi. Har-Row 1978.

One of the "I Can Read" History series, this story depicts the travels of Felipe and his family as they move from Mexico to California. Filomena, Felipe's burro, is to be left behind, but Felipe manages to hide her among some other animals making the trip. Even though it is a long, hard trip, the family and Filomena survive. An account of the 1775 expedition by Colonel Juan de Anza is related.

Greenfield, Eloise. **Africa Dream.** Illus. Carole Byard. John Day 1977.

A child tells of her dream in which she crossed the ocean and went to Africa. She lands in long-ago, visits cities, rides a donkey, goes to a village where she is greeted by her long-ago granddaddy, grandma, uncles, and cousins. The brief text is tucked into full-page black and white illustrations which appear dream-like but also depict the land of one's ancestors with dramatic emotion.

Hirsh, Marilyn. **One Little Goat: A Passover Song.** Illus. by author. Holiday 1979

This Jewish folksong (like the farmer in the dell) is sung at Passover. The father buys a goat, who is eaten by a cat, who is bitten by a dog, who is beaten by a stick, etc. The song continues to chain events and animals and soon the Holy One comes and kills the Angel of Death to put things right. The musical score is included along with brief information about Passover and the song.

Lattimore, Eleanor Frances. **A Smiling Face.** Illus. by author. Morrow 1973.

Seven-year-old Grace Piper has trouble understanding why the people in her small community in Kentucky ignore the new black family that moves into their neighborhood. The new family has a little girl Grace's age. Grace's best friend cannot play with the new girl, and Grace cannot understand why. Nevertheless Grace tries to become friends with the new girl and succeeds.

Leech, Jay, and Zane Spencer. **Bright Fawn and Me.** Illus. Glo Coalson. T Y Crowell 1979.

> Using an Indian trading fair as the setting, this story tells how one Cheyenne girl must look after her younger sister. The festive spirit of the fair is contrasted with the near-unpleasant experiences created by so much attention and approval being placed upon Bright Fawn, the younger sister. Illustrations glow in earth tones and depict life at such a fair in times past.

McDermott, Gerald. **Arrow to the Sun.** Illus. by author. Puffin. 1978.

> In this Pueblo Indian tale, the Lord of the Sun sends a spark to earth. The spark becomes the Boy who searches for his father. A wise Arrow Maker turns the Boy into an arrow and sends him to the sun. The Boy learns that the Sun Lord is his father. The Lord says that perhaps he is his son, but the Boy must first endure four trials to prove it. The father and son rejoice after the trials and the Boy goes to earth to bring the Lord's spirit to men. A brilliantly illustrated tale shows the Indians' reverence for the sun.

Miles, Miska. **Annie and the Old One.**

Ages 8 to 11

Baron, Virginia Olsen, editor. **Here I Am: An Anthology of Poems Written by Young People in Some of America's Minority Groups.** Illus. Emily A. McCully. Dutton 1969.

> Young people from Alaska, Utah, California, New Mexico, Oregon, Arizona, and New York wrote these poems, which tell what it is like to be black, Puerto Rican, Mexican, Indian, Eskimo, Cuban, Japanese—and American at the same time. The youngest poet is six years old and the oldest are in their early twenties. All speak in a moving way about the human condition as felt and seen by one who belongs to a minority group.

Bierhorst, John. **Songs of the Chippewa.** Illus. Joe Servello. FS&G 1974.

> Bierhorst has adapted Chippewa songs from the collections of Frances Densmore and Henry Rowe Schoolcraft which were made during the early 1900s, and has then arranged them for piano and guitar. Each song appears on a page with a full color illustration facing the song. There are lullabies and songs for the creatures of nature including the frog and owl.

Ethnic Cultures

Bulla, Clyde Robert, and Michael Syson. **Conquista!** Illus. Ronald Himler. T Y Crowell 1978.

During Coronado's time, a young Indian boy encounters his first horse. As he passes from boyhood into maturity, Little Wolf engages in conquests both for material gain and for something far more spiritual and personal. The sensitive black and white drawings reflect the inner strength Little Wolf achieves.

Burchard, Peter. **Chinwe.** Illus. by author. Putnam 1979.

Chinwe is a young Ibo maiden who delights in her African village life. It is 1838 and suddenly she is confronted with slave hunters who attack, killing the young man she admires. Violent deaths and imprisonment on a slave vessel follow. Chinwe learns quickly who can be trusted, both among the slavers and her own people, and she prepares for escape. The mutiny is short-lived, but she has found strength in hope. Choosing always to face difficulties with cautious consideration along with the determination to endure with dignity, she is able to face her unknown future.

Chaikin, Miriam. **I Should Worry, I Should Care.**

Clifton, Lucille. **The Lucky Stone.** Illus. Dale Payson. Delacorte 1979.

This is a collection of four tales about a very special black stone, three told by Tee's great-grandmother. The first tells of how, during slavery, the stone brought good fortune to a runaway, and in another story the stone seems responsible for bringing a husband to the great-grandmother. The final tale relates how Tee became the present owner of the stone.

Cunningham, Maggi. **The Cherokee Tale-Teller.** Illus. Patrick Des Jarlait. Dillon 1978.

Cherokee Indians in the Great Smoky Mountains liked to listen to Tale-Teller. He could only tell his tales during the winter so the corn wouldn't stop growing or the birds stop flying just to listen. They enjoyed hearing about the beginning of the world, spirits, and the Great Spirit.

Dionetti, Michelle. **Thalia Brown and the Blue Bug.** Illus. James Calvin. A-W 1979.

It seems as though no one has time or patience for Thalia. She finds a piece of blue chalk and begins to draw a bug on the walk but a quick rain washes the drawing away. Thalia finds paper and uses her brother's crayons to create another bug. Later she finds the picture thrown away and her brother refuses to let her use the crayons. A sign about an art fair excites her, and a neighbor assists her with materials. Her art work is admired by the family and displayed at the show.

Goble, Paul. **The Girl Who Loved Wild Horses.** Illus. by author. Bradbury Pr 1978.

Stampeding horses cárry a young girl far from the familiar grazing lands. Welcomed into the wild herd by the spotted stallion leader, she becomes one with the Horse People and a symbol of freedom to her people.

Goble, Paul, and Dorothy Goble. **The Friendly Wolf.** Illus. by authors. Bradbury Pr 1974.

Little Cloud and Bright Eyes are Plains Indians who get lost in the hills and find shelter in a wolf's den. The wolf befriends them and wolves have been Indians' friends ever since. Illustrations add to the appreciation of the life and lore of the early Indians.

Griese, Arnold A. **At the Mouth of the Luckiest River.** Illus. Glo Coalson. T Y Crowell 1973.

A lame Indian boy is feared by his tribe, but friendly Eskimos help him learn skills he needs. He attempts to prevent trouble between his medicine man and the Eskimos.

Griffin, Judith Berry. **Phoebe the Spy.**

Grimes, Niki. **Something on My Mind.** Illus. Tom Feelings. Dial 1978.

This collection of prose-poems speaks directly from the young black child's point of view and touches universal feelings of childhood—waiting for Daddy's visit, wondering what to write about summer vacation since the teacher does not want to hear about sneaking into the pool hall or Jimmy getting out of jail. Illustrations are strong, direct, gentle, sensitive, yet achieved with only halftones and line drawings.

Gustafson, Anita (retold by). **Monster Rolling Skull and Other Native American Tales.** Illus. John Stadler. T Y Crowell 1980.

Tales of the coyote are told by that often clever, often distrusted creature. The stories come from various Native American sources including Abnaki, Alsea, Seneca, Comanche, Okanagon, Sia, and Mandan-Hidatsa. In most of these stories humor is present, even during such a serious episode as the meat-eating skeleton.

Hays, Wilma Pitchford. **Yellow Fur and Little Hawk.** Illus. Anthony Rao. Coward 1980.

> Susanna's father is responsible for getting the Sioux Indians to move into the wooden houses that have been built on the reservation. It is 1915 in South Dakota, drought has come with summer, and Susanna learns from White Bull why his people refuse to give up their tepees.

Hodges, Margaret. **The Fire Bringer: A Paiute Indian Legend.** Illus. Peter Parnall. Little 1972.

> This is a legend about an Indian boy and his friend the Coyote who lead the Paiutes on a fearsome mission to seize fire from the Fire Spirits. Their journey makes an exciting and colorful tale. The dramatic illustrations add to the appeal of this story.

Lampman Evelyn Sibley. **Go up the Road.** Illus. Charles Robinson. McElderry Bk. Atheneum 1972.

> A Chicano girl's dream of finishing grade school is made almost impossible because of her family's annual journey north from New Mexico to harvest crops in Oregon and Washington. This is a sensitive portrayal of the life of the migrant farm worker.

Leech, Jay, and Zane Spencer. **Moon of the Big-Dog.** Illus. Mamoru Funai. T Y Crowell 1980.

> Three young Sioux braves are chosen to go to the big trading fair for their tribe. They encounter horses for the first time and Black Raven has a vision which convinces him to trade for two horses rather than for all of the items his people are expecting. The horses are costly and when he returns with them his people are not pleased. Yet, this is the beginning of a totally new way of life for the Teton Sioux.

Mathis, Sharon Bell. **The Hundred Penny Box.** Illus. Leo Dillon and Diane Dillon. Viking Pr. 1975.

> Michael loves his great-great-aunt Dew who has come to live with his family, but feels his mother does not understand the old lady's need to have her few remaining possessions close at hand. A favorite pastime is to count out the pennies in her box and hear Aunt Dew tell a significant moment in her life which each coin represents—from the year of her birth when slavery was over right up to the present, one hundred years later. The picture format suggests a younger reader, yet the content is particularly suited for older children who would gain from guided discussion about the universality of love between young and old.

Mobley, Jane. **The Star Husband.** Illus. Anna Vojtech. Doubleday 1979.

> Two Indian girls sit and watch the sky as night approaches. One wishes for a star husband, and when she awakens finds herself next to him in the sky. Though she has a son, the Moon, she becomes bored with nothing to do and misses the earth with its scent of green things growing and the pungent odors of animals. Finally she returns to earth where she spends the rest of her life. Upon dying she ascends to the sky and often can be seen now as the bright star close to her son, the Moon. Full-color illustrations complement this story of the natural life cycle.

O'Dell, Scott. **Island of the Blue Dolphins.** HM 1960.

> An Indian girl is forced to spend eighteen years alone on a harsh, bleak island off California. Courageously she makes the best of her circumstances, forages for food, makes animals her companions, and relies upon herself during her growing years. She is a young woman when rescued and taken to the mainland.

Rockwood, Joyce. **Groundhog's Horse.** Illus. Victor Kalin. HR&W 1978.

> This is the story of Groundhog, an eleven-year-old Cherokee boy who goes off alone to rescue his horse Midnight. Along his way, he meets other Cherokees and has various adventures.

San Souci, Robert. **The Legend of Scarface: A Blackfeet Indian Tale.** Illus. Daniel San Souci. Doubleday 1978.

> Scarface is teased because he is poor and because he was born with a scar on his cheek. He spends most of his time in the forest with the animals and learns their language. He falls in love with Singing Rains, the chief's daughter, but she has vowed to the Sun never to wed. Scarface sets out to speak with the sun, wins his favor, and is granted permission to marry Singing Rains.

Soyer, Abraham (translators Rebecca S. Beagle and Rebecca Soyer). **The Adventures of Yemima and Other Stories.** Illus. Raphael Soyer. Viking Pr 1979.

> This collection of six Hebrew stories, originally told by a Russian Jew and translated by his daughter and daughter-in-law, are filled with hopefulness and a firm belief in justice, yet they tell of hunger and povery. Included are stories of a courageous little girl who outwits a fox; of two very gullible and foolish animals; of a poor woman's tears that turn into jewels. The pencil drawings gently enhance each story.

Steele, William O. **Talking Bones: Secrets of Indian Burial Mounds.** Illus. Carlos Llerena-Aguirre. Har-Row 1978.

Archaeologists have uncovered graveyards of prehistoric American Indians. By studying the contents, they have reconstructed lifestyles and customs of several Indian tribes. Some of the remains include skeletons, beads, pots, tools, and weapons. Striking illustrations add authenticity to the text.

Thompson, Vivian L. **Hawaiian Tales of Heroes and Champions.** Illus. Herbert Kawainui Kane. Holiday 1971.

Kupua, or supernatural beings, roam the islands and do great deeds. The element of exaggeration adds to the excitement and entertainment in these tales. The illustrations give an authentic feeling of the islands. A glossary and excellent bibliography are included.

Yarbrough, Camille. **Cornrows.** Illus. Carole Byard. Coward 1979.

A story braided with love as Great-Grandmaw puts cornrows (plaits) into Mama's, Sister's, and Brother MeToo's hair along with the story of the origin of such styling in Africa is presented. Throughout the lyrical narrative is the power of love rising above hardship and imbuing families with a spirit of pride. The soft black and white illustrations evoke both the present hairstyling session and the past represented in Great-Grandmaw's tale.

Ages 11 to 14

Adoff, Arnold, editor. **Black Out Loud: An Anthology of Modern Poems by Black Americans.** Illus. Alvin Hollingsworth. Macmillan 1970.

Black poets of all ages—many under thirty—tell of the black experience in America. Adding much to the reading pleasure is the organization of the book into six theme areas, each poem complementing others within the group. This collection seems promising for classroom sharing in single or in choral readings.

Adoff, Arnold, editor. **I Am the Darker Brother: An Anthology of Modern Poems by Negro Americans.** Illus. Benny Andrews. Macmillan 1968.

These poems, by accomplished authors such as Langston Hughes, Richard Wright, and Gwendolyn Brooks, have been selected to reveal how the Negro feels about his condition in America.

Adoff, Arnold, editor. **My Black Me: A Beginning Book of Black Poetry.** Dutton 1974.

A joyful, proud introduction to black poets and poetry which should inspire further reading as well as personal efforts to create one's own poems. The editor encourages the reader to let these poems help one feel strong inside. These black poems are for all brothers and sisters of every race.

Anastas, Peter. **Glooskap's Children.** Illus. Mark Power. Beacon Pr 1973.

About 400 members of the Penobscot Nation live on Indian Island, all that is left of their ancestral lands in Maine. The narratives of legends, voices of the people, documents, personal journals, and photographs show a past and present of the descendants of Glooskap.

Anderson, Susanne (editor David R. Brower). **Song of the Earth Spirit.** Photographs by author. Friends Earth 1974.

The beliefs, life-styles, and customs of some Navajo families are brought to life by Susanne Anderson's beautiful photographs. She relates her experiences while living with the Navajo families, who accepted her although she was foreign to their ways.

Bales, Carol Ann. **Tales of the Elders: A Memory Book of Men and Women Who Came to America As Immigrants, 1900-1930.** Photographs by author. Follett 1977.

This collection provides twelve personal statements of naturalized Americans who came as children or young adults from such diverse countries as Japan, Greece, Holland, Italy, and Mexico during the early years of this century. They are written in a conversational style, rambling at times, but always revealing a lifetime of hope and fidelity to a new homeland.

Benchley, Nathaniel. **Only Earth and Sky Last Forever.** Trophy. Har-Row 1973.

This love story of a young Cheyenne, orphaned in 1868 and raised by the Oglala Sioux, is full of Indian lore as Dark Elk courts Lashuka. Her scornful grandmother opposes him with his one pony, no warrior "counting" or killing coups, and his adopted parents at Red Cloud Agency. When the Anglos flock crazily to the Black Hills for gold, Dark Elk has to join Crazy Horse to fight Custer at the Little Big Horn for his future and for Lashuka.

Bierhorst, John, editor. **The Girl Who Married a Ghost and Other Tales from the North American Indian.** Photographs by Edward S. Curtis. Four Winds. Schol Bk Serv 1978.

Ethnic Cultures 237

With this anthology of little-known American Indian folklore matched with Edward S. Curtis's photographs of Indian "monsters," maidens, and spirit persons, the reader "can enter an imaginary world that might otherwise remain permanently closed."

Bonham, Frank. **Durango Street.**

Bonham, Frank. **Viva Chicano.** LFL. Dell 1971.

In this story, Joaquin "Keeny" Duran struggles to rise above the influences of the urban, Mexican-American ghetto where he lives. Unjustly accused of pushing his brother out of the window, Keeny runs away and takes refuge in an abandoned police station. The book passes almost into the realm of fantasy when Keeny and his gang, the Aztecs, are given advice by a cardboard model of Emiliano Zapata which Keeny has stolen. The voice is later explained as being Keeny's conscience. The book returns to strict realism in the end.

Brooks, Charlotte K., editor. **African Rhythms: Selected Stories and Poems.** Photographs by Walter H. Brooks. WSP 1974.

This collection contains literary selections, including stories, poems, and photographic essays, by African writers from various regions. They reflect what Africa was once and is today.

Brown, Dee (adapted by Amy Ehrlich). **Wounded Knee: An Indian History of the American West.** HR&W 1974.

Amy Ehrlich has adapted for young readers Dee Brown's *Bury My Heart at Wounded Knee: An Indian History of the American West.* It is an account of how the Indians struggled to preserve their way of life in the face of the Westward Movement.

Bunting, Eve. **The Wild One.** Illus. Leo Summers. Schol Bk Serv 1974.

Snow Deer lives with his mother's people, the Cheyenne Indians, but he is blonde and blue-eyed like his white father. The tribal council has decided he should live with his grandmother and study art as his father did, but he is determined to run away rather than live with his grandmother. His bravery in warning the tribe of a Pawnee attack earns him a place as a true Cheyenne.

Burton, Jimalee. **Indian Heritage, Indian Pride: Stories That Touched My Life.** Illus. by author. U of Okla Pr 1974.

The author, who is also a talented Cherokee Indian artist, shares, through her illustrations and stories, memories of her Indian culture. She makes the American Indian aware and proud of their heritage.

Clifford, Eth. **The Year of the Three-Legged Deer.** Illus. Richard Cuffari. YB. Dell 1973.

This Indian story opens as a young man, Takawsu, half-Lenni Lenape, comes to visit his white father, Jesse Benton. An attack upon some Lenni Lenape by white men convinces Jesse's Indian wife and son to join her tribe during the mass removal of Indians to the Western lands.

Clifton, Lucille. **The Times They Used to Be.**

Fichter, George S. **How the Plains Indians Lived.** Illus. Alexander Farquharson. McKay 1980.

A carefully detailed text on over twenty Native American tribes who once lived on the Great Plains, with chapters on Indian dress, common sign language, the life of an Indian brave, women's work, games and sports, make up this book. Pen and ink drawings add considerable information to a rather thorough text.

Fox, Paula. **The Slave Dancer.**

George, Jean Craighead. **Julie of the Wolves.**

Gessner, Lynne. **To See a Witch.** Nelson 1978.

Kopi is jealous of the captive girl, Nawakna, now living in their Pueblo home. He scares her into leaving by convincing her a witch lives in their home. Kopi wants most to be admitted into the kiva, a sign of manhood, but the decision rests with his ceremonial father who knows what Kopi has done to Nawakna. Kopi's struggle involves learning to shoot a man's bow, providing for Nawakna, overcoming hatred of his cousin, and dealing with rumors of witchcraft.

Gordy, Berry, Sr. **Movin' Up: Pop Gordy Tells His Story.** Har-Row 1979.

"Pop" Gordy, founder of Motown Records and son of a former slave, recalls the highlights of his life. The story begins in Georgia, his childhood home, and ends in Detroit, where he lived most of his adult life. He and his family had many hard times; often they had to deal with unfair treatment of blacks. "Pop" Gordy's story shows his struggles in succeeding in the American business world.

Hamilton, Virginia. **Arilla Sun Down.**

Hamilton, Virginia. **M.C. Higgins, the Great.** Macmillan 1974.

An eleven-year-old black boy dreams of escape for himself and his family from his home on Sarah's Mountain, now spoiled by strip mining. M.C. must come to terms with family and heritage and his own desires.

Hamilton, Virginia. **W.E.B. DuBois: A Biography.** T Y Crowell 1972.

A thoughtfully documented biography of an intellectual giant, born three years after the Civil War into a black family that had lived free from the time of the Revolution. DuBois was a scholar and became an influential leader among black Americans, instrumental in founding the NAACP, and editor for over twenty years of an important black magazine, *The Crisis*. This biography deals forthrightly with DuBois' growing conviction of the need to embrace a socialistic viewpoint and eventual membership in the Communist Party during his later life, yet he never ceased to champion the right of dissent by loyal Americans, and he worked tirelessly for ninety-two years for the improvement of the quality of life of all black Americans.

Haskins, James. **The Creoles of Color of New Orleans.** Illus. Don Miller. T Y Crowell 1975.

This book presents the history of the group of people who "are the mixed descendants of the early French and Spanish colonists, African slaves, and West Indian refugees who settled in the Louisiana Territory." The author shows how they suffered great discrimination as they have tried to maintain their own life-style and culture.

Hassrick, Royal B. **The Colorful Story of North American Indians.** Octopus Bks 1974.

Over 180 illustrations in color and black and white, plus a narrative, tell the way of life, the struggle, and the religious beliefs and customs of the North American Indians. The author discusses the Indian in the modern world.

Haynes, Betsy. **Slave Girl.** Schol Bk Serv 1973.

Cowslip is a young black girl bought at a slave auction. At her new home, she encounters slaves who dream of being free and running away but Cowslip does not understand the meaning of free. The butler, an educated black man, secretly teaches her to read and write. When a close friend is killed while attempting to run away, she vows that someday she will be free.

Henderson, Nancy. **Walk Together: Five Plays on Human Rights.** Illus. Floyd Sowell. Messner 1974.

These plays are concerned with freedom and equality for all. "The Pledge" is based on historical facts about the American Indian-

Apaches and their right to live as they wish. "Harvest for Lola" shows problems of migrants and difficulties in education because they must move so often. "Get on Board, Little Children" tells of the Underground Railroad and the right for everyone to be free. "Look Behind the Mask" is about self-concept. "Automa" is a fantasy about children who lose the right to think and make decisions.

Highwater, Jamake. **Many Smokes, Many Moons.** Lippincott 1978.

An overview of history and culture in the Americas from the mythological explanation of the beginning through the present is given. The illustrations are of Indian artifacts and art pieces, and the writing is presented from the Indian point of view as interpreted by the Blackfeet/Cherokee author. The brief entries are presented in chronological order; an index and selected bibliography are included.

Holman, Felice. **The Murderer.** Scribner 1978.

This is the story of a Jewish boy's struggles in growing up during the Depression in a Jewish-Polish Pennsylvania mining town.

Houston, James. **Songs of the Dream People.** Illus by author. McElderry Bk. Atheneum 1972.

This collection by a distinguished Canadian author and artist arranges by regions the chants and poems of North American Indians and Eskimos.

Houston, James. **The White Archer.** Illus. by author. VoyB. HarBraceJ 1979.

An Eskimo legend portrays a young boy's experience with tragedy: the murder of his family and capture of his sister by Indians. Left alone, Kungo becomes absorbed in preparing himself for vengeance. Obsession is replaced by acceptance when later he finds his sister has married her captor.

Hunt, Irene. **William: A Novel.**

Ifkovic, Edward. **The Yugoslavs in America.** Illus. by author. Lerner Pubns 1977.

Information on Yugoslavian immigrants to America and the contributions they have made to science, arts, politics, entertainment, and other fields is outlined in this book.

Jones, Hettie, compiler. **The Trees Stand Shining: Poetry of the North American Indians.** Illus. Robert Andrew Parker. Dial 1971.

Ethnic Cultures

These brief poems are lullabies, prayers, and a few war chants. They have been used as songs for many generations, passed along orally until the nineteenth century.

Jones, Weyman. **Edge of Two Worlds.** Illus. J. C. Kocsis. YB. Dell 1970.

Calvin Harper is on his way to law school when his wagon train is ambushed by Comanches and he is the only survivor. He meets an old Indian, Sequoyah, the Cherokee who invented an alphabet for his tribe. Neither trusts the other and for days they travel together mainly for survival, but as they learn more about each other their trust and friendship grow. Both are on the edge of two worlds: the boy is on the edge of manhood and the Indian, because of his alphabet, feels alienated from both Indian and white men. When they part company both their lives have been changed.

Lampman, Evelyn Sibley. **The Potlatch Family.** Atheneum 1976.

A young Pacific coast Chinook Indian girl endures school but does not like it generally. Her family is poor as are many other Indian families in her area. She develops a new outlook, however, when her brother returns home from military service after a long stay in the hospital. He has an idea to help his family and people. To regain some pride as well as make a profit, he talks them into a potlatch, a custom of feasting and gift-giving. Success comes from the endeavor, but her brother dies before the final potlatch.

Lester, Julius. **To Be a Slave.** Illus. Tom Feelings. Dial 1968.

Through the words of the slave, interwoven with strongly sympathetic commentary, the reader learns what it is to be another man's property; how the slave feels about himself; and how he feels about others. Every aspect of slavery, regardless of how grim, has been painfully and unrelentingly described.

Lewis, Richard, compiler. **I Breathe a New Song: Poems of the Eskimo.** Illus. Oonark. S&S 1971.

This book provides an effective, representative collection of Eskimo poetry. Most of the pieces are anonymous but are identified by Eskimo group or geographical origin, and the book is illustrated with primitive drawings by an Eskimo artist. Combining forcefulness with simplicity, the poems include songs of joy, love, fear, and death. Anthropologist Carpenter's introduction explains Eskimo beliefs and manner of expression.

McDowell, Robert E., and Edward Lavitt. **Third World Voices for Children.** Illus. Barbara Kohn Isaac. Okpaku Communications 1971.

This is an anthology of stories, folktales, and poems for all children divided into four sections containing stories from Africa; the other three, stories from the West Indies, the United States and Papua-New Guinea point up the great influence of African folklore on cultures throughout the world. The same characters and concerns turn up repeatedly under different guises. Many of the stories included are traditional and many were written by contemporary authors.

Newlon, Clarke. **Famous Mexican Americans.** Illus. with photographs. Dodd 1972.

Mexican-Americans were building the Southwest long before the Pilgrims landed. This and other overlooked facts come to light in this collective biography of twenty Chicanos who have become known for their accomplishments. It contains a foreword by a Chicano psychiatrist, a list of source materials, and an index.

O'Dell, Scott. **Sing down the Moon.** YB. Dell 1979.

Navaho families of Canyon de Chelly, Arizona, are happily raising their sheep, when suddenly two fourteen-year-old girls are stolen by marauding Spanish slavers and sold in Fort Sumner, New Mexico, to be house servants. This is the story, in the 1860s, of the Navaho's 300 mile "Long March" from the four corners of Arizona, Utah, Colorado, and New Mexico to captivity at Bosque Redondo and Fort Sumner. In 1868, these Navajos are released and walk back to their ruined homeland.

Purdy, Susan Gold. **Jewish Holiday Cookbook.** Illus. by author. Watts 1979.

This cookbook is a delectable treat with clearly presented recipes for the Hebrew holidays. Information about each holiday is provided along with a useful calendar which compares the Jewish one with the Gregorian. Ingredients are measured in both metric and standard form. Helpful advice regarding numerous cooking techniques and explanations for unique dietary laws that should be followed by Jews are included. Recipes originate in Romania, Russia, Hungary, Poland, and Austria.

Sebestyen, Ouida. **Words by Heart.** Little 1979.

In 1910, Ben Sills, a black man of great courage and wisdom, moves his family to an all-white community where they will have more opportunities. He is especially close to his daughter Lena, and spends many hours encouraging her love of learning. When Ben is murdered, Lena and Claudie, her stepmother, draw on his beliefs and teachings to carry on their struggle for human dignity.

Sobol, Rose. **Woman Chief.**

Steele, Mary Q., and William O. Steele. **The Eye in the Forest.** Dutton 1975.

Kontu, a young apprentice medicine man, Yovo the priest, and two warriors begin a long journey to find the Eye in the Forest. They must find the Sacred Eye if the Adena people are once again to live without fear of death and terrible hardship. Kontu discovers during the journey that he possesses many doubts about his ability to assume the priest role when Yovo dies. The hardships and difficulties he encounters help him to overcome his self doubts.

Taylor, Mildred D. **Roll of Thunder, Hear My Cry.**

Wolf, Bernard. **In This Proud Land: The Story of a Mexican American Family.** Lippincott 1978.

This is the story of a Mexican-American family, David and Maria Hernandez and their seven children, as they make their yearly migration from their home in the Rio Grande Valley in South Texas to the sugar beet fields of Minnesota. Excellent photographs of the family at work and in their leisure accompany the text.

Wood, Nancy. **Hollering Son.** Photographs by Myron Wood. S&S 1972.

This book provides written and visual poetic expressions of the philosophy of the Taos Indians. Historical background intertwined with interpretations of Indian beliefs make the introduction of the book important to the basic understanding of this group of people.

Yellow Robe, Rosebud, retold by. **Tonweya and the Eagles and Other Lakota Indian Tales.** Illus. Jerry Pinkney. Dial 1979.

These Sioux tales have been retold by the eldest daughter of an hereditary chief and descendant of Sitting Bull. They are told as stories shared with the chief when he was a young boy, and each combines a legend or folktale with details of life before the white man came.

Yep, Laurence. **Child of the Owl.**

Yep, Laurence. **Dragonwings.**

Yep, Laurence. **Sea Glass.** Har-Row 1979.

> Craig Chin does not seem to fit in anywhere since his family moved from San Francisco's Chinatown to the small town of Concepcion. He does not measure up to "Western" standards; he is not the basketball player his father was and wants him to be. Only reclusive Uncle Quail understands him. Combining ideals from two cultures, Chinese and Western, Craig sees that being different has its beauty. He can find a niche as an individual with a heritage from two cultures.

Ages 14 and Up

Adoff, Arnold, compiler and editor. **Celebrations: A New Anthology of Black American Poetry.** Follett 1977.

> This anthology of African-American poetry covers several generations of literature, major poets and their works along with newer poets and pieces. It presents the past and the future of the black American.

Allen, Terry. **The Whispering Wind: Poetry by Young American Indians.** Doubleday 1972.

> These poems reflect the young Native Americans' dreams, hopes, yearnings, and flashes of insight, and are sensitive, vivid expressions of a valued but less well-known facet of American literature.

Allen, T. D., editor. **Arrows Four: Prose and Poetry by Young American Indians.** WSP 1974.

> This is the result of a creative writing project for high school Indian youth funded by the Bureau of Indian Affairs. The laconic three lines of "The Last Supper" are by a Mohave freshman; the lilting, loving "Spring At Home" is by an Eskimo at Wainwright, Alaska; and at Phoenix Indian School, a Navajo senior wrote a detailed love story to God's precious gift, "My Mother."

Angelou, Maya. **And Still I Rise.** Random 1978.

> A popular black poet celebrates life in her third book of verse.

Angelou, Maya. **Gather Together in My Name.** Bantam 1975.

> In this autobiography of a black woman's struggle to find security for herself and her son Guy, Angelou relates how she narrowly escaped drug addiction. This is the continuation of her life story begun in *I Know Why the Caged Bird Sings.*

Bierhorst, John. **A Cry from the Earth: Music of the North American Indians.** Four Winds. Schol Bk Serv 1979.

Information regarding the use of music by various Indian tribes including musical notation and explanations of instruments used for accompaniment such as drums, rattles, flutes, and whistles are offered. There are brief chapters on different types of music, prayers, war songs, songs for the dead, and dances. The book is enhanced by old, authentic photographs.

Bierhorst, John, editor. **In the Trail of the Wind: American Indian Poems and Ritual Orations.** Illus. with engravings. FS&G 1971.

This collection of poetry, prayers, incantations, myths, and omens gathered from the oral tradition of many Native American tribes of both North and South America (including Eskimo) includes poems of creation, life and death, love and war, fear and courage, and of dreams, omens, and prophecies of life to come. A glossary of tribes and languages as well as notes for each poem contribute greatly to the collection.

Brandon, William, editor. **The Magic World: American Indian Songs and Poems.** Morrow 1971.

These poems and songs are from many tribes—Eskimo, Kwakiutl, Tlingit, Aztec, Mayan—and from all over the United States. A Nahuatl poem describes the rituals a pagan endures as a human sacrifice of their society's most beautiful youth. There are poems and songs that may seem blunt in their references to sexuality and in their use of slang expressions for various physical processes.

Brooks, Gwendolyn. **Maud Martha (in The World of Gwendolyn Brooks).** Har-Row 1971.

A series of vignettes are presented about Maud Martha, a black girl who wants "to be cherished." The story tells of Maud from the age of seven through her school years, and into marriage and the birth of her first child. Although life does not fulfill her dreams, Maud Martha continues to feel a great joy in being alive.

Brown, Dee. **Bury My Heart at Wounded Knee: An Indian History of the American West.** Bantam 1972.

Rather than "how the West was won," this book relates how American Indian tribes lost their lands. The reader learns which new lands were given away when settlers and gold seekers flooded into the Indians' beloved homelands.

Brown, Dee. **Tepee Tales of the American Indian.** Illus. Louis Mofsie. HR&W 1979.

> These Indian legends, passed down from more than two dozen American Indian tribes, are retold as if they were originally told in English about today's world.

Brown, Dee, and Martin F. Schmitt. **Fighting Indians of the West.** Ballantine 1974.

> These fine old pictures of famous Indians, taken by intrepid photographers in the days of our grandfathers, are carefully worked into a text that delineates over twenty-five years of the Western Indians' tremendous, heartbreaking attempts to keep their lands.

Burt, Jesse, and Robert B. Ferguson. **Indians of the Southeast: Then and Now.** Illus. David Wilson. Abingdon 1973.

> In this overview of the Indians of the Southeast—the Cherokees, Choctaws, Seminoles, and other small tribes—from prehistoric times to now, the authors describe their languages, religions, life-styles, food, games, dances, and music. Numerous photographs and drawings complement the text.

Carter, Forrest. **Watch for Me on the Mountain.** Delacorte 1978.

> This is the story of Geronimo—a gifted and extraordinary leader of the Apaches. He was "a man with powers that cannot be explained by science; a sensitive mystic, fearlessly loyal, and fearlessly loving man who, more than any other of his people, carved a place in American life and legend."

Courlander, Harold. **The Mesa of Flowers.** Crown 1977.

> The Grey Fox Clan wanders across the Southwest in search of the prophesied Mesa of Flowers, meeting strange peoples and being strongly influenced by folklore, visions, and legendary interpretations of natural phenomena. This story presents a carefully detailed account of a people seeking a land of peace.

Craven, Margaret. **I Heard the Owl Call My Name.**

Davis, Christopher. **North American Indian.** Hamlyn-Amer 1972.

> Illustrated with maps and more than 150 prints, paintings, and photographs, the book tells the story of the North American Indians' fortunes since the discovery of the American continent. The first half traces the fall of the Indians' fortunes; the second half deals with the Indians today and their place in society.

Ethnic Cultures

Downs, James F. **The Navajo.** HR&W 1972.

This case study of a warm, loving, contemporary Navajo family shares both the present and the historical past of the Navajo who journeyed from northeast Asia to Arizona and New Mexico. The family's love is exemplified by those who go home to visit the sheep.

Ellis, Mel. **Sidewalk Indian.** HR&W 1974.

Charley Nightwind, an Indian living in the city, is falsely charged with murder during an Indian protest movement. Escaping to a northern Indian reservation, he encounters for the first time the reservation Indian and becomes acquainted with the ways of his ancestors.

Falk, Randolph. **Lelooska.** Celestial Arts 1976.

This story in words and pictures presents one family's fight to preserve the culture, ceremonies, and art work of the Northwest Coast Indians. The Lelooska family is Cherokee. They have and are restoring and recreating the art work, woodcraft, housing, and jewelry of this rapidly disappearing culture.

Fire, John, and Richard Erdoes. **Lame Deer: Seeker of Visions.** PB 1976.

Lame Deer, a Sioux medicine man, a *wićaśa wakan*, tells of his childhood, his days in the white man's school, and his life in the white man's world as a sheepherder, a policeman, and a rodeo performer. The history and folklore of the Sioux are illustrated with photographs.

Gaines, Ernest J. **The Autobiography of Miss Jane Pittman.** Bantam 1974.

This is the story of a 110-year-old black woman who has been both a slave and a witness to the black militancy of the 1960s. Her life summarizes the American history of her race.

Graham, Lorenz. **Return to South Town.** T Y Crowell 1976.

In a continuation of a character in Graham's earlier novels, *South Town, North Town,* and *Whose Town,* David Williams, now a doctor, returns to South Town, Virginia, to serve his people. He finds many changes have taken place, but he still has to struggle to create a new life as the first black doctor in the southern community.

Greene, Bette. **Morning Is a Long Time Coming.** Archway 1979.

In the sequel to *Summer of My German Soldier,* Patty, a Jewish girl tormented by memories of the German P.O.W. who was her friend and hoping to escape the prejudices of the community, leaves America for Europe. Her experiences there are influenced by the emotional pain of her childhood.

Griffin, John Howard. **A Time to Be Human.** Macmillan 1977.

The author of *Black Like Me* gives an account of race prejudices experienced as a white child in Texas, as a black man in the South, and again as a white man in the ghettos of the big cities and in many countries around the world.

Guy, Rosa. **The Disappearance.** Delacorte 1979.

Sixteen-year-old Imamu Jones lives with his alcoholic mother in Harlem. Upon his acquital of a murder charge, he is taken in by a middle-class family in Brooklyn. The adjustment to a different lifestyle is difficult for Imamu. Two days after his arrival, their young daughter disappears and Imamu is suspected of having something to do with her disappearance.

Guy, Rosa. **Edith Jackson.**

Guy, Rosa. **The Friends.** Bantam 1978.

Phyllisia, a black girl, has moved to Harlem from the West Indies. Because of her dialect and show of knowledge in class, she is rejected by her classmates. Phyllisia is ashamed of Edith, a poor, shabby girl who is the only one to offer friendship, but when Edith is rejected by Phyllisia's father, she becomes the center of conflict between Phyllisia and her father.

Hale, Janet Campbell. **The Owl's Song.** Avon 1976.

Billy White Hawk is a young Indian growing up on a reservation. He witnesses his cousin's suicide and, as a result, feels he must get away for awhile. His father sends Billy to stay with his half sister, Alice Fay, in California. The hostility and racial prejudice he encounters in school there eventually force him to return to the reservation.

Haley, Alex. **Roots.** Doubleday 1976.

Beginning with his own wise, alert grandmother's memories, a black writer succeeds in tracing his ancestors to a small African village where relatives still live. The horrors of slave ships are described as well as the years of slavery before the Civil War. Both joys and sorrows are vividly told in this beautifully written, carefully researched novel.

Halsell, Grace. **Bessie Yellowhair.** Warner PB Lib 1974.

The author, whose father had been a Texas rancher before 1900, grew up with his inexhaustible Indian stories. Years after her father's death, her deep interest in Native Americans caused her to fly to

Ethnic Cultures 249

> Albuquerque from where she drove an old VW to the Navajo Reservation, borrowed a friendly Navajo's name, "Bessie Yellowhair," and set out to find how an Indian maid was treated in a white home.

Hamilton, Virginia. **Paul Robeson: The Life and Times of a Free Black Man.** Har-Row 1974.

> This is the story of a black man who became a well-known actor and singer against many odds. He later became unpopular due to his political stance that grew out of his views on black liberation, prejudice, and bigotry. Now, many people realize the far-sightedness of the man and understand how timely his views were.

Hannum, Alberta. **Spin a Silver Dollar: The Story of a Desert Trading-Post.** Ballantine 1972.

> Jimmy (Little No Shirt) is a small, very shy, eight-year-old Navajo who fills reams of paper with his pictures. His father is the handyman at the Wide Ruins Trading Post in northern Arizona. Lots of life, laughter, and ceremony are recorded in this true story.

Harris, Marilyn. **Hatter Fox.** Random 1973.

> Teague Summer, fascinated by Hatter Fox, a wild, spirited, seventeen-year-old Navajo Indian girl, goes to the reformatory where she has been sent after stabbing a doctor in jail. He is determined to save her from complete isolation from society and mental collapse.

Haskins, James. **Barbara Jordan.** Dial 1978.

> This is the biography of a congresswoman from Texas who is a fast-rising figure in politics. She was the first black woman to represent a southern state in the House of Representatives, the first to sit on the House Judiciary Committee during the impeachment proceedings against a president, and the first to give the keynote address at a Democratic National Convention.

Houston, Jeanne Wakatsuki, and James D. Houston. **Farewell to Manzanar.** Bantam 1974.

> In this true story of one Japanese-American family's struggle for survival in the Manzanar Internment Camp during World War II, the Wakatsuki family life-style is permanently altered as a result of the internment and the racial discrimination they endure afterwards.

Jordan, June. **His Own Where.** T Y Crowell 1971.

> Buddy, a sixteen-year-old black boy, meets Angela at the hospital where his father lies dying. When his and Angela's world begins to

fall apart, they find love and solitude in an old shack in a cemetery where they can talk and make love.

Kroeber, Theodora. **Ishi in Two Worlds: A Biography of the Last Wild Indian in North America.** U of Cal Pr 1976.

Ishi is the last of the California Indians. Robbed of his home and bereft of his people, in final desperation he turns to the white man, his enemy. Yet it is with the white man that he lives out his final years in gentleness and peace.

Mohr, Nicholasa. **Nilda.**

Momaday, N. Scott. **The Gourd Dancer.** Illus. by author. Har-Row 1976.

Momaday, a Kiowa, is professor of English and Comparative Literature at Stanford and a Pulitzer Prize winner. This volume of exceedingly original poetry should invite the reader to seek other writing by this author. Students will enjoy his rhyming patterns from very simple in "Walk on the Moon" to more locked-in patterns (tercets) as in "Child Running." There are also many poems that do not rhyme. All of the poems can be enjoyed for their beauty and imagery.

Momaday, N. Scott. **The Way to Rainy Mountain.** Illus. Al Momaday. Ballantine 1974.

Rainy Mountain is an old landmark of the Kiowa in Oklahoma. Three hundred years ago, the Kiowa migrated from their Montana home on the Yellowstone River to the Oklahoma plains. The author, himself a Kiowa, made a pilgrimage to his grandmother's grave, travelling this old route. In telling his vivid story, Momaday shows his love for his grandmother and includes old legends like the origin of Devil's Tower in South Dakota and of the Big Dipper. He brings together Kiowa beliefs from Montana, old stories from along the journey's way, tales of the golden age of the Kiowa for about 100 years after 1740, and contemporary experiences of his own.

Morrison, Toni. **Song of Solomon.** Knopf 1977.

Macon Dead, Jr., accepted by neither the black nor the white community because he is the son of the richest black family in a midwestern town, is in constant conflict with his family. He heads south where he uncovers the unspoken truth about his family and his heritage. Harsh language seems appropriate to this complex adult novel.

Nabokov, Peter, editor. **Native American Testimony: An Anthology of Indian and White Relations.** T Y Crowell 1978.

Indian voices tell the documented history of four centuries of Native Americans and white relations. Famous and little-known events illuminate key historical issues.

Neihardt, John G. **Black Elk Speaks: Being the Life Story of a Holy Man of the Oglala Sioux.** Illus. Standing Bear. PB 1972.

Black Elk, medicine man of the Oglala Sioux, was just a boy when Custer died at the Little Big Horn. He saw great visions that he carried with him throughout his life. He applied the old visions to new situations; could predict coming bad times; was a good hunter and solider who seemed to live a charmed life in battle.

Norris, Clarence, and Sybil D. Washington. **The Last of the Scottsboro Boys: An Autobiography.** Putnam 1979.

During the Depression era, Clarence Norris and eight other black men were accused of raping a white woman. Pardoned from the death penalty, Mr. Norris recounts his struggles in prison, his days on death row, and his final vindication.

O'Dell, Scott. **Child of Fire.** LFL. Dell 1978.

A sixteen-year-old Chicano, Manuel Castillo, jumps into the ring to challenge a bull while trying to impress a girl. Two attendants pick him up for questioning. A parole officer visits him even though Manuel was not on his list for supervision; however, the man's efforts to help are repeatedly frustrated by the boy's fiery temper and involvement with youthful gangs who engage in gamecock fighting.

O'Dell, Scott. **Zia.** LFL. Dell 1978.

A storm off the Pacific Ocean deposits many odd things on the California mainland beaches. One morning, Zia, fourteen, and her twelve-year-old brother Mando find a long boat which they hide in a scary, bat cave. Using this boat Zia is able to row out toward the far island of the blue dolphins where their mother's sister was left behind and alone eighteen years before at the time their Indian tribe evacuated that island.

Qoyawayma, Polingaysi (Elizabeth Q. White). **No Turning Back.** U of NM Pr 1978.

Polingaysi's family met their first white man when her father worked for a Mennonite missionary. She spent her life trying to retain the best of Hopi culture and trying to introduce Hopis to the best of white learning. Her mother, in terror, hid her school-aged children, but this daughter let herself be taken to school. There was "no turning back" in her life. As a child, she stowed away in a wagon of children for Sherman Institute in California. With missionary encouragement, she worked at many jobs and eventually studied teaching.

Quam, Alvina, translator. **The Zunis: Self-Portrayals by the Zuni People.** U of NM Pr 1973.

Zunis chose forty-six tales from their extensive oral literature to be printed for the first time. Included are two useful maps and pictures of a dozen storytellers. Divided into six sections, there are hunting stories, history, fables including those "of moral instruction," religion, and war/defense. The tales move from days of hardship and famine to days of comfort and plenty.

Rockwood, Joyce. **To Spoil the Sun.** HR&W 1976.

Rain Dove's story, spanning two generations, tells of the foreboding omens of her childhood, the invasion of the strangers with light-colored skin, and the suffering during the invisible fire, smallpox. This story presents the unfolding of the beginning of the end of the Cherokee culture.

St. George, Judith. **The Halo Wind.** Putnam 1978.

In 1845 Ella Mae Thatcher and her family begin the long journey from Illinois to Willamette Valley in Oregon. When Yvette, a young Chinook Indian girl, joins the wagon, everything mysteriously begins to go wrong. Ella Mae comes to grips with the inevitable conflict that arose between two cultures as thousands of pioneers poured into the West.

Salerno, Nan F., and Rosamond M. Vanderburgh. **Shaman's Daughter.** P-H 1980.

A beautifully written novel about the Ojibwa Indians of Canada, with a strong, sensitive woman as central character, this story includes much detail on Ojibwa beliefs and customs. It covers the period from 1897–1967. One of the authors is a professor of anthropology and lived with the Ojibwas for twelve years.

Silko, Leslie Marmon. **Ceremony.** Sig. NAL 1978.

Tayo, a young American Indian returning to his tribal reservation after World War II, finds that drinking and sex are not the answers to his search for new meaning in his life. He finds the answer in the past rituals of his people.

Steiner, Stan. **The New Indians.** Delta. Dell 1968.

> One hundred years ago, West Point cadet George Custer wrote that the red man was on the verge of extinction. In 1911, 1932, and 1964, writers said the Indian cause was lost, but Sam Steiner, who wandered twenty years from tribe to tribe, has put together this book in which he shares a vital, growing, contributing group of people. It is told in the Indians' own words.

Sterling, Dorothy, editor. **The Trouble They Seen: Black People Tell the Story of Reconstruction.** Doubleday 1976.

> This documentary of black history during Reconstruction as seen through the eyes of the black people who lived it presents a realistic view through the use of numerous personal letters, diaries, official documents, and articles from black newspapers.

Stuart, Colin. **Walks Far Woman.** Popular Lib 1978.

> The stories that served as the basis for this novel were told to the author by two elderly Montana Indian women. Walks Far, a beautiful young Blackfoot who is married and widowed by age eighteen, walks to Sioux country and is present at Custer's final battle in June 1876.

Tamarin, Alfred. **We Have Not Vanished: Eastern Indians of the United States.** Follett 1974.

> This is the story of Native Americans on the East Coast, where and how they live as compared with yesterday. Some live in cities; some live on lands occupied by their ancestors and are still carrying out the duties handed down to them. The major tribes presented include Algonquian, Iroquois, Sioux, and Muskogee.

Thomas, Piri. **Down These Mean Streets.** Knopf 1967.

> This autobiography is set in the streets of Spanish Harlem where every form of human depravity seems commonplace. Rejected by his father because of his dark skin, Piri turns rebelliously to the street, which is a battleground where he earns his rights. Piri fights, steals, becomes a drug addict, and finally goes to prison after shooting a policeman. He survives drug withdrawal and the physical and mental degradation of prison.

Walker, Margaret. **Jubilee.** Bantam 1975.

> This powerful narrative of the Civil War is told through the central character, Vyry, daughter of a white father and a Negro slave mother.

This remarkable woman, even after she endured unbelievable physical mistreatment as a slave and cruel harassment of herself and her family by the Ku Klux Klan, could still say, "God knows I ain't got no hate in my heart for nobody." Vyry was the maternal great-grandmother of the author.

Walking Bull, Gilbert C., and Montana H. R. Walking Bull. **Mi Ta-Ku-Ye (About My People).** Itemizer Observer 1977.

In this collection of stories and poems, Gilbert C. Walking Bull, an Oglala Sioux Indian, and his wife Montana H. R. Walking Bull, an Oklahoma Cherokee, write of their experiences and the beliefs and values instilled in them by their Indian heritage.

Young, Alida E. **Land of the Iron Dragon.** Doubleday 1978.

Lim Yan-sung, a fourteen-year-old immigrant from China, lives with his father in the crowded Chinese section of San Francisco until one night their store is burned and his father is killed. Making his way to Sacramento, he joins the crews building the first transcontinental railroad where eventually he learns that all Americans are not cheaters or murderers.

Religious Cultures

Ages 5 to 8

de Paola, Tomie. **The Christmas Pageant.** Illus. by author. Winston Pr 1978.

This is a charmingly illustrated presentation of the typical Christmas pageant given by children. The childlike explanation of the text makes a good way to share the story of Christmas beliefs with young children.

Eisenberg, Phyllis Rose. **A Mitzvah Is Something Special.**

Greene, Laura. **I Am an Orthodox Jew.** Illus. Lisa C. Wesson. HR&W 1979.

Told from a young boy's point of view, this story describes the customs of a devout Jewish family. The tone, though informative, is matter-of-fact. Though some of the restrictions are difficult for the children in the family to accept, the close-knit relationship aids them in willingly accepting their religious obligations.

Moncure, Jane Belk. **Our Christmas Book.** Illus. Helen Endres. Childs World 1977.

An elementary class tells about the way they celebrate Christmas—they make their own decorations and clay ornaments for their Christmas tree, sing Christmas songs, make a toy shop, play Christmas games, send pictures to Santa Claus, make family gifts, and finally visit another class to see what they did.

Ruggill, Peter. **The Return of the Golem: A Chanukah Story.** Illus. by author. HR&W 1979.

This fanciful tale combines the traditional aspects of Chanukah with the contemporary possibility of a visit of strange beings from outer space. The Rabbi and two young children witness the force of the Golem to save the synagogue and set things right again. The children also learn the possible danger of a good force becoming evil itself. Detailed and humorous, the black line drawings are essential to the development of the story.

Ages 8 to 11

Aronin, Ben. **The Secret of the Sabbath Fish.** Illus. Shay Rieger. Jewish Pubn 1978.

> Tante Mashe listens to stories of great scholars and heroes at the synagogue, and wishes she, too, could do something special for her people. A strange visitor sells her an unusual fish and instructs her to think about what has been happening to the Jewish people as she prepares the fish, admonishing her not to fry or bake it. In an almost ritualistic manner, she finds each step of the food preparation reminds her symbolically of events, from the tears brought on by onions to the use of eggs, a symbol of life, to the boiling of the fish balls representing the sea of time bubbling in turmoil. And so gefilte fish are created.

Barker, Carol. **A Prince of Islam.** Illus. by author. A-W 1977.

> The book describes the training of a boy who would like to become Caliph in the Muslim Empire, like his father. It also details his family's trip to Mecca. Colorful illustrations provide a realistic view of Muslim life in Baghdad in 820 A.D.

Barth, Edna, compiler. **A Christmas Feast: Poems, Sayings, Greetings, and Wishes.** Illus. Ursula Arndt. Clarion. HM 1979.

> The material selected for this collection comes from various parts of the world and from authors both of the present day and from the past. The book is organized into sections including, "Christmas Is Coming," "At Christmas Time We Deck the Hall," "A Child Is Born," "The Friendly Beasts," and "Do Not Open Until Christmas."

Blume, Judy. **Are You There, God? It's Me, Margaret.** Bradbury Pr 1970.

> This is a story of family relationships in which the parents are of different religions. Margaret has two pressing problems in her life: one is deciding which religious faith to follow and the other is her impatience with her seemingly slow physical maturation. Her delightful grandmother is a sustaining influence.

Cobb, Vicki. **Truth on Trial: The Story of Galileo Galilei.** Illus. George Ulrich. Coward 1979.

> Galileo's logical mind leads him to doubt that the earth is the center of the universe. Through much of his life he is respected as a scholar and a teacher, but even his old friend, the Cardinal, later becoming Pope Urban, is influenced by potential enemies and approves of

calling Galileo to trial. The scientist, loyal both to his logical thought and to his Catholic faith, denies in his old age that the sun is the center of the universe, and in so doing is allowed to return to his home in Florence, Italy, where he goes right on studying and writing a book that becomes the beginning of modern physics.

Cone, Molly. **A Promise Is a Promise.** Illus. John Gretzer. HM 1964.

Ruthy Morgen develops a self-conscious attitude because she is Jewish. The neighborhood homes celebrating Christmas, the invitation to a party at the church, and the hidden feelings she holds about her brother's Bar Mitzvah all naturally intensify her desire to be like everyone else. The descriptions of Ruthy's perceptive inner thoughts and of exchanges with her gentile friend Sandra about religion, rituals, and customs contribute to her growing pride in her own heritage.

Cuyler, Margery. **Jewish Holidays.** Illus. Lisa C. Wesson. HR&W 1978.

Eleven holidays are explored here with many references to rituals and special foods and the meanings behind them. Craft projects, songs, and a unique calendar of Hebrew months, showing where each holiday falls, reflect the importance of the holidays in Jewish life.

de Paola, Tomie. **The Clown of God.**

Greenfeld, Howard. **Chanukah.** Illus. Elaine Grove. HR&W 1976.

Chanukah is a celebration of the right to religious freedom. In December, all Jews joyfully commemorate the heroic deeds of the Maccabees, who fought to preserve individuality of Jews. This book gives a brief history of that fight.

Hopkins, Lee Bennett, editor. **Easter Buds Are Springing: Poems for Easter.** Illus. Tomie de Paola. HarBraceJ 1979.

This collection of nineteen poems addresses both the secular and Christian aspects of Easter as well as its relationship to spring. Poets include David McCord, Aileen Fisher, Dorothy Aldis, and Myra Cohn Livingston. Illustrations add humor and depth to the various poems.

Kleeberg, Irene Cumming. **Christianity: A First Book.** Watts 1976.

This is a simple account of the growth and development of the Christian religion from the time of Jesus through the present day. It shows the early evolution from a form of Judaism to a separate religion that now encompasses many denominations all over the world.

L'Engle, Madeleine. **Ladder of Angels: Scenes from the Bible.** Seabury 1979.

A work of art throughout, especially in text and illustrations, this beautiful volume grew out of an art contest to make the International Year of the Child. The illustrations are paintings selected from the exhibition, "Children of the World Illustrate the Old Testament." The author, inspired by the children's interpretations, gives unforgettable commentaries in poetry and prose to accompany the colorful and creative paintings of the children.

Levitin, Sonia. **A Sound to Remember.**

Lisowski, Gabriel. **On the Little Hearth.** Illus. by author. HR&W 1978.

This illustrated lullaby, written during times of unrest for the Jews, describes the rabbi teaching little boys, stressing memorization of God's law and a love for the Torah. Hebrew words and the actual music are provided.

McDermott, Beverly Brodsky. **The Golem: A Jewish Legend.** Illus. by author. Lippincott 1976.

A Jewish legend is presented with masterful visual representations. A product of magic, the Golem was molded from clay into the form of man and given life. This Golem was meant to protect the Jewish ghetto people from evil; however, it grew to be more terrible than the evil itself and was returned to dust.

Monjo, F. N. **The House on Stink Alley: A Story About the Pilgrims in Holland.** Illus. Robert Quackenbush. HR&W 1977.

Based upon historical facts, this tale of English refugees living in Holland during the 1600s tells how events of religious persecution during King James' reign lead the Saints, known as Pilgrims, to the New World. Pictures are rendered in the style and period of the country.

Provensen, Alice, and Martin Provensen. **A Peaceable Kingdom: The Shaker Abecedarius.** Illus. by authors. Viking Pr 1978.

In this twenty-six-line poem, each line lists a variety of real and mythical animals and begins with a successive letter of the alphabet. Shaker life is portrayed with richness and imagination and the text provides historical insights with the inclusion of brief notes on Shaker history. Illustrations have a rural nineteenth-century motif.

Robinson, Barbara. **The Best Christmas Pageant Ever.**

Religious Cultures

Rowland, Florence Wightman. **Amish Boy.** Illus. Dale Payson. Putnam 1970.

Jonathan Lapp, a ten-year-old Amish boy anxious to help and please his family, demonstrates his ability to assume responsibility when lightning strikes, the barn burns, and the Amish neighbors cooperate in a barn raising.

Sorensen, Virginia. **Plain Girl.**

Weil, Lisl. **Esther.** Illus. by author. Atheneum 1980.

This is a simple retelling of the Old Testament story of the Persian Queen who saved her Hebrew people. The illustrations give a feeling of the times expressed with a child-like quality.

Ages 11 to 14

Branscum, Robbie. **The Ugliest Boy.** Illus. Michael Eagle. Lothrop 1978.

Fourteen-year-old Reb, a preacher's son, has just arrived with his family in a rural community in Arkansas. Somewhat of a loner, he avoids mixing with people because he feels so ugly. Yet within, Reb is gentle, loving, and responsible. He meets a girl and for the first time experiences a genuine friendship. A confrontation with a wandering snake cult group gives ideological contrast to the story.

Fellows, Lawrence. **A Gentle War: The Story of the Salvation Army.** Photographs by Janet Beller. Macmillan 1979.

From its beginning in the mid-nineteenth century in East London, the Salvation Army has led a persistent, yet gentle war against poverty, loneliness, alcoholism, and other misfortunes of men and women. This history is told in clear photographs and prose that both avoid sentimentality or over-adulation.

Hamley, Dennis. **Pageants of Despair.**

Hickman, Janet. **Zoar Blue.** Macmillan 1978.

Barbara Hoff, an orphan, had lived for a number of years under the protection and guidance of German Separatists in their community at Zoar, Ohio. At the outbreak of the Civil War, Barbara abandons the Separatists' teachings and makes her way to Pennsylvania to locate an unknown relative. Seventeen-year-old John Keffler also leaves his family in Zoar when he feels compelled to enlist in the Union Army. The war experiences for both Barbara and John contribute to their becoming better able to fit their religious beliefs into the fuller web of lives which recognize and accept the larger commitments of society.

Kherdian, David. **The Road from Home: The Story of an Armenian Girl.**

Levoy, Myron. **Alan and Naomi.** LFL. Dell 1979.

Naomi is a war refugee, a victim of the Holocaust. Her mind is shattered by the memory of her father's being beaten to death right before her eyes. As Alan and Naomi become friends, she begins to trust him until one day she is witness to a bloody fight that Alan has while defending her against ridicule.

Lingard, Joan. **The File on Fraulein Berg.** Elsevier-Nelson 1980.

Meeting a former classmate in London reminds a woman of her childhood in Northern Ireland where for several years she and her friends had a semi-distant view of World War II in Europe. She reminisces about their Protestant outlook and stance toward Eire, the Catholic country to the south, their suspicions of a German teacher who must surely be a spy, and their belated discovery that she was instead a Jewish refugee from Germany. Their preoccupation with Protestant and Catholic cultures has not left them room to consider the German-Jewish question.

MacKellar, William. **The Silent Bells.** Illus. Ted Lewin. Dodd 1978.

The bells in the cathedral have never rung, and it is believed that only a certain gift brought to the creche will cause them to ring. Anne-Marie hopes the shawl she has made will be the right gift, but she gives it to an old lady on the road to Geneva and receives a modest gift in return. In a series of encounters, she exchanges one gift for another, bringing comfort to those she meets including the rescue of a prince following an avalanche. The royal gift she receives will surely cause the bells to ring, but she is wrong. They do finally ring, though.

Meyer, Carolyn. **Amish People: Plain Living in a Complex World.** Photographs by **Michael Ramsey**, Gerald Dodds, and the author. Atheneum 1976.

Written by a non-Amish individual who grew up in central Pennsylvania amidst these seriously devout people, this seems to be a thoughtful and fair study of the Amish. The reader is introduced to a hypothetical family and follows them through customs associated with birth, marriage, death, schooling, farming, and religious services while they face and maintain their own plain way of living.

Smucker, Barbara Claassen. **Days of Terror.** Herald Pr 1979.

> During the Russian Revolution, thousands of Mennonite families, welcomed long ago by Catherine the Empress of all Russia, suddenly find themselves suspect because of their German heritage and equally suspect as friends of the current Tsar and his supporters. This story of the Neufeld family presents the adjustments and sorrows of a people forced to accommodate an alien group who invade their Ukraine valleys demanding food and supplies. Peter Neufeld sees his grandfather imprisoned, his older brother slip away to join a self-defense group against Mennonite beliefs, and his neighbors' homes burned. Finally he must face a mass migration to Canada.

Ages 14 and Up

Barrett, William E. **Lady of the Lotus.** Doubleday 1975.

> This tells the love story of Yasodhara and Prince Siddharta Gautama, who was to become Buddha. Understanding her husband's destiny and sacrificing their romantic idyll to a great Idea, she found fulfillment in the new religion.

Brancato, Robin F. **Blinded by the Light.**

Bryan, Ashley, editor. **Walk Together Children: Black American Spirituals.** Illus. by editor. Atheneum 1977.

> Bold, vibrant, full-paged black and white woodcuts accompany each of twenty-four spirituals that grew out of a variety of black experiences: slavery, Christianity, memories of African music, and themes of joy and sorrow. The melody line is provided for each song.

de Hartog, Jan. **The Lamb's War.** Har-Row 1980.

> The author, a Dutch Quaker now living in the United States, continues the story he began in *The Peaceable Kingdom*. This book begins with a young Dutch Quaker girl's tragic experiences with a Nazi concentration camp, continues with a journey to her American grandmother and some strange experiences at a Quaker mission in New Mexico among the Indians, and ends with the world-wide movement of the Quakers for needy children.

de Hartog, Jan. **The Peaceable Kingdom: An American Saga.** Atheneum 1971.

> This long, rather slow-moving story of the Quaker movement, begins with the founders, George Fox and Margaret Fell, and details the

cruelty and imprisonment of Quakers in England in Cromwell's time (1652). Cruel treatment also follows in America until William Penn establishes a Quaker colony in Pennsylvania in 1681. The second half of the book, "The Holy Experiment," describes early Quaker accomplishments in America: prison reforms, treatment of the insane, school for Indians, and abolition of slavery.

Dickinson, Peter. **Tulku.** Victor Gollancz (London) 1979.

Young Theodore is the only survivor when his father's Christian mission settlement in remote China is attacked and destroyed. He meets and joins Mrs. Jones, a brash, strong-willed Englishwoman, who is accompanied by Lung, a young Chinese man, who acts as her guide. The three journey into Tibet where they meet the old Lama, and he determines that the unborn baby Mrs. Jones now carries is the Tulku, or reincarnated leader of the Buddhist people. Theodore struggles with the shock of religious values seemingly foreign to his strong Christian background. His journey results in a readjusting of his convictions to reconcile the ideas met on his sojourn with the powerful influence of his father's teaching.

Dimont, Max I. **The Jews in America: The Roots, History, and Destiny of American Jews.** S&S 1978.

In this history of the Jews from 1659 to today, the author states that "American Judaism is a unique outgrowth of the American soil . . . and that American Judaism is destined to play the same role in the future of the Jews that rabbinic Judaism played in their past." He also contends that American Judaism will not only preserve the Jewish heritage but will serve as a vehicle for its enrichment.

Goldston, Robert. **Next Year in Jerusalem: A Short History of Zionism.** Little 1978.

The author traces the development of the Jewish national identity from Biblical times through the years of struggle, dispersal, exile, and slaughter to the emergence of the World Zionist movement and the establishment of the Zionist state of Israel. The book presents an objective, dramatic, and enlightening history.

Goldston, Robert. **The Sword of the Prophet: A History of the Arab World from the Time of Mohammed to the Present Day.**

Green, Gerald. **The Artists of Terezin.** Illus. The Inmates of Terezin. Hawthorn 1978.

The author of *Holocaust* writes of Terezin, a concentration camp in

Czechoslovakia, where the inmates turned to art, poetry, and philosophy in order to maintain their humanity. The paintings, drawings, and sketches that portray life in the camp serve as a tribute to the courage of the Jewish people.

Hesse, Hermann (translator Hilda Rosner). **Siddhartha.** New Directions 1951.

Siddhartha is a soul-searcher who meets the Buddha, a manifestation of the ultimate good. Siddhartha must find the ultimate good on his own; so he abandons his friends, rejects the teachings of his elders, and goes to the city to "learn" the life of man. After numerous experiences, he accepts the final renunciation and achieves self-knowledge.

Hickman, Janet. **The Valley of the Shadow.** Macmillan 1974.

Two Delaware Indian boys survive a brutal massacre of their entire community by the white Virginia militia who cannot accept the idea that a group of Indians could be pacifists. Yet these Delawares have been pacifists for several generations since their conversion to Christianity by German Moravians. The writing is particularly effective, calling upon vivid images appropriate to the time of the American Revolution and the Ohio wilderness. The story is based upon actual records of the Moravian missionaries.

Levin, Meyer. **The Harvest.** Bantam 1979.

After World War I, a Russian Jewish family, as a part of the world Zionist movement, settled in Palestine. Matis, who has been educated in Tel Aviv, goes to the United States to work his way through the University of Chicago but returns to help defend his home from hostile enemies.

Meltzer, Milton. **World of Our Fathers: The Jews of Eastern Europe.** LFL. Dell 1976.

Milton Meltzer writes of his Jewish heritage—the places they lived in Eastern Europe, the work they did, and the customs, habits, and values they lived by. It is the account of the cultural heritage of most of today's six million American Jews.

Michener, James A. **Hawaii.** Fawcett 1978.

This is the story of Abner and Jerusha Hale and their four children, but more important, it is the story of missionaries and their influence on life in Hawaii. The natives come to Hale's church, but in times of crisis they revert to the traditional pagan rites. It is Abner's son,

Hoxworth Hale, who sees the day when East and West can be united in the "new Hawaii."

O'Dell, Scott. **The Hawk That Dare Not Hunt by Day.** LFL. Dell 1979.

William Tyndale translated the Bible into English for the first time, had the book printed, and smuggled it into England. This story is told by sixteen-year-old Tom Barton who meets Tyndale, grows fond of him, and assists him in his efforts. The historical period of Henry VIII is richly developed, and the reader senses the conditions of both splendor and poverty, disease, treachery, life upon the Thames, and furtive crossings of the Channel.

Potok, Chaim. **The Chosen.** Fawcett 1978.

A portrayal of two young Jewish boys, *The Chosen* tells the story of Danny Saunders, whose father is a Hasidic rabbi, keeper of an ancient tradition, and Reuven Malter, whose father is an Orthodox rabbi, despised by the Hasidim. An accident brings the boys into unexpected contact. They experience the strains of ending adolescence and the conflicts between each boy and his father. The beauty of the novel lies in the expression of humanity, the demonstration of love and respect between father and son, and the transmitting of religious and intellectual traditions.

Potok, Chaim. **My Name Is Asher Lev.** Knopf 1972.

A young Jewish boy is compelled to be an artist. To do so he must immerse himself in the Christian tradition of the masters, tear himself away from his own ancestral heritage, and alienate himself from his orthodox Jewish family. There is great inner tension and conflict as he grows in art and life.

Potok, Chaim. **The Promise.**

Rice, Edward. **The Five Great Religions.** Four Winds. Schol Bk Serv 1973.

Hinduism, Buddhism, Islam, Judaism, and Christianity are traced from their beginnings to the present. Numerous pictures depicting each religion's cultural background and worship practices are included. The similarities and differences of these religions are discussed. A critical analysis of Christianity from the viewpoint of the other four is included in the closing summary.

Regional Cultures

Ages 1 to 5

Seeger, Ruth Crawford. **American Folk Songs for Children: In Home, School and Nursery School.** Illus. Barbara Cooney. Zephyr. Doubleday 1980.

Popular folksongs from all over the United States are embellished with joyful, tiny, detailed black and white drawings. Each song is on a full page with music and is identified by state of origin. Accompanying notes provide added information and suggestions for improvisation activities.

Ages 5 to 8

Baylor, Byrd. **Hawk, I'm Your Brother.** Illus. Peter Parnall. Scribner 1976.

Rudy Soto, living in the Santos Mountains of southwestern United States, dreams of flying, not like a cactus wren or sparrow, but like a hawk gliding smoother than anything else in the world. When he becomes the "brother" of a young hawk, his awareness of freedom is awakened as he feels his spirit flying in the wind with his winged brother.

Baylor, Byrd. **When Clay Sings.** Illus. Tom Bahti. Scribner 1972.

A lyrical tribute to an almost forgotten time of the prehistoric Indian of the desert West presents broken bits of pottery from this ancient time. The designs and drawings, done in rich earth tones, are derived from prehistoric pottery found in the American Southwest.

Caudill, Rebecca. **Did You Carry the Flag Today, Charley?**

Getz, Arthur. **Tar Beach.** Illus. by author. Dial 1979.

This picture book presents a day during the summer in New York City through the experiences of one family living in an apartment. One sees the children sleeping on the fire escape, everyone (including Pop) shopping at the supermarket, a multi-ethnic community playing and conversing on the street that is closed off so no cars can drive through. A highlight of the warm day is when the fire hydrant is opened and all sizes of kids play in the giant spray.

Gibbons, Gail. **The Missing Maple Syrup Sap Mystery.** Illus. by author. Warne 1979.

In this amusing picture book, Mr. and Mrs. Mapleworth discover their sap buckets are empty each morning when they check, and spend several nights trying to discover the cause. Once the problem is solved, the full process of making maple syrup is described through the remaining illustrations and text. A New England setting is implied.

Miles, Miska. **Hoagie's Rifle-Gun.**

Myers, Bernice. **Little John Bear in the Big City.** Illus. by author. Four Winds. Schol Bk Serv 1978.

Little John Bear won't go to his cousin's wedding because all he has is an old, worn-out coat. He sets out to borrow a coat from a friend who lives in the city. This is a first trip for this congenial bear, and he notes that the city has few trees, hardly any berries to eat, strange places like a cave entrance (for the subway), and strange moving monsters on which everyone rides through tunnels (the subway train, itself). The story provides an amusing introduction to cities for young children with equally humorous illustrations.

Sharmat, Marjorie Weinman. **The Trolls of Twelfth Street.** Illus. Ben Shecter. Coward 1979.

Trolls usually seem to live under bridges, so why not a family in a cave under Brooklyn Bridge? Young Eldred Troll persists in wishing his family could find out what it is like *up there,* and succeeding, the family discovers tall buildings, automobiles, the sun, and even a laundromat. Readers will be amused as troll customs are compared with those of city dwellers.

Spier, Peter. **The Legend of New Amsterdam.**

Watson, Clyde. **Father Fox's Pennyrhymes.** Illus. Wendy Watson. T Y Crowell 1971.

Good Father Fox in his stout work overalls is as American as barley corn. His exuberant rhymes and jingles, inspired by life on a Vermont farm, sing with the ring and the twang of a square-dance fiddler. The black line and watercolor illustrations are in keeping with the wit and language of the Pennyrhymes.

Regional Cultures 267

Ages 8 to 11

Adoff, Arnold. **Tornado!** Illus. Ronald Himler. Delacorte 1977.

> Powerful, stark lines of free verse commemorate the terrible tornado that hit Xenia, Ohio, in April of 1974. The turbulence and destruction as well as the drawing together of people are effectively presented in the black and white illustrations that enhance the poetic language of this book.

Evansen, Virginia B. **The Flea Market Mystery.** Illus. Ray Abel. Dodd 1978.

> Nancy and Tomas Perez set out ot solve the mystery of the robbery at the Senior Citizens' Coop Store where their grandparents' handwork has been included in the stolen items. The setting is a small town not far from Los Angeles. Information about garage sales leads to some significant sales and also plays a part in finding the guilty ones.

Frank, Phil, and Susan Frank. **Subee Lives on a Houseboat.** Photographs by Bruce Forrester. Messner 1980.

> Subee and her family live on a houseboat in the Sausalito Houseboat Community in the San Francisco Bay area. Daily life includes playing on friends' boats and visiting potters, welders, artists, carpenters, and the many other people who make a living on and near the waterfront. Black and white photographs depict the unique features of this houseboat community.

Gates, Doris. **Blue Willow.** Illus. Paul Lantz. Puffin 1976.

> Having to move from one migrant camp to another intensifies Janey Larkin's desire for a permanent home, friends, and school. The only beautiful possession the family has is a blue willow plate handed down from generation to generation. It is a reminder of happier days in Texas and represents dreams and promises for a better future. Reading about this itinerant family's ways of life, often filled with despair and yet always hopeful, leaves little room for the reader's indifference.

Griese, Arnold A. **The Way of Our People.** Illus. Haru Wells. T Y Crowell 1975.

> The Alaskan boy, Kano, is excited that he has shot his first moose, but he is afraid his people will learn he is afraid of hunting in the forest. Therefore he attempts to find other ways to help his tribe, such as driving a husky team in time of emergency. The story is set in Alaska of the early 1800s.

Jackson, Louise A. **Over on the River.** Photographs by George Ancona. Lothrop 1980.

Reverently told, this is a portrait of life early in the twentieth century in central Texas. The photographs are essential in evoking the spirit of a time now past when two girls cut out paper dolls from a mail-order catalog, folks travel by wagon, and an evening's entertainment could consist of Mama playing the old upright with the telephone earpiece placed on a nearby table so that families on the line could listen on their wall phones at home.

Lenski, Lois. **Cotton in My Sack.** Illus. by author. Dell 1966.

Joanda Huntler with other members of her sharecropper family picks cotton in the fields of Arkansas. She assumes many family responsibilities for overcoming the everyday hardships faced by the field workers. Joanda looks forward to the Saturday night pleasures in town when cotton-picking is good, even though that often means having little or no money for the next week. The colorful and descriptive language of this region reflects a cultural aspect of a way of life. Young readers have the opportunity to see how the joys, hopes, and beliefs of a group of people are closely interwoven with their means of earning a living and their environment.

Lenski, Lois. **Strawberry Girl.** Illus. by author. Dell 1967.

Birdie Boyer, "Strawberry Girl," seems as real to today's readers as she was to Lois Lenski when she first saw her plowing in a Florida field. With her many insecurities, Birdie faces adversities by dreaming of the future. The story contrasts the lives of the Boyer family with those of their less industrious neighbors in the backwoods of Florida. Readers can gain insight into life in this region with its dialect and traditions.

Lewis, Claudia. **Up and Down the River: Boat Poems.** Illus. Bruce Degen. Har-Row 1979.

This collection of poems, inspired by life upon the Hudson River, includes occasional rhyming, mostly free verse, describing gentle images of water in motion, reflections, the overriding sky, and changing seasons. These are useful poems to share with children unfamiliar with rivers.

Molnar, Joe, editor. **Graciela: A Mexican-American Tells Her Story.** Watts 1972.

One of ten children in a migrant Chicano family, twelve-year-old

Graciela describes the annual trip to pick produce in Michigan. She is candid about the prejudice her people face but does not dwell on it. Rather she comments on her family's efforts to improve their financial and educational condition.

Norris, Leslie. **Merline and the Snake's Egg.** Illus. Ted Lewin. Viking Pr 1978.

This is a collection of poems about such various circumstances as a fern buried in coal, buying a puppy, mice talking in a Bethlehem stable, the Kings' camels, and a coal mining grandpa. Black and white illustrations complement the verse.

Rawls, Wilson. **Where the Red Fern Grows.**

Schwartz, Alvin, compiler. **Chin Music: Tall Talk and Other Talk.** Illus. John O'Brien. Lippincott 1979.

"Chin music" is when you sit around talking and telling stories. Included here are all sorts of funny, yet interesting words and sayings that come from different parts of the United States. The examples of folk speech, representing the period 1815 to 1950, are identified by specific regions in a source list at the end of the book.

Shecter, Ben. **The River Witches.**

Smith, Doris Buchanan. **Kelly's Creek.** Illus. Alan Tiegreen. T Y Crowell 1975.

Kelly lives near the Atlantic coast in southeast Georgia where he spends all the time he can in the nearby marsh. He has a friend in the marsh, Phillip, a college student studying marine biology, and together they have learned much about fiddler crabs. His parents are unsure of this bearded stranger. At school Kelly is not making progress, seems to have a serious learning problem, and resists doing the perception exercises required. It's Phillip who encourages Kelly to share his knowledge about the marsh at school and thereby feel more sure of himself.

Snow, Richard. **The Iron Road: A Portrait of American Railroading.** Photographs by David Plowden. Four Winds. Schol Bk Serv 1978.

The author reminisces about his love for railroads and intersperses the history of railroading, blending it all with nostalgic, but informative photographs.

Snyder, Zilpha Keatley. **The Velvet Room.**

Stuart, Jesse. **The Beatinest Boy.** Illus. Robert Henneberger. McGraw 1961.

> David, a small orphaned boy, finds a real home with his grandmother who lives in the mountains of Kentucky. The understanding, esteem, and love that evolve between the two culminate in David's successful struggle to earn the money to buy a Christmas present for his grandfather.

Turkle, Brinton. **The Fiddler of High Lonesome.** Illus. by author. Viking Pr 1968.

> Sud, Deet, Hunk, and Old Man Fogle live at the top of High Lonesome. Lysander Bochamp goes there to claim his kin when his mother dies, for his "mammy were a Fogle from Chickasaw Creek." The boy decides that the Fogles are no kin of his, however, when they refuse to respect the lives of the "little critters" of the mountains. The book retains the flavor of the oral tale, and the timelessness of an important literary theme shows through the author's simple plot and style.

Yolen, Jane. **Rainbow Rider.** Illus. Michael Foreman. T Y Crowell 1974.

> Indian myths are reflected in this modern creation story of Rainbow Rider who needs a friend. Sand, weed, and cactus aren't suitable. Foreman's water colors are luminous and particularly effective in presenting the western desert of this tale.

Ages 11 to 14

Anderson, Madelyn Klein. **Counting on You: The United States Census.** Vanguard 1980.

> Providing both a history and current status of the census taken every ten years in our country, this book reflects present cultural attitudes. Changes include no longer assuming that the head of the household is male; increasing specificity of racial origin options beyond the historical "white or other"; and recognizing new household relationships such as single-parent families and unmarried couples. Explanations regarding the usefulness of the information requested are clearly made as are some of the concerns citizens have about the confidentiality of the information gathered.

Blos, Joan W. **A Gathering of Days: A New England Girl's Journal, 1830-32.** Scribner 1979.

> Fourteen-year-old Catherine records, rather faithfully, the day-to-day

events of her life on a small New Hampshire farm including the remarriage of her father, the death of a close friend, and her small contribution to assisting a fugitive slave. The gentle prose is written in the idiom of the early nineteenth century with carefully detailed customs recorded, such as making a quilt, reprimanding the young teacher for seeming to go beyond "reading, writing, and cyphering," and the 4th of July celebration in town. Readers can use this story to compare life in New England with midwestern life as presented in the Little House books. The diary format could serve to guide students in developing personal journals.

Burch, Robert. **Wilkin's Ghost.**

Clark, Ann Nolan. **All This Wild Land.** Viking Pr 1976.

A man, his wife, and eleven-year-old daughter arrive in the Minnesota wilderness from their native Finland. It is 1876, and they have come to join relatives in making this new land their home. They bring their customs, their unwavering love of their homeland, and their devotion to each other. Pioneering life is difficult, sometimes with tragic consequences, but each makes a willing commitment to the land. The portrait of the loving father is particularly effective.

Cleaver, Vera, and Bill Cleaver. **Trial Valley.**

Cleaver, Vera, and Bill Cleaver. **Where the Lilies Bloom.**

Constant, Alberta Wilson. **Does Anybody Care About Lou Emma Miller?** T Y Crowell 1979.

In this nostalgic view of rural Kansas early in the twentieth century, high school life and family relationships in a small town are clearly woven into this story of Lou Emma who struggles with algebra, envies her very competent debater sister, is fond of Tommy yet fearful he prefers haughty Zetta, and comes up with the idea of establishing a town library. An added line of interest is the election campaign of Tommy's mother for mayor in a time when people seemed firmly divided concerning women running for public office and women's suffrage was not yet a national right.

Demuth, Jack, and Patricia Demuth. **City Horse.** Dodd 1979.

A highly personal account of a New York City policeman and his horse, Hannon, begins with a nine-hundred mile trip from Tennessee Walker country to the city where the horse smells gas fumes and winter air for the first time. Hannon's training and duties provide insight into the life of this great city.

Distad, Audree. **Dakota Sons.** Illus. Tony Chen. Trophy. Har-Row 1972.

> In the summer Ted helps his father in the family general mercantile store in a South Dakota town. Ronnie Whitecloud, a Sioux, has a father who rides in rodeos, or at least that's Ronnie's explanation. Both boys are lonely this summer and develop a fine friendship—biking, shooting baskets, and taking in a local rodeo.

Edmonds, Walter D. **Bert Breen's Barn.** Illus. Eric Sloane. Little 1975.

> This novel, rich in the details of upstate New York at the turn of the century, deals with a boy's dreams of owning a barn, his growing maturity, and respectability. There are the elements of mystery, threat, and perpetual hard work that can make young readers sharply aware of the contrast between Tom Dolan's life and their contemporary one.

George, Jean Craighead. **The Cry of the Crow.** Har-Row 1980.

> Mandy's father and older brothers relentlessly hunt crows in order to keep them away from the family's strawberry crop on their farm in Piney Woods in the Florida Everglades country, but she has befriended an eyas—a baby crow—left helpless when the parent birds were shot by an unknown hunter. Naming it Nina Terrance, Mandy learns to communicate with it by imitating different sounds of the crows. She also knows that crows can be vindictive, that they recognize their enemies, and she fears someone in her family killed Nina's parents which means that person can be in danger.

Hamilton, Virginia. **M. C. Higgins, the Great.**

Haskins, James. **The Creoles of Color of New Orleans.**

Herbert, Wally. **Eskimos.** Watts 1977.

> In an overview of the history of the Eskimos and their most distinctive culture, the author questions whether the Eskimos were forced to accept the change in their life, or whether they chose of their own free will to abandon the old ways and try the new.

Hinton, S. E. **Rumble Fish.** Delacorte 1976.

> The "Rumble fish," Siamese fighting fish, kill each other if they can. Like them, Rusty James and his brother Motorcycle Boy rely more on their fists than they do their brains. Rusty James is the number one tough guy among the junior high kids; Motorcycle Boy is the most respected hood on his side of the river. But much as he would

like to think so, Rusty James is not really like Motorcycle Boy. This story provides an inside view of contemporary youth culture.

Holling, Holling Clancy. **Paddle-to-the-Sea.** Illus. by author. HM 1969.

In a meticulously researched tale of a Canadian Indian boy's carving which travels the Great Lakes on its way to the sea, handsome, full-paged pictures show significant moments in the carving's journey. Elaborately detailed sketches present a wealth of information about the life and industry of each of the Great Lakes.

Keith, Harold. **The Obstinate Land.** T Y Crowell 1977.

The Romberg family made the Oklahoma landrun of 1893. Fritz's father had previously identified a piece of land, but when the family arrives they find that the Cooper family had soonered—preceded the official run and settled the Romberg choice of land illegally. Without adequate law enforcement in those early days, the Rombergs must travel further and settle on less desirable land. The land is obstinate as the family faces drought, dust storms, hard winters, and unfriendly ranchers. Young Fritz also faces a great sorrow and finds the strength to carry on the family's determination to forge a home in this new, strange land.

Kornfeld, Anita Clay. **In a Bluebird's Eye.** HR&W 1975.

In an isolated coal-mining town in the Great Smoky Mountains of Tennessee, an eleven-year-old girl's best friend is a black woman who has served time in prison for killing a man. The story presents a strikingly authentic portrait of life in the rural South during the Depression.

Moore, Lilian. **Sam's Place: Poems from the Country.** Illus. Talivaldis Stubis. Atheneum 1973.

In the shadow of the Shawangunk Mountains of the northern Alleghenies, these poems have their setting. They trace through a country year and reflect upon the human experience and its relationship to the natural world. Strikingly apt images accompany the verse.

St. George, Judith. **The Amazing Voyage of the New Orleans.** Illus. Glen Rounds. Putnam 1980.

In 1811, Nicholas Roosevelt had studied rivers and navigation sufficiently to design the first deep-hulled steamboat to sail the Ohio and Mississippi Rivers. Hearing many disparaging voices, he never let loose of his dream and finally reached New Orleans. On the way the ship witnessed the Great Comet of 1811, experienced the strongest earthquake ever recorded in North America, and outdistanced a bark war canoe of the Chickasaws.

Strait, Treva Adams. **The Price of Free Land.** Lippincott 1979.

This biography of the author's parents details their homesteading in western Nebraska between 1914 and 1917. The Adams were a closely-knit family, and everyone worked hard both to survive and establish a home. Experiencing a tornado from a freshly dug cellar, walking several miles to the rural school, and building first a tent shelter and then a sod house are some of the events described.

Taylor, Theodore. **Teetoncey.**

Wilkinson, Brenda. **Ludell.** Bantam 1980.

Ludell is the first of three novels that chronicle the life of Ludell Wilson, a young black teenager living in Georgia. The author draws on her own childhood experiences to tell about life in the poor rural community. Ludell's days are filled with school, chores at home, summer in the cotton fields, and pleasures with her friends, especially Willie, her new boyfriend. She is aware, also, of the poverty surrounding her, the lost dreams of a teenage mother, the false glitter behind her own mother's infrequent visits, and an awareness that strengthens her dreams of a future beyond Waycross, Georgia.

Wolf, Bernard. **In This Proud Land: The Story of a Mexican-American Family.**

Ages 14 and Up

Childress, Alice. **A Hero Ain't Nothin' but a Sandwich.** Avon 1974.

Benjie Johnson, a thirteen-year-old black boy from the ghetto, is well on his way to being hooked on heroin. His mother, grandmother, stepfather, friends, and teachers tell the story of his troubles. Mature language is used in this picture of ghetto life.

Church, Peggy Pond. **The House at Otowi Bridge.** U of NM Pr 1976.

Edith Warner came from Pennsylvania around 1930 to live out her life across the Rio Grande River from San Ildefonso Pueblo and at the foot of Los Alamos Hill where great scientific advances were made in atomic energy before Hiroshima. She tried several odd jobs in her lifetime, but she found her greatest satisfaction in serving excellent meals at her little house to the famous scientists and in knowing the Indians at Ildefonso.

Conroy, Pat. **The Water Is Wide.** Photographs by William Keyserling and Paul Keyserling. HM 1972.

Pat Conroy accepts a most challenging teaching assignment—teaching the almost illiterate black children living on isolated Yamacraw Island off the coast of South Carolina. His unorthodox methods bring results for these children who were almost totally ignorant of the outside world.

Estes, Winston M. **Homefront.** Lippincott 1976.

The Holly family of Bentley, Georgia, was a closely-knit one before World War II. Their heartaches, joys, tribulations, faith, and patriotism are a reflection of all Americans during this era.

Graham, Lorenz. **Return to South Town.**

Greene, Bette. **Summer of My German Soldier.**

Haviland, Virginia, editor. **North American Legends.** Illus. Ann Strugnell. Collins Pubs 1979.

Using the broad term "legends," the editor has compiled an anthology of myths, legends, and tales from North America which originated from four main groups: American Indians and Eskimos, black Americans, European immigrants, and American "tall tales." There are useful notes on each of the stories as well as suggestions for further reading. This book should be a fine resource for teachers and young readers.

Jenkins, Peter. **A Walk Across America.** Morrow 1979.

A restless young college graduate sets out with his half malamute dog, Cooper, in October of 1973 to discover the heart of America. He begins his walk across the land in New York State on the eastern coast, then moves into Tennessee and Alabama, and finally concludes this book and the first half of his journey in New Orleans. He meets and lives with a loving black family for a period of time; works hard hours in a North Carolina sawmill; nearly dies in a storm; and buries his faithful companion.

Lawrence, R. D. **The North Runner.**

Lee, Mildred. **The People Therein.** Clarion. HM 1980.

A love story between a mountain girl with a crippled leg and an outsider from Boston, this novel steeps the reader in a Smoky Mountain setting at the early part of this century. The language and customs of the mountain people are deftly shown.

Massey, Ellen Gray, editor. **Bittersweet County.** Anchor Pr. Doubleday 1978.

> Included in this book are the best of the *Bittersweet* pieces from a magazine issued by a high school class in Lebanon, Missouri. They document the customs of the people of the Ozarks who established a culture that still exists there today, but has almost disappeared from the land.

Mohr, Nicholasa. **Nilda.** Illus. by author. Har-Row 1973.

> Nilda lives in a tenement building in the neighborhood known as El Barrio—Spanish Harlem. Nilda's mother is the strength that holds the large affectionate family together through many crises as Nilda learns to cope with the problems of youth, especially those of an adolescent Puerto Rican growing up in New York City.

Schellie, Don. **Maybe Next Summer.** Four Winds. Schol Bk Serv 1980.

> Seventeen-year-old Matt spends his summer vacation as a reporter for a small New Mexico newspaper, owned and operated by old family friends. The town of Crandall, just inside the United States border, is usually a quiet place with news of tea parties, weddings, and socials. While learning the newspaper business, Matt stumbles upon a big alien-smuggling ring through which hundreds of Mexicans each year slip into the United States illegally in hopes of finding a better way of life.

Specht, Robert. **Tisha: The Story of a Young Teacher in the Alaska Wilderness.** St. Martin 1976.

> This true story of a young white woman in the untamed northern gold-rush settlement of Chicken, Alaska, portrays warmth and love, violence and sudden death, prejudice and struggle as Ann Hobbs, a teacher, is pitted against the determination of the people that she will conform to their standards.

Wigginton, Eliot, editor. **The Foxfire Book.** Anchor Pr. Doubleday 1972.

> Since the first *Foxfire* was published in 1972, five successive volumes have been written. They are a collection of folklore, crafts, "how to" articles, home remedies, "affairs of plain living," and unique remembrances of the Appalachian mountain folk. The knowledge of their roots, heritage, and culture is collected and written by the Rabun Gap-Nacoochee School journalism class whose teacher and adviser is Eliot Wigginton.

Wilkinson, Brenda. **Ludell and Willie.** Har-Row 1977.

> Willie and Ludell, childhood friends, have developed a deeper relationship over the past six years. Now in their senior year, they face unexpected problems, such as the death of Ludell's grandmother and the return of her real mother from New York. Ludell is torn by these recent happenings, but her love for Willie gives her the courage to carry on. The character portrayals are sharp and the Southern black dialect enhances the story.

Wilkinson, Brenda. **Ludell's New York Time.** Har-Row 1980.

> Ludell, a young black girl, is forced to move to New York from Georgia to live with her mother after the death of her grandmother. She leaves behind her boyfriend, Willie. The new life-style, difficulty finding a job, and her loneliness and desire to marry Willie create problems that Ludell must learn to cope with.

Wright, Lawrence. **City Children, Country Summer.** Scribner 1979.

> A group of street-wise New York City ghetto children spend two weeks in a Pennsylvania Amish community. A striking contrast between cultures of young Americans, the story reveals enduring relationships that bridge differences of race, religion, and life-style.

World Cultures

Ages 1 to 5

Demi. Under the Shade of the Mulberry Tree. Illus. by author. P-H 1979.

A clever poor man buys the shade of a mulberry tree in the yard of a rich man in this Chinese tale. Owning the shade permits him to be wherever that shade is and that includes the yard, the steps, furniture, and even within until finally the rich man is routed. The Oriental appearance of the minutely detailed drawings complements the humor of the story while presenting the historic Chinese setting.

de Paola, Tomie. **Strega Nona.** Illus. by author. P-H 1975.

This is the retelling of an old folktale about "Grandmother Witch," Strega Nona. Everyone in her Calabrian town comes to Strega Nona for magic potions, but no one knows her secrets until Big Anthony overhears some incantations. The problems he runs into and the lessons he learns combine with boldly humorous pictures to make a delightful book.

Graham, Lorenz. **Song of the Boat.** Illus. Leo Dillon and Diane Dillon. T Y Crowell 1975.

Flumbo's dugout canoe has been destroyed by an alligator, and he begins the search for a tree suitable for building a new canoe. His son Mololu finds, through a dream, the perfect tree. Village customs, including the rituals performed around the chosen tree, are included. The idiomatic English of Liberia is rhythmic and provides fresh images.

Green, Norma. **The Hole in the Dike.** Illus. Eric Carle. T Y Crowell 1974.

This retelling of the familiar story of Peter's finger in the hole in the dike that saved Holland is enhanced greatly by the bold, lively illustrations. Personal courage and heroism are well communicated.

Ages 5 to 8

Aardema, Verna, retold by. **Half-a-Ball-of-Kenki: An Ashanti Tale.** Illus. Diane Stanley Zuromskis. Warne 1979.

In this humorous folktale, the leopard gains its spots and cornmeal mush (Half-a-Ball-of-Kenki) attracts flies. Bold, colorful illustrations include design motifs based upon Ashanti art. This story should be very good for telling aloud and for comparison with the Kipling "Just So" story.

Aardema, Verna, translated and retold by. **The Riddle of the Drum: A Tale from Tizapán, Mexico.** Illus. Tony Chen. Four Winds. Schol Bk Serv 1979.

In this folktale, a handsome prince must discover the material used to make the King's special drum in order to marry his beautiful daughter. On his journey to solve the riddle, he meets various people with unique talents which eventually become quite useful. There are echoes of "Rumpelstiltskin" and "Anansi the Spider" in this retelling of a familiar bit of folklore. The festive, colorful illustrations depict the Mexican setting of long ago.

Aardema, Verna. **Why Mosquitoes Buzz in People's Ears.** Illus. Leo Dillon and Diane Dillon. Dial 1975.

In this brilliantly illustrated African folktale, a mosquito angers an iguana and sets in motion a series of events that lead to the death of some owlets. Mother Owl is so saddened that she will not wake the sun until justice is done and the mosquito is properly punished. Readers can compare this story with myths from other cultures.

Anderson, Robin. **Sinabouda Lily: A Folktale from Papua New Guinea.** Illus. Jennifer Allen. Oxford U Pr 1979.

Sinabouda Lily loves to swing on a thick vine that goes out over an island where the wicked witch lives. Sinabouda Lily has a magic bunch of bananas that her father provided as protection when he and her mother are away. But Sinabouda Lily does not know that the magic spell will not work if she eats all the bananas and throws away the skins. And that is exactly what she does! Strong, vibrant pictures in greens, browns, and blues, quite appropriate to the locale of the story, illustrate the text.

Aruego, Jose, and Ariane Dewey. **We Hide, You Seek.** Illus. by authors. Greenwillow 1979.

> This almost wordless, full-color picture book of animals of East Africa develops the concept of camouflage through a very humorous story of a rhinoceros who is "it," and, in turn, tries to find the hiding creatures of the bush, desert, swamp, plains, river, and forest. End papers assist the reader in identifying each animal in the book. Rich in color and details, this book will be one children will examine over and over.

Bartoli, Jennifer. **The Story of the Grateful Crane.**

Baylor, Byrd. **The Way to Start a Day.** Illus. Peter Parnall. Scribner 1978.

> In a lyrical tribute to the sun and the beginning of each new day, Baylor shares how people throughout history and over the world today honor each new sunrise. Parnall's drawings flow from page to page in a fluid fashion, presenting the eternal wonder of every new day and creating a dramatic blending of prose and illustration.

Bunting, Eve. **St. Patrick's Day in the Morning.** Illus. Jan Brett. Clarion. HM 1980.

> It is very early morning and Jamie Donovan is first to awaken. He sets off with Nell, the sheepdog, to reach the top of Acorn Hill in order to prove that he can reach the top even though he is considered too young to walk in the parade to the hill. Strong, bold pictures with green dominant capture the rugged Irish countryside.

Dewey, Ariane, retold by. **The Fish Peri.** Illus. by author. Macmillan 1979.

> In this Turkish folktale, Ahmed catches a beautiful fish in his net and discovers that it changes into a lovely girl. The wicked Padishaw wants to marry her and she repeatedly sends Ahmed to the Genie in the sea to fulfill each of the impossible demands made by the royal leader. Illustrations, in a variety of muted colors, depict the ever-present sea as well as the Turkish style of building and costume.

Ets, Marie Hall, and Aurora Labastida. **Nine Days to Christmas.** Illus. by authors. Viking Pr 1959.

> Ceci, now old enough to participate in the Posadas, the festive Mexican parties given for the nine nights preceding Christmas, has difficulty choosing a special piñata. Her sadness at the thought of her star piñata being broken is overcome by the sight of the real

World Cultures

Christmas star. The illustrations and sensitive story, filled with myriad details, will supplement the reader's appreciation of Christmas life in Mexico.

Feelings, Muriel. **Moja Means One: A Swahili Counting Book.** Illus. Tom Feelings. Dial 1971.

Written to familiarize children with East African life, this picture book also teaches them to count from one to ten in Swahili. A map shows where Swahili is spoken.

Foreman, Michael. **Panda's Puzzle and His Voyage of Discovery.** Illus. by author. Bradbury Pr 1977.

Panda stared at his reflection in a can lid, wondering about himself. Was he a black and white bear, or a white and black bear? He travels down from the mountains where first he meets musicians and singers, then on into the city, then to a wide river that leads to the ocean which takes him to many countries. He discovers everyone is different and returns home happy. Illustrations reflect many cultures.

Fregosi, Claudia, adapted by. **Snow Maiden.** Illus. by author. P-H 1979.

This adaptation of the Russian version of the Persephone myth is told in simple, fluid prose and is enriched with illustrations that seem almost to swirl off the page. Snow Maiden strives to heed the warnings of her parents, Frost and Wind, when they permit her to go down to earth, but she falls in love with a kindly farmer and wants to stay on earth. At the end of the narrative are suggestions for developing the story into a drama.

Garrison, Christian. **The Dream Eater.** Illus. Diane Goode. Bradbury Pr 1978.

Everyone in Yukio's Japanese village is having bad dreams and waking tired and grouchy. Yukio is sent away by his father, mother, grandfather, and the old samurai. Yukio saves a baku, "dream eater," from the river and gives the baku a rice ball to eat. In return the baku eats everyone's bad dreams and they can sleep peacefully again.

Ginsburg, Mirra. **How the Sun Was Brought Back to the Sky.** Illus. Jose Aruego and Ariane Dewey. Macmillan 1975.

This adaptation of a Slovenian folktale attempts to explain how the sun is urged to return after a number of very cloudy days. The striking feature of this book is the humorous illustrations in bright, vivid colors which lead the reader from one page to another in this accumulative tale.

Ginsburg, Mirra, translator and editor. **The Lazies: Tales of the Peoples of Russia.** Illus. Marian Parry. Macmillan 1973.

In this collection of fifteen humorous tales, the stories generally emphasize the virtues of hard work, but a few have the lazy character winning in the end. Each story's setting reflects characteristics of Russia, including habits and beliefs.

Ginsburg, Mirra. **The Night It Rained Pancakes.** Illus. Douglas Florian. Greenwillow 1980.

In an adapted Russian folktale, one clever brother, Ivan, finds a pot of gold and tricks his simple brother, Stepan, with pancakes that seem to rain from the sky, a fish caught in a land-trap, and a rabbit caught in a fishnet, and so is able to keep his gold a secret even though Stepan talks too much.

Hou-tien, Cheng. **Six Chinese Brothers.** Illus. by author. HR&W 1979.

This is a tale of six brothers each of whom has a unique characteristic such as cleverness, the ability to stretch one's arms to the ends of the world, or a skin like iron. A doctor tells the boys that the only way to save their ailing father is to boil the great pearl from the King's palace and then offer the water to the father to drink. But when the king tries to execute the person responsible for the loss of the pearl, each brother's special quality is employed to save his life.

Howard, Moses L. **The Human Mandolin.** Illus. Barbara Morrow. HR&W 1974.

This is an original folktale about a mandolin in Africa that can bring joy back into people's lives with its beautiful music.

Lloyd, Errol. **Nini at Carnival.** Illus. by author. T Y Crowell 1978.

Nini's friends are all going to the Jamaican carnival in costumes. Nini wants to go but she has no costume. Her friend Betti talks Nini into going without a costume. At the carnival Betti puts on a mask, pretends to be Nini's fairy godmother, and gives her a costume. After the carnival, the girls go home together, and Nini seems not to realize that her friend Betti was the fairy godmother.

Löfgren, Ulf, retold by (translator Sheila LaFarge). **The Boy Who Ate More Than the Giant: And Other Swedish Folktales.** Illus. by author. Collins Pubs 1978.

World Cultures

These fanciful tales include a goatherd who outwits a giant; a troll who learns a lesson from goats; and a tailor who makes clothes that are fun. "Monstrously" funny illustrations accompany the text.

Maitland, Antony. **Idle Jack.** Illus. by author. FS&G 1979.

In this retelling of the familiar English folktale, a simple boy, who gets a different job each day, carries home some goods as payment in a most inappropriate manner because he uses yesterday's advice for today—i.e., when told to carry a coin in his pocket, he then attempts to transport an open jug of milk that way and most of the contents splash out. The bold, colorful illustrations are filled with action and should delight a young reader. A good book to compare with the Eve Merriam version of *Epaminandas* and Galdone's *Obedient Jack*.

McClenathan, Louise. **My Mother Sends Her Wisdom.** Illus. Rosekrans Hoffman. Morrow 1979.

This clever tale is set in pre-revolutionary Russia. In the story, an old woman tricks the moneylender into owing rubles to her. The writing and detailed illustrations are particularly effective in evoking the events and the setting of the time.

McDermott, Beverly Brodsky, adapted by. **Sedna: An Eskimo Myth.** Illus. by author. Viking Pr 1975.

In this myth of the Inuit, Sedna, the mother of all sea animals, tells how she has been deceived and now lives alone at the bottom of the sea. Angakok, the Inuit magic man, promises to respect Sedna by arranging her hair and ridding it of parasites. In return she guides seals toward the hungry hunters. Illustrations in indigo and violet suggest the cold, shadowy north.

McDermott, Gerald, adapted by. **The Magic Tree: A Tale from the Congo.** Illus. by author. HR&W 1975.

Two brothers live in the Congo. One gets everything and the other is left out. The lonely one leaves home, accidentally rescues people from the magic tree, and is rewarded but must keep it secret. He forgets and loses everything. Bold illustrations in intense colors will attract young readers.

Raynor, Dorka. **This Is My Father and Me.**

Reid, Barbara, and Ewa Reid. **The Cobbler's Reward.** Illus. Charles Mikolaycak. Macmillan 1978.

Janek, the young cobbler, decides to travel from village to village in

Old Poland seeking work. On his way, he assists some ants rebuilding their trampled nest, replaces fallen honeycombs in the bees' broken hive, and feeds a group of ducks. Later Janek is imprisoned by a witch who threatens to kill him unless he can accomplish three tasks. He is disheartened by the impossibility of each task but soon the creatures he has befriended help him out.

Rose, Anne, retold by. **Akimba and the Magic Cow: A Folktale from Africa.** Illus. Hope Meryman. Four Winds. Schol Bk Serv 1976.

The old man in the forest gives, in turn, a magic cow, sheep, and chicken to Akimba, and with appropriate magic words he amasses gold and silver coins and an unlimited supply of eggs. Shortly after receiving each gift Akimba leaves the animal with his neighbor, Bumba, in order to go on a journey. Bumba discovers the magic, and when Akimba returns he receives a different animal, one without magic. On Akimba's fourth visit to the forest, the old man gives him a magic stick that he uses to punish Bumba and regain his magic animals.

Rose, Anne. **The Triumphs of Fuzzy Fogtop.** Illus. Tomie de Paola. Dial 1979.

Fuzzy Fogtop is fuzzy-brained and even when he makes a list to keep his things in order, he loses himself. When he travels from Pinsk to Minsk, he doesn't realize that the train has not moved and discovers how exactly alike the towns are. The humorous illustrations are based upon the artist's study of village life of Eastern European Jews.

Roy, Ronald. **A Thousand Pails of Water.**

Smith, Jim. **Alphonse and the Stonehenge Mystery.** Illus. by author. Little 1979.

Mole McGrath and Alphonse le Flic set out to discover who is stealing the rocks at Stonehenge and leaving inflatable decoys in their place. The large, bold illustrations bounce with humor, detail the familiar English countryside, and present varying vantage points.

Spier, Peter. **People.** Illus. by author. Doubleday 1980.

This oversize picture book is actually a concept book about individual and cultural diversity.

Swados, Elizabeth. **Lullaby.** Illus. Faith Hubley. Har-Row 1980.

This lullaby is in celebration of the International Year of the Child.

The special love between parent and child is visually represented through pictures of different cultures from around the world. A recording of the text is attached to the inside back cover.

Titus, Eve. **Anatole and the Pied Piper.** Illus. Paul Galdone. McGraw 1979.

This book fairly sings the musical story it has to tell. Lilting language tells of the not-so-nice Grissac who plays the flute and writes music but has failed to compose a satisfactory Minuet for Mice until he becomes a Pied Piper of Paris. The story has a French setting and includes appropriate names for characters such as Claud and Claudette and Paul and Paulette, and adds an occasional French phrase in just the right place.

Waterton, Betty. **A Salmon for Simon.** Illus. Ann Blades. Atheneum 1980.

Simon lives on the west coast of Canada and all summer he has fished for a salmon without success. When he finally gets one, it comes in a most unusual way, from the sky dropped by an eagle, and lands in his sandy clam hole. Simon finds himself concerned and not eager to take his fish home, but the problem is how to get it back to the sea. The full-color pictures have an appropriate watery effect.

Wetterer, Margaret. **Patrick and the Fairy Thief.** Illus. Enrico Arno. Atheneum 1980.

In the foothills of the Connemara Mountains of Ireland, young Patrick's mother just disappears, and then he catches a trouble-making fairy stealing the cow. A great argument follows and, despite the fairy's persuasive ways, Patrick refuses to release his hold on the cow's horns and finds he has broken the spell and his mother returns after a tiring year of dancing.

Yolen, Jane. **The Seeing Stick.**

Zemach, Kaethe. **The Beautiful Rat.** Illus. by author. Four Winds. Schol Bk Serv 1979.

A family of rats in Japan decides it is time to marry off their lovely daughter, Yoshiko; but the mother and father cannot agree upon a suitable husband. Deciding that there is nothing greater than the sun, they go to offer her, but the sun has no time to marry and suggests the cloud as a more desirable husband. And so begins a chain of efforts to find the most powerful husband, a chain that leads right back to a rat. This is a good book to compare with Ginsburg's *The Strongest One of All.*

Ages 8 to 11

Aardema, Verna. **Who's in Rabbit's House?** Illus. Leo Dillon and Diane Dillon. Dial 1977.

> In this humorous Masai tale, the Long One has taken over Rabbit's house and won't let her in. Many friends unsuccessfully try to rid her house of the bad animal, but it takes a witty frog to flush out the Long One. The illustrations show Masai actors portraying the animals in the story and could serve as a model for puppetry.

Aliki. **Mummies Made in Egypt.** Illus. by author. T Y Crowell 1979.

> Simply told, this book describes in clear detail the process of mummification. Excellent drawings with appropriate captions accompany the text and present the step-by-step procedures of preparing and honoring the dead in ancient Egypt.

Bang, Betsy. **The Cucumber Stem.** Illus. Tony Chen. Greenwillow 1980.

> In this adaptation of a Bengali folktale, a woodcutter's wife wishes for a child, eats a magic cucumber but forgets to eat the stem, and suddenly has a tiny boy only two fingers tall. When the woodcutter sells himself to the Raja, Little Finger works to buy the man back. His work includes befriending a toad and capturing the king of a village of thieves. In the end, another magic cucumber assists Little Finger in his wedding to the once half-blind princess.

Bang, Garrett. **Men from the Village Deep in the Mountains.** Illus. by author. Macmillan 1973.

> These well-written stories from Japan provide an awareness of a different culture while also illustrating that people everywhere have similar virtues and faults.

Bible, Charles, adapted by. **Hamdaani: A Traditional Tale from Zanzibar.** Illus. by author. HR&W 1977.

> Hamdaani is a beggar who finds a dime. He buys a pet gazelle who happens to speak. Though the gazelle brings good fortune to the beggar, wealth goes to his head and he forgets his friend. The conclusion is one that shows what happens when one forgets to be grateful.

Bomans, Godfried (translator Patricia Crampton). **The Wily Witch and All the Other Fairy Tales and Fables.** Illus. Wouter Hoogendijk. Stemmer Hse 1977.

> These forty-five stories by a master storyteller have been translated

from the Dutch to reveal a book full of demons, witches, princesses, wizards, and other magic beings. Pervading almost every tale is a sense of the ridiculous. Each story is less than ten pages in length, making it a good choice for telling or reading aloud.

Bulla, Clyde Robert. **The Beast of Lor.** Illus. Ruth Sanderson. T Y Crowell 1977.

Lud, a boy of ancient England, is forced to fend for himself when his grandmother is taken captive by the villagers for witchcraft. While dodging the invading armies of Rome, he happens upon a strange and enormous beast never before seen in England. The beast and a "milky-white kingstone" enable Lud to defeat his foes and to help his new friends regain their kingdom.

Clark, Ann Nolan (retold by Dang Manh Kha). **In the Land of Small Dragon: A Vietnamese Folktale.** Illus. Tony Chen. Viking Pr 1979.

In a sensitive retelling of a Vietnamese variation of Cinderella, Number Two Wife is jealous of Tam, the child of Number One Wife, and sets out to make sure her own daughter, Cam, becomes Number One Daughter. There is a magic fish, a lovely silken dress, and a pair of jeweled shoes (hai). A crow carries away one of the hai and drops it in the Emperor's garden where the young prince determines he must find the maid who fits the shoe.

Coerr, Eleanor. **Sadako and the Thousand Paper Cranes.**

Cooper, Susan. **Jethro and the Jumbie.** Illus. Ashley Bryan. Atheneum 1979.

Jethro lives on the Caribbean island of Great Camanoe in the British Virgin Islands, and he is going to be eight. His older brother Thomas says he is not strong enough to go deep sea fishing, and angry with a broken promise, Jethro goes off where he meets a jumbie, the spirit of the dead who no longer remembers whose spirit. Jethro refuses to be intimidated, and in the end, he lets the jumbie work on changing Thomas's mind through a dream.

D'Aulaire, Ingri, and Edgar Parin D'Aulaire. **Book of Greek Myths.** Illus. by authors. Zephyr. Doubleday 1962.

Originally published in 1962, this handsome collection of Greek tales is now available in paperback. The soft, muted colors in this well-illustrated volume enhance the text. A most useful, though brief, index is included to assist one in locating familiar references to Greek gods and places.

Epstein, Sam, and Beryl Epstein. **A Year of Japanese Festivals.** Illus. Gordon Laite. Garrard 1974.

>Festivals are part of the way of life in Japan. In this book the reader is introduced to festivals that honor the gods and to some that honor people, festivals that relate to history, to the seasons, and to the beginning and ending of the year. A pronunciation guide and index are appended.

Fritz, Jean. **Brendan the Navigator: A History Mystery About the Discovery of America.**

Ginsburg, Mirra. **The Fisherman's Son.** Illus. Tony Chen. Greenwillow 1979.

>This is a Russian folktale about a boy who saves a fish, stork, deer, and fox and receives from each a promise of help in the future. As a young man, he meets and falls in love with a maiden who will only marry the person who can hide from her magic mirror. The animals then help him with this almost impossible quest. The illustrations alternate between full-color pages and pages with text and line drawings.

Ginsburg, Mirra, collected and adapted by. **The Twelve Clever Brothers and Other Fools.** Illus. Charles Mikolaycak. Lippincott 1979.

>These fourteen stories tell of very foolish folk in Russian lore. The tales are extremely short, many only one or two pages in length, and should be quite appropriate for early efforts in storytelling. They could also provide simple ideas for puppet shows.

Glubok, Shirley, and Alfred Tamarin. **Olympic Games in Ancient Greece.**

Goodall, John S. **The Story of an English Village.**

Griese, Arnold A. **The Wind Is Not a River.**

Harris, Peter, translator. **Monkey and the Three Wizards.** Illus. Michael Foreman. Bradbury Pr 1977.

>Written 400 years ago in China, stories of Monkey are still much loved. In this episode, a Buddhist monk, Tripitaka, and several wizards are outwitted by Monkey in a series of magic contests. Illustrations, alternating between bright water colors and single, gray tones, depict the pageantry of the Orient.

Harris, Rosemary. **The Child in the Bamboo Grove.** Illus. Errol LeCain. S G Phillips 1971.

An old Japanese bamboo cutter finds a child in a hollow reed and raises her. As an adult, she forces her suitors to do impossible tasks. Then she learns she is the daughter of the Sun and must return to him.

Holme, Bryan. **Tales from Times Past.** Viking Pr 1977.

Holme has selected twenty tales, six fables, and six rhymes including "Rumpelstiltskin" by the Brothers Grimm, illustrated by Cruikshank; "Cinderella" by Perrault, illustrated by Rackham; "Beauty and the Beast" by Beaumont, illustrated by Boyle; and "Bearskin" written and illustrated by Pyle. The illustrations are by artists from the "golden age of illustration" or from 1850 to 1920, and their varied talents make this book a visual banquet. A short biography of each author and illustrator is provided.

Hou-tien, Cheng. **The Chinese New Year.** Illus. by author. HR&W 1976.

Preparation and celebration of the Chinese New Year are represented through the unique art of paper-cutting. The scissor-cuts by the author create a visual description of daily life during the pageantries of the Little New Year, the New Year, and the Festival of Lanterns. This book provides an interpretation of the most festive of the holiday rituals in China.

Junne, I. K., editor. **Floating Clouds, Floating Dreams: Favorite Asian Folktales.** Doubleday 1974.

A collection of twenty-six myths and legends from ancient Asia, these stories come from Burma, Cambodia, China, India, Japan, Korea, Laos, Persia, Thailand, Tibet, and Vietnam. Some stories are very similar to folktales and legends found in other cultures.

Kendall, Carol, and Yao-wen Li, retold by. **Sweet and Sour: Tales from China.** Illus. Shirley Felts. Seabury 1979.

The oldest of the twenty-four brief Chinese tales in this collection was written in the third century B.C. and several more are from the Ch'ing Dynasty, which ended in 1911. All others fall somewhere between. Most are filled with humor and wit and they are especially well-suited for telling or reading aloud.

Kurelek, William. **A Prairie Boy's Summer.** Illus. by author. HM 1975.

Twenty somewhat disconnected "chapters" of one page each combine with twenty colorful, detailed paintings to tell the story of a young boy's summer experiences in the western prairies of Canada. The hard work connected with farm life is forcefully presented. William's difficulties in typical sports find a satisfying ending when he discovers his skill in archery.

Lasker, David. **The Boy Who Loved Music.** Illus. Joe Lasker. Viking Pr 1979.

In picture book format, this story tells of Karl, horn player in the Prince's orchestra. Haydn is the director, and all the musicians are eager to leave the Prince's summer castle and return to their families in Vienna. A new symphony composed by Haydn surprises the Prince and succeeds in achieving the musicians' desires. Illustrations are filled with information about the fashions and customs of eighteenth-century Europe.

Lewis, Richard, compiler. **Miracles: Poems by Children of English-Speaking Countries.** S&S 1966.

This selection of poems was written by children from English-speaking nations throughout the world. Through the eyes of these children, the reader realizes that no matter where they live or what their backgrounds may be, children have many of the same interests, the same reactions to fears and joys, ask the same questions, and wonder at the same things.

Lurie, Alison, retold by. **Clever Gretchen and Other Forgotten Folktales.** Illus. Margot Tomes. T Y Crowell 1980.

Fifteen seemingly forgotten tales in which fair maidens are resourceful, fearless, and clever are presented. This collection serves to balance the large number of folktales in which females generally are submissive or waiting patiently for rescue. At the end of each tale is a brief explanation of its origin, and specific literary sources are provided at the close of the book. These tales read easily and should lend themselves to oral telling.

Minard, Rosemary, editor. **Womenfolk and Fairy Tales.** Illus. Suzanna Klein. HM 1975.

In this book of folktales, women play the main roles, using their strength, courage, and wisdom to outwit foes. The stories are filled with adventure and quest and provide an excellent alternative to many traditional tales where female roles seem confined to the helpless damsel or wicked witch.

Monjo, F. N. **Prisoners of the Scrambling Dragon.**

Moore, Ruth Nulton. **Tomás and the Talking Birds.** Illus. Esther Rose Graber. Herald Pr 1979.

Tomas and his mother move from Puerto Rico to live on the mainland with an uncle. Americans seem pleasant enough to Tomas at first, but the language is hard for him to learn. His inability to talk with his classmates frustrates and isolates Tomas. He befriends a parrot from Mexico who is as lonely as Tomas and together they learn English.

Myers, Steven J. **The Enchanted Sticks.** Illus. Donna Diamond. Coward 1979.

This tale, set in old Japan, tells of an old man beset by robbers and left only with a bundle of sticks. But the sticks are magical and can spell out messages for the old man, play tic-tac-toe with him, dance, and participate in mock sword fights. When the robbers become more powerful, they imprison a young girl in a bamboo cage and force her to sing; hearing her, the old man and his unusual sticks come to her rescue. Exquisite line drawings evoke an oriental mood.

Ofek, Uriel. **Smoke over Golan: A Novel of the 1973 Yom Kippur War in Israel.**

O'Hare, Colette, collected by. **What Do You Feed Your Donkey On? Rhymes from a Belfast Childhood.** Illus. Jenny Rodwell. Collins Pubs 1978.

Most of these limericks, chants, and skipping rope songs are still heard today in Ireland and they have been accurately recorded in this book. The variety of pictures helps the reader in becoming acquainted with the culture. Explanations of games, foods, or songs are given at the end of the book.

Paterson, Katherine. **The Sign of the Chrysanthemum.** Illus. Peter Landa. T Y Crowell 1973.

A young Japanese boy who never knew his father is orphaned after his mother's death. She had told Muna (meaning no name) that his father was a great Samurai. Muna sets out to find his father, looking for a great man with a chrysanthemum tattoo. He meets a former Samurai, Takanobu, who rescues him from the wrath of the sea captain; a kind father with his daughter Aukiko, who feed him when he is hungry; but most important is the swordsmith, Fukji, who takes Muna in and helps him find his own identity. The inclusion of Japan's traditions and life-style enhances this story.

Price, Christine. **The Mystery of Masks.** Illus. by author. Scribner 1978.

This book details the use of masks throughout history in many cultures. The beliefs and rituals of various peoples are presented, and the accompanying pencil drawings depict the unique beauty of masks from all over the world. The illustrations are well labeled—there is a list of museums where the actual masks are located; and this list includes added information such as the materials from which the masks were made, the approximate dates when they were made or used, and their dimensions.

Reig, June. **Diary of the Boy King Tut-Ankh-Amen.** Illus. by author. Scribner 1978.

If the young Egyptian monarch had kept a diary during the year he became king (he was nine), this might have been it. Written from a child's point of view, it details the customs and way of life of Egypt in about 1334 B.C. and describes the circumstances of the boy marrying and becoming king.

Seed, Jenny. **The Bushman's Dream: African Tales of the Creation.** Illus. Bernard Brett. Bradbury Pr 1974.

The dream time was long ago when the animals and insects called themselves people. The grandfather of these people was Mantis, the maker of dreams. Finally as his magic moved him, Mantis discovered the dream was the passage of time.

Serwadda, W. Moses (transcriber and editor Hewitt Pantaleoni). **Songs and Stories from Uganda.** Illus. Leo Dillon and Diane Dillon. T Y Crowell 1974.

Thirteen stories with accompanying songs taken from Ugandan folklore are found in this colorful and authentic collection. Included are story songs, work songs, game songs, and lullabies. Song texts are given in both Lugandan and English, but should be sung in Lugandan to enjoy the full rhythm of the song. A pronunciation guide is provided.

Siberell, Anne. **Houses: Shelters from Prehistoric Times to Today.** Illus. by author. HR&W 1979.

Simplified explanations of various shelters—from isolated skin-covered poles to villages and cities made first from stone (Egyptian) and clay (Babylonian) and later elaborate homes of marble with porches and courtyards (Greek)—are detailed. Other cultures are represented: England and its castles, Native Americans with long houses and adobe pueblos and finally houses in different parts of the United States.

Smith, Edward, editor. **The Frogs Who Wanted a King and Other Songs from LaFontaine.** Illus. Margot Zemach. Four Winds. Schol Bk Serv 1977.

Fables, set to music (many adapted from Aesop), are presented here in French. The English translations could be used by older children to create their own lyrics for the accompanying music. The colorful illustrations by a former Caldecott winner are lively and humorous.

Steele, William O. **The Magic Amulet.** HarBraceJ 1979.

Tragg realizes his family has abandoned him since his seriously injured leg, the result of an attack by a saber-tooth tiger, makes him a burden. Through willful determination he recovers and sets out to find his family. Instead, he meets another nomadic band. There is dissension among the group about accepting Tragg, and he learns quickly to become both a part of the group and yet independent enough to rely primarily upon himself for survival. The story takes place in prehistoric time in southeastern America.

Toye, William, retold by. **The Mountain Goats of Temlaham.** Illus. Elizabeth Cleaver. Oxford U Pr 1969.

This legend of the Tsimshian Indians of British Columbia tells of when hunters in the village of Temlaham became thoughtlessly greedy and killed goats only for sport. One spring a kid was caught and brought back for the children to play with, but they followed their fathers' example by playing cruel games. When they throw the kid into the sea, only young Raven Feather feels ashamed and rescues the animal. Later the goats set out to punish the Indians. The illustrations are done in collage with brilliantly colored papers to represent water, rocky mountainsides, trees, goats, and people.

Weiss, Ann E. **What's That You Said? How Words Change.** Illus. Jim Arnosky. HarBraceJ 1980.

Every two facing pages present one or more words commonly used today with an explanation of the origin. A clever approach consists of a familiar expression modified to reflect an earlier meaning, i.e. "Wake up, Betsey! Time for *a rest.*" The word that should have been used, "school" in this instance, is presented along with its development: "school" from the Greek "skhole" originally meant a time to stop working and became the time during rest when Greek children were taught their lessons.

Williams, Jay. **Everyone Knows What a Dragon Looks Like.** Illus. Mercer Mayer. Four Winds. Schol Bk Serv 1976.

> This imaginative tale is supposed to take place in China just between that great land and the place where the Wild Horsemen live. When word comes that these men are going to destroy the city of Wu, the grand mandarin calls his counselors together. They decide to pray to the Great Cloud Dragon for his help, but when he arrives in the shape of a bald-headed, white-bearded, small, fat man, no one believes in him except young Han the gatekeeper. Because of the belief of one trusting citizen, the city is saved. Illustrations are lavish in color and oriental detail.

Williams, Jay. **The Surprising Things Maui Did.** Illus. Charles Mikolaycak. Four Winds. Schol Bk Serv 1979.

> In this tale taken from Hawaiian mythology, Maui does surprising things. He makes birds appear in the trees, he lifts the sky to let in light, he asks the sun to move more slowly across the sky so that days will be longer. All these tasks are accomplished to benefit his people. The illustrations are well done in bold color and sepia-and-white.

Wolff, Diane. **Chinese Writing: An Introduction.** Illus. Jeanette Chien. HR&W 1975.

> For the young reader or adult, this small volume introduces Chinese calligraphy and, through it, Chinese culture. Clear instructions encourage the reader to begin writing in "real" Chinese, and a lively text makes the reader want to learn more about Chinese culture.

Wolkstein, Diane, retold by. **Lazy Stories.** Illus. James Marshall. YB. Dell 1977.

> Three amusing tales, one each from Japan, Mexico, and Laos, tell about very lazy characters: Hiroko who had never learned to clean up and then married a man too poor to have servants; Mario who finds six chests of silver coins and seems too lazy to bring them home, so his friend attempts to take them himself; and Khotan who could not even feed himself. Excellent notes provided for telling each story effectively including approximate time each story takes to tell.

Wolkstein, Diane. **The Red Lion: A Tale of Ancient Persia.** Illus. Ed Young. T Y Crowell 1977.

> Before Azgid can succeed his father to the throne of Persia, he must prove his bravery by fighting the ferocious red lion. Out of fear,

Azgid runs away the night before his coronation. Everywhere he goes there is a lion waiting to fight him. Realizing he can never escape, Azgid returns home. When he fights the feared lion, it becomes a playful puppy. Azgid learned that it was only fear that would cause the red lion to be ferocious.

Wolkstein, Diane. **White Wave: A Chinese Tale.** Illus. Ed Young. T Y Crowell 1979.

A lonely, young farmer in the hills of southern China finds a snail in a white shell, takes it home, feeds it a few leaves each day, and each evening when he returns from the fields, he finds a warm dinner and a wild flower in a vase. Finally spying a moon goddess arising from the shell, he struggles never to touch, yet he must. And then she has to leave though she promises to help him if ever he has a great need. The softly shaded drawings enhance this sensitively expressed tale.

Yoo, Edward Yushin, retold by. **Bong Nam and the Pheasants.** Illus. Demi. P-H 1979.

A young Korean lad saves some pheasant chicks from a giant snake. Later, in the form of a beautiful girl, the snake entices Bong Nam with dinner and then threatens to kill him unless he can do the impossible tasks she sets for him. There is an edition of this little book that opens in an accordion-foldout and would serve as a model for children to create their own books.

Zimnik, Reiner (translator Nina Ignatowicz). **The Bear and the People.** Illus. by author. Har-Row 1971.

Loyalty, love, and reverence are woven into a German tale of friendship between a bear and his master. This tale captures the concept of good over evil through the lives of Bearman and his only friends, Brown One and Dear God. Upon the loss of his master, the bear continues to strive for love as the lasting melody of the Bearman's horn still rings.

Ages 11 to 14

Baron, Virginia Olsen, adapted by. **Sunset in a Spider Web: Sijo Poetry of Ancient Korea.** Illus. Minja Park Kim. HR&W 1974.

This collection of early Korean poetry known as Sijo was originally meant to be sung to the rhythm of drum or lute. Great philosophies of Korea are illustrated through these song-poems.

Blegvad, Erik. **Self-Portrait: Erik Blegvad.** Illus. by author. A-W 1979.

This excellent illustrator of children's books tells, briefly, of his boyhood growing up in Denmark where he was first helped to observe, listen, and learn by a loving grandfather who walked him all around Copenhagen, read fairy and folktales, and told stories of his own childhood on the west coast of Jutland. This slim volume is primarily a collection of Blegvad's paintings and sketches as well as some of the art work of friends who influenced him.

Burnford, Sheila. **One Woman's Arctic.** Little 1972.

Mrs. Burnford shares the happiness of the two summers that she spent with the Inuit (Eskimos) in the community of Pond Inlet near the North Pole. She tells of learning about the people and their courage, their gaiety, and their wise way with children.

Causley, Charles. **Figgie Hobbin.** Illus. Trina Schart Hyman. Walker & Co 1973.

Of these poems from Cornwall in England, many are humorous with a bit of satire. The droll illustrations give the reader a happy glimpse into the English world where these lyrical lines originate.

Clark, Ann Nolan. **To Stand Against the Wind.** Viking Pr 1978.

Young Em, now residing in America, is remembering the years leading up to and during the Vietnamese War. Family respect in all matters, ancestral worship, engagement/wedding customs, planting and harvesting rice are among the events detailed. Em develops a significant friendship with Sam, an American reporter, and also with a water buffalo who assists in the field work. The stark reality of the war is touched upon, and the strong will to endure is effectively presented.

Cooper, Gordon. **A Second Springtime.** Nelson 1975.

Hester begins a new life on a Nova Scotia farm in 1862, after eleven years as an orphan in England. The contrast between the harsh life of the orphanage and the care she experiences with her new family, the Clarkes, recurs throughout the book. However, her new life is not without problems—her "brother" Ben is less than eager to welcome her into the family, and her neighbor accuses her of stealing. Hester's tasks of overcoming these difficulties and adjusting to her new home make absorbing reading.

Cosner, Shaaron. **Masks Around the World: And How to Make Them.** Illus. Ann George. McKay 1979.

> Detailed descriptions of masks from various cultures including European, African, Far Eastern, South Pacific, Latin American, North American Indian, and Eskimo are presented. Explanations of the possible uses of masks such as fertility, coming-of-age, fear, humor, and exorcising demons are included. There is even a brief chapter on modern masks, usually for practical purposes, i.e. football helmet guard and firefighter's protection. The book also provides rather complete guidelines for personally creating several kinds of masks.

Davis, Douglas F. **The Lion's Tail.** Illus. Ronald Himler. Atheneum 1980.

> This original story is based upon a Masai creation myth in which Tambu, King of the lions, and Ndangaio, Chief of the Masai, engage in a struggle of wits as the lions attempt to steal the Masai cattle. Dramatic black and white illustrations accompany the text.

De Jong, Meindert. **The House of Sixty Fathers.** Illus. Maurice Sendak. Har-Row 1956.

> The river rises, and young Tien Pao, alone on his family sampan, is swept downriver into Japanese-occupied China. With only his little pet pig for a companion, Tien Pao makes his way back to find his family. All the terrors of a country at war are felt by the bewildered boy, whose unfaltering faith in his family pushes him forth against all odds.

Epstein, Sam, and Beryl Epstein. **She Never Looked Back: Margaret Mead in Samoa.** Illus. Victor Juhasz. Coward 1980.

> Focusing upon Margaret Mead's first significant study of adolescence in Samoa, this brief biography presents the commitment and energy necessary for one to study a different culture. The reader gains insight into learning the language of the host people as well as the very different customs of these young people as they existed in 1928. A short bibliography and glossary are also included.

Fife, Dale. **North of Danger.** Dutton 1978.

> This story is based upon a true incident that happened in August 1940 on a remote island not far from the North Pole and belonging to Norway. Twelve-year-old Arne Kristiansen has to hide while everyone is evacuating in the wake of the Nazi occupation because his scientist father is two hundred miles to the north and must be warned.

Fisher, Leonard Everett. **Across the Sea from Galway.** Illus. by author. Four Winds. Schol Bk Serv 1975.

>Not all immigrants reached our American shores safely at the time of the massive Irish migration in the mid-1800s. One ship, only a short distance from the Massachusetts coast, was destroyed in a violent storm. Three young Donovan children were on board and only Patrick survived. In a major flashback the bulk of this book is about the Donovan family facing increasing hardships in Ireland until finally the parents have enough money to send these three with plans that they and the infant twins will soon follow.

Gemming, Elizabeth. **Lost City in the Clouds: The Discovery of Machu Picchu.** Illus. Mike Eagle. Coward 1980.

>In 1911, Yale professor Hiram Bingham discovered a lost city of the Inca over 11,000 feet above the sea. The struggle to succeed drove Bingham to look where others had not, to persist in rugged, steep, jungle-dominated areas until he found an almost perfectly preserved city. An epilogue updates Bingham's early discoveries with additional finds in 1940 and 1965. A brief glossary, list of important dates, list of museums with South American departments, and a selected bibliography are included.

Glubok, Shirley. **The Art of China.** Illus. Gerard Nook. Macmillan 1973.

>This book introduces the reader to the beautiful silks, pottery, bronzes, and calligraphy of the Chinese. Glubok also explores Chinese history and traditions, providing insight into the rich heritage of China, and includes extensive illustrations.

Glubok, Shirley, and Alfred Tamarin. **The Mummy of Ramose: The Life and Death of an Ancient Egyptian Nobleman.** Photographs by Alfred Tamarin. Har-Row 1978.

>This is the story of Ramose, a high official of Egypt who saw the birth of King Tut. Life in Egypt is described in detail, including the elaborate preparations that are carried out when Ramose dies and is mummified. Photographs add to the authenticity.

Grimm, Jakob, and Wilhelm Grimm. **Fairy Tales of the Brothers Grimm.** Illus. Kay Nielsen. Viking Pr 1979.

>This facsimile edition makes this fine collection available to a new generation, who will delight in the lovely chapter-head decorations and ornamental letters done in Nielsen's style by Pierre Courtois for the original 1929 French edition. Elaborately ornate watercolor illustrations enhance the tales.

Hannam, Charles. **A Boy in That Situation.**

Huntington, Lee Pennock. **Simple Shelters.** Illus. Stefen Bernath. Coward 1979.

> Excellent, yet brief, text explains the specific shelters of various cultures including those of the Caribou Eskimo, Pueblo, Boro Indians of New Guinea, African Bushmen, and Kazaks of Central Asia. The text is clearly illustrated with line drawings which usually depict the interior of a shelter as well as its exterior.

Jenness, Aylette. **Along the Niger River: An African Way of Life.** Photographs by author. T Y Crowell 1974.

> A photodocumentary of life in an African town and the surrounding countryside explains how the different tribes of diverse religions, languages, and customs adapt successfully to changes brought on by mechanization.

Jenness Aylette, and Lisa W. Kroeber. **A Life of Their Own: An Indian Family in Latin America.** Photographs by authors. T Y Crowell 1975.

> In a photodocumentary of social life and customs in Guatemala, the details of the comings and goings of the Hernandez family tell the reader much about a family's way of life in Central America.

Keele, Luqman Lateef, and Daniel Pinkwater. **Java Jack.** T Y Crowell 1980.

> Adventure, mystery, violence, sinister characters, unexplained events, these all seem to happen to Java Jack, a young near-teen who returns to Indonesia to be with his parents after many years living in the United States with an aunt. A vivid picture of the sights and sounds of this part of the world combine with a tale of intrigue that stretches the plausible into possible fantasy before the lost are found, the wrongs are righted, and the future assured.

Lifton, Betty Jean, and Thomas C. Fox. **Children of Vietnam.** Illus. Thomas C. Fox. Atheneum 1972.

> Vietnamese children representing various aspects of life in their war-torn country are described in everyday situations. Through an expression of values, goals, and experiences in conflict, the author encourages understanding of the effects of crisis on all children.

Macaulay, David. **Pyramid.** Illus. by author. HM 1975.

> The author has combined his architectural training and research into Egypt to explain the mystery of the pyramids. Precise, detailed black

and white illustrations clearly describe the process behind the great wonder of the ancient world. In addition, the culture of ancient Egypt emerges through the description of pyramid construction.

Manton, Jo, and Robert Gittings. **The Flying Horses: Tales from China.** Illus. Derek Collard. HR&W 1977.

This fascinating collection of folktales, spanning 4,000 years of China's history, is taken from translations of real Chinese history and literature. Some are light-hearted and some are rather haunting. All are well written and most entertaining.

Marcus, Rebecca B. **Survivors of the Stone Age: Nine Tribes Today.** Hastings 1976.

This book serves as an excellent introduction to anthropology, written clearly and simply. It guides readers into an understanding of what life in a basic social group untouched by modern technology would be like. The distinctive features of the nine selected tribes are outlined, but it is easy for readers to pull together common threads among the tribes and see how they are all more "stone age" than modern in character, even though they are living at the present time.

Mathews, Janet. **Wurley & Wommera: Aboriginal Life and Craft.** Illus. Walter Stackpool. Collins Pubs 1979.

Originally published in Australia, this comprehensive book vividly recounts the daily life of the aborigines who live in a country where nature is harsh. A brief history of the early tribes is given. Tools and weapons, huts, family necessities, such as dilly bags and millstones, are described in detail. Tribal customs are explained and include the importance of magic in their lives. A glossary and index are appended.

Naylor, Penelope. **Black Images: The Art of West Africa.** Photographs by Lisa Little. Doubleday 1973.

The pages of this book are arranged with superb photographs of masks, fetish figures, headdresses, and sculptured heads, all made from a variety of materials including bronze, ivory, and wood. Words for songs and chants of specific African tribes as well as brief explanatory notes accompany the illustrations.

O'Dell, Scott. **The Captive.** HM 1979.

Julian, a young, blonde seminarian, leaves Spain on the *Santa Margarita* in the belief he will be bringing the message of Christ to the natives in the new world. He soon finds that the obsession of

World Cultures

the Spanish conquistadors is for gold and transcends humane treatment of those strangers they meet. The story is set in sixteenth-century Mayan culture, and is the first book in a series to be entitled *City of the Seven Serpents.*

Parks, Gordon. **Flavio.** Photographs by author. Norton 1978.

Flavio, a small boy living in the Catacumba slums of Brazil, cares for his starving brothers and sisters, fighting each day just to stay alive. Gordon Parks is his only hope for survival. The "before and after story" of a starving child is presented.

Paterson, Katherine. **The Master Puppeteer.**

Price, Christine. **Dance on the Dusty Earth.** Illus. by author. Scribner 1979.

Dance, a natural outgrowth of the rhythms of the body, the seasons, the plant world, has been essential to people throughout the world. Here the reader explores various essential aspects of dance: leaping and springing of legs in East Africa; storytelling with arms and hands in Polynesia, India, and Asia; dances of war where weapons are often used; magic circles from diverse groups including the American Indian, Voladores in Mexico, and traditional European Maytime dances. The drawings vibrantly express movement as discussed in the written text.

Rudstrom, Lennart. **Carl Larsson: A Family.** Illus. Carl Larsson. Putnam 1980.

Swedish artist Carl Larsson's biography is told with special emphasis upon his devotion to his large family which included seven children who became models for many of his paintings. Robust figures, rich, mellow colors, and elaborate detail help one visualize the countryside and life of a family in Sweden in the early 1900s.

Say, Allen. **The Ink-Keeper's Apprentice.**

Schlein, Miriam. **Antarctica: The Great White Continent.** Hastings 1980.

This book discusses the history of the discovery of Antarctica—from the early Greeks who theorized its existence, to England's Captain Cook who came close in the 1770s but never sighted land, to others from America, Russia, France, and Norway who eventually traveled upon its surface. There are considerations for the future that undoubtedly will include continued scientific investigations of minerals, temperatures and wind, the ice sheet, nutrients, and even modern man's impact via poisonous chemicals such as DDT which have found their way to this distant, nearly uninhabited land.

Simon, Seymour. **Strange Mysteries from Around the World.** Four Winds. Schol Bk Serv 1980.

Ten unexplained occurrences are described along with possible solutions. Included are the times that fish and frogs have appeared to rain down from the sky in different places such as Kansas City, Virginia, and Louisiana; an explosion in Siberia in 1908 that had the force of atomic energy; the people who walk on fire in remote areas such as Bora Bora, Tahiti, and Ceylon; and the discovery of a unique crystal skull in Central America.

Singer, Isaac Bashevis. **Naftali the Storyteller and His Horse, Sus, and Other Stories.** Illus. Margot Zemach. YB. Dell 1979.

Naftali and his horse, Sus, travel across Poland bringing books to children. When they become too old to travel, Naftali writes and prints the stories he has heard during his travels. Seven more Yiddish short stories follow. The setting for most of these tales is Poland.

Singer, Isaac Bashevis. **When Shlemiel Went to Warsaw & Other Stories.** Illus. Margot Zemach. YB. Dell 1979.

In this collection of eight stories, the characters range from rabbis, demons, devils, witches, wise and foolish men, to imps and crickets. Five of the stories are based on Yiddish folktales.

Suhl, Yuri. **Uncle Misha's Partisans.**

Synge, Ursula. **Weland: Smith of the Gods.** Illus. Charles Keeping. S G Phillips 1973.

This is a dramatic retelling of the story of Weland the Smith who is one of the heroic figures of Norse mythology. The story is a darkly fierce account of courage, endurance, and revenge. Woven into this narrative are other tales told by the Northmen.

Thiele, Colin. **The Hammerhead Light.** Har-Row 1976.

In Australia where warm weather comes at Christmas and the cold winter season touches June and July, young Tessa Noble lives in the small fishing village of Snapper Bay. Her close friend is seventy-two-year-old Axel Jorgenson, once the lighthouse keeper, now living in a shack near the old tower. Government authorities intend to tear down the lighthouse tower since a new, mechanical one has replaced it until the new beacon is incapacitated as a violent storm arises and Tessa's family is threatened as they return by boat from an outing.

Thiele, Colin. **Storm Boy.** Illus. John Schoenherr. Har-Row 1978.

Storm Boy lives with his father in a shack by the sea off the South

Australian coast. Fingerbone Bill, the Aborigine, is the only other person living near by, and he shares his extensive first-hand knowledge about fish, birds, and signs of wind and weather. Rescuing three baby pelicans after some ruthless men scatter their nests leads to a close, personal relationship between the weakest infant pelican and Storm Boy, and during a great storm, Mr. Percival, the young pelican, becomes a unique hero.

van Iterson, S. R. (translator Hilda van Stockum). **The Spirits of Chocamata.** Morrow 1977.

Chimi, native boy of Curacao, and Hans, who recently came from Holland to live with his aunt and uncle, embark upon an adventure in which they track an escaped convict. In their efforts the highly superstitious beliefs of Chimi are tested against Hans' more objective, rational approach to sickness, to mysterious lights and sounds in a "haunted" house and in several caves.

Walsh, Jill Paton. **A Chance Child.**

Walsh, Jill Paton. **Children of the Fox.** Illus. Robin Eaton. FS&G 1978.

Three stories of ancient Greece, each told from a young child's point of view, are based upon historical events such as Athenians escaping to a nearby island and then tricking the Persians into an ambush at sea; building a wall about Athens without the knowledge nor acceptance of Sparta; and the apparent fall of the great Greek general, Themistokles, known as the Fox.

Wuorio, Eva-Lis. **To Fight in Silence.** HR&W 1973.

This is a true story of how the Danes helped 8,000 Danish Jews slip away from the Nazis during three and a half years of occupation in Denmark. German occupation began in early 1940, and though Denmark believed its non-aggression pact would protect them, it was ignored. Soon, the young people were quietly hiding Jews and part-Jews whom the Nazis sought. While others fought with guns, Denmark fought with silence.

Zei, Alki (translator Edward Fenton). **The Sound of the Dragon's Feet.** Dutton 1979.

In early 1890 in Russia, Sasha, the only daughter of a tirelessly working doctor, lives comfortably with her bourgeois-intellectual family. One of her tutors, Pavel Grigorevitch, delights her in his revolutionary exhuberance and awes her with his history of imprisonment and three-year exile to Siberia. Sasha is devoted to her father and, despite his constant attention to countless, often nonpaying patients, he finds time to talk with her and to take her along on some of his calls. As the book closes the reader is becoming aware of the impending movement against the Tsar. Sasha learns that some like Pavel can be revolutionaries, ready to die, and others like her father can only offer assistance. Her love for both is equally great.

Zvorykin, Boris (editor Jacqueline Onassis). **The Firebird and Other Russian Fairy Tales.** Illus. by author. Viking Pr 1978.

These four Russian tales are accompanied by the original illustrations of a French edition published in the 1920s. Each story has three handsome, full-paged pictures with exquisite details that reflect the Russian culture at the time of the Tsars. Besides "The Firebird," the stories are "Maria Morevna," "The Snow Maiden," and the Russian version of Cinderella, "Vassilissa the Fair."

Ages 14 and Up

Balfour, Michael. **Stonehenge and Its Mysteries.** Scribner 1980.

Profusely illustrated with photographs, diagrams, and paintings, this detailed book describes how scientists, artists, politicians, and others have viewed Stonehenge and its neighboring prehistoric sites throughout history. These sites continue to yield new clues to their ancient past.

Bond, Nancy. **Country of Broken Stone.** Atheneum 1980.

In the north of England, fourteen-year-old Penelope, her brother, and author father have joined Valerie, a new stepmother, and her three children on an archeological dig of a second-century Roman fort. The local folk resent this intrusion, particularly a young boy, who, in spite of his intentions, grows fond of Penelope. The English countryside is vividly presented and the characterizations are equally distincitve. A dramatic sense of history is evoked along with the careful growth and development of a newly joined family.

Dawson, Raymond. **The Chinese Experience.** Scribner 1978.

Thirty centuries of Chinese human activity—political, philosophical, socioeconomic, and aesthetic experience—are covered. The four major categories are discussed separately but overlap each other, for Confucian culture has influenced every experience, past and present, of the Chinese. The author explains how China has been successful in sealing itself off from the world and retaining its own culture.

World Cultures

Ellis, Harry B. **Israel: One Land, Two Peoples.** Maps by Walter Hortens. T Y Crowell 1972.

Life and complex struggle in this rapidly developing country are illustrated as the author discusses the Arab-Jewish claims to Israel, the Jews from the time of Abraham, and the Arabs from the seventh century A.D.

Goldston, Robert. **The Sword of the Prophet: A History of the Arab World from the Time of Mohammed to the Present Day.** Dial 1979.

A highly readable account of a people who have and do exert powerful, political influence throughout the world is presented. Beginning with the life of Mohammed who became the Great Prophet of Islam, this book follows the ebb and flow of an empire that has stretched from the Pyrenees to the Himalayas. One can gain an understanding of the Arab culture, solidly based upon religious precepts, and follow its history to the current issues dealing with twentieth-century technology, radically different western values, relationships with Israel and the Jews, and also varying views within the Arab world.

Gregor, Arthur S. **Life Styles: An Introduction to Cultural Anthropology.**

Herriot, James. **James Herriot's Yorkshire.** Photographs by Derry Brabbs. St. Martin 1979.

Superb color photography on every page reveals Yorkshire in its apparently timeless beauty. This book illustrates its tranquil landscapes, proud ruins, and inviting byways. Clear, thoughtful prose throughout reminds both author and his readers of the setting of Herriot's popular books about his years as a local veterinarian.

Highwater, Jamake. **Journey to the Sky.** T Y Crowell 1978.

In 1839, American attorney John Lloyd Stephens and his British colleague Frederick Catherwood journeyed to Central America in search of the lost cities of the Maya. Catherwood's detailed drawings of the remnants of this ancient people are included. Though the book is considered a novel, it has been carefully researched and reads as a documented piece of nonfiction. Stephens' accounts of his travels provide a glimpse into the highly technological past of the Native American.

Jones, Toeckey. **Go Well, Stay Well.** Har-Row 1979.

A fragile, tense relationship develops between Candy, a privileged white girl, and Becky, a black child from the Soweto ghetto in South

Africa. Because of apartheid, it is nearly impossible for the fifteen-year-olds to get together, but persistent Candy finds a way. The book portrays the racial struggle of the time, seen from the perspective of both girls, and their maturing understanding of each other's rights and beliefs.

Karen, Ruth. **Feathered Serpent: The Rise and Fall of the Aztecs.** Four Winds. Schol Bk Serv 1979.

This is a presentation of the origins of the Aztecs, their great leaders, their fundamental religious beliefs including the primacy of sacrifice and reverence for death, their social structure, and their military successes and failures. Photographs of ancient sculpture and murals and architectural remnants are most helpful in presenting a picture of the culture.

Koehn, Ilse. **Mischling, Second Degree: My Childhood in Nazi Germany.** Greenwillow 1977.

Partly Jewish, Ilse Koehn is a Mischling, Second Degree, who survives the terror and horrors of war in Nazi Germany. To keep the family's deadly secret intact, Ilse joins the Hitler Youth Movement and spends two years in a paramilitary girls' camp in occupied Czechoslovakia. This account captures the inner world of childhood in Nazi Germany.

Laye, Camara. **The Dark Child.** FS&G 1977.

Twenty-year-old Camar was sent by his tribe to Paris to study engineering. He is descended from the black Sudanese of the fabled Mali empire. To relieve his severe homesickness for French Guinea, he wrote his autobiography. Although his family were professing Mohammedans, his life was shadowed by the supernatural, making this a fascinating account of contrasting cultures.

Ludwig, Charles. **He Freed Britain's Slaves.** Herald Pr 1977.

This is the biography of William Wilberforce, a tireless crusader against slave trade in the British Empire. The fight in Parliament lasted nearly half a century, but he believed that "a righteous cause, coupled with determination and motivation by faith in a loving God, could produce miracles." This is a story of extraordinary dedication.

Malamud, Bernard. **The Fixer.** PB 1975.

Yakov Bok, a simple Russian peasant of Jewish descent, is wrongly accused and convicted of murdering a boy. The setting is the city of

Kiev in tsarist Russia during a period of violent antisemitism. Bok becomes a hero because he refuses to confess to a crime he did not commit.

Moore, Janet Gaylord. **The Eastern Gate: An Invitation to the Arts of China and Japan.** Collins Pubs 1979.

Reproductions both in black and white and in color, photographs of sculpture, tapestries, vases, antique porcelain, and natural settings make this excellent, carefully written text a fine source for exploring the cultures of China and Japan via their centuries of significant arts and crafts.

Murphy, E. Jefferson. **Understanding Africa.** Illus. Louise E. Jefferson. T Y Crowell 1978.

This book provides an overview of the common and diverse traits that make up Africa as a whole, including the geography, ancient cultures, and the common experience under European colonialism. Special emphasis is given to countries south of the Sahara. The rise of African nationalism and the problems facing Africa today are discussed.

Oerke, Andrew. **Many Voices.** Celestial Arts 1974.

The author has written lines to match the famous people he has chosen: Buddha is thoughtful; Socrates instructs a servant with his last breath; and the magic numbers of Pythagoras relate the magic of the architect, the musician, and the geometer to the Greek's golden mean. In all, there are forty-two voices, many general like the seasons, directions, fire, water, peace, and mountain. Soft, two-color pictures come from various museums.

Ogilvie, Elisabeth. **The Devil in Tartan.** McGraw 1980.

A teacher from New England goes to a small farming community in Nova Scotia to do a genealogical report. She has ESP, and there is a haunted house, a large kindly Scottish family, some friendly teenagers, a murder, a villain, and a romance. An entertaining account of Nova Scotian adventure is presented.

Ojigbo, A. Okion, compiler. **Young and Black in Africa.** Random 1971.

The author believes that "if a non-African truly wants to understand Africans he should listen to what Africans have to say about their own way of life." In this book eight young Africans from six different countries write simply and with feeling of their struggle for education and independence, recognizing the clash that exists between the old world and the new. Educated mainly abroad, the majority have since returned to their native countries to continue their work.

Paterson, Katherine. **Of Nightingales That Weep.** Illus. Haru Wells. T Y Crowell 1974.

In twelfth-century Japan, Takiko's samurai father is killed during a clan power struggle. When her mother marries a potter, Takiko finds it difficult to accept this ugly man as her father. Because she is beautiful and musically gifted, Takiko is brought to court. Loyal to her own clan, she goes along when the royal family is exiled. There she has a love affair with a samurai from the opposing clan. When the war is ended, Takiko, transformed by war conditions, is deserted by her former lover and marries the widowed potter.

Price, Christine. **Made in the South Pacific: Arts of the Sea People.** Dutton 1979.

Excellent photographs of artifacts from the South Pacific are presented as well as illustrations of designs used in the art of tatu and on wood carvings, and pictures of present-day natives carving, dancing, and sailing. The accompanying text is thorough.

Remarque, Erich M. **All Quiet on the Western Front.** Fawcett 1979.

This is the journal of a young German man forced to serve in the German army during World War I. Written after his war experiences, he expresses his hate of war and love of humanity. As his many friends die, he becomes a broken man, wondering about the futility of life.

Ribner, Susan, and Dr. Richard Chin. **The Martial Arts.** Illus. Melanie Arwin. Har-Row 1978.

The authors trace the growth of the martial arts from their origin in China by the Shaolin monks and nuns to their new forms in the world today. The Shaolin orders spread their Zen Buddhist teachings and their martial arts knowledge throughout Europe and Asia, each people adapting them to its own culture and need.

Rice, Edward. **The Ganges: A Personal Encounter.** Photographs by author. Four Winds. Schol Bk Serv 1974.

In a personal tour of the Ganges, the land and the cities along her banks provide insight into her history and her influence on the history and civilization of India. Information on the recent conflict during which Bangladesh was born is included.

Rice, Edward. **Mother India's Children: Meeting Today's Generation in India.** Illus. by author. Pantheon 1971.

After several trips to India, the author crossed that country to interview twenty teenagers and to write thumbnail sketches of their occupations or daily lives. The reader meets Lata, a girl sweeper who cleans anything; Raj, a seventeen-year-old farm wife; Shyam, a seventeen-year-old guru or priest with seven years of study ahead; a nineteen-year-old engineering student, though he knows there are 60,000 unemployed; and others. The book provides a descriptive look at life through their eyes.

Risner, Robinson. **The Passing of the Night: My Seven Years as a Prisoner of the North Vietnamese.** Ballantine 1975.

The cruel and inhumane treatment during Risner's years as a prisoner of the North Vietnamese is described. After reflecting on his life, he says, "Don't ever by ashamed of your faith, nor of your wonderful heritage. Be proud of those things which made America great and which can, with our help, be even greater."

Skármeta, Antonio (translator Hortense Carpentier). **Chileno!** Morrow 1979.

Lucho, a teenager from Chile, is living in exile with his family in Berlin. He tells this tale in first person and it rambles as one might expect from a youngster talking intensely to the reader. He is experimenting with first love, assisting in a resistance effort for his native country, vacillating between affection and exasperation for his father, and trying to avoid a challenge to fight a young fellow who feels compelled to get even with Lucho.

Solzhenitsyn, Aleksandr I. (translator Thomas P. Whitney). **The Gulag Archipelago 1918-1956: An Experiment in Literary Investigation, Vols. I-II, III-IV.** Har-Row 1974, 1975.

These four volumes describe what life was like for the millions of political prisoners who became slave laborers in the vast network of penal institutions across Stalin's Russia.

Steinbeck, John. **The Pearl.** Viking Pr 1947.

This old Mexican folktale is simple, but moving. Kino the fisherman, his wife Juana, and their baby Coyotito have an indestructible closeness as they face the events following Kino's discovery of a priceless pearl. Portrayed poignantly is the people's superstition, which is supported by illiteracy and ignorance. The love of family and the patriarchal family structure are vividly described, as is the feeling of the Mexicans toward those who rule the village.

Sutcliff, Rosemary. **Song for a Dark Queen.** T Y Crowell 1979.

The Romans are in Britain conquering successfully the many tribes they find there. Queen Boudicca leads a forceful but futile attempt to push the Roman army back to the sea. The story is told from the point of view of Cadwan, the Queen's loyal Harper. It is a story of tribal tradition, violence, vengeance, and loyalty, and leads to possibilities for discussion.

Sutcliff, Rosemary. **Sun Horse, Moon Horse.**

Suyin, Han. **Birdless Summer.** Bantam 1972.

In 1938, Han Suyin prepares to sail from Marseilles to do what she can in China as war and revolution gather force. On shipboard she decides to marry Major Tang Paohuang (Pao), a graduate of Chiang Kaishek's military academy and now his aide. From 1938 to 1942, she follows him west. He has gone ahead to prepare for Chiang's army. He is safe, but she works in city hospitals, fleeing out the east side of a city as the invading Japanese storm in from the west. This third volume of her life takes Han Suyin through the Japanese attacks on China to the war's end, through medical aid in Szechuan slums, and to England as a Chinese diplomat's wife who remains to finish her M.D. degree.

Suyin, Han. **The Crippled Tree.** Putnam 1965.

The author's Chinese family migrated from Canton area to Szechuan, the breadbasket of China, about 1700. Chou, the first ancestor, was a very poor peddler. In 1908, Han Suyin's father was sent with 100 men to Belgium engineering schools in Brussels. There he met his high-spirited, Belgian, Catholic wife, and upon graduating they returned to his home in China. Life unfolds along the railroads of China as their Eurasian children are born. The Chinese culture is carefully detailed.

Suyin, Han. **A Mortal Flower.** Putnam 1966.

The second volume in this autobiography covers the years from 1928 to 1938 when Han Suyin is growing up in China. At eleven she reads that Chiang Kaishek will convert to Christianity and marry

Soong Meiling. Han Suyin's father has become an admirer of Mao Tse-tung but not of communism.

Suyin, Han. **Wind in the Tower: Mao Tsetung and the Chinese Revolution, 1949-1975.** Little 1976.

This volume of Han Suyin's autobiography concerns Mao Tse-tung and his structuring of "The People's Revolution" in China. Mao labored long and earnestly to keep Chinese Communism from following Russian Communism's pattern of letting ruling power go to a new technocratic class. During all the years that China was a closed door to Americans, Han Suyin had free access and went to China every year for twenty years. She also knew Mao personally.

Terrill, Ross, editor. **The China Difference.** Har-Row 1979.

This book presents a portrait of life today inside the country of one billion. This is a collection of addresses, essays, and lectures concerning the mind and heart of China. The writers evaluate the Chinese way in tradition and change, daily life, politics, and culture.

Thiele, Colin. **Fire in the Stone.** Har-Row 1974.

Opals of all colors were to be found beneath the arid landscape of Australia. Ernie, frequently left alone by his restless father and deserted by his mother, dreamed of making a great find. Along with his Aboriginal friend Willie Winowie and a Greek friend Nick, they work a mine claim. Excitement mounts after Ernie makes a rich strike and subsequently is robbed. Tracking the thief leads to a survival struggle and a successful test of friendship. The unique Australian countryside is well depicted, and though there is a useful glossary, most terms peculiar to this part of the world are easily understood through the context.

Walsh, Jill Paton. **The Emperor's Winding Sheet.** FS&G 1974.

Piers Barber, an English youth, is shipwrecked and then rescued by Turkish pirates. While fleeing from them, he encounters Constantine, last emperor of the Romans. He is renamed Vrethiki and becomes the emperor's talisman, remaining by his side throughout the siege of Constantinople by the Turks.

Willard, Barbara. **The Gardener's Grandchildren.** Illus. Gordon King. McGraw 1979.

Ella and Rob live on an island off the west coast of Scotland with their mother and grandfather, John Maitland, who has been entrusted with the maintenance of the lovely gardens. Ella and Rob resent the newly hired man who seems to be taking the place of their recently deceased father. Ella, eager for schooling, yearns to cross over to the mainland but must remain on the island where she and her brother help in the garden responsibilities.

Wrightson, Patricia. **The Dark Bright Water.** Atheneum 1979.

This dramatic, complex fantasy is set in Australia. Wirrun, a young Aborigine, is visited by older men from the interior urging him to come help. Strange things are happening. Wirrun is haunted by a singing of a woman's voice, and in time, he is drawn underground by troubled earth spirits. Wirrun's close friend, Ularra, accompanies him across the continent by plane, highway, and even a journey by wind. Most of the fairy and monster characters are drawn from the folklore of the Australian Aborigine.

Wrightson, Patricia. **The Ice Is Coming.** Atheneum 1977.

This elaborately complex fantasy set in modern Australia has references to the folk-spirits, gnomes, and monsters of the Aborigines. Wirrun, a young Aboriginal man becomes aware that the Ninya, ancient ice creatures, are attempting to create a new ice age. He and one of the Mimi, rock-spirits, set out on a long journey across the continent to the sea, seeking the eldest Nargun, a monster with power of fire to halt the coming of the ice.

Professional References

Carrier, Warren, ed. and Kenneth Oliver, associate ed. *Guide to World Literature.* Based upon the original work of Robert O'Neal. Urbana, Illinois: National Council of Teachers of English, 1980.

de la Garza, Rudolph O., Z. Anthony Kruszewski, and Tomas A. Arciniega, compilers. *Chicanos and Native Americans: The Territorial Minorities.* Englewood Cliffs, New Jersey: Prentice-Hall, Inc., 1973.

Haviland, Virginia, ed. *Children's Books of International Interest.* 2nd ed. Chicago: American Library Association, 1978.

Hinman, Dorothy and Ruth Zimmerman. *Reading for Young People: The Midwest.* Chicago: American Library Association, 1979.

Katz, William Loren. *Black People Who Made the Old West.* New York: T. Y. Crowell, 1977.

Laughlin, Mildred. *Reading for Young People: The Great Plains.* Chicago: American Library Association, 1979.

Laughlin, Mildred. *The Rocky Mountain Section.* Chicago: American Library Association, 1980.

Litwack, Leon F. *Been in the Storm So Long: The Aftermath of Slavery.* New York: Alfred A. Knopf, Inc., 1979.

Smith, Huston, *et al. Great Religions of the World.* Washington, D.C.: National Geographic Society, 1978.

Stanford, Barbara Dodds and Karima Amin. *Black Literature for High School Students.* Urbana, Illinois: National Council of Teachers of English, 1978.

Stensland, Anna Lee. *Literature by and About the American Indian: An Annotated Bibliography.* 2nd ed. Urbana, Illinois: National Council of Teachers of English, 1979.

Tudor, Bethany. *Drawn from New England: Tasha Tudor, A Portrait in Words and Pictures.* New York: William Collins, 1979.

Ladder V

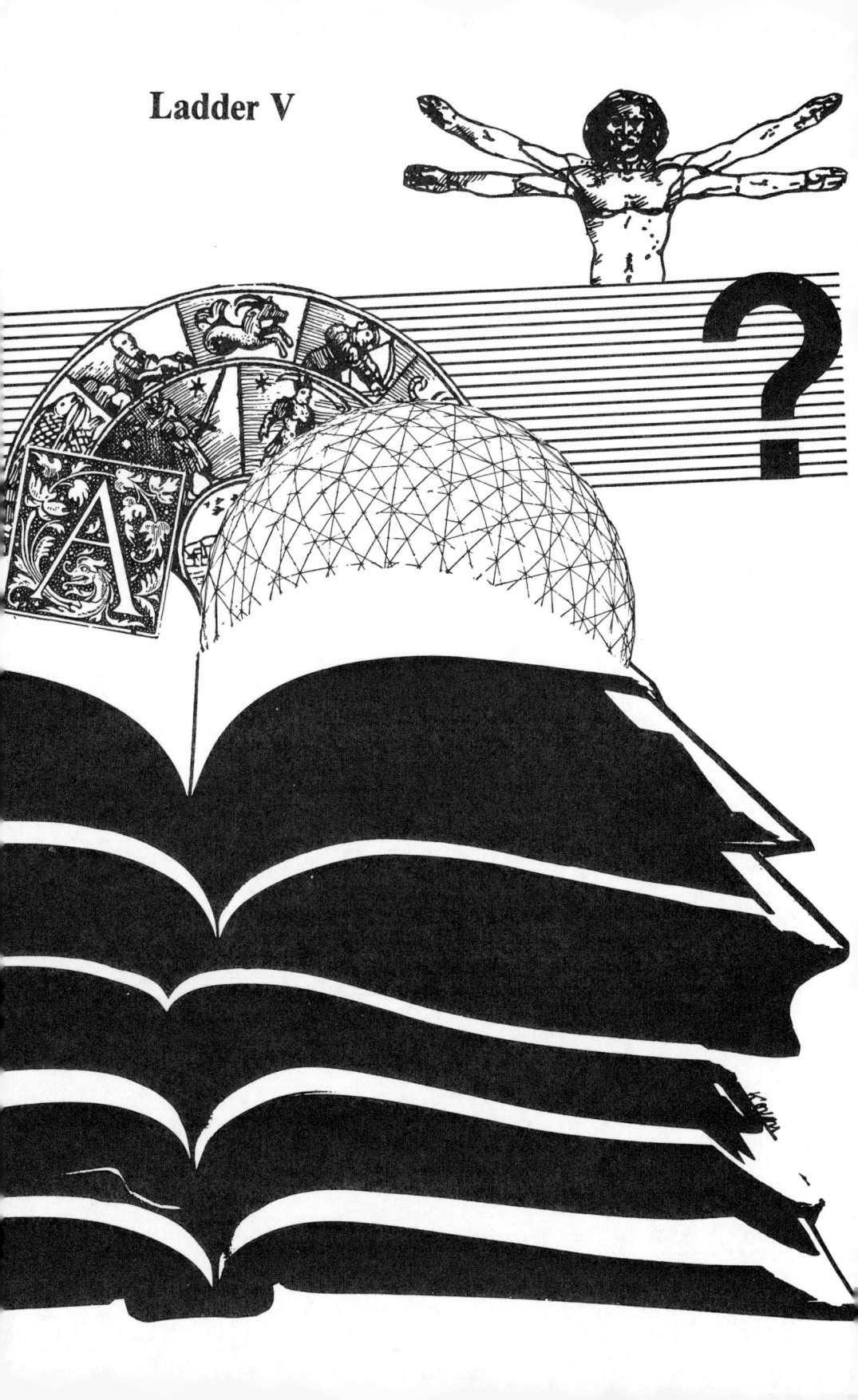

Coping in a Changing World

Children and young people need security and stability as they grow. Yet there is nothing so inevitable in their lives as change—from within, as they grow into self; and from without, as the world around them goes on its kaleidoscopic way. Although individuals have always had to deal with change, the pace of life in the last decades of the twentieth century demands the rapid assimilation of a diversity of changes. Technological, scientific, and political changes are increasingly becoming commonplace occurrences, which need to be dealt with in meaningful ways. Coming to accept change and learning to deal with it positively are important and continuing tasks. While Ladder I focuses on books which portray inner changes, this final Ladder looks at books that might help readers understand their own relationship to shifting patterns in the wider world of which they are a part.

The first division in this Ladder, "Understanding Life Cycles," is a category intended to deal with those natural changes that, although predictable, never come to seem ordinary. Birth or death in the family, among friends, even of a pet, substantially changes a young person's familiar world; stories that show others coping may help the reader do likewise. Until recently, death as a major event of plot had gone through a period of exclusion from children's books. Now we have a proliferation of books that explore the dimensions of grief, and it seems important to keep them in a reasonable perspective. Perhaps readers who grow up with poetry about the passage of the seasons, or with the life stories of animals, or with well-written information about other natural changes may be able to find analogs for stories of personal loss and to make better sense of the idea that endings are not only inevitable, but they are also beginnings.

The second category of the Ladder provides another perspective for coping with change. While adults can say, "How times have changed," young readers do not have such perspective. For them, literature is a window on history; thus the category "Learning from the Past." Books that give a memorable picture of life in a long-gone time, especially works which describe times of conflict and cultural change, are included here. Many of these are stories that introduce characters, real or fictional, whose vision and adaptability in dealing with crisis would be welcome today.

Other books in this category show contemporary characters looking backward, finding new respect for their own heritage and new understanding of the influence of the past upon the present.

Our third category, "Meeting Personal and Political Crises," also includes some works dealing with the recent past. Books on wars and political turmoil, the Holocaust, and the pursuit of diverse social causes are included here. Many of these books are written for adolescent readers, or written for adults and chosen by adolescents. Often the setting and scope of the book are beyond the reader's immediate experience, so that it is helpful for teachers to provide some background for the story. There is nothing remote, however, about the typical themes—justice, freedom, and perseverance. Such books are particularly valuable in promoting a wider view and understanding of the world, and provide excellent group discussion material.

Technological changes and advances introduce today's youngsters to worlds that did not exist for previous generations. The potential for the good of society, which could result from such innovations, is counterbalanced by the reality that technology has also made it possible for humankind to annihilate itself.

The fourth category, "Living in a Technological World," deals with works that describe life in contemporary times. A common theme in such literature is that technological changes are not without a price. Many authors have explored the dilemmas of living among machines, some humorously, some ominously. These books prompt value judgments from their readers; certainly the question of what is truly human, or humane, is brought into sharper focus when considered in the context of modern technology.

The last category in this Ladder builds upon the previous four, for there is little point in knowing the past or examining the present if such understandings fail to help us cope with what is to come. Our lives are governed by largely unspoken anticipations and predictions. "Facing the Future," then, may be the most crucial category of all. However, this is a theme which usually remains implicit in literature; it is left up to the reader to decide what relevance the story holds for a time to come. In this sense, all stories look to the future, although considerable discussion may be required to make that perspective clear. Only science fiction and some types of fantasy, along with futurist nonfiction, look explicitly at the future, and these are the books emphasized here.

Janet Hickman and Maia Pank Mertz

Understanding Life Cycles

Ages 1 to 5

Fisher, Aileen. **As the Leaves Fall Down.** Illus. Barbara Smith. Bowmar-Noble 1977.

> A pleasing combination of rhymed text and full-color pictures follows a "spry little rabbit" through the cycle of seasons in its natural habitat. The author's tone speaks reassuringly to a young child's discomfiture at unexpected changes.

Hallinan, P. K. **How Really Great to Walk This Way.** Childrens 1972.

> This book presents a variety of sensations in the life cycles of the world for a young boy and girl.

McCloskey, Robert. **Make Way for Ducklings.** Illus. by author. Puffin 1976.

> This story tells of a mother and father mallard finding a home for their children on an island in the Charles River in Boston. They adjust to a new life in the city, and the people of the city adjust to them.

Roy, Ron. **Three Ducks Went Wandering.** Illus. Paul Galdone. Clarion Bk. Seabury 1979.

> Three little ducks wander away from their mother's nest and into a circular journey of narrow escapes that only the reader can see. Home again under mother's wing makes for a satisfying ending.

Watson, Wendy. **Moving.** Illus. by author. T Y Crowell 1978.

> When Mom and Dad pack up to move, little Muffin says, "I'm staying here," and reserves her favorite possessions. As the old house is emptied, she decides it will be a lonely place and goes along to the new one. The parents' acceptance and sharing of Muffin's emotions are a comfort during a trying change.

Ages 5 to 8

Abbott, Sarah. **Where I Begin.** Coward 1970.

This quiet book intends to develop the concept that parents were once children, too. As a small girl looks through a family album, she discovers the many changes time brings in its wake.

Alexander, Martha. **Nobody Asked Me If I Wanted a Baby Sister.** Illus. by author. Dial 1971.

In this book Oliver, disgusted at all the to-do being made over his new sister, decides to give her away. Then he discovers he is the only one who can make the baby stop crying and decides that his baby sister is pretty smart after all. This book provides a realistic look at the older brother or sister who feels a bit neglected after the arrival of a younger sibling.

Anno, Mitsumasa. **Anno's Counting Book.** T Y Crowell 1977.

Children can compare and classify the pictures on each page to the specific number (0-12) corresponding with the pictures. Each picture shows a continuous change in the time of day, the change of seasons, and a change in the environment. These changes correspond with each number.

Bartoli, Jennifer. **Nonna.** Illus. Joan Drescher. Harvey 1975.

The continuity of life is emphasized in this gentle story of a grandmother's death. Nonna is remembered in a quilt, a mandolin, and a garden. Most of all she is remembered for her warmth and love. When little Amy bakes and shares Nonna's special cookies, she perpetuates her grandmother's spirit.

Bunting, Eve. **The Big Red Barn.** Illus. Howard Knotts. HarBraceJ 1979.

In this easy to read book, the big red barn means continuity and comfort for a child whose mother has died and who is not yet willing to accept a "new mom." When the barn burns and is replaced by a new aluminum one, it is Grandpa who helps him see that new things make their own place if given a chance.

Fisher, Aileen. **I Stood upon a Mountain.** Illus. Blair Lent. T Y Crowell 1979.

Greeting fellow travelers with "Wonderful world!" a small child moves from springtime mountains to deserts and oceans and finally to a winter hilltop. Each traveler shares a creation story that explains the wonder of the world. In the end the child gazes at the stars, "still filled with a wonder than needs no answer..."

Understanding Life Cycles 321

Fisher, Aileen. **Out in the Dark and Daylight.** Illus. Gail Owens. Har-Row 1980.

> The passage of seasons is celebrated in an attractively illustrated selection of verses. The focus is on changes in the weather and the habits of small creatures, and a child's sense of wonder that things are as they are.

Fox, Siv Cedering. **The Blue Horse and Other Night Poems.** Illus. Donald Carrick. Clarion Bk. Seabury 1979.

> Fourteen poems present thoughts and dreams between night and morning, touching a wide range of feelings. The imaginative illustrations are an important part of the whole, with images of disorientation like floating in space, and comfortably humorous ones like a tiger in flannel pajamas.

Gackenbach, Dick. **Ida Fanfanny.** Illus. by author. Har-Row 1978.

> Weather never touches Ida Fanfanny's mountain valley, so she sends peddlers packing back down the mountain with their galoshes, umbrellas, and weather vanes. Then one day Ida buys four magic paintings labeled *Spring, Summer, Winter,* and *Fall,* and things change in the valley. Humor and imagination accentuate the importance of the cycle of the seasons.

Greenfield, Eloise. **She Come Bringing Me That Little Baby Girl.** Illus. John Steptoe. Lippincott 1974.

> Kevin resents the new sister that upsets the familiar balance of his family until his mother helps him see that she too was once a baby girl, with a big brother to take care of her. The illustrations are bold and full of warmth.

Hegwood, Mamie. **My Friend Fish.** Illus. Diane de Groat. HR&W 1975.

> Moose catches a fish at day camp and takes it home for a pet, but it doesn't survive the night. His family understands his feelings and lets him decide an appropriate "good-bye" ritual—returning it to the lake where it was caught.

Hoban, Russell. **A Baby Sister for Frances.**

Keats, Ezra Jack. **Peter's Chair.** Har-Row 1967.

> Peter is unhappy because all of his baby furniture is being painted pink and being given to his baby sister. He takes his chair, his dog, his toy crocodile, a picture of himself when he was a baby, and runs away to settle in the front of his house. He finds his chair is too small and ends up helping his father paint it pink. The author-

illustrator creates a meaningful dramatization of the "new baby" problem being solved when the older child realizes his big brother status.

McCloskey, Robert. **Time of Wonder.** Illus. by author. Puffin 1977.

A family experiences the changes of nature in their vacation home. Along with the beauty of the storm comes destruction that the family has to deal with and adjust to. The award-winning illustrations help to dramatize the family's reaction to weather and seasonal changes.

Miles, Miska. **Annie and the Old One.**

Viorst, Judith. **The Tenth Good Thing About Barney.** Illus. Erik Blegvad. Atheneum 1971.

When Barney the cat dies, his owner tries to think of ten good things to say about him at the funeral, held under a tree in the yard. But the boy cannot name the tenth thing until he has talked to his father and helped plant seeds. As a part of the ground in the garden, Barney is "helping grow flowers."

Weil, Lisl. **The Little Chestnut Tree Story.** Illus. by author. Schol Bk Serv 1973.

A chestnut tree grows in the country. It is so beautiful a town is built around it. However, when the town becomes a city, the people cut the tree down so it will not be in the way of traffic. Some of the seeds from the tree drop to the ground. A bird picks up a seed and carries it away. Finally, a little sprout of a chestnut tree pushes its way out of the ground in the country.

Ages 8 to 11

Babbitt, Natalie. **Tuck Everlasting.** FS&G 1977.

In this fantasy, the Tuck family and young Winnie Foster know where to find a magic spring, the source of everlasting life. Will Winnie choose to drink from the spring? Will the sinister stranger find the water and sell it? Images of circles and wheels draw the reader to the central question: What if the cycle of life should stop, and the opportunity for growth and change were lost?

Bornstein, Ruth. **The Dancing Man.**

Understanding Life Cycles 323

Buck, Pearl. **The Big Wave.** Schol Bk Serv 1948.

> The Japanese boys, Kino, son of a mountain-side farmer, and Jiya, son of a fisherman, are only friends until the day a tidal wave sweeps away Jiya's family and village, and Jiya is alone. Kino's family helps Jiya through his grief, and the boys grow up as brothers. The lure of the sea is stronger for Jiya, and when grown, he returns to build again on the ocean's shore.

Cleaver, Vera, and Bill Cleaver. **Grover.**

Godden, Rumer. **The Rocking Horse Secret.**

Hopkins, Lee Bennett, editor. **Morning, Noon and Nighttime, Too.** Illus. Nancy Hannans. Har-Row 1980.

> This selection of poems follows the most familiar cycle of all—the progress of a single day. Child's-eye perspectives on getting up, going to school, coming home, and saying goodnight show a nice balance between lively verses and more reflective ones.

Hopkins, Lee Bennett, editor. **My Mane Catches the Wind.**

Jackson, Jacqueline. **The Taste of Spruce Gum.** Little 1966.

> Libby and her mother return to Vermont after Libby's father's death. Libby, recently left nearly hairless from a serious illness, self-consciously meets her father's family whom she has never known. Adjusting to a stepfather proves difficult, especially in the extremely rough environment of a logging camp. The fast-paced story suggests a believable adjustment to problems.

Langton, Jane. **The Fledgling.** Illus. Erik Blegvad. Har-Row 1980.

> Georgie is eight years old, light as thistledown, and so attuned to nature that she can fly—under the tutelage of the Goose Prince of Walden Pond. Busybody neighbors do not understand the strange moonlight soarings, and a self-styled duckhunter endangers Georgie's life as he finally kills the old goose. Georgie's grief is tempered by her realization that she is outgrowing her own capacity to fly, and by her discovery of the gift which the Prince has left her.

Little, Jean. **Home from Far.**

Lowry, Lois. **Anastasia Krupnik.** HM 1979.

> An only child of author/artist parents, ten-year-old Anastasia is about to become a sister and she's not happy. As appeasement, the

parents allow her to name the baby, and Anastasia vows to pick a bad one. The death of her senile but loved grandmother helps Anastasia to decide upon a name as well as to accept the new brother.

Mann, Peggy. **There Are Two Kinds of Terrible.** Doubleday 1977.

Robbie thinks that breaking his arm on the last day of school is terrible, but having his mother go into the hospital for minor surgery and stay there, dying of cancer, is another kind of terrible. Robbie's progress through his own sorrow and his new relationship with his father are realistic and moving.

Mathis, Sharon Bell. **The Hundred Penny Box.**

Mobley, Jane. **The Star Husband.**

Paterson, Katherine. **Bridge to Terabithia.**

Pringle, Lawrence. **Death Is Natural.** Four Winds. Schol Bk Serv 1977.

A simple and graphic text, complemented by the author's photographs, introduces the idea that life and beauty are the natural outgrowths of death. The effect of human choice on nature's cycle is discussed as it relates to the extinction of species and the death of individual humans.

Simon, Norma. **We Remember Philip.**

Simon, Seymour. **The Secret Clocks: Time Senses of Living Things.** Illus. Jan Brett. Viking Pr 1979.

The natural rhythms of living things—fish, bees, even potatoes—are explored in this easy-to-read book of information. Chapters on human perception of time and on biorhythms can broaden children's concepts about life cycles and changes.

Smith, Doris Buchanan. **A Taste of Blackberries.** Illus. Charles Robinson. T Y Crowell 1973.

When Jamie is stung by a bee and dies from an allergic reaction, his best friend must deal with grief and guilt: Could he have saved Jamie? The reader sees this death and the ensuing funeral through the child's eyes and can share both his bewilderment and his eventual satisfaction in giving a symbolic gift of fresh-picked blackberries to Jamie's mother.

Valens, Evans G. **Wildfire.** Illus. Clement Hurd. World 1963.

The devastating changes caused by a forest fire are described in poetic prose. How the birds and animals react and how the life cycle resumes after the fire are told with suspense and unusual sensitivity. Mr. Hurd's striking illustrations, making use of leaves and weeds lithographed on weathered wood, produce a remarkable forest before us.

Willard, Nancy. **The Island of the Grass King: The Further Adventures of Anatole.** Illus. David McPhail. HarBraceJ 1979.

A wish made on a rainbow sends Anatole on a hazardous and fantastic quest for fennel to cure Grandmother's asthma. Because his search is selfless, Anatole is empowered to free the King of Grass, allowing life to return to the island and a cure to appear for Grandmother.

Zim, Herbert S., and Sonia Bleeker. **Life and Death.** Morrow 1970.

Two distinguished authors have combined their talents to produce this unsentimental scientific explanation of the role of death in the life cycle of all things. There are many charts, diagrams, and sketches to explain the text. The authors show the difference between sleep and death and mention many burial customs past and present.

Zolotow, Charlotte. **River Winding.** Illus. Kazue Mizumura. T Y Crowell 1978.

Brief poems touch upon basic cycles of nature and encourage reflection in a contemplative mood. "Change" contrasts the return of the seasons with personal growth; "So Will I" and "Little Old Man" convey a child's intimation of the cycle of generations; "How Strange" suggests wonder at the idea of death.

Ages 11 to 14

Blos, Joan W. **A Gathering of Days: A New England Girl's Journal, 1830-32.**

Eyerly, Jeannette. **See Dave Run.** Lippincott 1978.

Several individuals, including an insensitive stepfather, an alcoholic mother, school friends, a truck driver, a waitress, a clinic doctor, and a small town sheriff, tell the story of fifteen-year-old Dave Hendry and his attempt to escape an intolerable home situation and locate his father. Mistaken for an escaped convict, Dave is arrested and later identified as a runaway. When the court threatens to send him home, Dave commits suicide in his jail cell.

Farley, Carol. **The Garden Is Doing Fine.**

Greene, Constance C. **Beat the Turtle Drum.**

Kjelgaard, Jim. **Big Red.** Illus. Carl Pfeuffer. Skylark. Bantam 1976.

>Danny Pickett's dream of owning the champion Irish setter, Red, becomes a reality when Mr. Haggin, the dog's owner, hires Danny to help train and show the dog. The exploits of this loyal dog and his master take them into the wicked Wintapi Wilderness where they must combat the elements, a bear, and a wolverine in an exciting tale of adventure and survival. Additionally, the reader traces Danny's development and his initiation into adult society.

Kjelgaard, Jim. **Outlaw Red.** Skylark. Bantam 1977.

>In this sequel to *Big Red*, Sean, a champion Irish setter, learns to survive in the Wintapi Wilderness when he is separated from his caretakers. Believing Sean is responsible for killing their livestock, several farmers hunt the setter and Sean becomes an outlaw until he kills the coyote responsible for the farmers' dilemma and is reunited with his caretaker, Billy Dash. Billy is also hunted for attempting to kill his Uncle Hat in self-defense. The story describes Sean's and Billy's adventures and Billy's decision to live up to his responsibilities.

Lowry, Lois. **A Summer to Die.** Illus. Jenni Oliver. HM 1977.

>During one fateful summer, thirteen-year-old Meg watches her beloved older sister Molly succumb to leukemia. She also watches a young neighbor couple prepare for and welcome the home birth of a son, an event which Meg, a skilled amateur photographer, is asked to record. The author's juxtaposition of ends and beginnings makes a powerful statement.

Peck, Robert Newton. **A Day No Pigs Would Die.**

Ages 14 and Up

Arrick, Fran. **Steffie Can't Come Out to Play.**

Bradbury, Bianca. **Red Sky at Night.** Washburn 1968.

>Jo Whittier's father buys a boat with television contest prize money. The boat is a delight for everyone except Jo, who is scared the moment it hits water. How Jo finally learns to accept the boat, the death her mother, and other aspects of her life make poignant reading for some teenagers.

Buchanan, William. **A Shining Season.**

Buck, Pearl S. **A Bridge for Passing.** John Day 1962.

> A famous writer, faced with the emptiness that comes with the death of her husband, tells of her adjustment to loss, her final acceptance, and the semipeace that comes with it.

Butterworth, W. E. **The Narc.** Four Winds. Schol Bk Serv 1973.

> Daniel Morton, a recent graduate of a police academy, receives his first assignment as an undercover narcotics agent investigating the trafficking of heroin at a local high school. Posing as a high school senior, Dan is exposed to the harsh realities of drug use and addiction which further motivates him in his successful effort to uncover and arrest the school's main drug supplier. The story reveals what drug abuse does to natural human cycles.

Craven, Margaret. **I Heard the Owl Call My Name.** Dell 1976.

> A dying priest is sent by his bishop to spend his remaining time with the Indians of British Columbia. From their way of life, he learns to accept death as an inevitable part of the life cycle. He also discovers the courage and pride which characterize the Indians' way of life. Craven also contrasts the basic values of the dying Indian culture to the values of contemporary technological society.

Elfman, Blossom. **A House for Jonnie O.** Bantam 1978.

> Sixteen years old, pregnant, unmarried—Jonnie O. is a rebellious, confused, tenacious, and thoroughly memorable character. The plot revolves on her determination to rent a house that she and some of her friends from "the pregnant school" can call home for themselves and their babies. Her eventual perception of herself as "a mother and a mother's daughter" is poignant testimony to the continuity of life.

Gregor, Arthur S. **Life Styles: An Introduction to Cultural Anthropology.** Scribner 1978.

> In this introduction to the study of culture ranging from studies of small tribes to contemporary cults, topics such as adolescence in America, the status of women, violence and war, magic, and cultural change are discussed. Terms and ideas are clearly explained.

Gunther, John. **Death Be Not Proud.** Har-Row 1965.

> John Gunther has written a step-by-step account of his seventeen-

year-old son's heroic battle against the inexorable progress of a tragic and fatal illness. Bravery and strength in the face of odds are the keynote of this personal story. Johnny's father and mother were divorced before his illness, but the entire book reveals their great love and devotion to Johnny throughout his gallant fight for life.

Lawrence, R. D. **The North Runner.** HR&W 1979.

A true story about the relationship between the author and a wild, savage half wolf, half Alaskan Malamute. Mistreated by his previous owner, the dog, Yukon, is gradually tamed as he grows to trust Lawrence. Vivid descriptions of nature and survival in the British Columbia wilderness enhance the main story.

Neigoff, Mike. **It Will Never Be the Same Again.** Illus. Gwen Brodkin. HR&W 1979.

When fifteen-year-old Sid Kaplan's father loses his job as a reporter, Sid takes a summer job developing film and doing odd jobs for a community newspaper. His goal is to earn enough money to finance his participation in a school-sponsored ski trip. Sid learns responsibility and gains maturity as he struggles to cope with the tedious tasks he must perform. Happily, Sid's summer employment leads to a permanent position for his father with the *Arbor News.*

Walsh, Jill Paton. **Unleaving.** FS&G 1976.

This story has a structure not unlike the life cycles it is portraying. It goes back and forth from the story of young Madge and her experiences in the house she inherited from her grandmother—to the story of the elderly Madge, herself a grandmother, reigning as grand dame in the house she has made her own. Her memories stretch back to the time her own grandmother was the "Gran" of the house. There is continuity here, a commentary on life cycles, as well as a love story, the prattling of young philosophers, and the recurring tragedies of the stormy seaside.

Learning from the Past

Ages 5 to 8

Aliki. **Corn Is Maize: The Gift of the Indians.**

Baylor, Byrd. **When Clay Sings.**

Brodsky, Beverly. **Secret Places.** Illus. by author. Lippincott 1979.

> Recollections of the author's childhood include many secret places, real and imagined, that serve as refuge and relief from an urban environment and as "the beginnings of everything that I am." Both the text and the dreamlike, full-color paintings encourage imagination and reflection.

Bulla, Clyde Robert. **Daniel's Duck.** Illus. Joan Sandin. Har-Row 1979.

> Daniel, who lives in a Tennessee cabin, plans to enter his hand-carved duck in the county fair. His older brother warns him that he didn't "do it right" and the fairgoers' laughter makes Daniel run angrily toward the river to throw the duck in. It takes master carver Henry Pettigrew to convince Daniel of the duck's value, and that there are different ways of seeing and of laughing.

Hall, Donald. **Ox-Cart Man.** Illus. Barbara Cooney. Viking Pr 1979.

> An early nineteenth-century New England farmer loads his ox-cart with goods the family has produced, travels to market, and sells everything—cart, ox, and all—then buys new items for his family to use in making more goods to sell. Full-color paintings show this simpler economic system in tune with the rhythm of the seasons.

Jackson, Louise A. **Grandpa Had a Windmill, Grandma Had a Churn.**

Ages 8 to 11

Aliki. **Mummies Made in Egypt.**

Avi. **Captain Grey.** Illus. Charles Mikolaycak. Skylark. Bantam 1978.

Kevin Cartwright becomes a pirate against his will. He learns well the violent trade plied by Captain Grey's "Free Nation," even winning the fierce captain's trust. Finally, Kevin turns trust and skill against the pirates. This book pictures the turbulent years of the Articles of Confederation.

Baker, Betty. **Shaman's Last Raid.** Illus. Leonard Shortall. Har-Row 1963.

Eban and his twin sister are excited because their great-grandfather from the Indian reservation is coming to spend the summer with them. They devise a plan to use their grandfather, a shaman who still believes in the old ways, to help them get in a TV movie being filmed at the reservation. Eban becomes absorbed in learning the old Apache ways. The book touches with humor on both the generation gap and the changing ways of a culture.

Barringer, D. Moreau. **And the Waters Prevailed.** Illus. P.A. Hutchison. Dutton 1956.

While on a reconnaissance trip, young Andor discovers that the Great Sea will eventually break through and inundate his Stone Age village. Andor spends much of his lifetime trying to convince his village of the danger; only a few believe him. When he is an old man the flood comes and he succumbs with most of his village—a dramatic example of failure to cope with changing conditions.

Blair, Ruth Van Ness. **Mary's Monster.** Illus. Richard Cuffari. Coward 1975.

Mary Anning, resident of the English harbor town of Lyme Regis, made her first significant geological discovery in 1811, the bones of a prehistoric fish-lizard, finally named Ichthyosaurus. Mary was only eleven years old, but she had always accompanied her father in hunting for "curiosities" along the river shore, and then these fossils were sold to summer tourists. She spent her entire life seeking fossils, and many of her discoveries are today in the British Museum. This book presents a clear picture of an historical time when the new science of geology was developing.

Chaikin, Miriam. **I Should Worry, I Should Care.** Illus. Richard Egielski. Har-Row 1979.

A gentle story about adjusting to a new home and neighborhood conveys a strong sense of the values and flavor of Jewish family life in pre-World War II Brooklyn. The author deals with prejudice at home as well as terror in distant Europe.

Clark, Ann Nolan. **Secret of the Andes.** Illus. Jean Charlot. Viking Pr 1970.

> A young South American Indian boy searchs for his destiny, eventually realizing that he wants to be a llama herder just as he has been trained to do. Interwoven into the story is the history of the Spanish conquerors and the value of continuing the ancient Incan traditions.

Foster, Genevieve. **The Year of the Flying Machine: 1903.** Illus. by author. Scribner 1977.

> Using her characteristic "horizontal history" format, the author provides a brief account of the Wright brothers' invention, plus contemporary achievements by Marconi, the Curies, Henry Ford, Einstein, and others, all set against a background of world politics. The organization helps readers make connections among events and develop a perspective on a "chunk" of history.

Fritz, Jean. **Brendan the Navigator: A History Mystery About the Discovery of America.** Illus. Enrico Arno. Coward 1979.

> This tale of St. Brendan of Ireland's sixth-century sea voyage to Paradise (or was it North America?) speculates about the relation of legend to fact. This brief book shows the author's characteristic sense of humor and fuels the popular debate on who "really" discovered America.

Gauch, Patricia Lee. **This Time, Tempe Wick?** Illus. Margot Tomes. Coward 1974.

> Trouble brings out the best in Temperance Wick, a real Revolutionary heroine whose spunk became legendary. When underpaid colonial troops threaten peace and property near her New Jersey home, Tempe hides her gray mare in the bedroom and outwits all the soldiers' efforts at horse thievery. Illustrations add humor and strengthen characterization.

Goodall, John S. **The Story of an English Village.** Illus. by author. Atheneum 1979.

> This wordless picture book traces the changes occurring in a British village over a period of several hundred years. Color illustrations show changes in home life, interiors and exteriors, clothing, and the daily occupations of the villagers. Countryside yields to condominiums as the castle overlooking the village gradually falls into ruin.

Haugaard, Erik Christian. **Orphans of the Wind.**

Mark, Jan. **Under the Autumn Garden.** Illus. Judith Gwyn Brown. T Y Crowell 1979.

> Matthew digs "under the autumn garden," hoping to find an historical artifact for a school project. What he turns up is trouble—with his teacher, his parents, and some unpleasant neighbor children. Only when the deadline has passed does he unearth a true relic. The English setting is crucial to Matthew's developing sense of history.

Meadowcroft, Enid La Monte. **By Secret Railway.** T Y Crowell 1948.

> David Morgan, who is twelve, makes friends with Jim, a young exslave, who comes to live at the Morgan home. When Jim is kidnapped and sold back into slavery, David goes on an adventure-filled journey to rescue Jim and bring him back to Chicago. Set in the period of Lincoln's election, this historical novel deals with the social and political problems of that day, as well as the warm and loyal friendship between two boys.

Monjo, F. N. **Prisoners of the Scrambling Dragon.** Illus. Arthur Geisert. HR&W 1980.

> Facts about the early nineteenth-century China trade provide the background for this story, told by a thirteen-year-old Yankee sailor who finds himself aboard an opium-smuggler's ship, a "scrambling dragon," not far from Canton. How he got there and how his older companion masterminds their escape is good adventure. The boy's language and the opinions that he repeats about politics, business, and culture could provide starting points for discussion of prejudice and fair play.

Morrow, Honore W. **On to Oregon.** Illus. Edward Shenton. Morrow 1946.

> The nine members of the Sager family are traveling westward with a large wagon train toward Oregon where they are to build their new home. After the death of his parents, thirteen-year-old John Sager is left responsible for his younger brothers and sisters. Facing near starvation and other perils of the wilderness trail, John and his tiny bank of children trek across the Rocky Mountains alone and follow the Snake River into Oregon.

Spier, Peter. **Tin Lizzie.** Illus. by author. Doubleday 1975.

> This is the story of one Model-T Ford touring car, from its creation in 1909, through hard use by three owners, to its restoration in the 1970s. Detailed watercolors tell as much as the text; backgrounds show houses, dress, and typical activities as the years pass. Endpapers provide a labeled diagram of "Tin Lizzie."

Walker, Barbara M. **The Little House Cookbook: Frontier Foods from Laura Ingalls Wilder's Classic Stories.** Illus. Garth Williams. Har-Row 1979.

> Excerpts from the Little House books are followed by recipes for the foods mentioned. Differences in the way food was obtained and prepared are dramatized by the carefully researched instructions for making each dish much as it would have been done 100 years ago. Many possibilities for discussion and comparision make this more than a recipe book.

Yates, Elizabeth. **Carolina's Courage.** Illus. Nora S. Unwin. Dutton 1964.

> When Carolina's father decides to leave their stony New Hampshire farm and move the family west to good rich land, much of what they love is left behind. Carolina is allowed to take only the clothes she wears and her beloved doll, Lydia-Lou. The journey is difficult but love within the family is a source of strength.

Ages 11 to 14

Baskin, John. **New Burlington: The Life and Death of an American Village.** NAL 1977.

> Elderly residents in an Ohio village about to be destroyed by the construction of a dam and reservoir share their memories about the town and about each other. The author's lyrical style is an effective counterpoint to the subjects' own words. This work of oral history encourages reflection on the theme "we learn values from things lost."

Bontemps, Arna. **Frederick Douglass: Slave-Fighter Freeman.** Illus. Harper Johnson. Knopf 1959.

> This dramatic short biography of Frederick Douglass is compelling reading. The changes in his character as a result of the trauma of slavery are characterized in the statement attributed to him: "If there is no struggle, there is no progress. Those who profess to favor freedom, and yet deprecate agitation are men who crop without plowing. . . . They want the ocean without the awful roar of its many waters." The struggles of this great American are sensitively presented.

Collier, James Lincoln, and Christopher Collier. **My Brother Sam Is Dead.**

Collier, James Lincoln, and Christopher Collier. **The Winter Hero.** Four Winds. Schol Bk Serv 1978.

> In the aftermath of the Revolution, it seemed to many Americans

that they had only exchanged one tyranny for another. Out of their bitterness grows Shays' Rebellion. Fourteen-year-old Justin Conklin joins the uprising to become a hero, but discovers that heroism is frequently in the eye of the beholder.

Forbes, Esther. **Johnny Tremain.**

Fox, Paula. **The Slave Dancer.** Illus. Eros Keith. Bradbury Pr 1973.

In this grim story, a thirteen-year-old New Orleans boy is shanghaied for the crew of a slave ship, to play his fife as the prisoners "dance" for exercise. The author shows the degradation and projected revulsion that eventually affect all those who are involved with the slave trade. Although the slave dancer survives a calamitous shipwreck, there is nothing joyful in his escape. Discussing the characters' assumptions and possible alternative courses of action may help students deal with the strong theme.

Hamley, Dennis. **Pageants of Despair.** S G Phillips 1974.

When Peter's mother is brutally mugged, he is sent to stay with his grandparents. On his way, Peter encounters Gilbert, a scribe who has traveled through time to seek assistance in combating a demon attempting to sabotage the mystery plays Gilbert has written. Peter returns to the Middle Ages with Gilbert in an effort to counter the evil forces threatening Gilbert's community. Following a series of terrifying experiences, Gilbert and Peter successfully complete their mission and the boy returns to his own time. The author's knowledge of Medieval drama makes this an extraordinary novel.

Hilton, Suzanne. **Who Do You Think You Are?**

Hunt, Irene. **Across Five Aprils.**

Hunter, Mollie. **The Third Eye.** Har-Row 1979.

The ancient Ballinford Doom and a mother's desire to spare her daughters from her own social and economic "doom" make a suspenseful backdrop for this story of Depression-era Scotland. As young Jinty considers her testimony about a fatal accident, she realizes how village and family history have shaped her life. Courage and a sense of vision are important themes.

Irwin, Constance. **Strange Footprints on the Land: Vikings in America.** Har-Row 1980.

In an examination of Norse exploration and settlement of North

America before Columbus, ancient Norse manuscripts, and findings, both old and new, of archaeologists, historians, and runologists are discussed.

Landau, Elaine. **Hidden Heroines: Women in American History.**

Monjo, F. N. **A Namesake for Nathan.**

Sonnleitner, A. Th. (translator Anthea Bell). **The Cave Children.** Illus. Katarina Freinthal. S G Phillips 1971.

When their grandmother is accused of being a witch, Peter and Eva are forced to flee with her to a remote Alpine valley. Shortly after their arrival in the Hidden Valley, she dies and the two children must become inventive and resourceful in order to survive. Peter and Eva's experience in securing shelter, food, and clothing, coping with the elements, and combating predatory animals closely parallels the early development of humanity.

Strait, Treva Adams. **The Price of Free Land.**

Suhl, Yuri. **Uncle Misha's Partisans.** Four Winds. Schol Bk Serv 1973.

Motele, whose family was massacred by Nazis, joins a band of partisans to avenge the crimes against the Jewish people of the Ukraine. The twelve-year-old gathers important military information while entertaining German officers with his violin.

Walsh, Jill Paton. **A Chance Child.**

Ages 14 and Up

Allen, Merritt P. **The White Feather.** McKay 1944.

Conflicts between loyalty to the North and to the South arise between an illiterate, tyrannical Kentucky mountaineer grandfather and his sensitive, well-educated seventeen-year-old grandson. The white feather, given as a symbol of cowardice and betrayal, becomes a badge of courage when the boy joins Morgan's Raiders. No reconciliation of conviction is possible but respect for honesty and idealism bridges the gap between generations.

Ellis, Mel. **Sidewalk Indian.**

Estes, Winston M. **Another Part of the House.** Avon 1978.

Larry Morrison is ten years old at the time of the Depression.

Through him, we experience a warm happy life in a small Texas Panhandle community, where his father is the local druggist. There are times, however, when adverse events shake Larry's secure world, and his reactions to such problems as death and dishonesty are revealed in this touching novel.

Harris, Janet. **Thursday's Daughters: The Story of Women Working in America.**

Jones, Douglas C. **Winding Stair.** HR&W 1979.

In 1890, Eben Pay, an inexperienced lawyer from St. Louis, accepts an appointment to celebrated "Hanging Judge" Parker's court in Fort Smith, Arkansas. As assistant to the U.S. prosecutor, Pay joins a posse to investigate the alleged rape and murder of an Indian woman. The trail leads the posse to a farmstead where a massacre has taken place. The story recounts the events leading to the capture of the men who committed these murders, as well as their trial and execution.

Rubin, Arnold P. **The Evil That Men Do: The Story of the Nazis.** Messner 1978.

This chronical of Nazi Germany offers a detailed account of the horrifying imprisonment and systematic extermination of European Jews during World War II. In addition to the events of the Holocaust, the author describes the rise of Nazi power and examines what, if any, effort the rest of the world made to stop these atrocities from continuing and provide relief for the Jews. First hand accounts by survivors are interspersed throughout the text.

Sterne, Emma Gelders. **They Took Their Stand.** Macmillan 1968.

In these biographical sketches, eleven men and women are described, who at various times in American history have worked selflessly for equal rights for blacks: a Southern colonial patriot who saw the need to emancipate the Negro during the American Revolution; a native Virginian and West Point graduate who was called a traitor when he chose to fight for the Union cause; several Southern clergymen who bravely spoke out against injustices as they saw them; and contemporary leaders in the struggle for open housing and equal education for all.

Stiller, Richard. **Queen of the Populists: The Story of Mary Elizabeth Lease.**

Suhl, Yuri. **Eloquent Crusader—Ernestine Rose.**

Werstein, Irving. **Pie in the Sky.** Delacorte 1969.

- The Industrial Workers of the World, or the IWW, played an important role in the development of industrial unions for the working class in America. From 1905 to 1924, this group, also known as "The Wobblies," helped organize workers. They also fought for improved conditions for black and migrant laborers. This book tells the history of the movement up to its final stages when the CIO rose to inherit its legacy.

Meeting Personal and Political Crises

Ages 5 to 8

Delton, Judy. **It Happened on Thursday.**

Haley, Gail E. **Jack Jouett's Ride.** Illus. by author. Viking Pr 1973.

>Personal courage is highlighted in this exciting true incident: A young man rides to warn Thomas Jefferson, Patrick Henry, and others that British troops threaten Charlottesville, Virginia. Jouett's words provide a theme: "'When men need to be free from tyrants, they will always find a way.'" Colored linoleum cuts provide drama and visual appeal.

Ages 8 to 11

Berger, Terry. **A Friend Can Help.** Photographs by Heinz Kluetmeier. Raintree Pubs Ltd 1975.

>A young child is troubled by the divorce of her parents. Even though she knows that her parents still love her, she is unhappy about the situation. By confiding in a friend she is able to reconstruct why it happened and why things are better now. Because of her friendship she is able to accept new ideas about herself and the family crisis.

Bourne, Miriam Anne. **Nabby Adams' Diary.** Illus. Stephen Gammell. Coward 1975.

>Nabby Adams, the daughter of John Adams, writes a very detailed day-to-day diary of her family's life during the pre-Revolutionary and Revolutionary War times. Times for the Adams family are personally difficult, and both personal struggles and the struggle for American independence are explicity revealed through the diary, as fictionalized by author Bourne.

Burchard, Peter. **Chinwe.**

Coerr, Eleanor. **Sadako and the Thousand Paper Cranes.** Illus. Ronald Himler. Putnam 1977.

> Based upon an actual event, this is the story of eleven-year-old Sadako who was a baby when Hiroshima was devastated by the atom bomb. When she contracts leukemia she wants to believe her friend's idea that making 1000 paper-folded cranes will help to make her well. This sad, realistic story should provoke serious discussion.

Foreman, Michael. **War and Peas.** Illus. by author. T Y Crowell 1974.

> This modern fable satirizes the conflict between the have's and have-not's as the overfed army of the Fat King unintentionally helps the starving subjects of King Lion to plant their crops. Big, colorful illustrations mixing food and weaponry make the book attractive to children too young to see its irony.

Gauch, Patricia Lee. **This Time, Tempe Wick?**

Griese, Arnold A. **The Wind Is Not a River.** Illus. Glo Coalson. T Y Crowell 1978.

> In 1942 when Japanese soldiers capture the tiny island of Attu in the Aleutians, two children escape discovery. Alone, they must aid their imprisoned neighbors. In doing so, Sasan and Sidak discover the wisdom and difficulty of their grandmother's admonition to love even one's enemy.

Haugaard, Erik Christian. **Orphans of the Wind.** Illus. Milton Johnson. Dell 1969.

> At twelve, Jim is signed on as deckboy for the Civil War blockade runner *Four Winds* by his selfish uncle. Leaving Bristol and sailing to Charleston, his life is changed by the people he meets and the things that happen. Many crewmen are concerned about slavery and question the ship's cargo of guns and powder. When the ship is burned Jim and three of his fellow crewmen row to shore. In order to travel North to join what they feel is the right cause, they travel with the Confederate Army. Their feelings as men in battle as well as their desire to do the right thing are well described.

Hays, Wilma Pitchford. **Trouble at Otter Creek.**

Jordan, June. **Fannie Lou Hamer.** Illus. Albert Williams. T Y Crowell 1972.

> Fannie Lou Hamer is tricked into picking cotton at the age of six. She never forgets this injustice and others that follow. Even as

a youngster, she talks with her people about the bad treatment they receive. As a grown-up, she does more than talk; she tries to get black people to vote, to stand up for their rights. She is beaten and thrown into jail, but with the help of Martin Luther King, she reaches Washington, D.C. where she tells of her treatment. With more help she starts the Freedom Farm Cooperative, where many people work and share the benefits of her fight against poverty and inhuman treatment.

Levitin, Sonia. **Journey to America.** Illus. Charles Robinson. Atheneum 1970.

As Jews are no longer safe in Hitler's Germany, Lisa and her family must abandon their home and go to America. Forced to wait in Switzerland while Papa earns their passage fare, the family courageously suffers poverty and loneliness, but they are able to survive with the help of new-found friends. This well-told and deeply moving story is both authentic and memorable.

Lifton, Betty Jean. **Return to Hiroshima.**

Ofek, Uriel (translator Israel I. Taslitt). **Smoke over Golan: A Novel of the 1973 Yom Kippur War in Israel.** Illus. Lloyd Bloom. Har-Row 1979.

Eitan's move to an isolated farm on the Golan Heights has its pleasures. There is the teacher for whom Eitan is sole pupil, and there is Saleem, the Syrian boy Eitan befriends. Political turmoil seems far away until war catches Eitan alone on his farm. Suddenly he is forced to contend with an enemy both real and very human. Although this is a story of the horrors of war, the value of love, peace, and friendship is felt throughout.

Putnam, Alice. **The Spy Doll.** Elsevier-Nelson 1979.

The Confederacy was desperate for medical supplies. Union troops kept close guard along the borders, searching and arresting suspected smugglers. No one, however, suspected a chip-nosed doll named Nina. This tale, set near the end of the Civil War, was inspired by a real doll now living in the Museum of the Confederacy in Richmond, Virginia.

Serraillier, Ian. **The Silver Sword.** Illus. C. Walter Hodges. S G Phillips 1959.

As a result of World War II, the Balicki family of Warsaw are separated from one another. Living in bombed-out cellars or the countryside, the children are helped by Edek until his arrest for smuggling and from then on by Jan, a sullen orphan. The privations of each member of the family, especially the children, are graphically described as each works toward their rendezvous, Switzerland, and freedom. A suspense-filled, exciting story.

Slote, Alfred. **Hang Tough, Paul Mather.** Lippincott 1973.

Twelve-year-old Paul Mather, a baseball enthusiast, is stricken with leukemia. His courageous struggle against the disease, his fight to continue playing baseball, and his relationship to his understanding doctor as they learn together about the course of Paul's disease, make this a story that is unforgettable. Paul's example will give readers renewed zest for life.

Smucker, Barbara. **Runaway to Freedom: A Story of the Underground Railway.** Illus. Charles Lilly. Trophy. Har-Row 1979.

Through the desperate adventures of four escaping slaves, Barbara Smucker describes the activities of the Underground Railroad and those, both black and white, who strove to aid fugitive slaves. Readers will learn of the infamous fugitive slave laws and the role Canada played in this political crisis.

Taylor, Mildred D. **Song of the Trees.**

Uchida, Yoshiko. **Journey to Topaz.** Illus. Donald Carrick. Scribner 1971.

The moving story of Yuki, an eleven-year-old Japanese-American girl who, in December of 1941, suddenly finds herself, her mother, and her older brother being sent from their comfortable home in Northern California to an internment camp in Utah, while her father is sent elsewhere. The humiliation and suffering inflicted on the Japanese during the war is made very evident in the story. The courage, the dignity, and the patriotism not only of Yuki and her family but of the other people in the camp come through very well.

Van Stockum, Hilda. **The Winged Watchman.** FS&G 1963.

During the occupation of Holland in World War II, the Verhagens adjust to the hardships—physical danger, cruelties, and food shortages. They maintain their loyalty to their country and participate in the underground movement. The book presents a dramatic picture of how political events can affect the daily life of individuals.

Watson, Sally. **Other Sandals.** HR&W 1966.

Debra Meyer, raised on a kibbutz, outspokenly despises all Arabs.

Eytan, her cousin, raised in the city of Haifa, indulges in self-pity over a permanent limp resulting from an accident. Their parents decide a "sandal swap" would profit both. Living in each others' shoes is quite an adjustment for both. After some painful events, they gain a wider view of their world and the consequences of living in an era of political and social upheaval.

Ages 11 to 14

Arnold, Elliott. **A Kind of Secret Weapon.** Scribner 1969.

Lars and Lise Anderson are deeply involved in the Danish underground. Their son, Peter, twelve, takes part as he helps to publish and distribute their underground newspaper. The changes which the Germans bring to their country are partially countered by such activities, and the emphasis on helping one's country in her hour of need is reiterated again and again. The ultimate consequence of such personal involvement is exemplified by Mr. Anderson's arrest, torture, and ultimate death as a martyr. Before they flee to Sweden, Peter, the new head of the family, asserts himself in order to publish and distribute his father's final edition which discredits the local German commander.

Bawden, Nina. **Rebel on a Rock.** Lippincott 1978.

Twelve-year-old Jo Popper, vacationing in a small Adriatic village with her family, discovers that a village boy, Alexis, is the son of a revolutionary planning to overthrow the current dictator. Jo suspects her stepfather may be a spy and must act soon in order to avoid a bloody revolution.

Beatty, Patricia. **I Want My Sunday, Stranger!** Morrow 1977.

A Mormon boy from California searches for his stolen horse, and his search takes him across the United States and right into the midst of the Civil War. The point is well made that war is anything but glamorous.

Blaine, Marge. **Dvora's Journey.** Illus. Gabriel Lisowski. HR&W 1979.

As life becomes increasingly difficult for Russian Jews in 1904, twelve-year-old Dvora and her family decide to flee their homeland for the promise of a better life in America. Their journey is successful until they reach Hamburg, Germany, and discover they must wait several weeks for passage across the Atlantic. The family becomes the victim of a con-artist who promises tickets on the next departing

Meeting Personal and Political Crises

ship. Left with only a limited amount of money, the family decides to send Dvora and her brother, Saul, to America where they will stay with their aunt and uncle until the family can be reunited.

Blume, Judy. **It's Not the End of the World.**

Clark, Ann Nolan. **All This Wild Land.**

Clark, Ann Nolan. **To Stand Against the Wind.**

Collier, James Lincoln, and Christopher Collier. **My Brother Sam Is Dead.** Four Winds. Schol Bk Serv 1974.

The ironies of war are highlighted in this story of a Connecticut family with divided loyalties. Sam takes up the Patriot cause, to the dismay of his Tory parents, but the ways in which they all suffer are unexpected. Sam's younger brother narrates the action and wonders in an epilogue if there might have been another way to achieve political freedom.

Collier, James Lincoln, and Christopher Collier. **The Winter Hero.**

David, Janina. **A Touch of Earth.** Grossman 1969.

Miss David escaped from the Warsaw ghetto in January 1943. Fleeing to a convent, she was forced to change her name and adopt the Catholic religion. She did so willingly, with conviction and relief. This is an autobiographical memoir recalling the feelings of a young girl adopting a strange way of life: making friends with a German soldier and weeping for the death of his family as the war, deprivation, and illness surround her.

Dunn, Mary Lois. **The Man in the Box: A Story from Vietnam.** Illus. Nicholas Fasciano. McGraw 1968.

Chau Li's father had been tortured and killed by the Viet Cong. Then a captured American is brought to his Montagnard village. The American is imprisoned in the tiny box in which Chau Li's father had suffered. The villagers had been too frightened and Chau Li had been too small to help his father. He is bigger now and he is determined to help the strange-looking foreigner. Chau Li overcomes fear and extraordinary difficulties to help a strange American escape, his only reward a feeling of personal satisfaction.

Fife, Dale. **North of Danger.**

Finlayson, Ann. **Rebecca's War.** YB. Dell. 1976.

Rebecca, at fourteen, is suddenly confronted with the responsibility of taking care of a small brother and sister when the British occupy Philadelphia during the War of Independence. Her situation is further complicated because her father has important government papers and gold ingots concealed in the house. When these are needed she must help the rebel soliders remove them, and she is also forced to house two enemy officers and their servants.

Fisher, Leonard Everett. **Across the Sea from Galway.**

Graham, Gail. **Cross Fire: A Vietnam Novel.** Illus. by author. Pantheon 1972.

A young American soldier, the only surviving member of a small scouting mission, and four Vietnamese children are the only survivors in a fire-bombed village. Beyond the barriers of languages and cultures, the soldier and the eldest girl reach out to each other, with gentleness and humor, as they share the responsibility for the younger children. The stark ending reveals far better than newspaper accounts the ugliness and violence of the Vietnamese War.

Greene, Constance C. **Beat the Turtle Drum.**

Hannam, Charles. **A Boy in That Situation: An Autobiography.** Har-Row 1978.

"That situation" is growing up a Jew in Nazi Germany. Plagued by the typical concerns facing young adolescents, as well as the extraordinary problem of being ostracized for his religious convictions, thirteen-year-old Karl Hartland, must flee his homeland for the security of England while leaving part of his family behind. In recreating his own childhood, the author provides a realistic and sensitive portrayal of a young adult confronting crises.

Harding, Lee. **Misplaced Persons.**

Haynes, Betsy. **Slave Girl.**

Hunt, Irene. **William: A Novel.**

Kaplan, Bess. **The Empty Chair.**

Kherdian, David. **The Road from Home: The Story of an Armenian Girl.** Greenwillow 1979.

Veron was born in the Armenian sector of a community in Turkey early in this century. This biography of the author's mother, narrated in first person, presents a much less well-known holocaust account but equally brutal and deliberate. The day-to-day life and customs of the Armenian Christians sharply contrast with sudden Moslem orders to pack and march eastward into the desert. Her courage, often sorely tested, sustains this gentle, sensitive girl as she grows into womanhood, finally becoming a mail-order bride as a means to flee to a better life in America.

Lawson, Don. **FDR's New Deal.** T Y Crowell 1979.

In a well-balanced description of Roosevelt's presidency, major aspects of the period, including the First Hundred Days, the Supreme Court debate, and the beginning of World War II are concisely and clearly discussed.

Lehmann, Linda. **Better Than a Princess.**

Leigh, Bill. **The Far Side of Fear.** Viking Pr 1978.

Kenny is frequently plagued by the vicious and violent assaults of Patrick, the local school bully. As a result of one such attack, both boys, Kenny's friend, and Patrick's sister find themselves trapped in a network of caves beneath the Irish countryside. In their frantic struggle to survive both physically and emotionally, the youngsters fight panic and fear. As a result of their plight, Kenny discovers his latent courage and leadership ability while Patrick learns to cooperate with others.

Lifton, Betty Jean, and Thomas C. Fox. **Children of Vietnam.**

O'Dell, Scott. **The 290.** LFL. Dell 1979.

In 1862, the 290 is built in secret at Laird's Shipyard of Liverpool, in neutral England for the United States Confederate Navy. Upon arriving in the Azores, her commander, Raphael Semmes, boards, and although on the losing side, he is said to have been the greatest raider of all times including those of World War II, U-boats, and navy bombers. This is mainly a story of the Civil War as seen by eighteen-year-old Jim Lynne, sailor second class aboard the Confederate raider.

Reboul, Antoine. **Thou Shalt Not Kill.** S G Phillips 1969.

This novel is set during the 1967 Arab-Israeli War. Both fourteen years old and separated from their troops, Slimane, an Egyptian boy, and Simmy, an Israeli girl, meet in the Sinai Desert. The first intent of each is to kill the other; instead they join forces and fight their immediate enemy—the desert. Their uneasy alliance quickly turns to respect, acceptance, and friendship.

Reiss, Johanna. **The Upstairs Room.** T Y Crowell 1972.

> Following the tradition of Anne Frank, Johanna Reiss details the events of her life during the Nazi occupation of Holland. She recalls the strengths and weaknesses of the Oosterveld family who offered their home as a hiding place to Johanna and her sister. Readers will sympathize with the limitations placed on the activities of this young girl, and will better understand the fear that permeated the lives of the Dutch Jews during World War II.

Smucker, Barbara Claasen. **Days of Terror.**

Stewart, A. C. **Dark Dove.** S G Phillips 1974.

> In northwestern Scotland, sixteen-year-old Margaret tries to cope with with her dour minister father and the problems connected with his premonitions of disaster. However, she is unable to avert her brother's death as it is predicted in her father's recurring nightmare.

Uchida, Yoshiko. **Journey Home.**

Walsh, Jill Paton. **Children of the Fox.**

Wuorio, Eva-Lis. **To Fight in Silence.**

Zei, Alki (translator Edward Fenton). **Wildcat Under Glass.** HR&W 1968.

> In 1936, fascism envelops all of Greece and reaches out to clutch at every facet of Greek daily life. In Melia's own family the threads of fascism are constantly at work changing lives, splitting loyalties, and capturing the minds of the youth.

Ages 14 and Up

Arnothy, Christine. **I Am Fifteen—And I Don't Want to Die . . .** Schol Bk Serv 1974.

> The author describes her experiences during the siege of Budapest in World War II when she was fifteen. She relates her fear of death and the uncertainties of life during this period.

Brancato, Robin. **Winning.**

Cormier, Robert. **I Am the Cheese.**

Greene, Bette. **Summer of My German Soldier.**

Hallstead, William F. **The Man Downstairs.** Elsevier-Nelson 1979.

After working as a draftsman for six months in Millbury's Department of Streets, Don Ellison becomes aware of a political kickback scheme which requires all city workers to make a "voluntary contribution" to the Party. When Don refuses, he and his wife are harassed until they finally decide to make this scandal known. In response, the Governor appoints a special committee to investigate the alleged corruption in Millbury's city government. Although Don's claims are documented and the committee's recommendations implemented, things quickly return to the status quo after the hearing and, as a result, Ellison resigns his position.

Hickman, Janet. **The Valley of the Shadow.**

Houston, Jeanne Wakatsuki, and James D. Houston. **Farewell to Manzanar.**

Hurwood, Bernhardt J. **Born Innocent.**

Joffo, Joseph (translator Martin Sokolinsky). **A Bag of Marbles.** Bantam 1977.

Robbed of their childhood by the events of World War II, two Jewish brothers journey across France in an effort to elude the Nazi holocaust. In this autobiographical novel, the adventures of ten-year-old Joseph Joffo and his twelve-year-old brother, Maurice, are woven together to reveal the courage and stamina which allowed these youngsters to triumph in their personal struggle to survive.

Kosinski, Jerzy. **The Painted Bird.** Bantam 1977.

A small boy, abandoned by his parents during World War II, wanders alone through Eastern Europe. He is treated with extreme cruelty and is confronted with superstition, ignorance, sadism, and hunger. Being a Jew or gypsy with dark hair and dark eyes among the blond peasants, he is the "painted bird" in their midst. Abnormal acts of cruelty may be offensive to readers, but the book is a powerful statement of the inhumanity of prejudice.

Lang, Othmar Franz. **If You Are Silenced, I Will Speak for You.** Collins Pubs 1978.

The issue of human rights and freedom for the victims of political imprisonment throughout the world is addressed in this fictionalized account of the actual efforts of a West German group of Amnesty

International. It is the story of the commitment and dedication exhibited by the young founders of the group as they struggle to secure the freedom of their adopted prisoners.

Lawrence, Louise. **Star Lord.** Har-Row 1978.

The unexpected crash of a spacecraft drastically alters the life of a Welsh family, who must decide whether to surrender the wounded star lord, Erlich, to the authorities or to help him escape capture. After much deliberation, the family chooses the latter option and is, therefore, forced to combat the military authorities and the supernatural powers of a mountain named Mawrrhyn. Erlich uses Mawrrhyn's power to return to Eridani Epsilon, but only at the personal expense of Rhys and his family.

Madison, Arnold. **Runaway Teens.** Elsevier-Nelson 1979.

Arnold Madison explores the plight of the adolescent runaway in the United States. He examines the principal reasons adolescents leave home and, through the use of several case studies, details what a potential runaway can expect to encounter after leaving home. Madison also delineates some alternatives to running away and provides the reader with a list of agencies that offer assistance to these adolescents.

Morrell, David. **First Blood.** M Evans 1972.

In this tense, psychological novel, Rambo, a returning Vietnam veteran, protests the prejudice he encounters upon his return to the United States. After repeatedly being escorted out of Madison, Kentucky, Rambo is finally arrested for vagrancy. This arrest reminds him of his treatment as a prisoner of war. Rambo escapes from the local jail by killing an officer and injuring another. He is then pursued through the mountains of Kentucky. In an effort to survive, Rambo utilizes his skill at guerrilla warfare until his inevitable destruction.

Morris, Edmund. **The Rise of Theodore Roosevelt.** Coward 1979.

This excellently written narrative traces Theodore Roosevelt from infancy to his first days as Vice-President, revealing major influences and trends in Roosevelt's formative years.

Orgel, Doris. **The Devil in Vienna.**

Rockwood, Joyce. **To Spoil the Sun.**

Meeting Personal and Political Crises 349

Sallis, Susan. **A Time for Everything.** Har-Row 1979.

> In the hills of England during World War II, adolescent Lily thinks she is faced with problems when Mavis, a refugee from London, arrives to stay for the duration. Her former problems pale into nothingness when Lily's dad leaves for service and her mother turns to another man. The village is scandalized when her mother becomes pregnant. Lily learns a lot about real sacrifice from Philippa, her mongoloid cousin, and also what real love is. The unexpected return of her father and his forgiveness of her mother also contribute to her growing understanding.

Samuels, Gertrude. **Run, Shelley, Run!** T Y Crowell 1974.

> Shelley's life is characterized by running. Initially she flees from foster homes, only to be neglected by her alcoholic mother. Sent to a detention center, she flees in order to escape the brutality of the other inmates. Shelley is mercilessly entangled in the bureaucracy of the juvenile justice system until she escapes the vicious cycle with the help of a humane judge. Psychologically, however, Shelley does not gain the freedom she so desperately desires until she decides not to return to her mother, but to build her life on her own strength and will.

Strassova, Helena (translator Peter Freixa). **The Path.** Grossman 1969.

> This is the story of a young Jewish girl alone during World War II, living as a fugitive, then a refugee. Nell, the narrator, is deeply attached to her parents and especially to her twin brother with whom she forms a remarkable bond. Her family is separated from her, never to be seen again. But in her flight, she meets people who influence the rest of her life.

Sutcliff, Rosemary. **Song for a Dark Queen.**

Trivelpiece, Laurel. **During Water Peaches.** Lippincott 1979.

> During the summer of 1943, Mexican migrant workers are brought into California to harvest the peach crop. Seventeen-year-old LaVerne Honeycutt accepts a job as a secretary in the government office which will supervise this World War II project. LaVerne's aspirations to extricate herself from an intolerable home situation and perhaps attend college are threatened by her loyalty to an unconventional boss, her love for a Mexican student, and her unwillingness to accept her family's poverty. However, LaVerne successfully emerges from these conflicts and later becomes the recipient of a college scholarship.

Uris, Leon. **Exodus.** Bantam 1975.

The establishment of a Jewish homeland is told dramatically through the personal experience of Jews and gentiles. The author controls the vast range of this novel and maintains reader interest in the characters as well as in the task of building a new nation. *Exodus* will be condemned by some critics for its partisan attitude toward Judaism. Despite this charge, it ranks as one of the fine novels in this century.

Wangerin, Walter, Jr. **The Book of the Dun Cow.**

Windsor, Patricia. **Diving for Roses.**

Interacting in a Technological World

Ages 5 to 8

Billout, Guy. **By Camel or by Car: A Look at Transportation.** Illus. by author. P-H 1979.

> Brief bits of information about fifteen different means of transportation are supplemented by the author's recollections of childhood feelings and experiences concerning each one. The full-page paintings are imaginative rather than informative, with an emphasis on isolation and sterile environments that would be worth discussing with older children.

Burton, Virginia Lee. **Mike Mulligan and His Steam Shovel.** HM 1977.

> This popular picture book tells the story of an old-fashioned steam shovel finding a useful occupation when more modern engines have replaced it.

Duvoisin, Roger. **Lonely Veronica.** Knopf 1963.

> When Veronica's peaceful river is invaded by men, machines, and a new city, the older hippopotami see the end of the good old days and leave. But young Veronica stays to find the good new days, and ends up in America where she is trapped in a construction site for a time, but finally finds her place on a farm.

Foreman, Michael. **Dinosaurs and All That Rubbish.** Illus. by author. T Y Crowell 1973.

> In a very pointed cautionary tale, the technology of building a rocket to carry a man to a star produces enough concrete and rubbish to cover the whole earth. Dinosaurs wakened by the heat and noise clean up the ruined planet and tell the rocket man on his return that the earth belongs to everyone and needs everyone's care. The illustrations are large, colorful, and exuberant.

Hoban, Russell. **Arthur's New Power.** Illus. Byron Barton. T Y Crowell 1978.

>The Crocodile family creates its own fuse-blowing energy crisis by using too many appliances. Even ingenious Arthur's water wheel generator suffers an overload, and he decides his guitar sounds fine "not plugged into anything." The dialogue and cartoonish illustrations invite laughter as well as thought.

Hurd, Edith Thacher. **Wilson's World.** Illus. Clement Hurd. Har-Row 1971.

>A little boy makes a picture of the world and keeps adding people, animals, factories, and cities until the earth is crowded and polluted. He looks upon his creation with disgust, tears up the picture, and starts again to make a world, this time a place where people care about each other and their environment.

Latham, Jean Lee. **Rachel Carson Who Loved the Sea.** Illus. Victor Mays. Garrard 1973.

>As a child, Rachel Carson loved writing stories. As an adult, she loved biology as well. By combining her two passions, she stirred Americans to care about chemicals poisoning the environment. This easy to read biography may help young children consider some of the dangers of modern technology.

McNulty, Faith. **How to Dig a Hole to the Other Side of the World.** Illus. Marc Simont. Har-Row 1979.

>McNulty's lively text combines with Simont's illustrations to give detailed instructions on how to dig, drill, and dive one's way to the center of the earth and out again. Along the way, readers learn about oil, magma, and futuristic technology. Children will enjoy this scientific adventure.

Mizumura, Kazue. **If I Built a Village . . .** Illus. by author. T Y Crowell 1971.

>In simple, poetic phrases and colorful, boldly outlined illustrations, Mizumura conveys a strong feeling that technology and urbanization should not destroy the natural environment. Along with her village, town, and city, there would also be rabbits and deer, geese and moles, and "people who would care and share."

Peet, Bill. **Farewell to Shady Glade.** Illus. by author. HM 1966.

>Sixteen animals have their own paradise in Shady Glade until they are threatened by urbanization. The wise old raccoon helps the group

through their difficulty by leading them on a long journey to other places until they find a suitable home.

Peet, Bill. **The Wump World.** Illus. by author. HM 1970.

The Wump creatures live simply and happily in their small Wump World. There is plenty to eat, they all get along beautifully and life is without problems. Suddenly from Outer Space come the Pollutions from the planet Pollutus. They take over everything everywhere and the Wumps are forced to go underground. The Wump World eventually becomes uninhabitable, the Pollutions take off for greener pastures and the Wumps are left to rebuild their world again. The message is there, subtly told in a simple straightforward manner.

Saul, Wendy. **Butcher, Baker, Cabinetmaker: Photographs of Women at Work.** Photographs by Abigail Heyman. T Y Crowell 1978.

Living in a world of technology means great diversity in the world of work. This photographic picture book focuses on women in a variety of jobs—airline pilot, taxi driver, architect, coal miner— once reserved for men.

Ages 8 to 11

Benchley, Nathaniel. **Kilroy and the Gull.** Illus. John Schoenherr. Trophy. Har-Row 1978.

In this mixture of fact and fantasy, a scientist studying the communication of killer whales doesn't quite realize that he too is being studied. Kilroy the orca and his unusual friend Morris the gull have the power of speech, and frequently discuss the strange habits of humans. This fun story invites discussion of man's proper relationship to other creatures.

Bradbury, Bianca. **Andy's Mountain.** Illus. Robert MacLean. HM 1969.

For six generations the farm has been in the Wheeler family. Now it is about to be taken by the state for a four-lane highway. Gramps, determined that his grandchildren Andy and Ellen will inherit the land, stubbornly refuses all offers and orders. When all his plans fail, eleven-year-old Andy finally comes up with a plan to satisfy both Gramps and the state.

Fleming, Susan. **Trapped on the Golden Flyer.** Illus. Alex Stein. Westminster 1978.

From the outset, Paul is not looking forward to his trip across the

Sierra Nevadas. Lonely and afraid, he feels abandoned by everyone. Then a blizzard freezes the train in the middle of the mountains and Paul discovers a community of caring people. In their struggle to survive, Paul finds courage to face his own future.

Goodall, John S. **The Story of an English Village.**

Jenness, Aylette. **The Bakery Factory: Who Puts Bread on Your Table.** Photographs by author. T Y Crowell 1978.

There is more to bread and coffee cake than dough. There are people—cake decorators, wrappers, truck drivers, assembly-line workers, and more. There are machines—enormous ovens, conveyor belts, cutting machines, icing machines. A tour through the bakery allows the reader to listen in on workers discussing the pleasures and frustrations of their jobs. The book includes suggestions for further investigations of our technological world.

Lifton, Betty Jean. **Return to Hiroshima.** Illus. Eikoh Hosoe. Atheneum 1970.

When the author went to live in Hiroshima with her husband, Robert J. Lifton, who was studying the psychological effects of the bomb on the survivors, she made a film of the young people. She asked the photographer to help her tell the story of the survivors in book form. The reader becomes a survivor and hopefully will grasp the nature of the weapons that man has created.

Müller, Jörg. **The Changing Countryside (vol. 1); The Changing City (vol. 2).** Illus. by author. Atheneum 1977.

Originally published in Switzerland, these two portfolios of foldout paintings show the effects of change on the environment and the development of an increasingly technological society. A versatile resource, the detailed pictures may suggest discussion of past or future, real changes or imagined ones.

O'Brien, Robert. **Mrs. Frisby and the Rats of NIMH.** Illus. Zena Bernstein. Atheneum 1971.

The rats of NIMH have been used for learning experiments, and they are such good students that they learn to read, to escape the laboratory, and to adapt modern technology to their colony under the rosebush. Their mouse friend, Mrs. Frisby, alerts them to the danger of exterminators so that most can flee to a valley where they hope to build a self-sufficient society. The "rat race" and the burden of labor-saving devices are two themes for discussion.

Spier, Peter. **Tin Lizzie.**

Steiner, Jörg (translator Ann Conrad Lammers). **Rabbit Island.** Illus. Jörg Müller. HarBraceJ 1978.

> Two rabbits escape from the antiseptic environment of a "factory" where others are fattened for slaughter. Even with the younger one as guide, the dangers of freedom in the countryside prove too unsettling for the older rabbit, who chooses to return to the factory. Allegorical implications and memorable pictures make this oversize book appropriate for discussion with all ages.

Ages 11 to 14

Jenness, Aylette. **Along the Niger River: An African Way of Life.**

Kirkpatrick, Doris. **Honey in the Rock.** Elsevier-Nelson 1979.

> Sixteen-year-old Linny was content to live with her grandparents on their rustic Vermont farm until the Power Company began purchasing property for the building of a dam. This novel, set in 1936, describes how the residents struggle to cope with the changes brought by the Power Company. This is also the story of Linny's maturation as she attempts to keep the farm running, meet property tax payments, combat the devastation wrought by a hurricane, and decide on her own future goals.

Meyer, Carolyn. **Amish People: Plain Living in a Complex World.**

Thiele, Colin. **The Hammerhead Light.**

Walsh, Jill Paton. **A Chance Child.** FS&G 1978.

> When Creep, a neglected English child, escapes the closet that confines him, he travels along a canal that takes him back in time to the early days of the Industrial Revolution. His involvement with the plight of child laborers invites discussion of the effects of industrialization. Suspense and mystery as Creep becomes part of the past add an unusual twist to the story.

Watson, Jane Werner. **Living Together in Tomorrow's World.** Abelard 1976.

> This book traces historic developments in housing, transportation, and communication, and invites the reader to speculate on how we will be living, traveling, and communicating in the twenty-first century. Watson maintains that the quality of life in tomorrow's world

is contingent upon the preparations we make today. Therefore, emphasis is placed on current plans to accommodate for future changes and needs.

Ages 14 and Up

Carothers, J. Edward. **Can Machines Replace Men?** Friend Pr 1966.

With the advent of computers, the relationship between men and machines has become more complex and is constantly changing. The author of this small pamphlet raises many provocative questions and shows how men's lives have been altered by machines in the past. He feels that a lag between religion and moral perception is causing society to be more the victim than the master of machines, and this trend must be reversed if humanity is to benefit.

Carson, Rachel. **Silent Spring.** Fawcett 1978.

A sensitive, distinguished scientist cites many examples of the dreadful effect chemicals have wrought upon our changing environment and the serious consequences which have developed. She examines and describes the pollution which has resulted from man's careless attempts to control unwanted plant and animal life and shows how disastrous this may be in upsetting the balance of nature both now and in the future.

Cox, John. **Overkill: Weapons of the Nuclear Age.** T Y Crowell 1978.

Frequently pessimistic in tone, this book traces the scientific and historical development of modern weapons systems. Cox also examines the current issues involved in the nuclear arms race and contends that nothing short of complete disarmament will insure the safety and survival of world civilization.

Cummings, Betty Sue. **Let a River *Be.***

Faber, Doris. **Wall Street: A Story of Fortunes and Finance.** Har-Row 1979.

A lively introduction to the history and current events of Wall Street, this book includes balanced treatments of famous financial figures such as Jay Gould, Cornelius Vanderbilt, and Andrew Carnegie, and discusses the various attempts to reform Wall Street. Faber also raises important issues about the function of this powerful institution.

Haskins, James. **Street Gangs: Yesterday and Today.**

Le Guin, Ursula K. **The Beginning Place.**

Parenteau, Shirley. **The Talking Coffins of Cryo-City.** Elsevier-Nelson 1979.

> This story is a rather shallow treatment of an intriguing future in which old people and criminals are frozen (cryonics) against the possibility of scientists learning how to reverse aging and cure criminal tendencies. The main value of this book lies in its provocative look at man versus machine and its warning not to let machines control human lives.

Perry, John. **Our Polluted World: Can Man Survive.** Watts 1967.

> The author believes that a crucial point in human development has been reached and that the overwhelming problem of wastes in the air and water must be solved. Our very survival depends upon this. With the naturalist's eye, he cites examples of changes in our environment which have resulted from misuse of natural resources and industrialization. While this is undoubtedly a complex concern with varying degrees of pessimism, Perry feels it is not too late to preserve ourselves from extinction.

Facing the Future

Ages 1 to 5

Hickman, Martha Whitmore. **I'm Moving.** Illus. Leigh Grant. Abingdon 1974.

> William tells of things he must leave behind and of things he may take with him as he and his family move from one city to another. He has mixed feelings about moving—he's glad because he can take his baby brother but sad because he cannot take his friend Jimmy; he can take his turtle but not the squirrel that visits him at the window. But he finds out that moving from his old home to a new home can be an exciting and enjoyable experience and means making new friends.

Ages 5 to 8

Kuskin, Karla. **A Space Story.** Illus. Marc Simont. Har-Row 1978.

> Speculation about life on faraway planets is handled with childlike perception and poetic text, although the book's primary purpose is to give information about our solar system. The illustrations evoke a sense of distance.

Ages 11 to 14

Ames, Mildred. **Without Hats, Who Can Tell the Good Guys?** Dutton 1976.

> Eleven-year-old Anthony is placed in a foster home after his mother dies and his father is out of work. He doesn't like any of the family, but feels it is only temporary until his father sends for him. When his father stops to see him, Anthony realizes he will never be sending for him. He also comes to the realization that he and the Diamond family really do care for each other, and that his future includes them.

Christopher, John. **The City of Gold and Lead.** Macmillan 1967.

In the second book of the trilogy, Will, Henry, and Jean-Paul train for the Olympic Games maintained by the Tripods who use the winners as slaves to work in their domed cities. Will and Fritz win their events and are taken to the dome. Their mission is to discover as much as possible about the Tripods so the information can be used to destroy them. While there, Will and Fritz uncover a diabolical plan to destroy all Earth inhabitants so the entire Tripod race can transfer from their dying planet.

Christopher, John. **The Guardians.** Macmillan 1970.

In the year 2052, England is a nation divided into the Conurb—a crowded megalopolis whose people are entertained with controlled riots and bloody sporting events—and the County, a quiet countryside reminiscent of the Victorian era. Rob Randall, a Conurban, sent to a grim boarding school after the death of his father, crosses the forbidden Barrier into the County. There he discovers that the price of true freedom is not what he thought. For he learns that English society is secretly conditioned and manipulated behind the scenes by power hungry men who wish to maintain the status quo. The story provides a thought-provoking look at a possible future.

Christopher, John. **The Pool of Fire.** Macmillan 1968.

In the final book of the "White Mountain Trilogy," Will, after his escape from the domed city, places the information he has gained into the hands of the rebels. After the rebels capture a Tripod, they find that alcohol incapacitates them. Will and Fritz are sent back into the dome. Once there, they treat the water with alcohol and, while the Tripods are incapacitated, shut off their life support systems. Using balloons, the other domed cities are destroyed and the Earth is left alone allowing human civilization to develop again. The success of this enterprise is left to the imagination of the reader.

Christopher, John. **The White Mountains.** Macmillan 1968.

In this first book of a series, the Tripods, a race from another planet, have taken over Earth. They control humans through the use of caps which regulate the brain-wave patterns. Will, Henry, and Jean-Paul, fearful of the capping ceremonies which occur at puberty, leave their homes and flee to the White Mountains, an area not controlled by the Tripods. There they join with a group of rebels intent on the overthrow of the Tripod domination.

Eldridge, Roger. **The Shadow of the Gloom-World.** Dutton 1978.

> Fernfeather, an inquisitive boy on the edge of puberty, is bothered by dreams of a world that lies beyond the dark caves (a subterranean society established by scientists to save part of the human race from a nuclear holocaust)—a world of fresh air and sunlight. Dreams, however, are forbidden by The Olden, keepers of the mystery. Fernfeather finds that dreams cannot be controlled. Banished to the Gloom World, he makes his way to the outside where he must learn to deal with a way of life totally different from the society in which he had been raised.

Gilbert, Harriett. **Running Away.**

Harding, Lee. **Misplaced Persons.** Har-Row 1979.

> Seventeen-year-old Graeme Drury of Melbourne, Australia, is perplexed and bewildered when everything in his world becomes grey and he loses his ability to make contact with people. Graeme believes he is suffering from a nervous breakdown until he realizes he has been transported into a parallel universe. Here he meets Jamie and Marion, who have also been temporarily misplaced. All three characters attempt to cope with their dilemma until they are mysteriously returned to their own world.

Hoover, H. M. **The Lost Star.** Viking Pr 1979.

> An observer at an archaeological dig on a seemingly "unpeopled" planet, Lian alone is able to communicate with the furry Lumpies, remnants of an advanced civilization whose starship lies buried inside a crater. If Lian reveals his knowledge to the wrong people, the Lumpies and their lost civilization will perish in exploitation and annihilation.

Kesteven, G. R. **The Awakening Water.** Hastings 1979.

> Set in the year 1997, this work of science fiction describes how the "awakening" water leads thirteen-year-old John to discoveries about the way life used to be. He begins to question the "Party" and the restrictions it places on life. The rediscovery of old values results in an affirmation of life.

Konwicki, Tadeusz (translators George Korwin-Rodziszewski and Audrey Korwin-Rodziszewski). **The Anthropos-Specter-Beast.** S G Phillips 1977.

> Peter, a terminally ill patient, vacillates between reality and a fantasy

he presumably created to alleviate his boredom while being hospitalized. The fantasy consists of being befriended by Sebastian, the Inspector Dog, who takes the young man on sojourns into a different world. Peter also meets the mysterious Anthropos-Specter-Beast and the prediction that the world is ending. Older children could discuss the probable, double meaning of the prediction.

L'Engle, Madeleine. **A Swiftly Tilting Planet.** FS&G 1978.

In a companion book to *A Wrinkle in Time* and *A Wind in the Door,* fifteen-year-old Charles Wallace rides a unicorn back through time to the Might Have Beens that, if changed, can save the world from imminent destruction at the hands of a dictator. Rich in allusions to history and myth as well as to theoretical science, this suspenseful fantasy encourages speculation about the relationship of past and future, and the significance of the individual in the affairs of the universe.

McKillip, Patricia. **Harpist in the Wind.** Atheneum 1979.

In this final book of the trilogy, Morgan and Raederle, now reunited, begin their journey to Lungold where the surviving wizards are assembling against the evil Ghisteslwchlohm. As they travel across the war-torn land where the mysterious shape changers battle against humankind, they are followed by Deth, the now crippled harpist, Morgan's friend and betrayer. In a final confrontation with evil at the Wind Plain Tower, Morgan meets and learns from the High One that he is the Starbearer destined to be the land heir of the High One, an awesome inheritance that includes reigning over all of the realm. Raederle learns to accept her powers of shape changing and finds that a power once associated with evil does not mean that one is inherently bad. The book ends with peace established once again in the kingdom.

McKillip, Patricia. **Heir of Sea and Fire.** Atheneum 1977.

In this second novel of the trilogy, Raederle sets out to learn the truth about herself. Her gift of magic seems too small to face the evil which roams the lands she must travel. She returns home, calling upon the Hosts of the Dead to protect herself and Morgan, who she believes is the man crossing the kingdom to join her. The man, however, turns out to be Deth, the Harpist, who has betrayed her. The book ends with the reuniting of Morgan and Raederle who realize that much still lies ahead in their desperate attempt to solve the riddle of the High One's disappearance and its connection with their individual destinies.

McKillip, Patricia. **The Riddle-Master of Hed.** Atheneum 1976.

> Morgan, prince of the farmers of Hed, proves himself a riddle-master when he stakes his life to win a crown from the dead Lord of Aum. But Morgan cannot solve the mystery of the three stars on his forehead. Accompanied by Deth, the High One's harpist, Morgan travels to Erlenstar Mountain, the mysterious home of the High One, to learn of his destiny and the meaning of the stars. Fighting the evil forces and shape changers who threaten him. Morgan reaches the mountain only to find the High One missing and himself betrayed to the evil wizard, Ghisteslwchlohm, by his friend, the harpist Deth. (First book of a trilogy.)

Watson, Jane Werner. **Living Together in Tomorrow's World.**

Ages 14 and Up

Bethancourt, T. Ernesto. **The Mortal Instruments.** Bantam 1979.

> Eddie Rodriguez, a Puerto Rican teenager from Spanish Harlem, becomes the host of a being from Earth's future and develops extrasensory perception, psychokinesthetic and telepathic abilities. When he takes over ODIN—a highly advanced computer that controls national security—the future of the planet is threatened. Eddie has developed a God complex and will use nuclear destruction, if necessary, to achieve his objectives.

Bova, Ben. **City of Darkness.** Scribner 1976.

> Ron Morgan, on holiday in the city, has his identification cards and money stolen. Without identification, Ron is locked in the city when the gates close on Labor Day. Surviving in the city until the following July, Ron learns the hard way that there are year-round residents of the city—gangs who must fight for power, money, and food in order to live. As he leaves the city, having retrieved his identification cards, Ron is determined to battle the injustice done to the minority groups and poor whites trapped in the city.

Brancato, Robin. **Winning.**

Carlisle, Olga. **Island in Time: A Memoir of Childhood.** HR&W 1980.

> This moving novel depicts accounts of the daily life of the Andreyev family during the Occupation. From 1939 to 1945, the family lived on Oléron, an island off the coast of France and part of Hitler's

Atlantic Wall fortifications. Carlisle describes ordinary events as well as the family's work with the Resistance. The novel presents the human aspects of trying to cope during the war and is a testament to individuals' ability to cope under extraordinary circumstances. Finally, as the war is coming to an end, the young daughter is able to look beyond day-to-day coping to the future.

deLarrabeiti, Michael. **The Borribles.** Macmillan 1976.

Eight Borribles—pointed-earred adults in children's bodies—from different parts of London, trained in guerilla warfare, are dispatched to liquidate the Rumble High Command—mole-like creatures. They discover that their mission also has a secret objective and that there is little chance of returning alive from their journey. The story presents a powerful allegory of military society and a destructive desire for power.

LeGuin, Ursula K. **The Beginning Place.** Har-Row 1980.

When Hugh and Irena separately discover the twilight world of Tembreabrezi, they find refuge from concrete and suburbs, frustration and human callousness. Refuge soon becomes nightmare, forcing the two outsiders to forge a human bond that will carry them back to the real world. Tembreabrezi provides a beginning place from which to face the future.

Lightner, A. M. **The Day of the Drones.** Norton 1969.

Amhara's people live in the African area ringed by radioactive wastelands. Their belief that they are the only humans who survived a nuclear disaster caused by the industrial nations of the world is shattered when N'Gobi, Amhara's cousin, finds a bird from the northern countries with the rope of a snare dangling from its leg. The expedition, which travels to England, discovers a white race that has established an apian society that literally worships large bees.

Murphy, E. Jefferson. **Understanding Africa.**

O'Brien, Robert C. **Z for Zachariah.** LFL. Dell 1977.

Sixteen-year-old Ann Burden suspects that she is the only survivor of a nuclear holocaust until John R. Loomis arrives in her valley wearing a safe-suit to protect him from radioactive fallout. Despite his caution, however, Loomis contracts radiation sickness and Ann nurses him back to health. During his illness, Loomis becomes delirious and admits to killing another man in a conflict over the safe-suit. This admission frightens Ann, who later decides to leave Loomis.

When he pursues and attempts to capture her, Ann steals the safe-suit and leaves the valley in an effort to find other survivors. The story demonstrates what desperation may do to human relations when the trappings of civilization are removed.

Obukhova, Lydia (translator Mirra Ginsburg). **Daughter of Night: A Tale of Three Worlds.** Macmillan 1974.

On earth, Lilith and Adam, forbidden to marry, have run away to live together. While searching for honey, Lilith sees a strange man step out of an egg-shaped module that has dropped from the sky. She overcomes her fears and superstitions and befriends the "Nameless One," her description of this being from another planet. This is an interesting retelling of the Sumerian myth of Adam and Lilith, interwoven with a science fiction theme of visitors from outer space during the dawn of earth's history. Past and future merge in this strange tale.

O'Dell, Scott. **Carlota.**

Orwell, George. **Animal Farm.**

Silverberg, Robert, editor. **The Androids Are Coming.** Elsevier-Nelson 1979.

This is an excellent collection of seven science fiction stories about androids—synthetic human beings. Though the plots revolve around androids, the story themes examine the foibles of being human. All the stories are very good, but particularly worth reading are "The Captain's Dog," "Evidence," and "Made in U.S.A."

Townsend, John Rowe. **The Creatures.** Lippincott 1980.

Vector and Harmony are two young people who live in the Colony, an isolated area of the Earth where the residents are protected from the "natives" of the Earth, the Creatures. In this future world, the Creatures are servants to the Persons—those who live and rule the Colony. This is a frightening view of what life can become when human feelings are denied and subjugated to the needs of the state. The story, however, is ultimately optimistic, as a spark of human feeling begins to emerge again.

Walton, Evangeline. **The Children of Llyr: The Second Branch of the Mabinogion.** Del Rey. Ballantine 1978.

In this retelling of the second branch of the Welsh Mabinogion,

Branwen, sister to Bran, King of the Island of the Mighty, is wed to Matholuch of Tara in the first state marriage of the Islands. Beaten and mistreated in Ireland, she requests assistance from her brother. The war that follows destroys Ireland and leaves only seven of Branwen's people alive. The book examines the conflict that arises when the state is considered more important than the individual.

Walton, Evangeline. **The Island of the Mighty: The Fourth Branch of the Mabinogion.** Del Rey. Ballantine 1979.

In this retelling of the fourth branch of the Welsh Mabinogion, Gwydion, heir of Math, King of Gwynedd, uses trickery to bring about the birth of a son by his sister Arianrhod. Angered by the trickery of her brother, Arianrhod lays three curses on her son Llew. Through the use of sorcery, Gwydion overcomes each curse, but in creating a bride from flowers for Llew, he does not foresee the terrible consequences that will result in the death of Llew's wife, his sister Arianrhod, and the loss of Llew. The book examines the consequence of a consuming desire for power which attempts to direct the lives of others.

Walton, Evangeline. **Prince of Annwn: The First Branch of the Mabinogion.** Del Rey. Ballantine 1978.

In this retelling of the first branch of the Welsh Mabinogion, Pwyll, King of Dyved, changes places with Arawn, King of Annwn (the Kingdom of Death). He must overcome fear, despair, and lust in order to defeat Havgen so that he might return to his own kingdom. While there, he meets Rhiannon, who later gives up eternal life to become his wife. A highly praised retelling, the book examines the conflicts which arise when two diverse cultures try to rule the same land.

Walton, Evangeline. **The Song of Rhiannon: The Third Branch of the Mabinogion.** Del Rey. Ballantine 1979.

In this retelling of the third branch of the Welsh Mabinogion, Manawyddan, one of the seven survivors of the war in Ireland, returns to the Island of the Mighty to marry Rhiannon, the widow of Pwyll. The recklessness of their son, Pryderi, releases the power of the Gray Man who enchants their kingdom and steals Rhiannon and Pryderi. Manawyddan challenges the Gray Man and by outwitting him ends the enchantment and arranges the release of his wife and son. The book examines the power inherent in the emotions of love and hate.

Professional References

Bernstein, Joanne E., compiler. *Books to Help Children Deal with Separation and Loss.* New York: Bowker, 1977.

Fassler, Joan. *Helping Children Cope.* New York: Free Press (A Division of Macmillan Company), 1978.

Toffler, Alvin. *Future Shock.* New York: Random House, 1970.

Toffler, Alvin. *The Third Wave.* New York: William Morrow and Co., Inc., 1980.

Directory of Publishers

A-W Addison-Wesley Publishing Co., Inc., Jacob Way, Reading, MA 01867
A Whitman Albert Whitman & Co., 560 W. Lake St., Chicago, IL 60606
Abelard Abelard-Schuman Ltd., c/o Harper & Row Pubs., Keystone Industrial Park, Scranton, PA 18512
Abingdon Abingdon Press, 201 Eighth Ave., S., Nashville, TN 37202
Ace Bks Ace Books, Div. of Charter Communications Inc., c/o Grosset & Dunlap, 51 Madison Ave., New York, NY 10010
Aladdin. Atheneum Aladdin Books. Imprint of Atheneum Pubs., 122 E. 42nd St., New York, NY 10017
Amecus St Amecus Street. Dist. by: Childrens Press, Inc. 1224 W. Van Buren St., Chicago, IL 60607
Anchor Pr. Doubleday Anchor Press. Imprint of Doubleday & Co., Inc., 501 Franklin Ave., Garden City, NY 11530
Apollo Eds Apollo Editions. Dist. by: Harper & Row Pubs., Scranton, PA 18512
Archway Archway Paperbacks, c/o Pocket Books, 1230 Ave. of the Americas, New York, NY 10020
Ata Bks Ata Books, 1920 Stuart St., Berkeley, CA 94703
Atheneum Atheneum Pubs. Dist. by: Book Warehouse, Inc., Vreeland Ave., Boro of Totowa, Paterson, NJ 07512
Avon Avon Books, 959 Eighth Ave., New York, NY 10019
Ballantine Ballantine Books, Inc., Div. of Random House, Inc., 400 Hahn Rd., Westminster, MD 21157
Bantam Bantam Books, Inc., 414 E. Golf Rd., Des Plaines, IL 60016
Beacon Pr Beacon Press, Inc. Dist. by: Harper & Row Pubs., Inc., Keystone Industrial Park, Scranton, PA 18512
Bowmar-Noble Bowmar/Noble Publishers Inc., 4563 Colorado Blvd., Los Angeles, CA 90039
Bradbury Pr Bradbury Press. Dist. by: E. P. Dutton & Co., Inc., 2 Park Ave., New York, NY 10016
Camelot. Avon Imprint of Avon Books, 959 Eighth Ave., New York, NY 10019
Carolrhoda Bks Carolrhoda Books, Inc., 241 First Ave., N., Minneapolis, MN 55401
Celestial Arts Celestial Arts Publishing Co., 231 Adrian Rd., Millbrae, CA 94030
Childrens Children's Press, Inc., Div. of Regensteiner Publishing Enterprises, Inc., 1224 W. Van Buren St., Chicago, IL 60607
Childs World Child's World, Inc. Dist. by: Children's Press, Inc., 1224 W. Van Buren St., Chicago, IL 60607

Chilton Chilton Book Co., School Library Services, 201 King of Prussia Rd., Radnor, PA 19089

Clarion. HM Imprint of Houghton Mifflin Co., Wayside Road, Burlington, MA 01803

Clarion Bk. Seabury Clarion Book. Imprint of Seabury Press, Inc., Seabury Service Center, Somers, CT 06071

Collins Pubs. William Collins Pubs., Inc., 2080 W. 117th St., Cleveland, OH 44111; 200 Madison Ave., Suite 1405, New York, NY 10016

Coward Coward, McCann & Geoghegan, Inc., 1050 W. Wall St., Lyndhurst, NJ 07071

Crest. Fawcett Crest Books. Imprint of Fawcett Book Group, 1515 Broadway, New York, NY 10036

Crown Crown Pubs., Inc., 1 Park Ave., New York, NY 10016

D White David White Co., 14 Vanderventer Ave., Port Washington, NY 11050

Dell Dell Publishing Co., Inc., 1 Dag Hammarskjold Plaza, 245 E. 47th St., New York, NY 10017

Delacorte Delacorte Press, c/o Dell Publishing Co., 1 Dag Hammarskjold Plaza, 245 E. 47th St., New York, NY 10017

Del Rey. Ballentine Imprint of Ballentine Books, Inc., Div. of Random House, Inc., 400 Hahn Rd., Westminster, MD 21157

Delta. Dell Delta Books. Imprint of Dell Publishing Co., Inc., 1 Dag Hammarskjold Plaza, 245 E. 47th St., New York, NY 10017

Dial Dial Press, 1 Dag Hammarskjold Plaza, 245 E. 47th St., New York, NY 10017

Dillon Dillon Press, Inc., 500 S. Third St., Minneapolis, MN 55415

Dodd Dodd, Mead & Co., 79 Madison Ave., New York, NY 10016

Doubleday Doubleday & Co., Inc., 501 Franklin Ave., Garden City, NY 11530

Dutton E. P. Dutton, 2 Park Ave., New York, NY 10016

Elsevier-Nelson Elsevier/Nelson Books, 30 E. 42 St., New York, NY 10017

EMC EMC Corp., 180 E. Sixth St., St. Paul, MN 55101

FS&G Farrar, Straus & Giroux, Inc., 19 Union Square, W., New York, NY 10003

Fawcett Fawcett Book Group, 1515 Broadway, New York, Ny 10036

Feminist Pr Feminist Press, SUNY/College at Old Westbury, Box 334, Old Westbury, NY 11568

Follett Follett Publishing Co., Div. of Follett Corp., 1010 W. Washington Blvd., Chicago, IL 60607

Four Winds. Schol Bk Serv Four Winds Press. Imprint of Scholastic Book Services, 906 Sylvan Ave., Englewood Cliffs, NJ 07632

Friend Pr Friendship Press, P.O. Box 37884, Cincinnati, OH 45237

Friends Earth Friends of the Earth, Inc., 124 Spear, San Francisco, CA 94105

G&D Grosset & Dunlap, Inc., 51 Madison Ave., New York, NY 10010

GM. Fawcett Gold Medal Books. Imprint of Fawcett Book Group, 1515 Broadway, New York, NY 10036

Garrard Garrard Publishing Co., 1607 N. Market St., Champaign, IL 61820

Directory of Publishers

Ginn Ginn & Company, Box 2649, 1250 Fairwood Ave., Columbus, OH 43216

Golden Gate. Childrens Golden Gate. Imprint of Childrens Press, Inc., 1224 W. Van Buren St., Chicago, IL 60607

Greenwillow Greenwillow Books, Div. of William Morrow & Co., Inc., Wilmor Warehouse, 6 Henderson Dr., West Caldwell, NJ 07006

Grossman Grossman Publishers, 625 Madison Ave., New York, NY 10022

HM Houghton Mifflin Co., Wayside Road, Burlington, MA 01803

HR&W Holt, Rinehart & Winston, Inc., 383 Madison Ave., New York, NY 10017

Hamlyn-Amer Hamlyn/American. Dist. by: A & W Pubs., 95 Madison Ave., New York, NY 10016

HarBraceJ Harcourt Brace Jovanovich, Inc., 757 Third Ave., New York, NY 10017

Har-Row Harper & Row Pubs., Inc., Keystone Industrial Park, Scranton, PA 18512

Harvey Harvey House, Pubs., 128 W. River St., Chippewa Falls, WI 54729

Hastings Hastings House Pubs., Inc., 10 E. 40th St., New York, NY 10016

Hawthorn Hawthorn Books, Inc., 260 Madison Ave., New York, NY 10016

Herald Pr Herald Press, 616 Walnut Ave., Scottdale, PA 15683

Hill & Wang Hill & Wang, Inc., Div. of Farrar, Straus & Giroux, Inc., 19 Union Square, New York, NY 10003

Holiday Holiday House, Inc., 18 E. 53rd St., New York, NY 10022

Human Sci Pr Human Sciences Press, Inc. Dist. by: Independent Publishers Group, 14 Vanderventer Ave., Port Washington, NY 11050

Island Her Island Heritage Ltd., 828 Fort St. Mall, Suite 400, Honolulu, HI 96813

Jewish Pubn Jewish Publication Society of America, 117 S. 17th St., Philadelphia, PA 19103

John Day John Day Co., Inc. Dist. by: Harper & Row, Keystone Industrial Park, Scranton, PA 18512

Knopf Alfred A. Knopf, Inc. Subs. of Random House, Inc., 400 Hahn Rd., Westminster, MD 21157

LFL. Dell Laurel Leaf Library. Imprint of Dell Publishing Co., Inc., 1 Dag Hammarskjold Plaza, 245 E. 47th St., New York, NY 10017

Lerner Pubns Lerner Publications Co., 241 First Ave., N., Minneapolis, MN 55401

Lippincott J. B. Lippincott, Co., c/o Harper & Row Publishers, Inc., Keystone Industrial Park, Scranton, PA 18512

Little Little, Brown & Co., 200 West St., Waltham, MA 02154

Lothrop Lothrop, Lee & Shepard Co., Div. of William Morrow & Co., Inc., Wilmor Warehouse, 6 Henderson Dr., West Caldwell, NJ 07006

M Evans Michael Evans & Co., Inc. Dist. by: E. P. Dutton, 2 Park Ave., New York, NY 10016

Macmillan Macmillan Publishing Co., Inc., Front & Brown Sts., Riverside, NJ 08075

McCormick-Mathers　McCormick-Mathers Publishing Co., Div. of Litton Educational Publishing, 7625 Empire Dr., Florence, KY 41042

McElderry Bk. Atheneum　McElderry Book. Imprint of Atheneum Pubs., Book Warehouse, Inc., Vreeland Ave., Boro of Totowa, Paterson, NJ 07512

McGraw　McGraw-Hill Book Co., 1221 Ave. of the Americas, New York, NY 10020

McKay　David McKay, Co., Inc., 2 Park Ave., New York, NY 10016

Messner　Messner, Julian, A Simon & Schuster, Div. of Gulf & Western Corp., 1230 Ave. of the Americas, New York, NY 10020

Morrow　William Morrow & Co., Inc., Wilmor Warehouse, 6 Henderson Dr., West Caldwell, NJ 07006

Natl Geog　National Geographic Society, 17th & "M" Sts., N.W., Washington, DC 20036

Nelson　Thomas Nelson, Inc., 407 Seventh Ave., S., Nashville, TN 37203

New Directions　New Directions Publishing Corp. Dist. by: W. W. Norton Co., 500 Fifth Ave., New York, NY 10036

Norton　W. W. Norton & Co., Inc., 500 Fifth Ave., New York, NY 10036

Octopus Bks　Octopus Books Ltd., 59 Grosvenor St., London W1

Okpaku Communications　Okpaku Communications, 444 Central Park, W., New York, NY 10025

Oxford U Pr　Oxford Univ. Press, Inc., 16-00 Pollitt Dr., Fair Lawn, NJ 07410

Pantheon　Pantheon Books, Div. of Random House, Inc., 400 Hahn Rd., Westminster, MD 21157

Parents　Parents Magazine Press. Dist. by: E. P. Dutton, 2 Park Ave., New York, NY 10016

Penguin　Penguin Books, Inc., 625 Madison Ave., New York, NY 10022

PB　Pocket Books, Inc., Div. of Simon & Schuster, Inc., 1230 Ave. of the Americas, New York, NY 10020

P-H　Prentice-Hall, Inc., Englewood Cliffs, NJ 06732

Popular Lib　Popular Library, Inc., Unit of CBS Pubns., 1515 Broadway, New York, NY 10036

Puffin　Puffin Books. Imprint of Penguin Books, Inc., 299 Murray Hill Pkwy., E. Rutherford, NJ 07073

Putnam　Putnam's, G. P., Sons, 390 Murray Hill Pkwy., East Rutherford, NJ 07073

Raintree Pubs Ltd　Raintree Pubs., Ltd. Dist. by: Childrens Press, Inc., 1224 W. Van Buren St., Chicago, IL 60607

Random　Random House, Inc., 400 Hahn Rd., Westminster, MD 21157

Rawson Wade　Rawson, Wade Pubs., Inc. Dist. by: Atheneum Pubs., 122 E. 42nd St., New York, NY 10017

S & S　Simon & Schuster, Inc., 1230 Ave. of the Americas, New York, NY 10020

S G Phillips　S.G. Phillips, Inc., 305 W. 86th St., New York, NY 10024

Schol Bk Serv　Scholastic Book Services, Div. of Scholastic Magazines, 906 Sylvan Ave., Englewood Cliffs, NJ 07632

Scribner　Charles Scribner's Sons, Shipping & Service Ctr., Vreeland Ave., Totowa, NJ 07512

Directory of Publishers 371

Seabury   The Seabury Press, Inc., Seabury Service Ctr., Somers, CT 06071

Serendipity Pr   Serendipity Press, Div. of Price/Stern, Sloan, 410 N. LaCienega Blvd., Los Angeles, CA 90048

Sey Lawr. Delacorte   Seymour Lawrence. Imprint of Delacorte Press. c/o Dell Publishing Co., 1 Dag Hammarskjold Plaza, 245 E. 47th St., New York, NY 10017

Sig Classics. NAL   Signet Classics. Imprint of New American Library, 1301 Ave. of the Americas, New York, NY 10019

Sig. NAL   Signet Books. Imprint of New American Library, 1301 Ave. of the Americas, New York, NY 10019

S Ill U Pr   Southern Illinois Univ. Press, P.O. Box 3697, Carbondale, IL 62901

Silver   Silver Burdett Co., Div. of General Learning Co., 250 James St., Morristown, NJ 07960

Skylark. Bantam   Imprint of Bantam Books, Inc., 414 E. Golf Rd., Des Plaines, IL 60016

Steck   Steck-Vaughn Company, Box 2028, Austin, TX 78768

Stemmer Hse   Stemmer House Pubs., Inc., 2627 Caves Rd., Owings Mills, MD 21117

St. Martin   St. Martin's Press, Inc., 175 Fifth Ave., New York, NY 10010

T Y Crowell   Thomas Y. Crowell Co. Dist. by: Harper & Row Pubs., Keystone Industrial Park, Scranton, PA 18512

Tempo. G&D   Tempo Books. Imprint of Grosset & Dunlap, Inc., 51 Madison Ave., New York, NY 10010

Trophy. Har-Row   Trophy. Imprint of Harper & Row Pubs., Inc., Keystone Industrial Park, Scranton, PA 18512

U of Cal Pr   Univ. of Califonia Press, 2223 Fulton St., Berkeley, CA 94720

U of NM Pr   Univ. of New Mexico Press, Albuquerque, NM 87131

U of Okla Pr   Univ. of Oklahoma Press, 1005 Asp Ave., Norman, OK 73019

Vanguard   Vanguard Press, Inc., 424 Madison Ave., New York, NY 10017

Victor Gollancz   Victor Gollancz Ltd., 14 Henrietta St., Covent Garden, London WC2E 8QJ

Viking Pr   Viking Press, Inc., c/o Vikeship Co., 299 Murray Hill Pkwy., E. Rutherford, NJ 07073

Vin. Random   Vintage Trade Books. Imprint of Random House, Inc., 400 Hahn Rd., Westminster, MD 21157

VoyB. HarBraceJ   Voyager Books. Imprint of Harcourt Brace Jovanovich, Inc., 757 Third Ave., New York, NY 10017

WSP   Washington Square Press, Inc., Div. of Simon & Schuster, Inc., 1230 Ave. of the Americas, New York, NY 10020

Walck   Henry Z. Walck, Inc., Div. of David McKay Co., Inc., 21-09 Borden Ave., Long Island City, NY 11101

Walker & Co   Walker & Co., Inc., 720 Fifth Ave., New York, NY 10019

Warne   Warne, Frederick, & Co., Inc., 2 Park Ave., New York, NY 10016

Warner PB Lib   Imprint of Warner Books Inc. Dist. by: Independent News Co., 75 Rockefeller Plaza, New York, NY 10019

Washburn Washburn, Ives, Inc., Subs. of David McKay Co., Inc., 750 Third Ave., New York, NY 10017

Watts Watts, Franklin, Inc., Subs. of Grolier Inc., 730 Fifth Ave., New York, NY 10019

Westminster Westminster Press, P.O. Box 718, Wm. Penn Annex, Philadelphia, PA 19105

Windmill. Dutton Imprint of E. P. Dutton, 2 Park Ave., New York, NY 10016

Winston Pr Winston Press, Inc., 430 Oak Grove, Suite 203, Minneapolis, MN 55403

Xerox Ed Pubns Xerox Education Publications, A Xerox Publishing Co., 245 Long Hill Rd., Middletown, CT 06457

YB. Dell Yearling Books. Imprint of Dell Publishing Co., Inc., 1 Dag Hammarskjold Plaza, 245 E. 47th St., New York, NY 10017

Young Scott Young Scott, c/o Addison-Wesley, 5851 Fuion Rd., Indianapolis, IN 45462

Zephyr. Doubleday Zephyr. Imprint of Doubleday & Co., Inc., 501 Franklin Ave., Garden City, NY 11530

Author Index

Aardema, Verna, 279, 286
Aaron, Chester, 87, 138, 170
Abbott, Sarah, 320
Adkins, Jan, 65
Adoff, Arnold, 19, 55, 151, 227, 235, 244, 267
Agee, James, 177
Albert, Louise, 99
Alcock, Gudrun, 138
Alexander, Lloyd, 65
Alexander, Martha, 320
Aliki, 51, 286, 329
Allard, Harry, 35, 60
Allen, Alex B., 25, 205
Allen, Merritt P., 335
Allen, T. D., 244
Allen, Terry, 244
Ambrus, Victor, 19
Ames, Mildred, 170, 192, 358
Amoss, Berthe, 203
Anastas, Peter, 236
Ancona, George, 85, 135
Anders, Rebecca, 82
Anderson, Madelyn Klein, 270
Anderson, Robin, 279
Anderson, Susanne, 236
Angell, Judie, 170, 209
Angelou, Maya, 244
Angier, Bradford, 128, 142
Anglund, Joan Walsh, 184
Anno, Mitsumasa, 60, 320
Ardizzone, Edward, 134
Arkin, Alan, 70
Armer, Alberta, 95
Armstrong, William H., 19, 161, 184
Arnold, Elliott, 342
Arnothy, Christine, 346
Arnstein, Helene S., 33, 149
Aronin, Ben, 256
Arrick, Fran, 48, 128, 326
Arthur, Catherine, 92
Aruego, Jose, 280
Asch, Frank, 40, 59, 149
Astrov, Margot, 57
Avi, 330

Babbitt, Natalie, 65, 87, 322
Bach, Alice, 20, 60, 82, 90, 128, 152
Baker, Betty, 217, 228, 330
Baker, Louise M., 105
Baker, Will, 199
Baldwin, Anne Norris, 99
Bales, Carol Ann, 87, 236
Balfour, Michael, 304
Bang, Betsy, 286
Bang, Garrett, 286
Barker, Carol, 256
Barkin, Carol, 214
Barnes, Nancy, 118
Baron, Virginia Olsen, 230, 295
Barrett, Judi, 33, 149
Barrett, William E., 218, 261
Barringer, D. Moreau, 330
Barth, Edna, 256
Bartoli, Jennifer, 60, 280, 320
Baskin, John, 333
Bates, Betty, 161
Bawden, Nina, 96, 192, 342
Baylor, Byrd, 20, 60, 65, 265, 280, 329
Beatty, Patricia, 342
Beckwith, Lillian, 100
Beim, Lorraine, 105
Bemelmans, Ludwig, 203
Benchley, Nathaniel, 228, 236, 353
Berger, Terry, 83, 149, 152, 184, 192, 205, 338
Bernstein, Margery, 228
Bethancourt, T. Ernesto, 362
Beyer, Audrey White, 70
Bible, Charles, 149, 286
Bierhorst, John, 230, 236, 245
Biesterveld, Betty, 205
Billout, Guy, 351
Blaine, Marge, 342
Blair, Ruth Van Ness, 330
Bleeker, Sonia, 325
Blegvad, Erik, 296
Blegvad, Lenore, 35, 60
Blos, Joan W., 170, 270, 325
Blue, Rose, 85, 228
Blume, Judy, 25, 44, 70, 100, 121, 139, 162, 170, 192, 205, 209, 256, 343

Bollinger, Max, 51
Bomans, Godfried, 286
Bond, Gladys Baker, 20, 152
Bond, Nancy, 57, 177, 304
Bonham, Frank, 209, 237
Bonsall, Crosby, 60
Bontemps, Arna, 333
Borack, Barbara, 149
Bornstein, Ruth, 65, 322
Bosse, Malcolm J., 70, 87, 196
Bottner, Barbara, 20
Bouchard, Lois, 92
Bourne, Miriam Anne, 162, 338
Bova, Ben, 362
Bradbury, Bianca, 25, 178, 192, 326, 353
Brancato, Robin, 105, 219, 261, 346, 362
Brandon, William, 245
Branscum, Robbie, 30, 121, 139, 209, 259
Brenner, Barbara, 51, 228
Bridgers, Sue Ellen, 70, 100, 121, 139, 170, 196
Brightman, Alan, 117
Brink, Carol Ryrie, 118, 135
Brittain, Bill, 70
Britton, Anna, 219
Brodsky, Beverly, 51, 329
Bronin, Andrew, 152
Brooke, Joshua, 105
Brooks, Charlotte K., 237
Brooks, Gwendolyn, 245
Brooks, Jerome, 100
Brooks, Ron, 152
Brower, David R., 236
Brown, Claude, 128
Brown, Dee, 237, 245, 246
Brown, Margaret Wise, 152
Bryan, Ashley, 261
Bryant, Dorothy, 90
Buchan, Stuart, 40
Buchanan, William, 106, 327
Buck, Pearl S., 85, 128, 323, 327
Buckley, Helen E., 149, 150
Bulla, Clyde Robert, 21, 40, 119, 152, 162, 192, 231, 287, 329
Bunting, Eve, 21, 55, 66, 153, 162, 209, 237, 280, 320
Burch, Robert, 83, 121, 162, 196, 209, 271
Burchard, Peter, 231, 338
Burleson, Elizabeth, 119
Burnford, Sheila, 196, 296
Burningham, John, 150, 203, 214
Burt, Jesse, 246
Burton, Jimalee, 237
Burton, Virginia Lee, 351
Butterworth, W. E., 73, 178, 199, 211, 327

Byars, Betsy, 25, 26, 40, 60, 85, 96, 121, 136, 162, 192, 205, 217

Caines, Jeannette Franklin, 150
Calhoun, Mary, 41, 184, 192
Callen, Larry, 197
Cameron, Eleanor, 48, 122, 139
Campanella, Roy, 106
Campbell, R. Wright, 178
Capote, Truman, 178
Carew, Jan, 70
Carle, Eric, 184
Carlisle, Olga, 362
Carlson, Dale, 142
Carlson, Natalie Savage, 35, 162, 163, 215
Carothers, J. Edward, 356
Carpelan, Bo, 100
Carrick, Carol, 33
Carson, Mary, 106
Carson, Rachel, 356
Carter, Forrest, 246
Cartman, Shirley, 211
Cather, Willa, 219
Caudill, Rebecca, 153, 265
Cauley, Lorinda Bryan, 92
Causley, Charles, 296
Chaikin, Miriam, 66, 215, 231, 330
Charlip, Remy, 61, 153
Child Study Children's Book Committee at Bank Street, 185
Childress, Alice, 274
Chin, Richard, 308
Christian, Mary Blount, 214
Christopher, John, 359
Christopher, Matt, 26, 66, 96, 206
Church, Peggy Pond, 274
Clapp, Patricia, 122
Clark, Ann Nolan, 55, 170, 271, 287, 296, 331, 343
Cleary, Beverly, 26, 66, 163, 206
Cleaver, Bill, 87, 122, 139, 164, 170, 271, 323
Cleaver, Vera, 87, 122, 139, 164, 170, 271, 323
Clewes, Dorothy, 106
Clifford, Eth, 238
Clifton, Lucille, 33, 44, 53, 55, 153, 164, 170, 185, 203, 228, 229, 231, 238
Clymer, Eleanor, 41, 66, 85, 136, 164, 193
Coatsworth, Elizabeth, 136
Cobb, Vicki, 256
Coerr, Eleanor, 287, 339
Cohen, Miriam, 185
Collier, Christopher, 333, **343**
Collier, James Lincoln, 178, 333, 334

Author Index

Colman, Hila, 41, 45, 179, 206
Conaway, Judith, 26, 61, 204
Cone, Molly, 257
Conford, Ellen, 114, 170, 206
Conroy, Pat, 275
Constant, Alberta Wilson, 71, 122, 209, 271
Conta, Marcia Maher, 165, 193, 215
Cook, Marjorie, 100
Cooper, Gordon, 45, 170, 296
Cooper, Susan, 287
Copeland, James, 106
Corcoran, Barbara, 101, 128, 142, 171
Corey, Dorothy, 33, 150, 227
Cormier, Robert, 73, 122, 179, 218, 346
Cosgrove, Stephen, 61
Cosner, Shaaron, 297
Courlander, Harold, 246
Coville, Bruce, 153
Cox, John, 356
Crane, Caroline, 139, 171
Craven Margaret, 73, 246, 327
Crawford, Charles P., 73, 212
Cresswell, Helen, 114
Cretan, Gladys Yessayan, 26, 112
Crichton, Michael, 107
Croll, Carolyn, 185
Crompton, Anne Eliot, 128
Cummings, Betty Sue, 90, 107, 356
Cunningham, Julia, 30, 197
Cunningham, Maggi, 231
Cuyler, Margery, 257

D'Ambrosio, Richard, 107
D'Aulaire, Edgar Parin, 287
D'Aulaire, Ingri, 287
Danziger, Paula, 45, 114, 171
Dauer, Rosamond, 34, 185
David, Janina, 343
Davis, Christopher, 246
Davis, Douglas F., 297
Dawson, Raymond, 304
de Hartog, Jan, 261
De Jong, Meindert, 297
de Larrabeiti, Michael, 363
Delton, Judy, 21, 34, 35, 150, 154, 186, 193, 338
Demi, 278
Demuth, Jack, 271
Demuth, Patricia, 271
Denker, Henry, 90
de Paola, Tomie, 27, 61, 117, 154, 229, 255, 257, 278
Dewey, Ariane, 280
Dickinson, Peter, 73, 262

Dimont, Max I., 262
Dionetti, Michelle, 27, 165, 231
Distad, Audree, 30, 197, 272
Donovan, John, 30, 48, 122
Dooley, Thomas A., 107
Doss, Helen, 171
Downs, James F., 247
Dumas, Philippe, 21
Duncan, Lois, 112, 154
Dunlop, Eileen, 171
Dunn, Mary Lois, 343
Duvoisin, Roger, 61, 204, 351

Edmonds, Walter D., 71, 272
Eisenberg, Phyllis Rose, 51, 154, 255
Eldridge, Roger, 360
Elfman, Blossom, 179, 327
Elliott, David, 107
Ellis, Harry B., 305
Ellis, Mel, 57, 247, 335
Emberly, Ed, 184
Engebrecht, P. A., 122, 140, 172
Engel, Beth Bland, 197
Epstein, Beryl, 288, 297
Epstein, Sam, 288, 297
Erdoes, Richard, 247
Erickson, Russell E., 215
Estes, Eleanor, 136, 165, 206
Estes, Winston M., 275, 335
Ets, Marie Hall, 18, 280
Evans, Mari, 35
Evansen, Virginia B., 267
Ewing, Kathryn, 193
Eyerly, Jeannette, 325

Faber, Doris, 356
Falk, Randolph, 247
Fanshawe, Elizabeth, 92
Farley, Carol, 172, 325
Fassler, Joan, 21, 93
Feelings, Muriel, 281
Fellows, Lawrence, 259
Ferguson, Robert B., 246
Ferry, Charles, 179
Fichter, George S., 238
Fife, Dale, 297, 343
Finlayson, Ann, 343
Fire, John, 247
First, Julia, 96, 119
Fisher, Aileen, 154, 186, 319, 320, 321
Fisher, Leonard Everett, 55, 298, 344
Fisher, Ronald M., 66
Fitzhugh, Louise, 34, 45, 123, 172, 207
Flack, Marjorie, 150
Fleischer, Leonore, 101

Fleischman, Paul, 52, 96
Fleming, Susan, 353
Flournoy, Valerie, 150
Fogel, Julianna A., 27
Forbes, Esther, 101, 334
Forbes, Kathryn, 179
Foreman, Michael, 216, 281, 339, 351
Foster, Genevieve, 331
Fox, Paula, 154, 165, 216, 238, 334
Fox, Siv Cedering, 321
Fox, Thomas C., 299, 345
Frank, Anne, 45
Frank, Phil, 267
Frank, Susan, 267
Freeman, Don, 186
Fregosi, Claudia, 186, 281
Fremlin, Robert, 204
Freschet, Berniece, 21
Friis-Baastad, Babbis, 27, 96, 101
Fritz, Jean, 288, 331
Fukada, Hanako, 119
Fuller, Miriam Morris, 112

Gackenbach, Dick, 61, 154, 321
Gaines, Ernest J., 247
Garfield, James B., 97
Garfield, Leon, 102, 140
Garrigue, Sheila, 71, 102, 197
Garrison, Christian, 281
Gates, Doris, 165, 267
Gauch, Patricia Lee, 209, 331, 339
Gemme, Leila Boyle, 119
Gemming, Elizabeth, 298
George, Jean Craighead, 55, 73, 172, 238, 272
Gerson, Corinne, 172, 212
Gessner, Lynne, 30, 238
Getz, Arthur, 265
Gibbons, Gail, 266
Gilbert, Harriett, 71, 197, 360
Gill, Derek, 110
Gill, Joan, 155
Ginsburg, Mirra, 281, 282, 288
Giovanni, Nikki, 227
Girion, Barbara, 27, 86, 179, 207
Gittings, Robert, 300
Glaser, Dianne, 129
Glasgow, Aline, 136
Glass, Frankcina, 199
Glubok, Shirley, 53, 288, 298
Goble, Dorothy, 232
Goble, Paul, 54, 232
Godden, Rumer, 66, 142, 323
Goffstein, M. B., 186
Golding, William, 210

Goldman, Susan, 155
Goldston, Robert, 57, 262, 305
Goodall, John S., 288, 331, 354
Goodman, Robert B., 67
Gordon, Barbara, 74
Gordon, Shirley, 165, 186, 187
Gordy, Berry, Sr., 140, 238
Graber, Richard, 172
Graham, Gail, 344
Graham, Lorenz, 247, 275, 278
Gray, Genevieve, 229
Gray, Nigel, 62
Greaves, Margaret, 67
Green, Gerald, 262
Green, Hannah, 31
Green, Norma, 278
Green, Phyllis, 27, 102, 207
Greenberg, Joanne, 107, 108
Greene, Bette, 48, 67, 74, 200, 247, 275, 346
Greene, Constance C., 67, 86, 119, 172, 193, 197, 326, 344
Greene, Laura, 52, 155, 255
Greenfeld, Howard, 257
Greenfield, Eloise, 34, 52, 150, 155, 157, 166, 173, 229, 321
Gregor, Arthur S., 305, 327
Griese, Arnold A., 216, 232, 267, 288, 339
Griffin, John Howard, 248
Griffin, Judith Berry, 54, 232
Grimes, Niki, 232
Grimm, Jakob, 298
Grimm, Wilhelm, 298
Gripe, Maria, 112
Grisé, Jeannette, 41, 207
Guest, Judith, 180
Gunther, John, 327
Gustafson, Anita, 232
Guy, Rosa, 74, 129, 180, 200, 219, 248

Hale, Janet Campbell, 248
Haley, Alex, 57, 248
Haley, Gail E., 338
Hall, Adelaide, 187
Hall, Donald, 329
Hall, Lynn, 88, 123, 129, 140
Hallinan, P. K., 18, 22, 155, 187, 204, 319
Hallstead, William F., 347
Halsell, Grace, 248
Hamilton, Dorothy, 136
Hamilton, Virginia, 54, 55, 56, 114, 173, 218, 238, 239, 273
Hamley, Dennis, 71, 259, 334
Hanlon, Emily, 108, 200, 210

Author Index

Hannam, Charles, 299, 344
Hannum, Alberta, 249
Hansberry, Lorraine, 130
Hansen, Joyce, 193
Harding, Lee, 344, 360
Harper, Anita, 134
Harris, Janet, 57, 336
Harris, Marilyn, 249
Harris, Peter, 288
Harris, Rosemary, 288
Harrison, Deloris, 166
Haskins, James, 219, 239, 249, 272, 356
Hassrick, Royal B., 239
Haugaard, Erik Christian, 331, 339
Haviland, Virginia, 275
Hayes, Kent, 180
Hayes, Sheila, 140, 198
Haynes, Betsy, 30, 239, 344
Hays, Wilma Pitchford, 41, 166, 233, 339
Hazen, Barbara Shook, 34, 59, 134, 155
Hegwood, Mamie, 321
Heide, Florence Parry, 71, 88, 108, 115, 130
Henderson, Nancy, 239
Hentoff, Nat, 30, 210
Herbert, Wally, 272
Herman, Charlotte, 86, 166
Hermes, Patricia, 97
Herriot, James, 305
Hesse, Hermann, 74, 130, 219, 263
Heyward, Du Bose, 117
Hickman, Janet, 56, 67, 259, 263, 347
Hickman, Martha Whitmore, 187, 358
Hickok, Lorena A., 97
Hicks, Clifford B., 27
Highwater, Jamake, 240, 305
Hill, Elizabeth S., 134, 155
Hill, Grace L., 108
Hill, Margaret, 130
Hilton, Suzanne, 56, 334
Hinton, S. E., 45, 180, 272
Hirsch, Karen, 97, 166
Hirsh, Marilyn, 229
Hoban, Lillian, 35, 117, 155
Hoban, Russell, 93, 156, 321, 352
Hodges, Margaret, 216, 233
Hoff, Syd, 22, 204, 207
Holding, James Jr., 22
Holland, Barbara, 123
Holland, Isabelle, 180, 200
Holland, Marion, 166
Holling, Holling Clancy, 273
Holman, Felice, 140, 218, 240
Holme, Bryan, 289
Holmes, Efner Tudor, 36
Holt, Deloris L., 187

Hoover, H. M., 360
Hopkins, Lee Bennett, 22, 36, 46, 52, 68, 123, 137, 166, 210, 257, 323
Horvath, Betty, 36
Hou-tien, Cheng, 282, 289
Houston, James D., 86, 227, 240, 249, 347
Houston, Jeanne Wakatsuki, 249, 347
Howard, Moses L., 282
Hugo, Victor, 108
Hunt, Irene, 27, 71, 97, 173, 198, 240, 334, 344
Hunter, Mollie, 46, 114, 173, 334
Huntington, Lee Pennock, 299
Hurd, Edith Thacher, 352
Hurmence, Belinda, 173
Hurwood, Bernhardt J., 48, 219, 347
Hutchins, Pat, 36

Ifkovic, Edward, 240
Irwin, Constance, 334
Irwin, Hadley, 42, 86
Isadora, Rachel, 62, 117
Iverson, Genie, 34

Jackson, Jacqueline, 323
Jackson, Louise A., 52, 268, 329
Jacobs, William Jay, 119
James, Elizabeth, 214
Jenkins, Peter, 49, 275
Jeness, Aylette, 299, 354, 355
Jeschke, Susan, 83, 156
Joffo, Joseph, 49, 347
Johnson, Annabel, 120, 166
Johnson, D. William, 62
Johnson, Edgar, 120, 166
Johnston, Johanna, 54, 151
Johnston, Norma, 181, 200
Jones, Adrienne, 42, 74
Jones, Douglas C., 336
Jones, Hettie, 240
Jones, Ron, 102
Jones, Toeckey, 305
Jones, Weyman, 241
Jordan, June, 54, 156, 249, 339
Joseph, Stephen M., 31
Junne, I. K., 289

Kamien, Janet, 97
Kaplan, Bess, 56, 173, 344
Karen, Ruth, 306
Karp, Naomi J., 137
Kay, Helen, 36
Keats, Ezra Jack, 93, 188, 321
Keele, Luqman Lateef, 299

Keeping, Charles, 37
Keith, Harold, 46, 273
Keller, Beverly, 112
Kellogg, Steven, 37, 157
Kendall, Carol, 216, 289
Kennedy, Richard, 207
Kent, Deborah, 212
Kent, Jack, 22
Kerr, Judith, 157
Kerr, M. E., 130, 142, 143, 181
Kesteven, G. R., 360
Keyes, Daniel, 108, 115
Kherdian, David, 260, 344
Kidd, Ronald, 198
Killilea, Marie L., 108
King, Clive, 71
King, Cynthia, 28
Kingman, Lee, 174
Kirkpatrick, Doris, 46, 355
Kjelgaard, Jim, 46, 71, 326
Kleeberg, Irene Cumming, 257
Klein, Norma, 118, 167, 174
Knowles, John, 74, 212
Knox-Wagner, Elaine, 34, 150
Knudson, R. R., 123
Kobrin, Janet, 228
Koehn, Ilse, 306
Konigsburg, E. L., 42, 113, 114, 194, 207
Konwicki, Tadeusz, 360
Kornfeld, Anita Clay, 72, 273
Kosinski, Jerzy, 347
Krahn, Fernando, 37
Krasilovsky, Phyllis, 23
Kraus, Robert, 23. 93, 157
Krents, Harold, 109
Kroeber, Lisa W., 299
Kroeber, Theodora, 250
Kroll, Steven, 37
Krumgold, Joseph, 113, 120, 194
Kurelek, William, 42, 289
Kuskin, Karla, 23, 37, 358

L'Engle, Madeleine, 68, 113, 167, 218, 258, 361
Labastida, Aurora, 280
Lader, Lawrence, 131
Lampman, Evelyn Sibley, 120, 233, 241
Landau, Elaine, 123, 335
Lang, Othmar Franz, 347
Langton, Jane, 42, 323
Lapsley, Susan, 151
Larrick, Nancy, 54
Larsen, Hanne, 93
Lasker, David, 290
Lasker, Joe, 93, 157
Lasky, Kathryn, 83, 118, 157

Latham, Jean Lee, 352
Lattimore, Eleanor Frances, 167, 229
Lavitt, Edward, 242
Lawrence, Louise, 348
Lawrence, Marjorie, 109
Lawrence, R. D., 275, 328
Lawson, Don, 345
Laye, Camara, 306
Lazzarino, Alex, 180
LaFarge, Phyllis, 83
LeGuin, Ursula K., 42, 201, 357, 363
Lee, H. Alton, 46
Lee, Harper, 181
Lee, Josephine, 140
Lee, Mildred, 102, 200, 210, 213, 275
Leech, Jay, 157, 230, 233
Lehmann, Linda, 56, 345
Leigh, Bill, 345
Lenski, Lois, 268
LeRoy, Gen, 49, 131, 219
LeShan, Eda, 46, 174
Lester, Julius, 241
Levin, Meyer, 57, 263
Levitin, Sonia, 28, 98, 115, 140, 258, 340
Levoy, Myron, 102, 260
Levy, Elizabeth, 28
Lewis, Claudia, 268
Lewis, Richard, 241, 290
Lewiton, Mina, 54
Lexau, Joan M., 43, 134, 157
Li, Yao-wen, 289
Lifton, Betty Jean, 299, 340, 345, 354
Lightner, A. M., 363
Lindbergh, Anne Morrow, 75
Lingard, Joan, 260
Lionni, Leo, 62
Lipsyte, Robert, 31
Lisowski, Gabriel, 134, 258
Litchfield, Ada B., 94
Little, Jean, 28, 98, 137, 167, 194, 323
Little, Lessie Jones, 34, 157
Lloyd, Errol, 157, 282
Lobel, Arnold, 189
Löfgren, Ulf, 282
Lofts, Norah, 124
Long, Judy, 102
Lowry, Lois, 164, 174, 181, 323, 326
Ludwig, Charles, 306
Lundgren, Max, 83, 157
Lurie, Alison, 120, 290
Lyle, Katie Letcher, 131

Macaulay, David, 299
Mack, Nancy, 94, 204, 207
MacKellar, William, 260
MacLachlan, Patricia, 35, 82, 151
Madison, Arnold, 49, 348

Author Index

Madison, Winifred, 31, 116
Mahy, Margaret, 86
Maitland, Antony, 283
Malamud, Bernard, 306
Mancini, Pat McNees, 109
Mann, Peggy, 115, 168, 324
Manton, Jo, 300
Marcus, Rebecca B., 300
Mark, Jan, 28, 198, 332
Martin, Bill, Jr., 62
Marzollo, Jean, 157
Massey, Ellen Gray, 276
Mathews, Janet, 300
Mathis, Sharon Bell, 87, 109, 116, 143, 168, 181, 233, 324
Matsuno, Masako, 84
Matthew, Scott, 124
Mauermann, Mary Anne, 131
Maugham, W. Somerset, 109
Mayer, Marianna, 68
Mayerson, Charlotte Leon, 143
Mazer, Harry, 46, 124, 174
Mazer, Norma Fox, 88, 131, 174
McClenathan, Louise, 283
McCloskey, Robert, 319, 322
McCullers, Carson, 219
McDermott, Beverly Brodsky, 258, 283
McDermott, Gerald, 230, 283
McDonnell, Lois Eddy, 98
McDowell, Robert E., 242
McGovern, Ann, 120, 137
McKillip, Patricia, 362
McNaughton, Colin, 18
McNulty, Faith, 189, 352
Meadowcroft, Enid La Monte, 332
Means, Florence C., 57
Melton, David, 103
Meltzer, Milton, 124, 131, 263
Merriam, Eve, 62, 131
Merrill, Jean, 113
Meyer, Carolyn, 174, 260, 355
Michener, James A., 263
Miles, Betty, 72, 124, 140
Miles, Miska, 63, 84, 158, 230, 266, 322
Miller, Arthur, 143
Milord, Jerry, 189
Milord, Sue, 189
Minard, Rosemary, 120, 290
Minarik, Else H., 158
Mizumura, Kazue, 352
Mobley, Jane, 234, 324
Mohr, Nicholasa, 250, 276
Molarsky, Osmond, 23, 215
Molnar, Joe, 268
Momaday, N. Scott, 58, 250
Moncure, Jane Belk, 18, 23, 204, 255

Monjo, F. N., 56, 258, 290, 332, 335
Montgomery, Elizabeth Rider, 94
Moore, Janet Gaylord, 307
Moore, Lilian, 61, 153, 273
Moore, Ruth Nulton, 290
Morgenroth, Barbara, 116
Morrell, David, 348
Morris, Edmund, 348
Morrison, Toni, 250
Morrow, Honore W., 332
Morse, Ann, 137
Morse, Charles, 137
Moskin, Marietta D., 37, 88
Müller, Jörg, 354
Murphy, E. Jefferson, 307, 363
Murray, Michele, 182
Myers, Bernice, 266
Myers, Steven J., 291
Myers, Walter Dean, 124, 175, 218

Nabokov, Peter, 250
Nason, Donna, 109
Nason, Michael, 109
Naylor, Penelope, 300
Neigoff, Mike, 49, 328
Neihardt, John G., 251
Ness, Evaline, 63
Neufeld, John, 103, 175, 198
Neville, Emily Cheney, 217
Newlon, Clarke, 242
Newman, Shirlee P., 52
Newton, Suzanne, 88
Ney, John, 140, 175
Niemeyer, Marie, 120
Noble, June, 158
Norris, Clarence, 251
Norris, Leslie, 269

O'Brien, Robert C., 354, 363
O'Dell, Scott, 32, 72, 75, 220, 234, 242, 251, 264, 300, 345, 364
O'Hare, Colette, 291
Obukhova, Lydia, 364
Odor, Ruth, 59
Oerke, Andrew, 307
Ofek, Uriel, 291, 340
Ogilvie, Elisabeth, 307
Ojigbo, A. Okion, 307
Olsen, Tillie, 143
Oppenheimer, Joan, 140
Orgel, Doris, 194, 201, 348
Orwell, George, 143, 364

Parenteau, Shirley, 357
Parks, Gordon, 301
Pascal, Francine, 175

Paterson, Katherine, 68, 72, 75, 115, 195, 218, 291, 301, 308, 324
Peare, Catherine Owens, 143
Peck, Richard, 182, 213, 220
Peck, Robert Newton, 46, 120, 175, 326
Peet, Bill, 352, 353
Pepe, Phil, 110
Perl, Lila, 175, 210
Perry, John, 357
Peter, Diana, 24, 94
Petersen, Palle, 28, 99
Peterson, Jeanne Whitehouse, 92
Pevsner, Stella, 46, 72, 176, 210
Peyton, K. M., 75, 116
Pfeffer, Susan Beth, 68
Pinkwater, Daniel M., 63, 141, 158, 299
Platt, Kin, 103
Potok, Chaim, 49, 131, 182, 264
Power, Barbara, 38, 158
Prager, Annabelle, 38
Price, Christine, 291, 301, 308
Pringle, Lawrence, 324
Provensen, Alice, 258
Provensen, Martin, 258
Purdy, Susan Gold, 242
Putnam, Alice, 340

Qoyawayma, Polingaysi (Elizabeth Q. White), 251
Quam, Alvina, 252

Rabe, Berniece, 125, 141, 176
Rabinowich, Ellen, 211
Rainbolt, Richard, 113
Raucher, Herman, 131
Rawls, Wilson, 43, 168, 269
Raynor, Dorka, 52, 158, 283
Reardon, Maureen, 165, 193, 215
Reboul, Antoine, 345
Reid, Barbara, 283
Reid, Ewa, 283
Reig, June, 292
Reinach, Jacquelyn, 38, 63
Reiss, Johanna, 47, 346
Reit, Ann, 132
Remarque, Erich M., 308
Renter, Margaret, 95
Reyher, Becky, 158
Ribner, Susan, 308
Rice, Edward, 264, 308, 309
Richards, Arlene Kramer, 182, 201
Riley, Susan, 38, 63, 204
Rinkoff, Barbara, 217
Risner, Robinson, 309
Rivera, Geraldo, 103, 141
Robertson, Keith, 121

Robinet, Harriette, 24, 95
Robinson, Barbara, 68, 208, 258
Robinson, Veronica, 99
Rockwood, Joyce, 234, 252, 348
Rodgers, Mary, 47, 114, 115, 176
Rodowsky, Colby F., 110
Rogers, Pamela, 89, 176
Rose, Anne, 125, 284
Rosen, Winifred, 28, 135
Rosenberg, Janet, 135
Ross, Geraldine, 24
Rowland, Florence Wightman, 259
Roy, Ronald, 53, 284, 319
Rubin, Arnold P., 336
Ruby, Lois, 132
Rudstrom, Lennart, 301
Ruggill, Peter, 255

Sachs, Marilyn, 29, 103, 114, 195, 208
Salerno, Nan F., 252
Sallis, Susan, 349
Samuels, Gertrude, 49, 182, 349
San Souci, Robert, 234
Sarton, May, 64, 90
Sauer, Julia, 215
Saul, Wendy, 118, 353
Say, Allen, 47, 301
Schellie, Don, 276
Schlein, Miriam, 301
Schmidt, J. H., 220
Schmitt, Martin F., 246
Schulman, L. M., 91
Schwartz, Alvin, 269
Schwartz, Delmore, 18
Schwartz, Sheila, 182
Scott, Ann Herbert, 59, 151, 227
Scott, J. M., 91
Scott, John Anthony, 125
Sebestyen, Ouida, 72, 176, 242
Seed, Jenny, 292
Seeger, Ruth Crawford, 265
Seixas, Judith S., 176
Sendak, Maurice, 64, 158
Sergeant, Elizabeth, 132
Serraillier, Ian, 340
Serwadda, W. Moses, 292
Seuling, Barbara, 82
Seuss, Dr. (Theodor Geisel), 214
Sharmat, Marjorie Weinman, 38, 64, 190, 266
Shecter, Ben, 69, 269
Sherburne, Zoa, 103, 176
Showers, Paul, 53
Shreve, Susan, 125
Shyer, Marlene Fanta, 47, 104, 177
Siberell, Anne, 292

Author Index

Silko, Leslie Marmon, 58, 252
Silman, Roberta, 43, 168
Silverberg, Robert, 364
Simon, Marcia L., 126
Simon, Norma, 19, 43, 159, 324
Simon, Seymour, 302, 324
Singer, Isaac Bashevis, 302
Sivers, Brenda, 195
Skármeta, Antonio, 49, 213, 309
Skorpen, Liesel Moak, 19, 39, 64, 82, 84, 151
Slote, Alfred, 99, 341
Smith, Alison, 115, 126
Smith, Doris Buchanan, 29, 47, 99, 211, 269, 324
Smith, Edward, 293
Smith, Gene, 104
Smith, Jim, 284
Smith, Lucia B., 95, 159
Smith, Nancy Covert, 137, 217
Smith, Robert Kimmel, 29, 168
Smucker, Barbara Claasen, 261, 341, 346
Snow, Richard, 269
Snyder, Zilpha Keatley, 138, 208, 269
Sobol, Rose, 126, 243
Solzhenitsyn, Aleksandr I., 309.
Sonnleitner, A. T., 335
Sorensen, Virginia, 55, 259
Southall, Ivan, 99
Soyer, Abraham, 234
Specht, Robert, 276
Spencer, Elizabeth, 110, 144
Spencer, Zane, 157, 230, 233
Sperry, Armstrong, 29
Spicer, Robert A., 67
Spier, Peter, 53, 266, 284, 332, 355
St. George, Judith, 252, 273
Stanton, Elizabeth, 19
Stanton, Henry, 19
Steele, Mary Q., 31, 243
Steele, William O., 31, 168, 217, 235, 243, 293
Steig, William, 69, 190
Steinbeck, John, 49, 110, 144, 201, 309
Steiner, Jörg, 69, 355
Steiner, Stan, 253
Steinmetz, Leon, 24
Steptoe, John, 169
Sterling, Dorothy, 253
Sterne, Emma Gelders, 336
Stevens, Margaret, 84
Stevenson, Robert Louis, 75
Stewart, A. C., 47, 346
Stiller, Richard, 132, 336
Stolz, Mary, 43, 47, 177, 183, 195, 208
Stoutenburg, Adrien, 47

Strachan, Margaret Pitcairn, 144
Strait, Treva Adams, 177, 274, 335
Strassova, Helena, 349
Stren, Patti, 19, 84, 112, 159, 190
Stuart, Colin, 253
Stuart, Jesse, 270
Stubbs, Joanna, 203
Suhl, Yuri, 133, 302, 335, 337
Sullivan, Tom, 110
Sutcliff, Rosemary, 49, 104, 310, 349
Suyin, Han, 310, 311
Swados, Elizabeth, 284
Swearingen, Martha, 198
Synge, Ursula, 302
Syson, Michael, 231

Tamarin, Alfred, 53, 253, 288, 298
Taylor, Mildred D., 56, 126, 138, 177, 243, 341
Taylor, Sydney, 169
Taylor, Theodore, 47, 199, 274
Teague, Bob, 75
Tennant, Veronica, 114
Terrill, Ross, 311
Terris, Susan, 32, 43, 121
Tester, Sylvia Root, 159
Thiele, Colin, 31, 72, 89, 201, 302, 311, 355
Thoger, Marie, 126
Thomas, Ianthe, 39, 84, 190
Thomas, Piri, 253
Thompson, Jean, 39, 159
Thompson, Vivian L., 235
Titus, Eve, 285
Tobias, Tobi, 44, 121
Tolan, Stephanie S., 89, 133, 201
Tolles, Martha, 44, 121, 208
Tolstoy, Leo, 75
Towne, Mary, 127
Townsend, John Rowe, 364
Toye, William, 293
Trivelpiece, Laurel, 349
Trumbo, Dalton, 110
Turkle, Brinton, 159, 190, 270

Uchida, Yoshiko, 47, 341, 346
Udry, Janice M., 190
Ullman, James Ramsey, 72
Uris, Leon, 350

Valens, Evans G., 324
Van Iterson, S. R., 56, 303
Van Leeuwen, Jean, 31, 211
Van Steenwyk, Elizabeth, 72
Van Stockum, Hilda, 341

Vanderburgh, Rosamond M., 252
Vestly, Anne-Cath, 118, 160
Vigna, Judith, 64, 191, 204
Viorst, Judith, 39, 135, 322

Waber, Bernard, 24, 39, 53, 160, 205
Wahl, Jan, 160
Waldron, Ann, 211
Walker, Barbara M., 333
Walker, Margaret, 253
Walking Bull, Gilbert C., 254
Walking Bull, Montana H. R., 254
Wallace, Barbara Brooks, 69, 87, 208
Walsh, Jill Paton, 73, 202, 303, 311, 328, 335, 346, 353
Walton, Evangeline, 364, 365
Walton, Todd, 111
Wangerin, Walter, Jr., 58, 202, 350
Washington, Sybil D., 251
Waterton, Betty, 64, 285
Watson, Clyde, 266
Watson, Jane Werner, 355, 362
Watson, Pauline, 169
Watson, Sally, 341
Watson, Wendy, 151, 319
Watts, Marjorie Ann, 191
Wayne, Bennett, 127
Weik, Mary Hayes, 104
Weil, Lisl, 64, 191, 259, 322
Weiss, Ann E., 293
Wersba, Barbara, 48, 89, 127, 141, 183, 199
Werstein, Irving, 337
West, Jessamyn, 183
Westheimer, David, 202
Weston, John, 141, 199
Wetterer, Margaret, 285
Wharton, Edith, 111, 220
Wheeler, Shirley P., 76
White, E. B., 196
White, Paul, 95
Wigginton, Eliot, 276
Wilde, Oscar, 69
Wilder, Laura Ingalls, 169
Wilder, Thornton, 183
Wilkinson, Brenda, 48, 141, 202, 213, 274, 277

Wilkinson, Sylvia, 89
Willard, Barbara, 311
Willard, Nancy, 325
Williams, Barbara, 40, 65, 160
Williams, Jay, 294
Williams, Margery, 24, 69
Williams, Tennessee, 111
Willis, Irene, 182, 201
Windsor, Patricia, 50, 350
Winthrop, Elizabeth, 104, 183, 199
Wise, William, 25
Wojciechowska, Maia, 127
Wolf, Bernard, 243, 274
Wolff, Diane, 294
Wolitzer, Hilma, 177
Wolkstein, Diane, 44, 294, 295
Wong, Jade Snow, 133
Wood, Nancy, 243
Woody, Regina J., 133
Wright, Lawrence, 277
Wrightson, Patricia, 196, 312
Wulf, Kathleen, 19, 59
Wuorio, Eva-Lis, 303, 346

Yarbrough, Camille, 55, 169, 235
Yashima, Taro, 205, 208
Yates, Elizabeth, 111, 169, 333
Yellow Robe, Rosebud, 243
Yep, Laurence, 56, 57, 105, 141, 177, 243, 244
Yolen, Jane, 29, 44, 53, 65, 73, 95, 151, 196, 270, 285
Yoo, Edward Yushin, 295
Young, Alida E., 50, 220, 254
Young, Miriam, 160
Young, Scott, 208

Zei, Alki, 303, 346
Zemach, Kaethe, 285
Zim, Herbert S., 325
Zimnik, Reiner, 295
Zindel, Paul, 89, 211
Zolotow, Charlotte, 118, 160, 161, 191, 325
Zvorykin, Boris, 304

Title Index

When the book has been cross-referenced, the page where the full annotation appears is listed in italic type.

Aaron's Door, 158
Abby, 150
Abel's Island, 69
About Me, 23
About the B'Nai Bagels, 207
Absolute Zero, 114
Accident, The, 33
Acorn People, The, 102
Across Five Aprils, 71, 173, 334
Across the Sea from Galway, 55, 298, 344
Adam's Daughter, 182
Adventures of Yemima and Other Stories, The, 234
Afraid: What Does It Mean?, 38
Africa Dream, 52, 229
African Rhythms, 237
After the First Death, 179
After the Goat Man, 25, 85, 192
Akavak: An Eskimo Journey, 86
Akimba and the Magic Cow: A Folktale from Africa, 284
Alan and Naomi, 102, 260
Alexander, Who Used to Be Rich Last Sunday, 135
All by Myself, 18
All Except Sammy, 26, 112
All Kinds of Families, 159
All Quiet on the Western Front, 308
All the Money in the World, 70
All This Wild Land, 170, 271, 343
All Together Now, 100, 196
All-of-a-Kind Family, 169
Along the Niger River: An African Way of Life, 299, 355
Alphonse and the Stonehenge Mystery, 284
Alvin's Swap Shop, 27
Amazing Voyage of the New Orleans, The, 273
American Folk Songs for Children: In Home, School and Nursery School, 265

American Indian Prose and Poetry, 57
Amifika, 153, 228
Amish Boy, 259
Amish People: Plain Living in a Complex World, 174, 260, 355
Amos and Boris, 190
Amy's Goose, 36
An Egg Is for Wishing, 36
Anastasia Krupnik, 168, 323
Anatole and the Pied Piper, 285
And Now Miguel, 120
And Still I Rise, 244
And the Waters Prevailed, 330
And This Is Laura, 114, 170
And You Give Me a Pain, Elaine, 176
Androids Are Coming, The, 364
Andy's Mountain, 353
Angry: What Does It Mean?, 63, 204
Animal Farm, 143, 364
Anna Karenina, 75
Anne Frank: The Diary of a Young Girl, 45
Annie and the Old One, 84, 230, 322
Anno's Counting Book, 320
Another Part of the House, 335
Antarctica: The Great White Continent, 301
Anthropos-Specter-Beast, The, 360
Any Me I Want to Be, 23
Anyhow, I'm Glad I Tried, 64, 204
Apprentices, The, 140
April Fools, 37
Apt. 3, 93
Are You There, God? It's Me, Margaret, 256
Arilla Sun Down, 55, 173, 238
Arrow to the Sun, 230
Arrows Four: Prose and Poetry by Young American Indians, 244
Art of China, The, 298
Arthur Mitchell, 121
Arthur's Honey Bear, 35

383

Title Index

Arthur's New Power, 352
Arthur's Pen Pal, 117, *155*
Artists of Terezin, The, 262
As the Leaves Fall Down, 319
As We Are Now, 90
Ask for Love and They Give You Rice Pudding, 128, *142*
Ask Mr. Bear, 150
At the Mouth of the Luckiest River, 216, *232*
Autobiography of Miss Jane Pittman, The, 247
Autumn Light: Illuminations of Age, 91
Awakening Water, The, 360

Baby Sister for Frances, A, *156*, 321
Baby, The, 150
Bad Fall, 212
Bag of Marbles, A, 49, *347*
Bakery Factory, The, 354
Bannekers of Bannaky Springs, The, 166
Banner in the Sky, 72
Barbara Jordan, 249
Basketball Toss-Up, *25*, 205
Bear and the People, The, 295
Bear Who Saw the Spring, The, 37
Beast of Lor, The, 287
Beat the Turtle Drum, *172*, 326, 344
Beatinest Boy, The, 270
Beautiful Rat, The, 285
Beauty and the Beast, 68
Bedtime for Frances, 156
Beech Tree, The, 85
Beezus and Ramona, 163
Beginning Place, The, 357, *363*
Being Alone, Being Together, 205
Being Poor, 135
Belonging: A Novel, 212
Benjie, 157
Bert Breen's Barn, 71, *272*
Bessie Yellowhair, 248
Best Christmas Pageant Ever, The, *68*, 208, 258
Best Mom in the World, The, *34*, 150
Best Time of the Day, The, 150
Better Than a Princess, *56*, 345
Better Than Laughter, *87*, 138, 170
Between Friends, 71, *102*, 197
Beyond Another Door, 115
Big Brother, 157
Big Dipper Marathon, The, 100
Big Orange Splot, The, 63
Big Red, 46, *326*
Big Red Barn, The, 153, *320*
Big Sister Tells Me That I'm Black, *19*, 227
Big Sister, Little Brother, 152

Big Wave, The, 323
Billion for Boris, A, 114
Billy and Our New Baby, *33*, 149
Birdless Summer, 310
Birthday for Frances, A, 156
Birthday Tree, The, 52
Birthday Wish, A, 184
Bittersweet County, 276
Black BC's, The, 228
Black Elk Speaks: Being the Life Story of a Holy Man of the Oglala Sioux, 251
Black Images: The Art of West Africa, 300
Black Is Brown Is Tan, 151
Black Out Loud: An Anthology of Modern Poems by Black Americans, 55, *235*
Blinded by the Light, *219*, 261
Blubber, 205
Blue Fin, 31
Blue Horse and Other Night Poems, The, 321
Blue Willow, 165, *267*
Bong Nam and the Pheasants, 295
Book of Greek Myths, 287
Book of the Dun Cow, The, *58*, 202, 350
Born Innocent, *48*, 219, 347
Borribles, The, 363
Bow Island, 100
Boy Called Hopeless by M. J., A, 103
Boy Friends, Girl Friends, Just Friends, 201
Boy in That Situation, A: An Autobiography, 299, *344*
Boy in the Middle, *20*, 152
Boy Who Ate More Than the Giant: And Other Swedish Folktales, 282
Boy Who Could Make Himself Disappear, The, 103
Boy Who Didn't Believe in Spring, The, 185
Boy Who Had Wings, The, 29
Boy Who Loved Music, The, 290
Boy Who Sang the Birds, The, *141*, 199
Boy Who Wanted a Family, The, 165
Boy Who Wouldn't Talk, The, 92
Bread and Jam for Frances, 156
Brendan the Navigator: A History Mystery About the Discovery of America, 288, *331*
Bridge for Passing, A, 327
Bridge to Terabithia, 68, *195*, 324
Bright Fawn and Me, 157, *230*
Broken Promise, 180
Brother for the Orphelines, A, 215
Bullfrog Builds a House, 185
Bullfrog Grows Up, 34

Title Index

Bully of Barkham Street, The, 208
Bury My Heart at Wounded Knee, 245
Bushman's Dream, The: African Tales of the Creation, 292
But I'm Ready to Go, 99
But Names Will Never Hurt Me, *53*, 160
Butcher, Baker, Cabinetmaker: Photographs of Women at Work, 118, *353*
By Camel or by Car, 351
By Myself, 36
By Secret Railway, 332

Caddie Woodlawn, 118
Call It Courage, 29
Can Machines Replace Men?, 356
Can You Sue Your Parents for Malpractice?, 171
Candita's Choice, 54
Cane in Her Hand, A, 94
Captain Grey, 330
Captive, The, 300
Carl Larsson: A Family, 301
Carlota, *32, 364*
Carolina's Courage, 333
Carousel Horse, The, 140, *198*
Cartoonist, The, 26, *162*
Cat Ate My Gymsuit, The, *45*, 114, 171
Cave Children, The, 335
Cay, The, 199
Celebrations: A New Anthology of Black American Poetry, 244
Ceremony, 58, *252*
Chance Child, A, 303, 335, *355*
Changing Countryside, The, (Vol. 1); The Changing City (Vol. 2), 354
Chanukah, 257
Charlotte's Web, 196
Cherokee Tale Teller, The, 231
Child in the Bamboo Grove, The, 288
Child of Fire, 220, 251
Child of the Owl, 56, *141*, 177, 243
Children of Llyr, The (2nd Branch of "The Mabinogion"), 364
Children of the Fox, 73, *303*, 346
Children of Vietnam, *299*, 345
Chileno!, 49, 213, *309*
Chin Music: Tall Talk and Other Talk, 269
China Difference, The, 311
Chinese Experience, The, 304
Chinese New Year, The, 289
Chinese Writing: An Introduction, 294
Chinwe, *231*, 338
Chip, 199
Chocolate Fever, *29*, 168
Chocolate War, The, *122*, 218
Chosen, The, 182, *264*

Christianity—A First Book, 257
Christmas Feast, A: Poems, Sayings, Greetings, and Wishes, 256
Christmas Memory, A, 178
Christmas Pageant, The, 255
Christmas Tree Crisis, The, 166
Cider Days, 195
City Children, Country Summer: A Story of Ghetto Children Among the Amish, 277
City Horse, 271
City of Darkness, 362
City of Gold and Lead, The, 359
Claire and Emma, 24, *94*
Classmates by Request, 206
Clever Gretchen and Other Forgotten Folktales, 120, *290*
Clocks in the Woods, 24
Close Your Eyes, 157
Clown of God, The, *27*, 257
Cobbler's Reward, The, 283
Cold Feet, *49*, 131, 219
Colorful Story of North American Indians, The, 239
Come to the Edge, *30*, 197
Confessions of an Only Child, 167
Conquista, 231
Constance: A Story of Early Plymouth, 122
Corduroy, 186
Corn Is Maize: The Gift of the Indians, *51*, 329
Cornrows, 55, 169, *235*
Cotton in My Sack, 268
Counting on You: The United States Census, 270
Country Bunny and the Little Gold Shoes, The, 117
Country of Broken Stone, *57, 177, 304*
Cousins Are Special, 155
Cowboy Surprise, The, 25
Creatures, The, 364
Creoles of Color of New Orleans, The, *239, 272*
Crippled Tree, The, 310
Crocodile Medicine, 191
Cross Fire, 344
Crow Boy, 208
Cry from the Earth, A: Music of the North American Indians, 245
Cry of the Crow, The, 172, *272*
Crystal Is My Friend, 186
Crystal Is the New Girl, 187
Crystal Nights, The, 182
Cucumber Stem, The, 286
Cute Is a Four-Letter Word, *72, 210*

D.J.'s Worst Enemy, 162
Dakota Sons, 197, *272*
Dance on the Dusty Earth, 301
Dance to Still Music, A, 101
Dancing Man, The, *65,* 322
Daniel's Duck, 21, *329*
Dark Bright Water, The, 312
Dark Child, The, 306
Dark Dove, 47, *346*
Dark Princess, The, 207
Dark Venture, 70
Daughter of Night: A Tale of Three Worlds, 364
David in Silence, 99
David Was Mad, 62
Day After Christmas, The, 60
Day in the Woods, A, 66
Day No Pigs Would Die, A, 46, *175,* 326
Day of the Drones, 363
Days of Terror, *261,* 346
Dear Bill, Remember Me?, 131
Death Be Not Proud, 327
Death Comes for the Archbishop, 219
Death in the Family, A, 177
Death Is Natural, 324
Death of a Salesman, 143
Deenie, 44, *100,* 209
Demian, 130, *219*
Devil in Tartan, The, 307
Devil in Vienna, The, *201,* 348
Diary of the Boy King Tut-Ankh-Amen, 292
Diary of Trilby Frost, The, 129
Did You Carry the Flag Today, Charley?, *153,* 265
Dinky Hocker Shoots Smack, 181
Dinosaurs and All That Rubbish, 351
Disappearance, The, 219, *248*
Diving for Roses, *50,* 350
Do You Love Me?, 61
Do You Want to Be My Friend?, 184
Does Anybody Care About Lou Emma Miller?, 71, 122, 209, *271*
Dog on Barkham Street, A, *195,* 208
Dollar Man, The, 124, *174*
Don't Ask Miranda, 210
Don't Forget the Bacon!, 36
Don't Forget Tom, 93
Don't Look at Me That Way, *139,* 171
Don't Take Teddy, 101
Dorrie's Book, 103
Down These Mean Streets, 253
Dr. Nina and the Panther, 76
Dragonwings, *57,* 177, 243
Dream Eater, The, 281
Dream Runner, The, 30

Dream Watcher, The, 89, *199*
Drowning Boy, The, 32
Dumb Old Casey Is a Fat Tree, 20
Durango Street, *209,* 237
During Water Peaches, 349
Dvora's Journey, 342

Easter Buds Are Springing: Poems for Easter, 257
Eastern Gate, The, 307
Edgar Allen, 175
Edge of Next Year, The, 183
Edge of Two Worlds, 241
Edie Changes Her Mind, 151
Edith Jackson, *180,* 248
Egypt Game, The, 208
18th Emergency, The, *121,* 205
Elf Who Didn't Believe in Himself, The, 24
Eloquent Crusader—Ernestine Rose, *133,* 337
Emperor's Winding Sheet, The, 311
Empty Chair, The, 56, *173,* 344
Enchanted Sticks, The, 291
Episode of Sparrows, An, 142
Eskimos, 272
Esther, 259
Ethan Frome, *111,* 220
Evan's Corner, 134, *155*
Everett Anderson's Friend, 203
Everett Anderson's 1.2.3., 164
Everyone Knows What a Dragon Looks Like, 294
Evil That Men Do, The: The Story of the Nazis, 336
Evonne Goolagong, 137
Exodus, 350
Eye in the Forest, The, 31, *243*
Eyes of the Amaryllis, The, 87

Fabulous Manticora, The, 140
Fairy Tales of the Brothers Grimm, 298
Family Nobody Wanted, The, 171
Family Under the Bridge, The, 162
Famous Mexican Americans, 242
Fannie Lou Hamer, 54, *339*
Far Side of Fear, The, 345
Farewell to Manzanar, *249,* 347
Farewell to Shady Glade, 352
Fast Sam, Cool Clyde, and Stuff, *124,* 218
Fastest Quitter in Town, The, *27,* 207
Father Figure, 182
Father Fox's Pennyrhymes, 266
Father's Arcane Daughter, 114
FDR's New Deal, 345
F.D.R. Story, The, 143

Title Index

Feathered Serpent: The Rise and Fall of the Aztecs, 306
Feeling Angry, 159
Feelings Between Kids and Parents, 165
Feelings Between Brothers and Sisters, 165
Feelings Between Friends, 193
Feelings Between Kids and Grownups, 215
Felicia the Critic, 206
Ferris Wheel, *43,* 195
Fiddler of High Lonesome, The, 270
Fifth Chinese Daughter, 133
Figgie Hobbin, 296
Fighting Indians of the West, 246
Figure of Speech, A, *88,* 174
Fike's Point, 219
File on Fraulein Berg, The, 260
Find a Stranger, Say Goodbye, 181
Fire Bringer, The: A Paiute Indian Legend, 233
Fire in the Stone, 201, *311*
Firebird and Other Russian Fairy Tales, 304
Fireflies, The, 51
Fireweed, 202
First Blood, 348
First Pink Light, 150
First Serve, 127
First Woman of Medicine, The: The Story of Elizabeth Blackwell, 124
Fish Peri, The, 280
Fisherman's Son, The, 288
Five Great Religions, The, 264
Fixer, The, 306
Flat on My Face, *96,* 119
Flavio, 301
Flea Market Mystery, The, 267
Fledgling, The, 42, *323*
Floating Clouds, Floating Dreams: Favorite Asian Folktales, 289
Flowers for Algernon, *108,* 115
Flying Horses, The: Tales from China, 300
Fog, 213
Follow My Leader, 97
Football's Clever Quarterbacks, 113
For the Love of Ann, 106
Four Donkeys, The, 65
Fox Farm, 171
Foxfire Book, The, 276
Freaky Friday, 47, *115,* 176
Frederick, 62
Frederick Douglass: Slave-Fighter Freeman, 333
Friday's Child, 109
Fridays, 209
Friend Can Help, A, 192, *338*

Friend Is Someone Who Likes You, A, 184
Friend, The, 203
Friendly Persuasion, 183
Friendly Wolf, The, 232
Friends Are Like That! Stories to Read to Yourself, 185
Friends, The, 74, 200, *248*
Frog and Toad All Year, 189
Frog and Toad Are Friends, 189
Frog and Toad Together, 189
Frogs Who Wanted a King and Other Songs from LaFontaine, The, 293
From Anna, 28, *98*
From the Mixed-Up Files of Mrs. Basil E. Frankweiler, 42

Gammage Cup, The, 216
Ganges, A Personal Encounter, The, 308
Garden Is Doing Fine, The, *172,* 325
Gardener's Grandchildren, The, 311
Gather Together in My Name, 244
Gathering of Days, A: A New England Girl's Journal, 1830-32, 170, *270,* 325
Gentle War, A: The Story of the Salvation Army, 259
Gentlehands, *142,* 181
Gently Touch the Milkweed, 129
Genuine, Ingenious, Thrift Shop Genie, Clarissa Mae Bean, and Me, The, 112
(George), 113
Gertie & Gus, 64
Getting Along: How to Be Happy with Yourself and Others, 220
Getting Nowhere, 172
Gia and the One Hundred Dollars Worth of Bubblegum, 40
Gift from the Sea, 75
Gift of Magic, A, 112
Gift-Giver, The, 193
Ginny, 106
Girl Called Al, A, 193
Girl Who Had No Name, The, *125,* 141
Girl Who Loved Wild Horses, The, 54, *232*
Girl Who Married a Ghost and Other Tales from the North American Indian, 236
Girls Can Be Anything, 118
Girls Can Too: A Book of Poems, 22
Give Dad My Best, 178
Giving Away Suzanne, 154
Glass Menagerie, The, 111
Glooskap's Children, 236
Glue Fingers, *26,* 206
Go and Catch a Flying Fish, 177
Go up the Road, 120, *233*
Go Well, Stay Well, 305

Goggles!, 188
Going to the Sun, 73
Golden Shores of Heaven, The, 131
Golem, The, 258
Good Friends Come in Many Shapes, 187
Good-Bye, Chicken Little, *40,* 121
Gorilla Did It, The, *34, 59*
Gourd Dancer, The, 250
Graciela: A Mexican-American Tells Her Story, 268
Grandfather and I, 149
Grandma Didn't Wave Back, 85
Grandmother and I, 150
Grandpa, 149
Grandpa—and Me, 89
Grandpa Had a Windmill, Grandma Had a Churn, *52, 329*
Granny's Fish Story, 83
Grapes of Wrath, The, 144
Great Gilly Hopkins, The, *72,* 115, *218*
Grizzly, The, 120, *166*
Grouchy Uncle Otto, *20,* 82, 152
Groundhog's Horse, 234
Grover, *164, 323*
Growing Anyway Up, 115, *130*
Growing Older, *85,* 135
Growing Up Female in America: Ten Lives, 131
Guardians, The, 359
Guess Who My Favorite Person Is, 65
Guide Dog, 106
Gulag Archipelago, The: An Experiment in Literary Investigation, 309
Gus and Buster Work Things Out, 152

Half Sisters, The, 163
Half-a-Ball-of-Kenki: An Ashanti Tale, 279
Half-a-Moon Inn, The, 96
Halo Wind, The, 252
Hamdaani: A Traditional Tale from Zanzibar, 286
Hammerhead Light, The, 89, *302, 355*
Hand-Me-Down Kid, The, 175
Hang Tough, Paul Mather, 99, *341*
Happy Bear's Day, 203
Happy Dromedary, The, 21
Harpist in the Wind (3rd), 361
Harriet and the Runaway Book, 54
Harriet the Spy, 207
Harvest, The, 57, *263*
Hatching of Joshua Cobb, The, 216
Hating Book, The, 191
Hatter Fox, 249
Hattie Be Quiet, Hattie Be Good, 154
Hawaii, 263
Hawaiian Tales of Heroes and Champions, 235

Hawk That Dare Not Hunt by Day, The, 75, *264*
Hawk, I'm Your Brother, 20, *265*
Hawkins, 69, *87*
Hawks of Chelney, The, 74
Hayburners, The, 104
He Freed Britain's Slaves, 306
He's My Brother, *93,* 157
Heir of Sea and Fire (2nd), 361
Helga's Dowry: A Troll Love Story, 61
Hello, Aurora, 118, *160*
Henrietta and the Day of the Iguana, 135
Henrietta, the Wild Woman of Borneo, 28
Henry Reed's Babysitting Service, 121
Henry Three, 113
Here I Am, 230
Hero Ain't Nothin' but a Sandwich, A, 274
Hi, Mrs. Mallory!, 39, *84,* 190
Hidden Heroines: Women in American History, *123,* 335
Hiding House, The, 191
Higglety Pigglety Pop!, 64
His Mother's Dog, 39
His Own Where, 249
Hoagie's Rifle-Gun, *63, 266*
Hole in the Dike, The, 278
Hollering Sun, 243
Home Before Dark, 70, 121, *139,* 170
Home from Far, 167, *323*
Homefront, 275
Honestly, Katie John, 192
Honey in the Rock, 46, *355*
Hooray for Me!, *61,* 153
Horowitz and Mrs. Washington, 90
Horton Hears a Who!, 214
House at Otowi Bridge, The, 274
House for Jonnie O., A, 327
House Made of Dawn, 58
House of Sixty Fathers, The, 297
House of Wings, The, 85, 136, *162*
House on Stink Alley, The, 258
Houses: Shelters from Prehistoric Times to Today, 292
How Far, Felipe?, 229
How Many Miles to Babylon?, 216
How Really Great to Walk This Way, 319
How Tevye Became a Milkman, 134
How the Plains Indians Lived, 238
How the Sun Made a Promise and Kept It: A Canadian Indian Myth, 228
How the Sun Was Brought Back to the Sky, 281
How to Dig a Hole to the Other Side of the World, 352
How to Get It Together When Your Parents Are Coming Apart, 182

Title Index

How We Live, 134
Howie Helps Himself, *21*, 93
Hucklebug, 61
Hug Me, 19, *190*
Hugo and Josephine, 112
Human Mandolin, The, 282
Hunchback of Notre Dame, The, 108
Hundred Dresses, The, 136, *206*
Hundred Penny Box, The, 87, 168, *233*, 324
Hundredth Dove and Other Tales, The, 73
Hush, Jon, 155

I Am Adopted, 151
I Am an Orthodox Jew, 52, 155, *255*
"I Am Cherry Alive," the Little Girl Sang, 18
I Am Fifteen—and I Don't Want to Die . . . , 346
I Am Five, 34
I Am Here, Yo Estoy Aqui, 228
I Am the Cheese, *73*, 346
I Am the Darker Brother: An Anthology of Modern Poems by Negro Americans, 235
I Breathe a New Song: Poems of the Eskimo, 241
I Can Do It by Myself, *34*, 157
I Don't Care, 38
I Hate to Go to Bed, *33*, 149
I Have a Sister: My Sister Is Deaf, 92
I Have Four Names for My Grandfather, *83*, 118
I Heard the Owl Call My Name, 73, 246, *327*
I Know You, Al, 197
I Never Promised You a Rose Garden, 31, *107*
I Should Worry, I Should Care, 66, 215, 231, *330*
I Stood upon a Mountain, 320
I Want My Sunday, Stranger, 342
I Want to Be Big, 34
I Was a 98-Pound Duckling, *31*, 211
I Wish Laura's Mommy Was My Mommy, *38*, 158
I'll Get Even, *61*, 204
I'll Get There: It Better Be Worth the Trip, *30*, 122
I'll Love You When You're More Like Me, 130
I'm Dancing as Fast as I Can, 74
I'm Glad I'm Little, 19, *59*
I'm Glad to Be Me, 18
I'm Going to Run Away, 39, *159*
I'm Moving, 358

I'm Not Oscar's Friend Anymore, 38
I'm Terrific, 64
Ice Castles, 101
Ice Is Coming, The, 312
Ida Fanfanny, 321
Idle Jack, 283
If Anything, 198
If He's My Brother, 40, *65*, 160
If I Built a Village . . . , 352
If It Weren't for You, 160
If You Are Silenced, I Will Speak for You, 347
If You Could See What I Hear, 110
If You Love Me, Let Me Go, 200
In a Beautiful Pea Green Boat, 91
In a Bluebird's Eye, 72, *273*
In the Land of Small Dragon: A Vietnamese Folktale, 287
In the Trail of the Wind: American Indian Poems and Ritual Orations, 245
In This Proud Land: The Story of a Mexican American Family, *243*, 274
In This Sign, 107
Incredible Journey, The, 196
Indian Heritage, Indian Pride: Stories That Touched My Life, 237
Indians of the Southeast: Then and Now, 246
Ink-Keeper's Apprentice, The, *47*, 301
Inside Moves, 111
Integration of Mary-Larkin Thornhill, The, 211
Interrupted Melody, 109
Ira Sleeps Over, *39*, 205
Iron Road: A Portrait of American Railroading, The, 269
Ishi in Two Worlds: A Biography of the Last Wild Indian in North America, 250
Island in Time: A Memoir of Childhood, 362
Island of the Blue Dolphins, 234
Island of the Grass King, The, 325
Island of the Mighty, The (4th Branch of "The Mabinogion"), 365
Israel: One Land, Two Peoples, 305
It Ain't All for Nothin', 175
It Happened on Thursday, 35, *154*, 338
It Isn't Easy Being a Teenage Millionaire, 140
It Will Never Be the Same Again, 49, *328*
It'll All Come Out in the Wash, 62
It's Good to Be Alive, 106
It's Not the End of the World, *170*, 343
It's So Nice to Have a Wolf Around the House, *35*, 60
It's Too Late for Sorry, 108, *200*

Jack Jouett's Ride, 338
James Herriot's Yorkshire, 305
Janet at School, 95
Java Jack, 299
Jay and the Marigold, *24,* 95
Jazz Man, The, 104
Jennifer, Hecate, Macbeth, William McKinley, and Me, Elizabeth, 194
Jennifer's New Chair, 149
Jethro and the Jumbie, 287
Jewish Holiday Cookbook, 242
Jewish Holidays, 257
Jews in America, The: The Roots and Destiny of American Jews, 262
Jim Flying High, 35
Johnny Got His Gun, 110
Johnny Tremain, *101,* 334
Joshua, the Czar, and the Chicken Bone Wish, 27, *86,* 207
Josie's Handful of Quietness, *137,* 217
Journey Home, *47,* 346
Journey to America, 140, *340*
Journey to the Sky, 305
Journey to Topaz, 341
Jubilee, 253
Julie of the Wolves, *55,* 238
Just a Little Inconvenience, 105
Just Being Alone, 22
Just Me, 18
Just the Beginning, 140

Karen, 108
Katie and Those Boys, *44,* 121, 208
Keep Running, Allen, *21,* 152
Keeping Days, The, 181
Kelly's Creek, 29, 99, *269*
Kick a Stone Home, 47, *211*
Kid Power, 68
Killer-of-Death, 228
Killing Frost, A, 89
Kilroy and the Gull, 353
Kind of Secret Weapon, A, 342
King on the Court: Billie Jean King, 119
King's Flower, The, 60
Kisses and Fishes, 39
Kiviok's Magic Journey: An Eskimo Legend, 227
Knock, Knock, Who's There?, 183
Kristy's Courage, 27, *96*

Lace Snail, The, 60
Ladder of Angels, 258
Lady Ellen Grae, 164
Lady of the Lotus, 261
Lamb's War, The, 261
Lame Deer—Seeker of Visions, 247

Land of the Iron Dragon, 50, 220, *254*
Lands End, 47
Last Guru, The, 141
Last Look, 192
Last of Eden, The, 133, *201*
Last of the Scottsboro Boys, The, 251
Lazies, The: Tales of the Peoples of Russia, 282
Lazy Stories, 294
Learning to Be Captain, 208
Lee Henry's Best Friend, 193
Legend of New Amsterdam, The, *53,* 266
Legend of Scarface, The, 234
Lelooska, 247
Lemming Condition, The, 70
Leo the Late Bloomer, 23, *93*
Leroy and the Old Man, 73, *178*
Let a River Be, *90,* 107, 356
Let the Balloon Go, 99
Let's Be Enemies, 190
Letter Perfect, 73, *212*
Letter to Amy, A, 188
Letters to a Black Boy, 75
Life and Death, 325
Life of Their Own, A: An Indian Family in Latin America, 299
Life Styles: An Introduction to Cultural Anthropology, 305, *327*
Light in the Piazza, The, *110,* 144
Lighted Heart, The, 111
Like Me, 117
Like Mother Like Me, 182
Lilith Summer, The, 42, *86*
Lillies of the Field, 218
Linda's Rain Tree, 136
Lion's Tail, The, 297
Lisa, Bright and Dark, 103, *198*
Listen for the Fig Tree, *109,* 143
Listen to the Silence, 107
Little Bear, 158
Little Breathing Room, A, 172
Little Chestnut Tree Story, The, 322
Little House Cookbook, The: Frontier Foods from Laura Ingalls, 333
Little House, The, 169
Little John Bear in the Big City, 266
Little Time, A, 99
Littlest Leaguer, The, 22, *204,* 207
Living Together in Tomorrow's World, *355,* 362
Living with a Parent Who Drinks Too Much, 176
Lizzie Lies a Lot, 28
Lonely Veronica, 351
Long Shot for Paul, 96
Look at Aging, A, 82

Title Index

Look Through My Window, 137
Lord of the Flies, 210
Lost City in the Clouds: The Discovery of Machu Picchu, 298
Lost Star, The, 360
Lottery Rose, The, 27, *97*
Louie, 189
Lucky Ones, The: Five Journeys Toward a Home, 136
Lucky Stone, The, 53, *231*
Ludell, 48, 141, *274*
Ludell and Willie, 202, *277*
Ludell's New York Time, 213, *277*
Luke Was There, 66
Lullaby, 284
Lysbet and the Fire Kittens, 37

M. C. Higgins, the Great, 56, *238*, *272*
Made in the South Pacific: Arts of the Sea People, 308
Madeline, 203
Maggie and the Goodbye Gift, 189
Magic Amulet, The, 217, *293*
Magic and the Night River, *66*, 162
Magic Brush, The, 67
Magic Tree: A Tale from the Congo, 283
Magic World, The: American Indian Songs and Poems, 245
Make Way for Ducklings, 319
Mama, *68*, 137, 166
Mama's Bank Account, 179
Man Downstairs, The, 347
Man in the Box, The: A Story from Vietnam, 343
Man Without a Face, The, 200
Manchild in the Promised Land, 128
Mandy's Grandmother, *82*, 151
Many Smokes, Many Moons, 240
Many Voices, 307
Marathon Miranda, *104*, 199
Marcella's Guardian Angel, 63
Margaret Sanger: Pioneer of Birth Control, 131
Maria's House, 113
Martial Arts, The, 308
Marv, *29*, 114
Marvin and Tige, 199
Mary's Monster, 330
Masks Around the World: And How to Make Them, 297
Master Puppeteer, The, *72*, 301
Matt's Grandfather, *83*, 157
Maud Martha, 245
Maude Reed Tale, The, 124
Maurice's Room, 154
Max, 117

Maybe Next Summer, 276
Me and My Family Tree, 53
Me and My Million, 71
Me and the Eggman, *41*, 85
Me and the Terrible Two, 206
Me Day, *43*, 157
Me Nobody Knows, The: Children's Voices from the Ghetto, 31
Meat in the Sandwich, The, 128
Meet the Austins, 167
Member of the Gang, 217
Member of the Wedding, 219
Men from the Village Deep in the Mountains, 286
Merline and the Snake's Egg, 269
Merrily Comes Our Harvest In, 52
Mesa of Flowers, The, 246
Mi Ta-Ku-Ye (About My People), 254
Mia, Grandma and the Genie, *83*, 156
Michael, *19*, 64, 151
Middl'un, 119
Midsummer Night's Death, A, 75
Mike Mulligan and His Steam Shovel, 351
Mike's House, 215
Millicent the Magnificent, 20
Mine for Keeps, 98
Mine's the Best, 60
Miracles: Poems by Children of English-Speaking Countries, 290
Mischling, Second Degree: My Childhood in Nazi Germany, 306
Mishka, 19
Misplaced Persons, 344, *360*
Miss Giardino, 90
Miss Susy's Birthday, 160
Missing Maple Syrup Mystery, The, 266
Mitzvah Is Something Special, A, *51*, 154, 255
Moffats, The, 165
Mog's Christmas, 157
Moja Means One: A Swahili Counting Book, 281
Mollie Make-Believe, 90
Mom, the Wolf Man and Me, 174
Monday Voices, The, 108
Monkey and the Three Wizards, 288
Monkey Face, *59*, 149
Monster Rolling Skull and Other Native American Tales, 232
Moon Guitar, The, 120
Moon of the Big-Dog, 233
Moon-Watch Summer, 35, *60*
Morning Is a Long Time Coming, 48, *247*
Morning, Noon and Nighttime, Too, 323
Mortal Flower, A, 310
Mortal Instruments, The, 362

Mother India's Children: Meeting Today's Generation in India, 309
Mother, Aunt Susan and Me: The First Fight for Women's Rights, 119
Mountain Goats of Temlaham, The, 293
Mouse and Tim, 189
Movin' Up, 140, *238*
Moving, 151, *319*
Moving On: Stories of Four Travelers, 65
Mr. Grumpy's Motor Car, 214
Mr. Rabbit and the Lovely Present, 161
Mrs. Frisby and the Rats of NIMH, 354
Much Bigger than Martin, *37,* 157
Mummies Made in Egypt, *286,* 329
Mummy of Ramose, The: The Life and Death of an Ancient Egyptian Nobleman, 298
Murderer, The, 240
My Black Me: A Beginning Book of Black Poetry, 235
My Brother Fine with Me, *153,* 229
My Brother Sam Is Dead, 333, *343*
My Brother Stevie, *164,* 193
My Dad Lives in a Downtown Hotel, 168
My Friend Fish, 321
My Friend John, 191
My Friend William Moved Away, 187
My Island Grandma, 157
My Mane Catches the Wind, *68,* 323
My Mom Got a Job, 159
My Mom, the Money Nut, 161
My Mother and I, 154
My Mother Is Blind, 95
My Mother Is the Most Beautiful Woman in the World, 158
My Mother Sends Her Wisdom, 283
My Name Is Asher Lev, 49, *264*
My Sister, 97, *166*
My Sister's Silent World, 92
My Sweet Charlie, 202
Mystery of Masks, The, 291
Mystery of the Boy Next Door, The, 94

Nabby Adams' Diary, 162, *338*
Naftali the Storyteller and His Horse, Sus, and Other Stories, 302
Namesake for Nathan, A, *56,* 335
Nanny Goat and the Fierce Dog, The, 37
Narc, The, 211, *327*
Native American Testimony, 250
Navajo, The, 247
Neighbors, 186
Net to Catch the Wind, A, 67
New Baby, A, 149
New Boy in Kindergarten, A, 204

New Burlington: The Life and Death of an American Village, 333
New Indians, The, 253
New Life: New Room, 156
Next Door to Xanadu, 194
Next Year in Jerusalem: A Short History of Zionism, 57, *262*
Night It Rained Pancakes, The, 282
Night They Burned the Mountain, The, 107
Nightmares of Geranium Street, The, 125
Nilda, 250, *276*
Nine Days to Christmas, 280
Nini at Carnival, 157, *282*
No Bath Tonight, 151
No Boys Allowed, *43,* 121
No Language but a Cry, 107
No Promises in the Wind, 198
No Turning Back, 251
Nobody Asked Me If I Wanted a Baby Sister, 320
Nobody's Family Is Going to Change, *45,* 123, 172
Nonna, 320
North American Indian, 246
North American Legends, 275
North of Danger, *297,* 343
North Runner, The, 275, *328*
Nothing Rhymes with April, 137

O Zebron Falls!, 179
Obadiah the Bold, 159
Obstinate Land, The, *46, 273*
Ode to Billy Joe, 131
Of Human Bondage, 109
Of Love and Death and Other Journeys, 180
Of Mice and Men, 110, *201*
Of Nightingales That Weep, 75, *308*
Old Arthur, 84
Old Hippo's Easter Egg, 160
Oliver Button Is a Sissy, 117
Olympic Games in Ancient Greece, *53,* 288
On City Streets, 54
On Mother's Lap, *59,* 151, 227
On Stage, Please, 114
On the Little Hearth, 258
On to Oregon, 332
Once We Went on a Picnic, 186
One Fat Summer, 31
One Little Goat: A Passover Song, 229
One Woman's Arctic, 296
Onion John, 194
Only Earth and Sky Last Forever, 236

Title Index

Ordinary People, 180
Orphans of the Wind, 331, *339*
Orphans, The, 176
Other Sandals, 341
Otherwise Known as Sheila the Great, *25*, 192
Otis Spofford, 206
Our Christmas Book, 255
Our Cup Is Broken, 57
Our Polluted World: Can Man Survive, 357
Our Snowman Had Olive Eyes, *86*, 166
Our Town, 183
Out in the Dark and Daylight, 321
Out on a Limb, 105
Outlaw Red, 71, *326*
Over on the River, 268
Overkill: Weapons of the Nuclear Age, 356
Owl's Song, The, 248
Ownself, 41
Ox-Cart Man, 329
Ox: The Story of a Kid at the Top, 140, *175*

Paddle-to-the-Sea, 273
Pageants of Despair, 71, *259*, *334*
Painted Bird, The, 347
Pair of Red Clogs, A, 84
Pair of Shoes, 136
Panda's Puzzle, and His Voyage of Discovery, 281
Paper Dragon, A, 88
Passing of the Night, 309
Passing Through, 212
Patch of Blue, A, 108
Path, The, 349
Patrick and the Fairy Thief, 285
Paul Robeson: The Life and Times of a Free Black Man, 249
Peaceable Kingdom, A: The Shaker Abecedarius, 258
Peaceable Kingdom, The: An American Saga, 261
Pearl, The, 309
Pennington's Last Term, 116
People Therein, The, 275
Pepe's Private Christmas, 227
Perilous Road, The, 168
Peter Camenzind, 74
Peter's Chair, 321
Petunia's Treasure, *61*, 204
Philip Hall Likes Me. I Reckon Maybe, 67
Phillis Wheatley: America's First Black Poetess, 112
Phoebe the Spy, *54*, 232

Pie in the Sky, 337
Pieface and Daphne, 175
Pigman, The, *89*, 211
Pinballs, The, 217
Pistachio Prescription, The, 171
Place for Peter, A, 169
Plain Girl, *55*, 259
Planet of Junior Brown, The, 114, *218*
Pony Problem, The, 123
Pool of Fire, The, 359
Portrait of Ivan, 216
Portrait of Myself, A, 31, *116*
Potlatch Family, The, 241
Power Play, *66*, 206
Prairie Boy's Summer, A, 42, *289*
Price of Free Land, The, 177, *274*, 335
Prince of Annwn (1st Branch of "The Mabinogion"), 365
Prince of Islam, A, 256
Prisoners of the Scrambling Dragon, 290, *332*
Private Matter, A, 193
Promise Is a Promise, A, 257
Promise, The, *131*, 264
Pyramid, 299

Quarreling Book, The, 161
Queen of Hearts, *87*, 170
Queen of the Populists: The Story of Mary Elizabeth Lease, *132*, 336
Queenie Peavy, 121, *209*
Quitting Deal, The, 44

Rabbit Island, 69, *355*
Racecourse for Andy, A, 196
Rachel, 92
Rachel Carson, 352
Rainbow Rider, 270
Raisin in the Sun, 130
Ramona and Her Father, 66, *163*
Ramona and Her Mother, 163
Ramona the Brave, *26*, 163
Ramona the Pest, 163
Rare One, The, *89*, 176
Rat Race, The, 18
Real Me, The, *72*, 124
Rebecca's War, 343
Rebel on a Rock, 342
Red Lion: A Tale of Ancient Persia, The, 44, *294*
Red Pony, The, 49
Red Sky at Night, 326
Remove Protective Coating a Little at a Time, 48

Renfroe's Christmas, 162
Representing Super Doll, *213*, 220
Reserved for Mark Anthony Crowder, *115*, 126
Return of the Golem, The: A Chanukah Story, 255
Return to Hiroshima, 340, *354*
Return to South Town, *247*, 275
Reubella and the Old Focus Home, 88
Riddle of the Drum, The: A Tale from Tizapan, Mexico, 279
Riddle-Master of Hed, The (1st), 362
Ride a Wild Dream, 123
Ride the Pine Sapling, 197
Rise of Theodore Roosevelt, The, 348
Rivals on Ice, 72
River Winding, 325
River Witches, The, *69*, 269
Road from Home, The: The Story of an Armenian Girl, 260, *344*
Robert Benjamin and the Great Blue Dog Joke, *41*, 207
Robert Frost: The Trial by Existence, 132
Rocking Horse Secret, The, *66*, 323
Roll of Thunder, Hear My Cry, 56, *126*, 177, 243
Ronnie and Rosey, 170
Roots, 57, *248*
Ruby, 129
Rumble Fish, 45, *272*
Run Softly, Go Fast, 183
Run, Reddy, Run, 205
Run, Shelley, Run!, 49, *349*
Runaway Bunny, The, 152
Runaway Marie Louise, 35
Runaway Summer, The, 192
Runaway Teens, 49, *348*
Runaway to Freedom, 341
Running Away, *71*, 197, 360
Running Owl the Hunter, 228

Sadako and the Thousand Paper Cranes, 287, *339*
Sail, Calypso, 42
Sally Can't See, *28*, 99
Salmon for Simon, A, 64, *285*
Sam's Place: Poems from the Country, 273
Sand Lot, The, 214
Sarah and Simon and No Red Paint, 134
Sarah Lou's Untied Shoe, 59
Screwball, 95
Sea Glass, 177, *224*
Sarah's Unicorn, 153

Second Springtime, A, 45, 170, *296*
Secret Clocks, The: Time Senses of Living Things, 324
Secret Dreamer, Secret Dreams, 108
Secret Friend, A, 195
Secret Life of Harold the Bird Watcher, The, 41
Secret of the Andes, 331
Secret of the Sabbath Fish, The, 256
Secret Places, 51, *329*
Secret Selves, 209
Secret Soldier, The: The Story of Deborah Sampson, *120*, 137
Secret Summer of L.E.B., The, *69*, 208
Sedna: An Eskimo Myth, 238
See Dave Run, 325
"Seeing" in the Dark, 94
Seeing Stick, The, 53, *95*, 285
Self-Portrait: Erik Blegvad, 296
Separate Peace, A, *74*, 212
Seven Feet Four and Growing, 46
Seventeenth-Street Gang, The, 217
79 Squares, The, *70*, 87, 196
Shadow of a Bull, 127
Shadow of the Gloom-World, 360
Shadow on the Hills, The, *72*, 89
Shaman's Daughter, 252
Shaman's Last Ride, 330
Shanta, 126
She Come Bringing Me That Little Baby Girl, 155, *321*
She Never Looked Back: Margaret Mead in Samoa, 297
Shining Season, A, *106*, 327
Shoeshine Girl, *40*, 119, 162
Shy Little Girl, The, 23
Siddhartha, 263
Sidewalk Indian, 57, *247*, 335
Siege of Silent Henry, The, *88*, 140
Sign of the Chrysanthemum, The, 291
Silent Bells, The, 260
Silent Spring, 356
Silver Sword, The, 340
Simple Prince, The, 65
Simple Shelters, 299
Sinabouda Lily: A Folktale from Papau New Guinea, 279
Sing Down the Moon, 242
Single Light, A, 127
Sister, 173
Six Chinese Brothers, 282
Sister Act, The 179
Skates!, 188
Skating Rink, The, 102, *210*

Title Index

Slake's Limbo, 140, *218*
Slave Dancer, The, 238, *334*
Slave Girl, 30, *239*, 344
Small Bear Builds a Playhouse, 187
Smart Kid Like You, A, 46, *176*
Smartest Bear and His Brother Oliver, The, 20
Smiling Face, A, 229
Smith, 102
Smoke over Golan: A Novel of the 1973 Yom Kippur War in Israel, 291, *340*
Snailman, The, 195
Snow Maiden, 186, *281*
Snow Bound, 46
Some of the Days of Everett Anderson, 33
Somebody Else's Child, *43*, 168
Something on My mind, 232
Sometimes I Don't Love My Mother, 179
Sometimes I Hate School, 214
Sometimes I Like to Cry, 19
Son of Someone Famous, The, 143, *181*
Song for a Dark Queen, *310*, 349
Song of Rhiannon, The (3rd Branch of "The Mabinogion"), 365
Song of Solomon, 250
Song of the Boat, 278
Song of the Earth Spirit, 236
Song of the Empty Bottles, *23*, 215
Song of the Trees, *138*, 341
Songs and Stories from Uganda, 292
Songs of the Chippewa, 230
Songs of the Dream People, 240
Sorrow's Song, 197
Sound of Chariots, A, 114
Sound of the Dragon's Feet, The, 303
Sound to Remember, A, 28, *98*, 258
Sounder, 161
Space Story, A, 358
Special Friends, *83*, 184
Special Gift, A, 126
Special Kind of Courage, A, *103*, 141
Special Kind of Sister, A, 95
Spin a Silver Dollar: The Story of a Desert Trading-Post, 249
Spin a Soft Black Song, 227
Spirits of Chocamata, The, 56, *303*
Spuddy, The, 100
Spy Doll, The, 340
St. Patrick's Day in the Morning, 21, *280*
Star Child, The, 69
Star Husband, The, *234*, 324
Star Lord, 348
Steffie Can't Come Out to Play, 48, *128*, 326
Stevie, 169

Sticks and Stones, 129
Stolen Key, The, 211
Stone-Faced Boy, The, 165
Stonehenge and Its Mysteries, 304
Stones, The, 67
Storm Boy, 302
Story of an English Village, The, 288, *331*, 354
Story of Edward, The, 21
Story of Helen Keller, The, 97
Story of the Grateful Crane, The, *60*, 280
Strange Footprints on the Land: Vikings in America, 334
Strange Mysteries from Around the World, 302
Stranger in the House, 176
Strangers into Friends, 131
Strawberry Girl, 268
Street Gangs: Yesterday and Today, *219*, 356
Strega Nona, 278
Striped Ice Cream, 134
Subee Lives on a Houseboat, 267
Summer of My German Soldier, 74, *200*, 275, 346
Summer of the Monkeys, 43, *168*
Summer of the Swans, *96*, 162
Summer to Die, A, 174, *326*
Sun Horse, Moon Horse, *49*, 310
Sunset in a Spider Web (Sijo Poetry of Ancient Korea), 295
Surprise for Mother, A, 169
Surprise Party, The, 38
Surprising Things Maui Did, The, 294
Survivors of the Stone Age: Nine Tribes Today, 300
Susan Comes Through the Fire, 98
Sweet and Sour: Tales from China, 289
Sweetwater, 105
Swiftly Tilting Planet, A, 361
Swing, The, 210
Sword of the Prophet, The, 262, *305*
Sycamore Year, 200

Take Wing, 194
Tale of Tawny and Dingo, The, 19, *184*
Tales from Times Past, 289
Tales of a Fourth Grade Nothing, *25*, 162
Tales of the Elders, 87, *236*
Talk About a Family, 166
Talking Bones: Secrets of Indian Burial Mounds, 235
Talking Coffins of Cryo-City, 357
Tangle of Roots, A, 179
Tar Beach, 265

Title Index

109
e of Blackberries, A, 324
te of Spruce Gum, The, 323
eacup Full of Roses, 116, *181*
Teeny Tiny Woman, The, 82
Teetoncey, *47*, 274
Tell Me No Lies, 45
Tell Me, Grandma Tell Me, Grandpa, 52
Tenth Good Thing About Barney, The, 322
Tepee Tales of the American Indian, 246
Terminal Man, The, 107
Tex, 180
Thalia Brown and the Blue Bug, 27, 165, *231*
That Makes Me Mad, 37
That's What a Friend Is, 187
That's What Friends Are For, 198
Then Again, Maybe I Won't, 70, 121, *139*
There Are Two Kinds of Terrible, 168, *324*
There Is a Season, 125
There's a Rainbow in My Closet, *84*, 112, 159
They Took Their Stand, 336
Third Eye, The, 46, 173, *334*
Third Gift, The, 70
Third World Voices for Children, 242
This Is My Father and Me, *52*, 158, 283
This School Is Driving Me Crazy, *30*, 210
This Time, Tempe Wick?, *331*, 339
Thornton the Worrier, 190
Thou Shalt Not Kill, 345
Thousand Pails of Water, A, *53*, 284
Three Ducks Went Wandering, 319
Three Friends, 204
Three-Legged Race, 212
Through Grandpa's Eyes, 35, *82*, 151
Thunder and Lightnings, 198
Thursday's Daughters: The Story of Women Working in America, *57*, 336
Thy Friend, Obadiah, 190
Tight Times, 134, *155*
Time for Everything, A, 349
Time of Wonder, 322
Time to Be Human, A, 248
Time to Quit Running, 130
Times They Used to Be, The, *44*, 55, 170, 238
Timothy and Gramps, 152
Tin Lizzie, *332*, 355
Tisha: The Story of a Young Teacher in the Alaska Wilderness, 276
To Be a Slave, 241
To Fight in Silence, *303*, 346
To Kill a Mockingbird, 181

To My Daughter, with Love, 128
To Race the Wind, 109
To See a Witch, 30, *238*
To Spoil the Sun, *252*, 348
To Stand Against the Wind, 55, *296*, 343
To the Green Mountains, *48*, 122, 139
To Walk on Two Feet, 100
Toby Lived Here, 177
Toby, Granny and George, 121, *139*
Tomas and the Talking Birds, 290
Tongue of Flame: The Life of Lydia Maria Child, 124
Toni's Crowd, 211
Tonweya and the Eagles and Other Lakota Indian Tales, 243
Too Many Babas, 185
Tornado!, 267
Touch of Earth, A, 343
Touchstone, The, 75
Tough Tiffany, 173
Tracy, *94*, 204
Tramps Like Us, 116
Transfigured Hart, The, *44*, 196
Trapped on the Golden Flyer, 353
Tread Softly, 172
Trees Stand Shining, The: Poetry of the North American Indians, 240
Trial Valley, *122*, 139, 271
Trig, 120
Triumph Clear, 105
Triumphs of Fuzzy Fogtop, The, 284
Trolls of Twelfth Street, The, 266
Trouble at Otter Creek, *41*, 166, 339
Trouble at Torrent Creek, 144
Trouble River, *85*, 162
Trouble They Seen: Black People Tell the Story of Reconstruction, 253
Truth on Trial: The Story of Galileo Galilei, 256
Try It Again, Sam, 39
Tuck Everlasting, 65, *322*
Tulku, 73, *262*
Tunes for a Small Harmonica, 48, *127*, 141
Turn the Next Corner, 138
Twelve Clever Brothers and Other Fools, The, 288
Two Are Better Than One, 118
Two Blocks Apart: Juan Gonzalez and Peter Quinn, 143
Two Good Friends, *21*, 186
Two Homes for Lynn, 158
Two Is Company, 186
Two That Were Tough, 83
290, The, 72, *345*

Title Index

Ugliest Boy, The, 30, 209, *259*
Ugliest Dog in the World, The, 22
Ugly Bird, 93
Ugly Duckling, The, 92
Ultra-Violet Catastrophe!, 86
Uncle Misha's Partisans, 302, *335*
Under the Autumn Garden, 28, *332*
Under the Haystack, *122*, 140, 172
Under the Influence, 199
Under the Shade of the Mulberry Tree, 278
Understanding Africa, *307*, 363
Unhurry Harry, 62
Unleaving, 328
Unmaking of Rabbit, The, 67, 86, *119*
Up and Down the River: Boat Poems, 268
Upstairs Room, The, 47, *346*

Valley of the Shadow, The, *263*, 347
Velvet Room, The, *138*, 269
Velveteen Rabbit, The, *24*, 69
Veronica Ganz, 208
Very Far Away from Anywhere Else, 201
Very Worst Thing, The, 203
Visiting Pamela, 188
Viva Chicano, 237
Volunteer Spring, 102

W.E.B. Dubois: A Biography, 239
Wagon Wheels, *51*, 228
Walk Across America, A, 49, *275*
Walk the World's Rim, 217
Walk Through the Woods, A, 64
Walk Together Children: Black American Spirituals, 261
Walk Together: Five Plays on Human Rights, 239
Walkie-Talkie, 102
Walks Far Woman, 253
Wall Street: A Story of Fortunes and Finance, 356
Walt and Pepper, 191
War and Peas, 216, *339*
War on Villa Street, The, 174
Warrior Scarlet, 104
Warton and Morton, 215
Watch for Me on the Mountain, 246
Watch Out for the Chicken Feet in Your Soup, *154*, 229
Watching Eyes, The, 171
Water Is Wide, The, 275
Way of Our People, The, 216, *267*
Way to Rainy Mountain, The, 250
Way to Start a Day, The, 60, *280*

We Have Not Vanished: Eastern Indians of the United States, 253
We Hide, You Seek, 280
We Lived in the Almont, 136
We Remember Philip, *43*, 324
We're Very Good Friends, My Brother and I, 155
Weland: Smith of the Gods, 302
Welcome Home, Jellybean, 47, *104*, 177
Wesley Paul, Marathon Runner, 27
What About Me?, 110
What Are Friends For?, 192
What Do You Do in Quicksand?, 132
What Do You Feed Your Donkey On? Rhymes from a Belfast Childhood, 291
What if They Knew, 97
What if You Couldn't . . .?, 97
What's Going to Happen to Me? When Parents Separate or Divorce, *46*, 174
What's That You Said: How Words Change, 293
When Clay Sings, *265*, 329
When Grandpa Died, 84
When Shlemiel Went to Warsaw & Other Stories, 302
When the Sad One Comes to Stay, 71, *88*
When We Lived with Pete, 40
Where I Begin, 320
Where Pigeons Go to Die, 178
Where the Lilies Bloom, *170*, 271
Where the Red Fern Grows, *168*, 269
Where the Wild Things Are, 64, *158*
Where to Now, Blue?, 47
Where's Jim Now?, 178
Where's Michael?, *22*, 204
Which Way, Black Cat?, 167
Whispering Wind, The: Poetry by Young American Indians, 244
White Archer, The, 240
White Feather, The, 335
White Mountains, The, 359
White Wave, 295
Whitney Young, Jr.: Crusader for Equality, 115
Who Do You Think You Are?, *56*, 334
Who Stole Alligator's Shoe?, 38, *63*
Who's in Rabbit's House?, 286
Why Am I Different?, 19
Why Have the Birds Stopped Singing?, 103
Why Me?, 207
Why Mosquitoes Buzz in People's Ears, 279
Wild Heart, A, 142
Wild One, The, 55, 209, *237*
Wildcat Under Glass, 346

Wildfire, 324
Wilkin's Ghost, *196*, 271
Will I Ever Be Good Enough?, 26
Will I Have a Friend?, 185
Will the Real Tommy Wilson Please Stand Up, 36
Willaby, 62
William: A Novel, *173*, 240, 344
William's Doll, 118, *161*
Willow Flute, The: A North Country Tale, 62
Wilson's World, 352
Wily Witch and All the Other Fairy Tales and Fables, The, 286
Wind in My Hand, 119
Wind in the Door, A, 113
Wind in the Tower: Mao Tsetung and the Chinese Revolution, 1949-1975, 311
Wind Is Not a River, The, 288, *339*
Winding Stair, 336
Winged Watchman, The, 341
Winners Never Quit, 110
Winning, *105*, 346, 362
Winter Cottage, 135
Winter Hero, The, *333*, 343
Witch Who Lost Her Shadow, The, 184
Witch's Daughter, The, 96
Without Hats, Who Can Tell the Good Guys?, 170, *358*
Wizard of Earthsea, 42
Wizard of Wallaby Wallow, The, 22
Woman Against Slavery: The Story of Harriet Beecher Stowe, 125
Woman Chief, *126*, 243
Woman's Place, A, 128
Women Who Dared to Be Different, 127
Womenfolk and Fairy Tales, 120, *290*
Wonder Wheels, *46*, 123, 210
Wonderful Year, The, 118

Words by Heart, 72, 176, *242*
World of Our Fathers: The Jews of Eastern Europe, 263
World Outside, The: Collected Short Fiction About Women at Work, 132
Wounded Knee, 237
Wrinkle in Time, A, 68, *167*
Wuggie Norple Story, The, 158
Wump World, The, 353
Wurley & Wommera: Aboriginal Life and Craft, 300

Year of Japanese Festivals, A, 288
Year of Mr. Nobody, The, 28
Year of the Flying Machine, The: 1903, 331
Year of the Raccoon, The, 174
Year of the Three-Legged Deer, The, 238
Yellow Fur and Little Hawk, 233
Yonnondio from the Thirties, 143
You Go Away, 33, *150*
You Look Ridiculous Said the Rhinoceros to the Hippopotamus, 24
Young and Black in Africa, 307
Young Loner, The, *25*, 192
Young Medics, The, 133
Young Unicorns, The, 218
Youngest One, 205
Your Old Pal, Al, 197
Yugoslavs in America, The, 240

Z for Zachariah, 363
Zanballer, 123
Zeely, 54
Zia, 251
Zoar Blue, 56, *259*
Zunis, The: Self-Portrayals by the Zuni People, 252